Petrified Utopia

Petrified Utopia

Happiness Soviet Style

Edited by

MARINA BALINA
EVGENY DOBRENKO

ANTHEM PRESS
LONDON · NEW YORK · DELHI

Anthem Press
An imprint of Wimbledon Publishing Company
www.anthempress.com

This edition first published in UK and USA 2011
by ANTHEM PRESS
75-76 Blackfriars Road, London SE1 8HA, UK
or PO Box 9779, London SW19 7ZG, UK
and
244 Madison Ave. #116, New York, NY 10016, USA

British Library Cataloguing in Publication Data
A catalogue record for this book is available from the British Library.

Library of Congress Cataloging in Publication Data
The Library of Congress has catalogued the hardcover edition as follows:
Petrified utopia : happiness Soviet-style/edited by Marina Balina and Evgeny Dobrenko.
p. cm.
ISBN-13: 978-1-84331-310-6 (hbk.)
ISBN-10: 1-84331-310-3 (hbk.)
1. Soviet Union—Social life and customs. 2. Soviet Union—Social conditions. 3. Soviet
Union—Intellectual life. 4. Happiness—Social aspects—Soviet Union—History.
5. Happiness—Political aspects—Soviet Union—History. 6. Utopias—Soviet Union—
History. 7. Communism and culture—Soviet Union—History. 8. Social values—Soviet
Union—History. 9. Identity (Psychology)—Soviet Union—History. 10. Group identity—
Soviet Union—History. I. Balina, Marina. II. Dobrenko, E. A. (Evgenii Aleksandrovich)
DK266.4.P46 2009
947.084—dc22
2009018737

ISBN-13: 978 0 85728 390 0 (Pbk)
ISBN-10: 0 85728 390 1 (Pbk)

This title is also available as an eBook.

TABLE OF CONTENTS

LIST OF ILLUSTRATIONS

ACKNOWLEDGMENTS

This project originated from the conference 'Happiness Soviet Style' in May of 2006, which took place at the University of Nottingham. We would like to express our gratitude to the Department of Critical Theory and Cultural Studies and the Centre for the Study of Post-Conflict Cultures at the University of Nottingham, and in particular, to Professors Bernard McGuirk and Nick Hewitt for their support of the conference. We express our appreciation to David Parker for his technical assistance in preparing this volume for publication. We owe a particular debt to Jesse Savage for his dedication to this project, his helpful readings of the manuscript, and his skilful translations. We would also like to thank the Leverhulme Trust for their funding of the initial research related to this project, and to extend our gratitude to the Isaac Funk Foundation at Illinois Wesleyan University for providing financial assistance to the preparation of this volume for publication. Finally, we are grateful to Alexander Beecroft and Tej P. S. Sood at Anthem Press for their support, confidence, and patience during the completion of this volume.

LIST OF CONTRIBUTORS

Albert Baiburin is Professor in the Anthropology Faculty of the European University, St. Petersburg. He specialises in cultural anthropology and is the author of many books and articles about ritual in traditional culture and about Russian cultural history. His major publications include *Dwelling in Ceremonies and Notions of Eastern Slavs* (1983), *Ritual in Traditional Culture* (1993) and *Half-forgotten Words and Meanings* (co-edited, 2004).

Marina Balina is Isaac Funk Professor of Russian Studies at Illinois Wesleyan University. She is the author of numerous articles and book chapters and co-editor of *Endquote: Sots-Art Literature and Soviet Grand Style* (1999), *Soviet Riches: Essays on Culture, Literature and Film* (2002), *Dictionary of Literary Biography: Russian Writers Since 1980* (2003), *Politicizing Magic: An Anthology of Russian and Soviet Fairy Tales* (2005), and *Russian Children's Literature and Culture* (2008).

Philip Ross Bullock is University Lecturer in Russian at Oxford. He is the author of *The Feminine in the Prose of Andrey Platonov* (2005) and numerous articles on literature and music.

Katerina Clark is Professor of Comparative Literature and of Slavic Languages and Literatures at Yale University. She is the author of *The Soviet Novel: History As Ritual* (1981), *Petersburg: Crucible of Cultural Revolution* (1995), co-author of *Mikhail Bakhtin* (1984) and co-editor of *Soviet Culture and Power: A History in Documents, 1917–1953* (2007).

Evgeny Dobrenko is Professor in the Department of Russian and Slavonic Studies at the University of Sheffield. He is the author of the *Metaphor of Power: Literature of the Stalin Era in Historical Context* (1993), *The Making of the State Reader: Social and Aesthetic Contexts of the Reception of Soviet Literature* (1997), *The Making of the State Writer: Social and Aesthetic Origins of Soviet Literary Culture* (2001), *Aesthetics of Alienation: Reassessment of Early Soviet Cultural Theories* (2005),

Political Economy of Socialist Realism (2007), *Stalinist Cinema and the Production of History: Museum of the Revolution* (2008) and co-editor of *Socialist Realism without Shores* (1997), *Endquote: Sots-Art Literature and Soviet Grand Style* (1999), *Socialist Realist Canon* (2000), *Soviet Riches: Essays on Culture, Literature and Film* (2002), *The Landscape of Stalinism: The Art and Ideology of Soviet Space* (2003), *Soviet Culture and Power: A History in Documents, 1917–1953* (2007).

Helena Goscilo is Professor and Chair of the Slavic Department at Ohio State University. She is the author of *TNT: The Explosive World of Tatyana Tolstaya's Fiction* (1996) and *Dehexing Sex: Russian Womanhood Before and After Glasnost* (1996) and the editor and co-editor of numerous books including *Russian and Polish Women's Fiction* (1985), *Balancing Acts* (1989), *Glasnost': New Soviet Prose* (1990), *Skirted Issues: The Discreteness and Indiscretions of Russian Women's Prose* (1992), *Fruits of her Plume* (1994), *Lives in Transit* (1995), *Russia*Women*Culture* (1996), *Russian Culture of the 1990s* (2000), *Politicizing Magic: An Anthology of Russian and Soviet Fairy Tales* (2005), *Gender and National Identity in Twentieth-century Russian Culture* (2006), *Preserving Petersburg: History, Memory, Nostalgia* (2008), *Cinepaternity: Fathers and Sons in Soviet and Post-Soviet Film* (forthcoming, 2010).

Julian Graffy is Professor in the Department of Russian at the School of Slavonic and East European Studies, University College London. He is the co-editor of *The BFI Companion to Eastern European and Russian Cinema* (2000) and the author of *Gogol's The Overcoat* (2000), *Bed and Sofa: The Film Companion* (2001) and *Chapaev: The Film Companion* (2009) as well as numerous articles on Russian film. He is the translator of *Lines of Resistance: Dziga Vertov and the Twenties* (2004).

Catriona Kelly is Professor in the Department of Slavonic Studies at Oxford University. She is the author of *Petrushka: The Russian Carnival Puppet Theatre* (1990), *A History of Russian Women's Writing* (1994), *Russian Literature: A Very Short Introduction* (2001), *Refining Russia: Advice Literature, Polite Culture, and Gender from Catherine to Yeltsin* (2001), *Comrade Pavlik: The Life and Legend of a Soviet Boy Hero* (2004), *Children's World: Growing Up in Russia, 1890–1991* (2007) and co-editor of *Russian Cultural Studies: An Introduction* and *Constructing Russian Culture in the Age of Revolution* (both 1998).

Alexandra Piir is a researcher in the Anthropology Faculty of the European University, St. Petersburg. She works on the anthropology of Leningrad and St. Petersburg and has published articles on the culture of the Leningrad courtyard.

Gian Piero Piretto is Professor of Russian at the University of Milan. He is the author of numerous books including *Derelitti, Bohémiens e Malaffari: Il Mito Povero di Pietroburgo* (1989), *Il Radioso Avvenire. Mitologie Culturali Sovietiche* (2001), *Parole, Immagini, Suoni di Russia: Saggi di Metodologia della Cultura* (2002).

Susan E. Reid is Reader in the Department of Russian and Slavonic Studies at the University of Sheffield. She is the author of numerous articles and the co-editor of *Style and Socialism: Modernity and Material Culture in Post-war Eastern Europe* (2000), *Socialist Spaces: Sites of Everyday Life in the Eastern Bloc* (2002), *Women in the Khrushchev Era* (2004), *Russian Art and the West: A Century of Dialogue in Painting, Architecture, and the Decorative Arts* (2006). She is currently completing a book on homemaking, consumption and everyday aesthetics in Khrushchev-era apartments.

Maya Turovskaya is a major film and theatre critic and historian of Soviet cinema. She is the author of numerous books including *Babanova: Legend and Biography* (1981), *Frontiers of the Arts: Brecht and Cinema* (1985), *Recollections of the Present Moment: Sketches, Portraits, Notes* (1987), *Tarkovsky: Cinema as Poetry* (1990) and *Blow Up!* (2003). Turovskaya is also the author of a series of film scenarios, including Mikhail Romm's famous *Ordinary Fascism* (1966, co-authored). In 1989 she organised a retrospective of the cinema of the totalitarian era.

Emma Widdis is Senior Lecturer in the Department of Slavonic Studies at Cambridge University, and Fellow of Trinity College. She is the author of *Visions of a New Land: Soviet Cinema from the Revolution to the Second World War* (2003) and *Alexander Medvedkin* (2004), and co-editor of *National Identity in Russian Culture: An Introduction* (2004). She has published articles on the cinema, literature and architecture of the Soviet and post-Soviet period in several journals and edited volumes.

INTRODUCTION

Marina Balina and Evgeny Dobrenko

In his new book *Happiness: A History*, Darrin McMahon refers to the observation made by Hegel: 'One may contemplate history from the point of view of happiness, but history is not the soil in which happiness grows. The periods of happiness in it are the blank pages of history.' But what are the 'periods of happiness' in history, and were there, in fact, such periods in history (even if we allow them to be 'blank pages')? Obviously, the yearning for happiness is one of mankind's fundamental needs, and its fulfilment is the basis for a person's creative activity, filling the sphere of his/her imagination. The yearning for happiness is a quite individual need, and this is why drama arises from the historical impossibility of harmonising individual happiness with the overall social project. Without doubt, the Soviet era attempted to achieve just this harmony. It was, however, an era of shortages everywhere. The only thing that it provided in abundance was the historical cataclysms that followed hard upon each other, any one of which might well comprise an entire era in the history of a nation. The Russian revolution was an attempt to fast-forward history. Today, what it produced—the Soviet era—has itself become history.

Marxism, which the Russian revolutionaries invoked, was least of all concerned with the private (or bourgeois) ideal of happiness. It operated with the masses and the classes, and was concerned with the problems of equality and social justice. The individual, and his/her yearning for happiness, were present in it only in an indirect way. Only in the general class struggle was the attainment of the 'centuries-old dream of mankind' possible.

The pursuit of collective happiness is traditionally considered a utopian ideal that structured multiple aspects of Soviet culture, a fact recognised not only by literati, but also by numerous scholars in varied disciplines ranging from cultural and literary studies to sociology, history, anthropology and political science. Several groundbreaking studies in the literary and cultural history of the former Soviet Union have changed our understanding of the Soviet past. However, none of these studies has paid enough attention to an important theme in the cultural history of Soviet society—the pursuit of happiness. Although specialists in Soviet culture repeatedly invoke various manifestations of happiness in works of literature and film in their research, it has yet to be investigated as an independent subject.

Social Utopia is always aimed towards the pursuit of happiness; but contrary to individualistic bourgeois ideals, socialist Utopia (much like a nationalist or religious Utopia) is rooted in the impossibility of achieving individual happiness without first embracing collective happiness. As such, socialist Utopia is built upon the fundamental assertion that individual salvation is not possible without collective salvation, a concept that in Russia had a long history tied in with Orthodoxy, and which left a profound stamp on the Russian national consciousness. From a social and cultural point of view, the most interesting aspect of this dynamic is the tension between committing oneself to the collective ideal and the natural human desire to pursue individual happiness. In the process of adaptation to collective values, individual aspirations must be adjusted accordingly, not the least of which are the changes to the formation of self-identity. Given this context, the problem of happiness extends beyond our understanding of the historical Soviet or East European experience, and thus demands a greater perspective regarding our perception of the ways in which the individual and collective understanding of happiness play out, as well as the exploration of the means of achieving happiness within this polemic. Of particular importance is the study of how the personal and intimate are subordinated to social conventions, and how this process transforms personal ideals, such as moral or material values, among others.

The aim of this book is to investigate the various social and artistic practices through which the idea of happiness in Soviet culture is manifested and to analyse the formative influences of this key notion on social sensitivities, identity, and society's sense of meanings and values. Our objective is to introduce the reader to the most representative ideas of happiness and the common practices of its pursuit that shaped everyday Soviet life and cultural discourse from the early postrevolutionary years to the later period of Stalinist and late Soviet culture. This volume examines different manifestations of happiness in literature and visual culture—from children's literature to official high literary canon, from architecture to popular film, from cookbooks to textiles, and from the culture of consumerism to the paradise of goods depicted in Soviet posters and paintings. This book will redefine the preconceived notion of Soviet happiness as a product of official ideology imposed from above and expressed predominantly through collective experience. The articles in this collection will provide evidence that the formation of the concept of individual happiness was not contained by the limitations of the important state projects that were controlled by state policies and aimed towards the creation of a new society. The state-sanctioned blueprint for happiness in socialist society was provided for its citizens in various forms of media, but a closer reading of these artifacts reveals the 'slippage' between the public and private spheres of the Soviet experience.

The very concept of happiness is an integral part of the individual human code, but by virtue of its social significance, it could not be ignored by the socialist state, which strove to swallow up any enclaves of autonomy. The concept of happiness is not a phenomenon that is defined simply. It is a product of societal and individual aspirations and values, which in turn are a product of the interaction between societal and individual experience and which thus constantly change in tandem with these experiences. One could say that happiness is the product of personal, public, and ideological design. Any Utopia (which is implicit in the very etymology of this word) has something to do with a nonexistent *topos*. In other words, the two sides of a Utopia are the modal and the spatial. As a social *Utopia*, happiness has for its reverse side the *reality* of living societal and personal experience, which at the same time is also the experience of consuming the ideological constructs of happiness. The other key aspect of the Utopia is the problem of *topoi*. This book is constructed in accordance with these interconnected basic aspects of our subject.

The utopian aspect of happiness under Soviet conditions is most of all linked to the social modelling of consciousness. In the foreground of this are the strategies for inculcating the notions about happiness constructed by authority into the individual consciousness of the people. The criteria for collective happiness, just as the criteria for personal success and the prerequisites for social mobility, are subjected to continual transformation and correctives in accordance with the changing directives of the state. Soviet society itself was in a process of constant dynamics that was unprecedented in Russian history. But no matter what the differing social situations that took shape in Soviet society were (as the result of emigrations of the cultural elites, civil war, collectivisation, forced industrialisation, the Great Terror, devastating war and de-Stalinisation), the authorities were not only obliged to 'include' private aspirations (which changed in tandem with the social structure of Soviet society itself) in the model of collective happiness, but also to fit them into a constantly redrawn ideological frame. What 'happiness' officially meant and what it meant at the level of personal aspirations never coincided; what is more, this disparity was different in 1917, 1937, 1956 and 1987.

The prototype of the Soviet Utopia was childhood, which was projected onto both the sphere of personal life and the realm of national history. As Catriona Kelly demonstrates, the 'happy Soviet childhood', since it was the product not only of social policy and the activities of the new political and ideological institutions, but also of ideological manipulation (for example, through the creation of a steadfast aversion to the image of prerevolutionary childhood), by the 1930s began to be perceived as the most visible indicator of the success of the new government in materialising its concern for its small citizens, and as proof of the inalienable right of Soviet children to a happy life; thus, it was consolidated in the masses' consciousness. Adducing numerous interviews, Kelly demonstrates the striking stability of this utopian construct even in the post-Soviet period, which manifested itself in a consistent unwillingness to reject the image of collective Utopia shaped in the Soviet person and led to a negative perception of post-Soviet reality.

Indeed, the task of removing the negative turned the process of presenting reality into a key political problem for Soviet culture. The revolutionary discourse of Utopia had run its course by the late 1920s. The Stalin era was a time of already-triumphant Utopia, and the orientation towards the future of revolutionary era was replaced by the apologetics of already-present happiness—'Socialism in One Country'. The Stalinist revolution that occurred in 1929 was tied to forced collectivisation, which, in peasant Russia, became a true civil war. This is what makes the strategies through which the 'domestication' of *kolkhozes* (a form of collective farming in the Soviet Union) took place in Stalinism all the more interesting. This transformation reached its apogee in the genre of the 'kolkhoz epic poem', which flourished in the postwar decade. As Evgeny Dobrenko demonstrates, the kolkhoz epic became the consummate embodiment of happiness achieved because it found a unique stylistic formalisation for the world simulated in it.

Another quite significant aspect is the visual demonstration of materialised communist 'abundance'. As Helena Goscilo shows, when the ascetic ideology of the earliest days of the Soviet republic was replaced by the Stalinist promise of a 'cultured, prosperous life', the mythical amenities of the Soviet Utopia began to take on a material dimension. In anticipation of a consumers' paradise, Soviet citizens were obliged to learn the 'culture of consumption'. This new problem was primarily solved with the aid of advertising and representational art.

However, being constantly 'nourished' in a visual way, Soviet utopian consciousness had to be brought back down to reality. One of the most famous examples of this was the publication, in the late 1930s, of the *Book About Tasty and Healthy Food (Kniga o Vkusnoi i Zdorovoi Pishche)*. In his analysis of this book, perhaps one of the most popular books ever issued by

Soviet publishers, Gian Piero Piretto examines the process of adaptively applying the collective Utopia to the family: the consumers' Utopia 'In One Family' became a projection of 'Socialism in One Country'. The utopian impulse assumes the form of culinary recipes in a country experiencing complete shortages, as if confirming the 'reality' of the collective dream of abundance and happiness for all. In his scrutiny of the Stalin-era editions of this book, Piretto examines the strategies for propagandising the new Soviet 'culturedness' as a most significant component of the Soviet conception of 'happiness' (beginning with the numerous colourful illustrations and ending with the likewise numerous and detailed demands for proper table service and rules for 'cultured' behaviour at the table). This book not only described an already-realised abundance but also transformed it into an almost tangible (and even edible!) product, thereby instilling confidence about the attainability of the promised dream: one need only follow the established rules and the happiness of the 'full cup' table would become possible, neutralising the absence in Soviet stores of the majority of the ingredients needed to make this or that dish, the absence of anything like suitable conditions for preparing them in communal kitchens and the impossibility of finding the utensils and accommodations needed for 'table service'.

The dissonance between the ideological construct of Soviet happiness—the 'horizon of expectations' offered by the government—and the practical embodiment of the Soviet Utopia led to the appearance of an extraordinarily protean model of reality, wherein the boundaries of the ideal itself constructed by power were constantly 'eroded' under the influence of everyday Soviet life.

The new state collided with the already-formed 'human material' that it was faced with remaking after the patterns of new social and aesthetic norms. It seemed that this problem could be most easily solved in the children's collective, where the 'relics of the past' had not yet firmly enough taken root. The cataclysms of the first decade of Soviet history (revolution, civil war, hunger, large-scale migration of the rural population in the early 1920s, as well as the 'de-*kulak*-ing' and destruction of the countryside) turned millions of children in Russia into homeless orphans. Children's homes and colonies for underage offenders were transformed into breeding grounds for Soviet anthropological experimentation. On the basis of 1920s and 1930s children's literature, Marina Balina demonstrates how the notion of happiness was transformed in the children's collective, where the greatest pains were taken to squeeze the idea of family—this traditionally necessary element of a child's happiness—out of the children's consciousness. Despite the great demand for texts in which the privacy of family happiness is supplanted by the collective Utopia of depersonalised collective happiness, the stories about the reformed vagrants usually conclude in a complete 'family-like' vein: the authors either allow their heroes to find their lost parents or else offer them new ties that reproduce family relationships—older mentors that replace fathers and mothers, close friends who become almost siblings, and love affairs. In all of this, the collective is deliberately reduced to the dimensions of a manageable, but nevertheless happy, small union.

The privatisation of happiness extends to various spheres of everyday practices. With the 1930s arrival of the Stalinist 'culture of abundance', the very concept of the lifestyle of Soviet people changed as well. The long-standing debate about beauty versus utility that had coursed through classic Russian literature came to an end in the Stalinist era—as did everything else—with the triumph of harmony: synthesis of the useful and the beautiful. Soviet happiness not only had to be tasty and beautifully served, but also pleasant to the touch. As Emma Widdis demonstrates in the case of the culture of texture and textile, the idea of prettification of one's living space, which, in the ascetic revolutionary culture, had been considered petty bourgeois, became newly legitimate and thus part of the vocabulary of the Soviet media. Thus, in Soviet women's journals, practical advice about how to best 'dress up' one's space and oneself became widely touted, and room was made for sewing patterns, as well as samples of embroidery and appliqués. Needlework, an activity that combines texture and touch, became an important instrument for concretising the aesthetic aspirations of the new way of life. The powers that be embarked on an attempt to shape sensory experience and to mastermind the creation of a new sensuous world for the Soviet people. At the same time, all these homemade (or rather, home-altered, given the constant shortages) items bore the stamp of individual taste, although it was a taste harmonised in accordance with the new Soviet aesthetic code.

The culmination of private happiness in the 1950s was the move from overcrowded postwar *kommunalki* into the separate apartments that Nikita Khrushchev began to bestow on his fellow citizens. An apartment for a single family was an extremely personal space, although the setting was limited by the authorities: there was no right to choose the neighbourhood, and there were strict limits on the metric area allotted to each member of the family. And no matter how ironically these apartments are remembered today—with their tiny bathrooms, diminutive hallways, narrow kitchens into which one could barely squeeze a table and chairs, and incredible 'sound proofing' that made the voices of neighbours in the enclosed stairways penetrate the thin walls even more—they were nonetheless a step towards private happiness, and the collective remained outside, more and more displaced into the arena of annoying 'idle newspaper talk'. The authorities had long instructed Soviet citizens in a 'culture of consumption' that was merely theoretical, due to the absence of goods; at last, these citizens got an opportunity to put this knowledge into practice. Susan Reid shows how the large-scale transformation of Soviet people into new apartment dwellers turned them into 'happy and duly grateful' citizens—'but not carefree'. The move to a new apartment was equated with the beginning of a new life upon which one had to embark equipped with new furniture, new technology (a vacuum cleaner and a television) and a new understanding of cosiness and beauty. The culture of consumerism became an important component of Soviet life in the 1950s and 1960s; more surprisingly, perhaps, the values of the new Soviet consumer also manifested an unexpected resemblance to those in Western culture, as far as the acquisition of goods was concerned.

The *re-privatisation of the private sphere* that began in the post-Stalin era took the Soviet person further and further away from an important postulate of Stalinist culture—the collective principle of Soviet happiness. The private and personal took precedence over the public and universal in everyday life. However, during state holidays, this breached priority was quickly restored. Albert Baiburin and Alexandra Piir provide an analysis of how the peculiar coexistence of two models of happiness, private and collective, was entrenched in the memories of a Soviet generation. Holidays like November 7 (the anniversary of the October Revolution) and May 1 (International Solidarity Day), with the ritual nationwide demonstrations, military parades and salutes, assumed the role of a reinstated Utopia of the common unity of the Soviet people. A state holiday was organised as an extremely propagandistic measure. However, once it left the public square, the holiday itself receded into the background and was reduced to the level of a family meal that, at times, had nothing whatsoever connecting it to the just-resurrected Utopia of collective unity; and, as the analysis of reminiscences about Soviet holidays from various generations of contemporary Russians shows, this was just how they were preserved in individual memory.

One of the most difficult problems to solve in the materialisation of a Utopia becomes that of the *topos* as a physical location. A Utopia has no place in real life, and never can—and this is the key difference between a utopian dream and wishes rooted in reality. The paradox of the Soviet Utopia is that the authorities, in striving to define and build a specific space for this Utopia, constantly defer the attainment of utopian happiness in time. The temporal coordinates of the Utopia are always located beyond the boundaries of the present and are fixed on the future. In Stalinism, however, the Utopia is proclaimed to be already built, the future has already arrived, and the only thing that remains is to experience the Utopia and equip the world for a new and even greater prosperity. This makes the practices of mystification of reality even more important, a reality replete with what Sheila Fitzpatrick called 'preview[s] of the coming attractions of socialism',[1]—but which Stalin called 'the miracles of new achievements'.[2] Katerina Clark shows how the projects aimed at rebuilding Moscow in the 1930s transformed the Soviet capital into just this kind of utopian *locus*. The plans for reconstructing old Moscow did not simply task the architects with renewal of a Soviet city; Moscow had to be rebuilt as a new *socialist* city in which the architecture was allotted a propagandistic function on a level equal to that of the Word. From these Moscow reconstruction plans, one can see how literature-centric Stalinist culture was and the extent to which politics was saturated with aesthetics. Numerous descriptions of new projects and architectural solutions took precedence over the process of construction itself: in fact, the majority of the contemplated plans for rebuilding Moscow were never realised. Nonetheless, in the form of scale models of the new Utopia, exhibited for all to see in the shop windows of Moscow, Soviet architecture fulfilled the function of a visual narrative about the bright future that was already coming, while not hinting at any timetables whatsoever for its realisation.

Returning to the issue of the literature-centredness of Stalinist culture, we find ourselves not only in a new medium, but also in a space of tradition. The literary text is locked in self-referentiality. The most obvious example of such isolation is Andrei Platonov's novel entitled *Happy Moscow* (*Schastlivaia Moskva*), in which the Stalinist capital is construed as a city of happiness and a direct affirmation of Stalin's words. Platonov's characters employ various strategies for finding happiness: rejection of personal happiness in the name of work, rejection of an elite job for the purpose of finding oneself and personal happiness, or through some combination of the two, as the main heroine of the novel, Moscow Chestnova (yes, 'Moscow' is her first name!), employs. Moscow is the place of the privileged life of the new elite (which sets this *topos* apart from Platonov's traditional provincial *loci*). Indeed, the idea of happiness as a personal and intimate notion about life is revealed in this novel, as distinct from Platonov's *Foundation Pit* (*Kotlovan*) or *Chevengur*, in which the concept of happiness is tied to politics, philosophy or ideology. As in Aleksandr Medvekin's film *Happiness* (*Schast'e*), personal success is affirmed in this novel through an arrival in Moscow, and the recognition of the metropolis is tantamount to the recognition of success. Philip Ross Bullock suggests reading *Happy Moscow* intertextually with Lev Tolstoi's *Anna Karenina*, wherein the characters are also engaged in the quest for an extremely personal happiness. The transition to a *locus classicus* and the immersion into literary tradition allows one to decode Platonov's text. Platonov embraces Tolstoi's idea that happy moments are full of sorrow and anguish. But since the quest of Platonov's characters for happiness takes place not in the past and not in the unattainable future, merriment (or happiness) in the novel is perceived as a facade and as self-deceit.

If, in the case of Moscow's planned reconstruction, the visual arena is transformed into the Word, and in the instance of Platonov the Word becomes self-referential and immersed in strata of literary tradition, then in Soviet cinema the Word relinquishes the space of literature in order to bring the recipient a recipe for happiness in a new, onscreen medium. With reference to the films of the Khrushchev Thaw, Julian Graffy demonstrates that the Thaw restores a personal dimension to the search for happiness; the films emphasise, however, that one must *struggle* for happiness, in a never-ending effort. By intensifying the social dimension of personal happiness, Thaw cinema expands the space for romantic conflict between the hero eager for happiness and a reality that is mired in materialism and petty bourgeois values. An important aspect of overcoming this reality is space. The Thaw cinematographer generally rejects Moscow; one can find oneself and overcome difficulties only by relinquishing Moscow's comforts and setting out for the periphery, towards a complicated but interesting life. The relocation in space is a sort of journey of errors; the characters often do not understand where they should seek happiness. It was no coincidence that de-Stalinisation provoked new debates about happiness, as it placed a concern for everyday life—alongside 'high ideology', of course—at the centre of public discourse. It humanised the face of socialism, but, in a paradoxical way, intensified the utopian element in it even more. Suffice it to recall Khrushchev's promise that in twenty years the Soviet people would live under communism; that is, in the categories of Soviet discourse, they would find complete happiness.

The examination of Soviet strategies for realising happiness would be incomplete if one examined Soviet culture only outside the context of other twentieth-century totalitarian regimes that attempted to solve similar problems originating from completely opposite political ideologies. As Maya Turovskaya shows, these ideologies are begotten from similar cultural situations in mass societies. Two important popular illustrated journals—*Ogonek* in the USSR and the *Berliner Illustrierte Zeitung* (*BIZ*) in Germany—like two mirrors, demonstrate the similarities and differences between the two cultural models of happiness, the Stalinist and the Nazist. By examining their propaganda strategies, Turovskaya shows the evolution of the journals. *Ogonek* was the face of a peasant population at the moment of its exodus from the countryside into the cities as a result of collectivisation. It was a sort of USSR-wide factory newspaper, in which politics predominated. *BIZ* was another story; a journal about and for the city, in which the driving force was sensationalism, and there was a bare minimum of politics. (Interestingly, this 'dialogue of dictatorships' sometimes became rather obvious—*BIZ*, for example, would sometimes reprint photographs from *Ogonek*). Significant, too, was the difference in advertising: there was very little in *Ogonek*, while *BIZ* was replete with advertisements aimed at female readers—from soups to household appliances. The female readership of each journal found a different model with which to identify. In *Ogonek*, a woman was only a working entity (the journal was intended for both male and female workers); but in *BIZ*, a woman was not only a soldier's mother but also a sex object. The two journals were closer, however, on the theme of leader and people and in the type of quasi-religion common to both regimes (but Hitler is basically portrayed through photographs, while Stalin is chiefly represented in words). They are also similar in the theme of the hero; both publications engage in the production of living demigods, in heroic rhetoric in time with the growth of militarisation and in the creation of cults of youth and iron (from the car to the tank). The two regimes are similar in their passionate desire to present politically, socially, and ideologically acceptable models to the individual for the realisation of each person's inherent yearning for happiness; this yearning always begets discontent, dooming the totalitarian regime to ultimate defeat.

Utopias live intense but short lives. When they begin to petrify, they cease to satisfy the human pursuit of happiness and give rise to a new cycle of utopian creation. But perhaps the most interesting thing about a petrified Utopia is the trail of evidence for this pursuit of happiness. And it is perhaps the most significant and instructive thing in the experience of the lost Soviet civilisation.

Petrified Utopia

Part One

UTOPICS

Chapter One

A JOYFUL SOVIET CHILDHOOD: LICENSED HAPPINESS FOR LITTLE ONES

Catriona Kelly

In a recent essay, the Russian ethnolinguist Anna Zaliznyak claimed that the word *schast'e*, usually rendered in English by 'happiness', actually represents a quite specific emotional state.[1] 'Happy' is adequately translated, she asserts, only by *dovol'nyi*, which suggests a comparable sense of well-anticipated and serene contentment. *Schast'e*, on the other hand, refers to a kind of elation that is extreme, sudden, and not to be relied on; it is a type of 'earthly bliss' that exists mainly in the future or in the past (i.e., is a potential force), and that cannot be attained by 'some algorithmic means—deserved or earned'. So unusual and accidental is the feeling, that it is also 'slightly shameful'.[2] As always with this kind of exercise in comparative definition, one is tempted to dispute the nationally specific tenor of the analysis; the fact that 'happiness' is not the *right* translation for *schast'e* surely does not mean that there is *no* translation for *schast'e* ('bliss' would be fairly close), or that the emotional state so defined is unrecognizable to a person without that term in their linguistic range. However, there are two directions in which discussion can usefully run. One is that Zaliznyak foregrounds an association—which is indeed difficult to capture in English—between 'happiness' in the emotional sense and good luck (compare the Latinate term 'fortunate'). The other is that a perception of Russians' exceptional relationship with happiness is an important element in the national autostereotype, or, to put it more simply, in how Russians like to perceive themselves. Unhappiness (or 'bad luck') is, so the idea goes, fatalistically accepted, while happiness descends like manna from heaven and is definitely not going to last; perceiving happiness as somehow deserved or merited would be both foolish and arrogant. An indication of the pervasiveness of such views in what might be termed 'the performance of being Russian' is that the Russian teacher at my London school in the 1970s, a member of the 'first wave' of Russian emigration (she was born in Moscow in 1913 and brought up in a completely Russophone environment in Serbia), emphasised the exceptional meaning of *schast'e* when she first taught us the word (I can still remember the pantomime of ecstasy into which she contorted her rather set, if not actually lugubrious, small, snub-nosed face).

In terms of a generalisation about Russian culture, as opposed to a self-defining statement by Russians, the claims about *schast'e* have some limitations. Certainly, according to a perhaps apocryphal but plausible story, silent films made before 1917 had two endings, the 'happy end' for Western Europe, and the sad one for Russia. Indeed, the term 'happy end' usually gets used by Russians in transliteration, *kheppi end*, as though to emphasise the alien nature of the concept.

In classic Russian literature, love affairs, as is well known, generally end badly; the contrast between *Pride and Prejudice* and *Evgeny Onegin*, to name two works of roughly similar date by authors of comparable temperament, is instructive. Just so in Tolstoy; happiness is an elusive emotion, as is suggested not only by the cryptic aphorism about happy and unhappy families at the beginning of *Anna Karenina*, but by, say, the heart-searching of Olenin, the protagonist of *The Cossacks*. For the Cossacks themselves, *schast'e* is an opportunity to be seized; thus in the older woman Usten'ka's question to Mar'yana when the latter, courted by Olenin, is reluctant to respond, *Schast'ya sebe ne khochesh'?*[3] This translates literally as 'So you don't want happiness?' but might more appropriately be rendered, 'Don't you recognise good luck when you see it?' The Russian intellectual outsider's view of happiness is, in contrast, not pragmatic; it means following a course of action that is unlikely to bring social or, indeed emotional, advantage, and happiness is an unreliable and temporary emotional state; *Kak ya byl vlyublen v etu noch', kak ya byl schastliv!* (How much in love I was that night, how happy (or more appropriately, 'ecstatic')!)[4]

Yet, as always with national stereotypes, the notion that suffering is proper to Russian culture (and a sign of the distinctiveness, even moral superiority, of same) has not gone unchallenged. Russian radical culture (Chernyshevsky's novel of blissful extramarital love, *What is to be Done?*, for example), posits quite a different model of human existence, one according to which it actually is possible to enjoy happiness, and indeed to create it. This attitude to happiness was absorbed into official Soviet culture, where—at least from Stalin's declaration in 1935 that 'life had become more joyful' (*zhit' stalo veselee*)—not recognising one's own happiness/good fortune as a Soviet citizen became tantamount to a political crime. Depressive states were branded 'decadent moods' (*upadochnicheskie nastroeniya*), and, like British citizens of the wartime years, those suffering such afflictions were expected to 'keep their pecker up' (*ne padat' nosom*) and not to 'whine' (*khnykat'*).

From the mid-1930s until Stalin's death, with the signal exception of the war years, it was impermissible to acknowledge suffering on the part of any Soviet citizen who was not in one way or another beyond the pale. It followed that admitting to being unhappy was potentially shameful, an act of self-exposure. At the same time, happiness did not simply descend from above; it had to be worked for, and obtaining access to it became a demonstration of righteousness. Honoured citizens of the late 1930s and 1940s, such as Stakhanovite workers or record-breaking pilots, were among those who were understood to deserve happiness, a point registered not just in their privileged access to scarce goods (bicycles, pianos, family flats),[5] but in the fact that they were usually represented in propaganda images with beaming smiles, gazing upwards into radiant sunshine. Yet such an emotion was too precious to be squandered in everyday contexts; thus, official photographs for identity papers (*dokumenty*), such as the Soviet passport, required that the subject pose face-on and without a smile, and business portraits, such as those of Party members for the 'boards of honour' or for double-page spreads in *Pravda*, were equally somber. *Schast'e* belonged to the world of the Soviet holiday or celebration (*prazdnik*) and not to ordinary days (*budni*); to leisure (*otdykh, dosug*) rather than to business (*delo*).[6]

Something of an exception to this generally operating binary divide was, however, represented by the case of Soviet children, or at any rate, by younger children (*malen'kie deti*), who were by definition too young to be involved in 'business', and who had not yet reached the stage when they could be perceived as a political threat. The trope of 'happy childhood' was not invented in the Stalin era. An extremely influential example from classic Russian literature is Tolstoy's *Childhood* (*Detstvo*), where, in a famous passage later set for learning by heart in the schoolroom, the narrator meditated on his own good fortune:

> Happy, happy time of childhood, never to return! How could one not love it, cherish one's memories of it? These memories refresh and elevate my soul and are a source of the greatest delights for me.

In other narratives by Tolstoy as well—for example, *The Cossacks*—childhood was also represented as a time of heedless happiness, retrievable by adults only if they became 'like children':

> And suddenly such a bizarre feeling of causeless delight (*schast'e*) and love for everything came upon him that, falling into a habit that went back to childhood, he started crossing himself and expressing thanks to someone or other.[7]

Children were recognised from the early days of Soviet power as a key target group of propaganda and agitation, and, given the importance of *schast'e* to Soviet ideology, it was natural that the idea of 'happy childhood' should be absorbed into propaganda for and about them. In the 1920s, the picture was still mixed: the slogan 'happy childhood' was sometimes used, and it was common for children's stories to have an optimistic flavor (Socialist Realist before their time!). Still, the real heyday of 'happy childhood' began in the mid-1930s. The years 1934 and 1935 witnessed an upsurge of 'joy and happiness' stories in the press; child readers of *Pioneer Pravda* could read about 'The Happy Life of Children in the Land of the Bolsheviks', 'We are the Children of a Happy Country', 'There is no End to the Joy', and so on.[8] This was the period when 1 September, the start of the school year, was turned into a festival for 'happy children'; in the words of a poem printed in *Pioneer Pravda* in 1935:

> Radiant, joyful, and cheery,
> The day rises over the city.
> Good day, autumn! Good day, school!
> Good day, school year![9]

Also in late 1935 the famous slogan according to which children themselves expressed gratitude to Stalin (and through him to the Party and the state) for their good fortune was introduced: 'Thank You Comrade Stalin for [Our] Happy Childhood!' The forms of address varied—Stalin was sometimes invoked as 'dear' Comrade Stalin, *rodnoi*, an epithet usually reserved for family members, lovers or very close friends—but the adjective attached to 'childhood' was much more stable (the variant *radostnoe*, or 'joyful', was occasionally found, but rarely).[10]

Official literature of the day also harped relentlessly on children's happiness, as in Aleksei Surkov's 'A Song about Stalin', written for the leader's sixtieth birthday in 1939, which was repeatedly anthologised, including in the official primer for the postwar Soviet schoolroom, *Rodnaya rech'* (Native Tongue, 1946, etc.):

> Fairer than the first dawns of Spring
> Is the happy time of youth.
> Warmed by Stalin's smile
> Our children play joyfully.
>
> Stalin is our battle glory,
> Stalin is the soaring of our youth,
> Singing, fighting and winning,
> Our nation follows Stalin.
> (Aleksei Surkov, 'Pesnya o Staline' (Song of Stalin), 1939)

As the second stanza quoted here suggests, children were also exposed to the idea of happiness for adults—heroes on the one hand, the entire 'nation' or 'people' on the other. The ethos of 'happiness through self-sacrifice' was impressed upon them, particularly upon older children. In 1935, for example, the newspaper *Pioneer Pravda* illustrated a topos of the times, 'we are happy/lucky to live in such a wonderful new society,' with the words uttered by a member of the crew of the *stratostat* (supersonic airliner) USSR-1 Bis in June 1935: 'There is no greater joy than the joy of being the son of a country that is the hope of working people all over the world. There is no greater happiness than the happiness of living and working under the supervision of the great Communist Party. There is no greater happiness than reporting to the Leader about one's achievements.'[11] Young readers learned about heroes such as Pavlik Morozov, who sacrificed the 'personal' in favor of the 'social' and 'collective' when reporting his father's misdemeanors to the authorities,[12] or (in the postwar years) Aleksandr Matrosov, who died when using his own body to defend his comrades from a German gun position. All the same, children were seen, both in texts for children and in texts for adults, as the central group guaranteed happiness in the Soviet nation, a happiness directly conferred upon them by the Party and Leader of the nation.

A direct result of this situation was that it became difficult, from the mid-1930s, to address in print cases of childhood unhappiness within the Soviet Union itself. Unhappiness was the lot of children and adults abroad—in poor families within the rich West, and in Russia before 1917. 'I Don't Remember a Single Happy Day,' read the headline to a piece in *Pioneer Pravda* about one Petros Muradyan from the Collective Farm of the Name of Stalin: 'Over the seventy years of my life I have seen and experienced many things. Over the fifty-six years before Soviet Armenia was created, I don't remember a single happy day.'[13] A common strategy was to juxtapose the unhappiness of one of these groups with the joyous life lived by Soviet children. An article in *Our Achievements* magazine contrasted the daughter of a textile worker in Moscow (who had such a talent for the piano that she had been selected as one of only two children to be loaned an instrument by the local House of Culture) with her mother, who in her girlhood had wistfully heard the strains of music played on a mysterious black box drifting from the windows of the local manor-house.[14] By extension, while the Soviet authorities regularly collected reports of abuses in children's institutions, these were not usually made public; and news reports about cases where children had been disruptive or violent, or engaged in misdemeanors, attributed blame not to hardship or want, but to deficiencies in moral education.

The emphasis on happiness as the essential state of Soviet children did not vanish at the point when little Soviet citizens stopped thanking Stalin for their happy childhood. A child's poem published by Kornei Chukovsky in 1960 retained the emotional stereotypes of the past, while reconfiguring the cast of human actors represented:

> Let there always be sunshine,
> Let there always be blue skies,
> Let there always be mama,
> Let there always be me.[15]

Shortly afterwards, in 1962, the poem was recycled by L. Oshanin and A. Ostrovsky as the chorus to a children's song for peace; here, it was described as a text written on a child's drawing (a gloss that had not been provided by Chukovsky). Whatever its true origins (was it perhaps even made up by Chukovsky himself?), it became hugely popular, yet the piece, seen as heralding a new era of children's creativity, was, in fact, thoroughly conventional in terms of its sentiments. One only needs to alter 'mama' to 'Stalin' to have a poem that might well have been published fifteen years earlier.

Yet the perception that children's happiness now had different causes ('nature' and 'mama', not the fiat of a political leader) was significant. The phrasing of the poem quoted by Chukovsky drew attention to a 'privatisation' of ideals of happiness that had a significant impact on propaganda during the post-Stalin era. The 1960s, and more particularly the 1970s and 1980s, saw increasing uncertainty about whether institutional life was best for children, and celebration of the (virtuous, Soviet) home as the ideal place for raising useful and well-balanced citizens.[16] What persisted was the conviction that happiness was children's essential condition, a dogma that remained undisputed throughout the Soviet period, and that continued to be widely accepted after 1991. This might in itself seem obvious—what culture does not think that children's happiness is important?—but, in fact, a concern for children's well-being and a desire to make them happy are not necessarily the same thing. The Princess Royal (Princess Anne), the patron of the charity Save the Children, was recorded in the early 2000s as saying, 'One doesn't have to like children to think that they deserve a better deal in life.' She was articulating the rationalistic spirit (care and concern, but without emotional attachment) that was often behind the creation of total institutions for children, from boarding schools to orphanages, right across the world.

Thus, concern for 'happiness' and beneficence are not necessarily to be linked; the emphasis on childhood 'happiness' (as opposed to health, security, adequate education) had as much to do with the Soviet state's own presentation of itself as uniquely humane as it did with actual commitment to improving children's lives. Indeed, in terms of this commitment, Soviet policy often looked notably flawed. For example, children's welfare was cited as an argument against nuclear proliferation, yet the Soviet state itself maintained a formidable array of atomic weapons. The state's commitment to ensuring the highest level of educational and medical services for children was regularly celebrated in the Soviet press and in publications aimed at foreign audiences, yet schools and hospitals were funded on the so-called *ostatochnyi printsip*, or on the basis of what was 'left over' from funding the military-industrial base. Representation of achievement all too often produced statistics that were misleading, if not actually mendacious. Favourable comparison of the Soviet record relating to infant mortality with the record of Western European countries and the US ignored the fact that Soviet statistics omitted still births and spontaneous abortions, which were included in mortality records elsewhere; published statistics for numbers of new institutions founded in recent months were not adjusted to account for institutions that had been closed, thus making advances seem larger than they were.

Childhood happiness was thus not only (or even mainly) a goal of Soviet culture, it was a legitimating sacred value. The state's ability to guarantee happiness to children was both a key instance of the country's status as a kind of earthly paradise (in the loose sense),[17] and a way of assuring adults that, whatever else might be unsatisfactory, at least one section of the population was well looked after. The identification of 'childhood happiness' and 'the Soviet state' in turn meant that, if the latter inspired suspicion, so did the former. It became common for satirical commentators on Soviet reality during the post-Stalin era to represent the country as a place with an infantilised population. An example was a sketch by the famous Odessa stand-up comedian Mikhail Zhvanetsky beginning, 'This isn't a country, it's a kindergarten. Radio and television announcers talk to us all as though we were feeble-minded, or children.'[18] Thus, the standing of the ideal of 'childhood happiness' became closely associated with the observer's views of Soviet social control more generally; the 'care and attention' (*zabota i vnimanie*) lavished on children stood for a broader model of paternalism to which by no means all Soviet citizens wished to subscribe, and which led them in turn to see 'childhood happiness' as tinged with hypocrisy.

During the era of *glasnost'*, when material about the dire condition of many children's institutions began to flood the Soviet press, the ethos of 'childhood happiness' provoked sarcasm and contempt. Accusations arose that this mythology had been actively detrimental to children's happiness, rather than fostering it. Exemplary was an article by a pediatrician, Mariya Rakhmanova, published in *Nedelya* in 1989. 'For decades we have placed the adjective "happy" next to the word "children", and insisted that "the only privileged class in our country is children,"' Rakhmanova lamented. 'These slogans gradually drove out of our head any concern for children in real life.' In support of her argument, she cited hair-raising statistics: 30 per cent of Soviet children were born with severe damage to the central nervous system, and 40 per cent with slight damage. The infant mortality rate of 2.5–2.6 per cent was around five hundred times higher than the rate in Japan. Equally worrying were the high levels of malaise among schoolchildren—almost 50 per cent suffered from problems of the central nervous system.[19]

A sardonic attitude to the slogans of the past was characteristic well beyond journalism. Typical was a 1998 publication by two Moscow historians assembling archival documents that presented a dismal catalogue of deprivation: malnutrition, neglect, abuse and mismanagement in children's institutions. The title 'A Happy Childhood' emerged as grotesque in the extreme (though in fact, the documents dated from before the time when it had become essential in the Soviet press to write only about children's happiness).[20] In a similar gesture, David Samoilov's bittersweet 1935 diary of adolescent experience was published in 1999 under the title *The Diary of a Happy Boy*,[21] even though a sardonic juxtaposition of slogans and reality was in fact not characteristic of Samoilov's own view of the world.

This ironic representation of 'happiness', seen in retrospect, captures the attitude of some ordinary people in the post-Soviet period, too. A man born in a Tver Province village in 1928 and recorded in 2004, humorously remembered the effects of school sermons about 'happy childhood' on his particular group:

> They'd tell us first off that we was living better than anyone, and we was better off than everyone, and so on and so on. Eh-eh-eh... As for us, of course, we couldn't get our heads round that, and specially not in Class One. Well, how was we supposed to understand, living better than everyone... better... and better off? When we, excuse me for being so crude, was sitting there with bare bottoms, and all...[22]

Yet this was not the only type of recollection to be found. It was also common for informants, looking back from the post-Soviet period, to sum up their childhood as happy:

> **Interviewer:** OK, Nina, let's sum up, then. How would you assess what you got out of your youth, your childhood, in your family, and how do you sum up your life? Let's sum up.
> **Informant:** Well, I think we had the best childhood you could possibly have, and the best we had was what we had in childhood. And now I'd like my children to have a childhood like that, a cloud-free, happy childhood.

Interviewer: So you think that all the social muddle and confusion reflects…
Informant: I don't 'think.' I **know**.[23]
And so what were the history lessons like [in the early 1990s]? I can remember one really well. We were all one form, but they divided us in two. So one form [i.e., one half of it] talked [about] the advantages of socialism, and the other the advantages of capitalism. I get to be a Soviet person! Well, fine by me! Everyone gives me this look: like, turned Communist, have you? Want to live under socialism, do you? And I'm like, Well, I think things were OK then (*Vot ya schitayu, chto eto bylo normal'no*). If we have to stand up for that system, no problem. I trotted out the arguments. But they was all so up with the times! (*O, u nas vse prodvinutye*—meant sarcastically) Sort of, like, free market and all that stuff. Ooo, the mood they was in! Bite your head off soon as look at you. They're all for emergencies all over the place, free enterprise. And so what was going on when we were in the top form, eh? Barricades all over the street, all that stuff was starting. I couldn't buy any bread for my parents, for instance, in the village where I was studying or working. Well, though, I did have a happy childhood, all in all, it was an OK childhood (*Nu tak, v printsipe u menya bylo schastlivoe detstvo. Takoe normal'noe*).[24]

The informants cited were people from rank-and-file Soviet backgrounds. In the first case, the person concerned had become, through education, a member of the intelligentsia, though her parents were manual workers; but in the second, the speaker was still a manual worker at the time of the interview. So there is not a direct link between social status and the experience of 'happy childhood', as is sometimes argued.[25] And not all positive testimony is retrospective. There is an interesting contrast, in the unpublished memoirs of Boris Rodoman (born 1931, memoirs written 1949–1952), between the author's own state of melancholy, as an adolescent, and his recollection of an acquaintance who entirely espoused the Stalinist ideal of happiness, despite being an orphan:

When my father […] launched into a rather tactless expression of sympathy, saying that living with your uncle and aunt couldn't be the same as with your parents, Genya politely but decisively interrupted and said some words that sank so deeply into my soul that I haven't simply remembered them by heart, but keep hearing them resounding in my ears: 'No! I don't miss my papa and mama! I'm having a good life with them [i.e., his uncle and aunt], and I wish everyone could have as good a life! I'm very happy!' He, an eleven-year old Pioneer, said this so simply and with such conviction, so seriously and so joyously […] Not every boy of this age thinks so seriously about happiness and the purpose of his life, but Genya, saying this, expressed the feelings of all Pioneers, of all our happy Soviet children.[26]

In this particular case, the orphaned child had stayed in the family, but people brought up in orphanages could also be positive about their experiences. In our interviews with such people, the term *schast'e* was seldom used, but informants usually described their childhood experiences as *normal'nye* (not so much 'normal' as 'fine', and, in some contexts, the most appropriate translation of English 'happy') or even *prekrasnye* (wonderful). And this despite the fact that recollections sometimes recorded what, to an external observer, sounded like horrendous discomfort or even physical suffering. For instance, a woman born in 1938 who was in an orphanage in the Perm' area between the ages of nine and fifteen remembered that the children were made to kneel on dried peas as a punishment, that they only ever had cold water to wash in, and that they were never able to clean their teeth. But she also said she relished the sense of discipline that was imparted by her orphanage upbringing, and had many positive memories. 'It was good. That was a good time,' she summed up.[27]

Thus, a sense that life had improved (most informants interviewed in 2003–2006 firmly believed that their children were better off materially, if nothing else) turned out not to devalue the sense that one's own childhood (or at worst, someone else's childhood) had been happy, if not necessarily blissfully so. Sometimes, such reminiscences had a didactic ring, as in the words of a village informant: 'We weren't allowed to hang round idle. But we'd go berry picking, we'd swim, we'd lie in the sun, we'd read, we'd study plenty, so we didn't give any grief. We had fun, but we worked too.'[28] Here, one has a clear case of 'narrative double-voicing' in the phrase 'we didn't give any grief' (*gorya s nami ne bylo*), which identifies 'happiness' with 'causing no trouble', and gives a nudge in the ribs to 'modern youngsters', who, by implication, are forever pestering others to get what they want. But in many other recollections, there is a stronger sense of the viewpoint of the child back then, as in the following happy memories associated with the unexpected discovery of an ordinary object recounted by a woman born into a Perm' working-class family in 1960:

Interviewer: So what are your earliest memories of childhood?
Informant: Our own house, a big family. We only had two rooms. And there's this story I always tell my children. We didn't have much to live on; no one did back then. (*My zhili bedno, da vse v to vremya zhili nebogato.*) And next door they were pulling down this house; everyone had moved out. And it was raining. And someone must have gone there to shelter

and left their raincoat behind. It was this thin one, made of kind of oilcloth. And we went out for a walk, and I found that raincoat. Oooh, was I overjoyed! (*I u menya byli radosti!*) But then they came for the coat, and I had to give it back.[29]

In similar vein, a woman born in 1938, whose family moved from Leningrad to a settlement in Leningrad province when she was a small child, recalled the impact of exploring round what had once (before the Finno-Soviet War) been a Finnish village:

My most vivid memory is when we went round the Finnish farms—it used to be a Finnish area here—and... it was so beautiful, those Finnish houses, those Finnish gardens... We climbed through all the attics, the rooms, their Finnish vegetable gardens, it was so... I still remember how beautiful it all was...[30]

According to these recollections, children are gifted with a capacity to respond vividly to experience, and this can be manifested in the most unpropitious circumstances. One informant even remembered listening with great enjoyment to her uncle's memories of the dreadful things that had been done to him under interrogation after his arrest in 1937.[31] Eager curiosity could, it seems, extend even to areas that adults find repellent.

Obviously, it would be a considerable leap of faith to move from these recollections, recorded years after the event, to a judgment about how happy children actually were in the Soviet period. Overall assessments of the emotional, psychological, and moral impact of socialisation are one of the areas where informants' recollections are most subject to permeation by official discourse. In the words of a woman who was raised in a Leningrad orphanage, 'I have really good memories of childhood [...] Even now, I tell the children I teach, I say to them: "We should be grateful to the state because no one knows what would have become of us if state bodies hadn't taken us in." '[32] This last statement is a commonplace of recollections from informants brought up in orphanages; while without doubt completely sincere, it does not necessarily reflect the view of children themselves at a time when they were living in orphanages. If asked for their recollections in detail, as opposed to a summary of what they feel about orphanage life, informants make clear that children were quite capable of being 'ungrateful'—of, for instance, using their status as war orphans to negotiate for favors. 'We used to dwell on our rights: "What have we got to do with it, we're not to blame for having lost everything in the war." '[33] The stereotype of orphan experience, though, conforms to the redemptive patterns ('happy to be saved') common in Soviet culture generally.[34] In the other direction, informants from villages tended to integrate childhood into the pattern of lamentation in which they remain engaged, denying that they ever experienced a 'real childhood' ('What kind of childhood did I have?!' (*Da kakoe detstvo bylo?!*)), though their recollections at a microscopic level usually indicated that they in fact possessed toys (albeit simple, home-made ones), played games, engaged in mischief and experienced other aspects of what would generally have been understood as a 'normal childhood' in the Soviet period.

It is easier to generalise about the extent to which memoirists recall moments of happiness, and in which contexts they occurred. Not surprisingly, those brought up in the post-Stalin era recorded many more 'happy moments', and interviews with informants who were raised at this time generally lacked the recollections of truly tragic events—the arrest of a parent, wartime displacement, starvation or persistent hunger—that were recalled by many informants who grew up before the mid-1950s. But equally important was the divide between urban and rural childhood. An open question about first memories ('What are your most vivid memories of childhood?') often produced positive recollections from people who grew up in cities even before the late 1950s:

> Well, my first memory—my parents don't believe this by the way—goes back to when I wasn't much more [older] than one. I had an uncle who was in the army, so he lived in the Baltic states, somewhere across the border, he had money, and we lived in Yaroslavl', and life was quite hard, well, it wasn't the kind of childhood you'd have now. And for us, he was as good as GUM and TsUM combined, and who knows what else too. I remember well how my uncle arrived and brought a bar of chocolate and some absolutely amazing lollies, we still have the box, by the way. And my mum said, 'No, you can't possibly.' Then I did a map for her of who was sitting where, and she was astonished, but she did agree in principle that it really had happened like that.[35]

By contrast, village memories tended to begin not just with lamentatory formulae, but with deprivation in concrete detail:

> **Interviewer:** So before you started working, do you remember anything, from when you were really little, anything back then?
> **Informant:** Well, what am I sposed to say? There was no grain, our parents worked for next to nothing (*za palochki*), they cut corn from one day's end to the other, half-starved, we was, we grated potatoes and made bread ourselves. With goosegrass (*lebeda*).
> **Interviewer:** And you children grated the potatoes?

Informant: Yes.
Interviewer: Really?
Informant: Yes. So we never had enough bread in our mouths, but then my parents got signed up and we left for the north. Until the… We left in '42, then we started living up north. My parents got signed up, they promised them the moon, but when we arrived… water everywhere, you could only use boats, and it was ex-kulaks living there. They'd done well enough for themselves, of course, they all had two-storey houses…[36]

Certainly, there are exceptions—such as the memories of wandering round Finnish farms quoted earlier. But here, of course, the informant was emphasising her contact with out-of-the-ordinary experience, with something 'foreign' (in a positive sense). Mostly, village informants began by speaking of what was always familiar, and very often the 'familiar' meant misery.

Even in villages, there were some lighter moments, though. Festivals were always a high point. Children would enjoy egg rolling at Easter, or go out to watch the drinking, dancing, and fighting with which adults and young people passed the time on festival days.[37] But nothing special was organised for village children at such events, at any rate before the 1960s. Thus, one of the big changes that took place in the twentieth century—the development of a sense that children ought to be entertained over holidays, and that special foods and entertainments should be provided for them—affected city children much earlier than village ones. Already by 1917, the Christmas-tree party (*elka*) was becoming quite widespread as a festival in well-off families, and in institutions; in the late 1930s, this festival was reinvented as New Year. For most urban children brought up in the second half of the twentieth century, New Year was a particularly happy memory:

And I have these memories, I remember them all the time—how the Chinese would put long stilts on for New Year and walk at the end of the procession, bringing up the rear. I always wondered—how could they walk like that? Lots and lots of balloons, lots and lots of flowers out of people's gardens. Everyone out walking, everyone giving each other good wishes, all so happy. (*Vse idut, drug druga pozdravlyaut, schastlivye takie.*)[38]

Birthdays, another recently invented festival,[39] were another highlight. Often, informants also recount their joy at receiving presents:

Informant: The presents I looked forward to most were from my grandmother, because my grandparents lived in the south. My birthday comes in mid-Spring, and the first fruit was already around by then. Right. And we'd always go and meet that parcel.[40] There'd be maybe one or two boxes (nice big heavy ones). And it was hard work getting them home. Right. And they smelled so delicious. I'll remember the smell forever. It was a kind of train smell, mixed up with the smell of those early fruits, there was lots of fresh green leaves, and presents too, sweets, jam—that is, all in all, something really tasty, and nice, and really a proper celebration. But my birthday generally? Well, really, they gave me what I wanted, what I asked for, see.

Interviewer: So your mother asked what you wanted?

Informant: No, she didn't ask, I just told her. It was simpler. Right. I just needed to start whining for something... Well, see, there'd be heaps of things, so if me and mum went to a toyshop, you could just see, a child's eyes'll light up when he sees some toy or other. I'd say, I want that. Right. She'd say, no no, that's really dear, we can't possibly buy that. And then maybe she'd save up, or she'd borrow some money, but anyway, on big days—New Year and my birthday—I'd get things. But on the twenty-third of February,[41] it'd be some really small present, for whatever reason. So maybe [that's why] I don't like the twenty-third of February.[42]

Again, such moments proliferated in the memories of informants brought up from the late 1950s onward. This was a period when home celebrations such as New Year and birthday parties were encouraged, both as a way of reinforcing family solidarity and as a way of fostering secular, as opposed to religious, practices (the era saw a revival of atheist propaganda, with associated attacks on Easter, Christmas, and traditional saints' days such as the *prestol'nyi prazdnik* ('pattern day', the feast day of the patron saint of a local church).[43]

This is not to say that unhappiness had vanished from the records. Indeed, as informants recount, hostile feelings towards an era could become all the more bitter when problems often came from within the family, rather than from outside. Parental drinking was one case in point:

I'm not saying that he [the informant's father] hurt us in a physical sense, it was just that all the swearing we heard had an impact, because there were families where they didn't say things like that and didn't drink [...] I wanted to write down all those nasty words, that's what the effect was. Because I kept hearing them, probably. [...] I wrote a few words down on a bit of paper, three or four words, and with mistakes in too—going by the sound. And so I got a thrashing.[44]

According to recollections, another cause of unhappiness was the imposition of punishment, which inspired indignation even when recalled years later:

> You get a smack on the bum, you stand in the corner, and then you have to ask forgiveness for not eating some revolting meatballs?[45]

The punishment involved did not have to be physical: being forced to stand in the corner could provoke equal rage, while some informants also recall feeling deeply hurt by parents' shouting, or indeed by the 'softest' form of punishment—pantomimes of rejection, such as refusing to speak to a child.[46]

The nature of remembered happiness also varied according to the phase of childhood being remembered. Positive memories of early childhood were above all associated with the family; thereafter, the peer group was usually the dominant space associated with happiness, and, indeed, unhappiness. Children came across their peers in official institutions, such as schools, children's homes and Pioneer camps, but they also came across them in less formal associations, such as streets or the large city courtyards (*dvory*) that acted as playspaces for youngsters in the larger cities, particularly Moscow and Leningrad.[47] While encounters in these areas did not tend to be bathed in the roseate glow that saturates earlier memories, they were recalled as interesting and exciting; and even for children who did not much enjoy formal education, the opportunity to make friends with other children was often a redeeming feature of life at school.

In themselves, the happy moments recalled by those remembering their Soviet childhood emerged as generally compatible with official views of happiness as expressed in Soviet propaganda. Satirists might pour scorn on the infantile nature of the Soviet population, but the Soviet concatenation of concern and control (*zabota i vnimanie*) was expressed in its most appealing form with reference to childhood experience. When people remembered childhood, especially late Soviet childhood, in the early twenty-first century, what they remembered was often a 'happiness' or contentment born of security, familiarity, a sense of certainty and a sense of purpose. While undoubtedly fed by post-Soviet anomie, this vision of the past at the same time itself fuelled anomie; informants' sense of the disintegration that they were witnessing in the present was exacerbated by a conviction that life had not always been like this, that someone had once cared about them (and that, by extension, people in society generally had once cared about each other).

Thus, though the question of whether children actually *were* happy under Soviet power is essentially unanswerable, the fact that many, perhaps most, adults looking back on their experiences in the late Soviet period *believed* themselves to have been happy (and contrasted this with the experiences of today's children) had an important emotional, cultural and, indeed, political resonance. In *Speak, Memory*, Nabokov provocatively claimed that his main grudge against the Bolsheviks was that they had stolen his childhood. It would not be too fanciful to suggest that many of Russia's citizens during the late 1990s and early 2000s believed that current social and political circumstances had tarnished the sense of innocent happiness they felt as children and deprived their own children of the chance to experience this, and that these parents' response was one of anger—and resentment against the forces blamed for having brought about the changes, which were often identified with 'the West' in general.[48]

Chapter Two

UTOPIAN NATURALISM: THE EPIC POEM OF KOLKHOZ HAPPINESS

Evgeny Dobrenko

... essential, it seems,
That a poem's style fit its themes.
— Nikolai Nekrasov, *Imitation of Schiller*

1

Soviet 'Great Style' is primarily associated with the 'grand' genre forms. In painting, this means ceremonial portraits and battle scenes; in music, it means opera, oratorios, cantatas, symphonies; in city planning, architectural complexes; in prose, novels; and in poetry, the epic poem. As a sort of narrative in verse, the epic poem, like operas and programmatic music, was narrative in form, and the connection to heroic style made it the embodiment of 'epic thinking', and made it especially close to the Socialist Realist aesthetic—much closer than lyric poetry, and it was no coincidence that the first glimmers of the thaw in Soviet literature were connected precisely to the 'discussion about lyric poetry'.

The genre hierarchy in Stalinism can infallibly be reconstructed according to the preferences in awarding the Stalin Prizes (Stalin, as is well known, personally participated in distributing these prizes). Thus, in the period spanning 1934 to 1952, there was not a single year in which a Stalin Prize for poetry was not conferred on an epic poem (the others were for poem cycles, anthologies of poetry, lyrics of popular songs, and translations of poetry). And although the Soviet epic poem had a broad thematic range—about Stalin, the army, war victories, youth, achievements in industry, heroism, history, and so forth—none of these themes enjoyed more steadfast support than that of the *kolkhoz*. Beginning with Aleksandr Tvardovskii's 'The Land of Muravia' (*Strana Muraviia*), which consolidated the canon of the 'kolkhoz poem' itself, kolkhoz poems were awarded seven prizes. For the period 1934–1940 (the first wave of Stalin Prizes, which were established in 1939), Tvardovskii's work received the 'first degree' prize in 1941. For 1947, Nikolai Gribachev's 'The "Bolshevik" Kolzhoz' (*Kolkhoz 'Bol'shevik'*) and Aleksei Nedogonov's 'Flag over the Village Soviet' (*Flag nad sel'sovetom*) both took first degree prizes. For 1948, the prizes went to Belorussian poet Arkadii Kuleshov's poem 'A New Channel' (*Novoe ruslo*) and Gribachev's 'Spring in 'Pobeda' (*Vesna v 'Pobede'*). For 1949, it went to Aleksandr Iashin's 'Alena Fomina.' And for 1951, the prize went to another kolkhoz poem, Vladimir Zamiatin's 'The Green Shelterbelt' (*Zelenyi zaslon*). (1952, when the prizes for 1951 were announced, was the last year in which Stalin Prizes were given.) What function did the kolkhoz poem fulfill, and why did it invariably have such support from Stalin?

Nowhere else did the conservative Utopia of Stalin's 'socialist modernisation' manifest itself so obviously, nor was the 'Russification of Marxism' expressed so brightly, as in collectivisation, with its reliance on the patriarchal Russian commune. The kolkhoz poem, which first came together in the times of collectivisation and then flourished during late Stalinism, fulfilled a function in the representation of communal agrarian socialism as a realisation of the Marxist modernisation project and of the mode of the patriarchal commune as contemporary collective agriculture. If the kolkhoz poem was in this sense national in content and socialist in form, then the kolkhoz system that it 'reflected' was itself a national form of socialist content. There is a complex symbiosis of revolutionary-socialist utopian Marxist fantasizing and a thousand-year-old communal tradition that had a profoundly patriarchal form; imposed on this form was an ideologically alien but socially akin form of socialist ('according to Marx') economy. The kolkhoz poem was supposed to accommodate a communal, essentially feudal structure with its *lubok* aesthetics in a bed of Marxist ideology. But since political-ideological representation and aesthetic 'packaging' were so much more important in Stalinism than reality itself, the kolkhoz poem had been allotted maximally high status against the backdrop of a most perilous Stalinist economic project: If industrialisation did have positive effects, then collectivisation reduced them to nothing, impoverishing the Soviet economy once and for all. In a sense, the kolkhoz era became an extended farewell to the commune, a sort of requiem for the loss of the thousand-year-old Russian village. This requiem was fully in the spirit of Stalinist art; a feast during a time of plague, frolicking at a wake.

If, as Roland Barthes observed, mythology is based on the transformation of *history* into nature, then Socialist Realism is based on the transformation of

Utopia into nature. For this naturalisation to find aesthetic dimensions and to be transformed into a sort of *utopian naturalism*, the Utopia had to possess some sort of fascination beyond rationality. Only thus is it capable of being realised in traditional (albeit transformed, as well) genre forms. Marxist Utopias in a peasant country were transformed into ready-made constructs that by no means always found a genre canon corresponding to the Russian literary tradition. However, it was precisely the communal Utopia that remained closest to both the tradition of Russian popular culture (to *lubok*, of course, first and foremost) and the Russian literary tradition (primarily to populist poetry, going back to the poetic school of the Surikovians, all the way back to Nekrasov).

When discussion turns to the 'kolkhoz genres' of Stalinist art, what is primarily recalled is *lubok*, which traditionally falls somewhere between high culture and folklore, between the professional culture of the educated strata of the populace and peasant culture. Popular literature, which Iurii Lotman defined as 'the folklore of literature' and the 'literature of folklore',[1] and to which, undoubtedly, *lubok* belongs, occupied a special place in Soviet culture by virtue of the social structure that came together in Russia on the eve of the Revolution, and following it. The enormous rift between the cultural level of the few in the educated stratum and that of the overwhelming mass of the peasant population was intensified many-fold as a result of the Revolution and the Civil War, which in fact swept away the former social elites in Russia. Cultural revolution and the landslide of urbanisation led to a dramatic growth of the so-called intermediate stratum, which had lost its ties to peasant culture, but had not yet found its link with urban culture (or had acquired only a superficial acquaintance with it). This was the social stratum that became the fundamental class under Stalinism, in essence remaining in the same intraintellectual position in which the cities' lower classes found themselves before the Revolution—with their alienation from high culture and their attraction to cultural compensation. And it was Socialist Realist *lubok*— accessible, festive, institutionalised and ideologically consecrated, all at the same time—that promised them this compensation. For the fundamental mass of the Soviet population, with its cultural self-identity split in half, this art form created a comfort zone, an 'illusion of harmony' and of cultural homogeneity.[2]

Living parasitically from both high culture and folklore, *lubok* is a simulative phenomenon par excellence. What chiefly distinguishes it from the cultural phenomena that it uses is not only the fact that it does not produce anything original, but also that it contains nothing that is real; everything that falls into this arena is transformed into a simulation and loses its dimensionality. Styles, genres, speech patterns and laughter are all simulated in it. Forms developed by high culture descend to the lower strata of the cities' 'common folk', where they are reshaped into 'mass culture' (*lubok*), with its characteristic eclecticism of styles, images and motifs. As a result of the tectonic cultural shift that took place because of the Revolution, however, entire layers of high culture went 'downward'. From their fragments, at the boundary between the two cultures, the formation of a new, unique culture began—a culture that was simultaneously mass-oriented and semi-official, accessible but status-bearing; though it 'belonged to the people', it was reinforced by the might of state institutions. This culture of aestheticised and politicised *lubok* was Socialist Realism.

Lubok is organically tied to acting and folk theatre—Christmastime show booths, folk drama, puppet shows, *skomorokh*, and in the broadest sense, to the culture of fairs. It is connected not simply to any festival event, but specifically with the fair, that is, to a *commercial* festival, a marketplace. As one of the most authoritative researchers of *lubok*, Boris Sokolov, observed, '*lubok* can be distinguished from "non-*lubok*" only according to aesthetic criteria. But since *lubok*, a product of mass art, reflects not so much the interests of its creator as those of its consumer, the aesthetic nature of each page is determined by its function.'[3] In other words, the 'aesthetic criteria' are directly dependent on the social functions of *lubok* and on its nature *as a commodity*. In this sense, *lubok* is the ideal ready-made model for Socialist Realism, which was also created to the 'taste' of the purchaser-state and of 'the people' as consumer.

This obliges us to ponder the figure of the 'creator'. As Sokolov asserts, 'the commodity in festive urban folklore … was not so much a spectacle as a game, collective playful improvisation and jollity.'[4] The transformation of the game—that is, of the artistic act per se—into a commodity was the key element of the political economy of *lubok*. To paraphrase Pushkin's famous dictum, 'Inspiration is not for sale, but one may sell a manuscript,' we might say that for the lack of a 'manuscript', the commodity in *lubok* was 'inspiration' per se, which we might more precisely call simulation or trade-fair-style trickery.

The Soviet writer was moulded, in fact, into a 'producer' bureaucrat to create the kind of 'artistic production' that was to 'reflect the interests of the consumer'. This had important consequences for the 'creative process': adapting to the 'interests of the consumer' presupposes a reduction of the principle of 'playfulness' and a simulation of artistry, a commodification and, effectively, a simulation of the creative artistic process.[5] Thus, against the background of the starving country, the cheerless merriment in Ivan Pyr'ev's kolkhoz films, Semen Babaevskii's kolkhoz novels, or Gribachev's kolkhoz poems, was the product of sheer aestheticisation of reality. The social function of this aestheticisation was the derealisation of life, an ideological sublimation of life meant to induce social amnesia. Socialist Realism inevitably was transformed into *lubok*, which by its social and aesthetic nature was also a 'merry art' created 'in the interests of the consumer'. Once it became a highly prized ideological commodity in Socialist Realism, *lubok* required an industrialised, assembly line mode of production.

2

Peasant poetry (from Ivan Nikitin to Ivan Surikov) inherited the traditions of 'folk culture' directly; but for Nekrasov, literary *reworking* of folklore (and, in part, aestheticisation of *lubok*) became a defining feature. Soviet criticism, which canonised Nekrasov, wrote tirelessly about the folklore tradition in his work. Kornei Chukovskii did more than anyone else for the study of Nekrasov, in his book *Nekrasov's Craftsmanship*.

Nekrasov in all respects remains an important starting point for any discussion of the kolkhoz poem. As Chukovskii noted on this subject, 'the old countryside had to completely disappear, and Nekrasov's Nenilas, Oref'evnas, Naums, and Vlases had to retreat into the irretrievable past, so that [Mikhail] Isakovskii, Tvardovskii, and other great poets continuing Nekrasov's literary work could arise from the folk milieu.'[6] Chukovskii perceived this continuation in the fact that 'in "The Land of Muravia" and in "Vasilii Terkin", Tvardovskii's verse is so connected to popular thinking and to popular forms of speech that, as is also the case with [Nekrasov's] "Who is to Live Well in Russia?" it is impossible to clearly delineate the author's own creation from the folk sayings, nursery rhymes, and proverbs with which his text is so abundantly larded.'[7]

Chukovskii welcomed the folklorisation of Soviet poetry, but he discerned completely new qualities in Soviet folklore. For example, if the old folklore was sad (the ceremonial lamentations and ritual wedding songs, for instance), then Soviet folklore was, on the contrary, happy. And everything new and joyous that the Soviet government and kolkhoz life brought found expression in this happiness of the new folklore. Chukovskii was so pleased by Tvardovskii's 'jollifying' of the ceremonial songs in 'The Land of Muravia' that he exclaimed, 'These verses are so folksy that it would not be at all surprising if kolkhoz weddings started to be celebrated with these verses.'[8] Clearly, there could not have been such happiness in Nekrasov: 'Nekrasov did not know these rollicking *chastushki* forms. He would not have been the mouthpiece for the moods of the peasant serfs if he had not conveyed, in the melodies themselves of his poetry, the mournful sound of the songs begotten of thousands of years of slavery.'[9] In the drafts of his *Who is to Live Well in Russia?* Nekrasov wrote, 'All the songs are unhappy, / All the songs are forced. / There were no others at that time / And still, there are not any!' However, Nekrasov envisioned something else: 'Other times / Will come, yes!—God is gracious—/ Other songs will arise / And there will be no complaints / About the slavish lot in them. / Not slavish grief / But the joy, now laughing, / Of the Russian people's soul / The soul, bounced back / From gloom and despair!'[10]

Chukovskii suggested that 'now that "the people's soul" has finally "begun to laugh", the people's new songs have lost their former plaintiveness,' and opined that Soviet poetry, 'even in its sound and rhythm has now become much more in the major key.'[11] Optimism, the major key, and happiness were all to become the main qualities of Soviet poetry. Finally, we can see the 'soul … now laughing'—in the kolkhoz poem.

3

Isakovskii and Tvardovskii were the founders of kolkhoz poetry, and their work represented its peak. But the kolkhoz poem did not arrive immediately at the synthesis of Nekrasov and *lubok*. At the beginning, it had no place for literary tradition. Nikolai Zabolotskii's poem 'The Triumph of Farming' gives us an idea of the 'grass-roots kolkhoz poetry' of the second half of the 1920s and the first half of the 1930s, nurtured first by the Peasant Writers' Union and then by the Russian Organisation of Proletarian-Kolkhoz Writers. Written in 1929 and 1930, it not only stands as one of the apical accomplishments of the Russian avant-garde, but is also a pointed parody of the developing canon of kolkhoz poetry, just as Andrei Platonov's *Foundation Pit* was a parody of another nascent super-genre of Socialist Realism, the industrial novel. Moreover, the parody in many respects anticipated its object. Many of the lines in Zabolotskii's work (including those in the prologue, 'Nature here was all a-sprawl / In frightful disarray…') read, in fact, like rhymed versions of Platonov's prose. It goes without saying, however, that this definition cannot by any means provide an exhaustive characterisation of either Platonov's novel or Zabolotskii's poem.[12] The parodic layer of Zabolotskii's work is tied not only to the author's philosophy of nature, but also to the genesis of the work itself.

It is worth noting that aesthetic criticism, which dealt only with the material of 'high literature' and ignored such phenomena as 'grass-roots poetry' or 'popular literature', overlooked this connection. It was noticed, however, by Viacheslav Zavalishin, who got his own start in the 1930s in the 'Chisel' (*Rezets*) group of young working-class poets in Leningrad. Once he emigrated, Zavalishin readily observed 'from what kind of rubbish' Zabolotskii's genial poem arose—from worker-peasant poetry: 'Zabolotskii did not start out so much from Khlebnikov, as Gleb Struve not quite accurately states, as he did from what actually harked back to Khlebnikov—the grotesquely satirical current of post-October poetry to which A. Zviagin's collection of poems, *Khlebnukha*, and Vasilii Kazin's 'Newspaper' both belong.'[13] The name Vasilii

Kazin, one of the leading proletarian poets and organisers of the 'Smithy' (*Kuznitsa*) group, needs no comment. Aleksei Zviagin was one of the 'peasant poets', and his anthology, *Khlebnukha: Songs of Earth and Sky, 1924–1925*, with an introductory article by Grigorii Deev-Khomiakovskii, chairman of both the 'Surikov Circle of Writers From the People' and the 'Peasant Writers' Society', was published by the All-Russian Union of Peasant Writers in 1926.

The structure itself of Zabolotskii's work reproduces the 'sensible peasant conversation', so beloved in kolkhoz poetry, about the soul and God (the character Nikita Morgunok in 'The Land of Muravia' would discuss just these subjects). This conversation goes on, as usual, at a school, where the pupils are asleep. Also present are a backward peasant, a kulak, and a positive hero—the Soldier, who has 'progressive ideas'. These characters are drawn in a way that is not even so much parodic and satirical as it is 'overdone', *lubok*-like. Dmitrii Prigov might well have written the same about a kulak:

> Rich peasant, master of his men for hire,
> Sat there, magnified by riches,
> He, self-centred in his world,
> Which o'er many clouds was higher.

The Soldier's debate with the ancestors, as well as his debate with the animals that figure as simple kolkhozniks from a kolkhoz poem, is full of parodic energy bent on neutralising the utopian potential of kolkhoz poetry. His daydream about the future is similar to the dream of Marfa Lapkina, a character in Sergei Eisenstein's film *Old and New* (or *The General Line*), which also came out in 1929; in the film, Lapkina, who has no horse, bands together with a local agronomist and *bedniak* peasants to organise a dairy cooperative in the village; the local kulaks actively oppose this, and not all the *bedniaks* understand the meaning of collectivisation. Lapkina's dreams of the future abundance of milk can be easily linked to the dream of 'The Land of Muravia' in Tvardovskii's work and to the dreams about communism in numerous kolkhoz poems. What Zabolotskii's Soldier dreamed about represents a parodic mishmash of the social, industrial and scientific Utopias on which the kolkhoz poem was based: 'Then I saw a redden'd torch / In the clever ox's palace. / Th'assembly, pensive, of the cows / Worked out all their business there. [...] / The donkey wandered through the hills, / Gnawing at cast-iron potatoes, / But, mountainside, the temple of Machine / Made pancakes all of oxygen. / Chemistry's friends, the horses there / Gulped down hundred-moleculed *shchi*, / Yet others, hanging there midair, / Watched to see who else would come. / The cow, on formulas, on ribbons, / Baked a pie from elements, / And by her, there, within a jar / Chemical oats grew tall and lush.'

The very last part of this excerpt is noteworthy: Lapkina's dream and Zabolotskii's 'chemical oats' both acquire a new dimension in art—the 'free milkmaids and workers' believe in them. Alongside Aleksandr Medvedkin's films *Happiness* (1934) and *The Miracle Worker* (1936), we can define these texts, as does Oleg Kovalov, as 'neo-Utopias,' wherein 'the features of reality are not magically transfigured by a stream of light from the beautiful future, but rather are so deformed by a press of mythological strata that even the things glorified seem distorted, defective or deformed.'[14] The artist in this situation 'is constrained more and more into an artificial state of reserve, from which stepping out into the territory of reality is more dangerous than stepping onto a mine. Boxed in, he has endeavoured to find freedom, if not in the expression of reality, then in the forms of glorifying it', which, of course, could not be successful when 'even extolling reality was permitted [only] according to a standard form and a fixed canon—by the permission of a grudgingly allocated coupon indulgently pushed towards the supplicant with a little finger, on a first-come, first-served basis, with a probing stare that went all down one's back and with stinking radish breath in one's face.'[15] This gave rise to a strained atmosphere in which the artist began to play the fool or behave outrageously, finding *lubok* to be just the ready-made 'national form' that he needed. Soviet *lubok*, this poisoned draught of freedom, restricts one's breathing. The artist 'now and then chokes from the absurdity, as if from underneath the peeling lacquer of the *Palekh* makers' lyrical *lubok*, the lurid, membranous wing of a Goyan batfish had stuck out: the kolkhoz Eden begins to gleam with the deceptively optimistic tints of a Potemkin village.'[16]

'The Triumph of Farming' was literature's response to the grass-roots 'proletarian-kolkhoz poetry' of the latter half of the 1920s. We can at least partially judge the state in which this poetry found itself in the following decade by what turned up in the public arena in the mid-1930s: At this time, the leading publishing houses and journals printed either panegyric poems glorifying the kolkhozes (such as, for example, Tvardovskii's first poem entitled 'The Path to Socialism', published in 1931) or unabashedly *lubok*-style kolkhoz fairy-tale poems. An example of the latter is the poem of Nikolai Nezlobin (a much-published figure of the 1930s) entitled 'Treasure: A tale in verse about the landless peasant Eremei, the village blacksmith Iakun, a priest, a miller, a prince, and three *bogatyrs*', which was blatantly written in the style of *lubok*. This poem was not only published as a separate book issued by the 'Soviet Writer' publishing house in 1935, but was also excerpted in the leading Soviet 'thick' journal, *Novyi mir*. The main character in this fairy tale, Eremei, steals the moon. As a result, the sun no longer set upon the Soviet lands. So, 'hiding the bright moon 'neath his side', Eremei sets off for the Kremlin, where he ascends 'on the carpets of the broad staircases' until he finally reaches the top: 'The hall was like the wide,

wide world, / and packed it was with people— / the smallest mouse could not squeeze in— / They'd gathered to make nature / subject to the power of man.'

The hall in the Kremlin is a metaphor for the Soviet country: 'Experts of the highest rank, / famous breed of kolkhoz fields, / stalwart growers of the grain, / the eminent collective. // They gathered as one family / from regions and republics, / heroes there, with sunburn brown, / of battles waged in fields.' In it, there are 'Cossacks from the Seven Rivers, herders, shepherds', as well as 'gray-eyed milkmaids from the steep-banked Oka'; right alongside them are an 'academician, and a people's commissar'. The culmination is the appearance of Stalin in the hall, an event described in the style of the new 'Soviet folklore': 'The hour struck, all present stood / the delegates, as one— / Comrade Stalin had come in, / from side doors, not the main one. // And not a downpour, not a downpour, / not thunder, whirlwind, squall— / the hall, so great, / began to roar / wider than the sea, and stronger. // Stalin gaily nods his head, / smiles through his mustaches, / from his pocket takes his watch / the one with clear glass face. // With his smile and with his watch / he tries to shush the noisy throng / as if to say, "It's time, / you know, to start the meeting." // But, hardly was the stormy sea / becalmed, when, suddenly, / a voice from someone there is heard / louder than the blizzard of applause. // Another downpour through the hall, / again a whirlwind blows! / Happier then than all on earth / was every soul within that hall.'

This is the moment when Eremei's magical transformation takes place: 'Not a trace remained / of his past, rabid life.' On the contrary, now 'Erema's suit is light gray finest twill.[17] / Soft his sweater, many-coloured, / fitted with a silken collar, / the corner of a notebook shows / from his outer pocket.' All of this occurs thanks to his encounter with Stalin: 'Who has helped Erema out? / Who the way to him did show / from rural village, hard to find, / to sunlight, and the Kremlin, / and to this mighty hall? // Now here he stands, with fear of no one, / as if he were right at home… / Stalin gazes at Erema, / and Erema, back at him.' In his conversation with Stalin, Eremei finally reveals the secret of his treasure: 'Weighed down by life I was, / dearest Comrade Stalin, / believing in the demons and the oaths, / in old traditions and in witchcraft, // Black cats, icons, held their sway, / and treasures buried in the woods, / but to the kolkhoz, like a garden, / I came, and saw in *it* that treasure!'

Eremei has brought, 'as a gift to the conference', the moon, which he has kept in his tobacco pouch. This gift highly pleases all the delegates. It was not needed so that day and night could be switched in the Soviet lands, but rather so that the joyous kolkhozniks, when leaving to go home, could leave their greeting for Stalin: 'Now fly, our brilliant moon / up to ancient Kremlin walls. / Take our greeting, clearest moon, / to our Soviet capital / and to the leader of our native land!'

4

Nezlobin's clownish eruption of *lubok* found a place in official literature thanks
to the peculiarities of the workings of Stalinist culture. We should keep in mind
that by the mid-1930s, collectivisation had by no means become a forgotten
part of the past. On the contrary, it was a still-open wound; in 1933 alone,
millions of people died from starvation, which was a direct result of
collectivisation, and the severe impoverishment of the countryside resulted in
millions of peasants pouring into the cities and living there in barracks. The
development of the bravura-laden kolkhoz poetry in the first half of the 1930s
was possible only because of a sharp compartmentalisation of the media
under Stalinism: It was as if urban literary production and the real life of the
collectivised countryside existed in different dimensions. Thus, when today one
reads the kolkhoz poetry of the era in tandem with the thousands of
contemporary documents reproduced in the multivolume publications
produced between 1999 and 2005, *The Soviet Countryside Through the Eyes of the
VChK-OGPU-NKVD, 1918–1939* and *The Tragedy of the Soviet Countryside:
Collectivisation and De-Kulakisation, 1927–1939,* one could easily believe that they
existed in different countries and even in different languages.

As a literary phenomenon, the kolkhoz poem begins with 'The Land of
Muravia'. Tvardovskii combined folklore with the literary poetic tradition that
harked back to Nekrasov. Although he introduced a literary current into an
established genre, he rejected *lubok*. The literariness of 'The Land of Muravia'
is characteristic: the homage to Nekrasov and the use of living folkloric forms
are both evident. Tvardovskii constructs the poem with the motif of the
roadway and the quest for a peasant Utopia. Morgunok knew details of the
Land of Muravia that he sought: 'Standing on a steep small hill, / A little
farm, just like a little shrub. / As far and wide as you can see, / Everything is
yours. / You sow a single tiny grain, / And that grain, too, is yours.' This ' little
farm' is the land of the 'petty proprietor', whose main value is freedom: 'And
you don't have to ask a soul, / Respecting self alone. / Time to harvest? You
decide! / Choose to go when best you think.' This is just what makes Muravia
faithful to 'all the peasant rules'. The main thing that stands opposed to it is
'*communia*' (or '*kolkhozia*').

With a narrative based on Morgunok's search for Muravia and his stolen
horse, the poem unfolds as a derealisation of peasant Utopia. And although
Tvardovskii rejects the flat *lubok* picture stylistically, the effect of the new
literariness, with respect to its perspective and ideology, is similar. The poem
is somewhat like a Möbius strip; the surface of its inner ideological plot is
deceptive—it is a true political-ideological circle that, incredible as it may
seem, in fact has only one surface.

'The Land of Muravia' was written between 1934 and 1936, hot on the heels of collectivisation. The traumatic experience is quite palpable in it (it mentions kulak deportations, forced labour, famine and poverty). Nonetheless, the author neutralises this experience by an alternation of time shifts. The collectivisation that affected 'a hundred thousand villages, a hundred million people', for example, is temporally shifted to 1929. The reference to the 'great break' transforms it into history: 'Never before did folk bethink, / in worry and in struggle, / their life, nor hope for living.' Stalin is, of course, present in the poem, but is distanced with a completely folkloric device: According to 'hearsay,' he arrives in the village 'on a raven horse'; 'He rides upright, with pipe in hand, / And in his overcoat [...] / He looks all 'round and chats with people. / In his little book he writes, / In detail, all that needs recording.' But, whereas Nezlobin's Eremei announces how happy he is to live in the kolkhoz when talking with the leader, Tvardovskii's Morgunok, when imagining his own conversation with Stalin, wants to ask the leader to allow him to 'live a little, just once, off my own farm' and 'to leave the little farm alone awhile'. He agrees to remain 'the only one in the whole realm'; however, the seventh chapter of the poem concludes with a peculiar image from the famous poster of the collectivisation era:

> The native land is very great.
> It's spring! The year, too, grand!
> And, calling, 'Forward!', far outstretched,
> A hand is raised o'er all the land.

When portraying the 'little farm', Tvardovskii creates a frightening spectacle of the kulaks who have broken away from kolkhoz life, made all the more sinister by the singsong rhythm, 'The wheat of all the 'people' people, / By the wind is loved and shaken. / But for monstr'ous people, straw / is all that we have flying 'round. // The children of the 'people' people / While the day away in playing, / Then line up, sit themselves at table, / Like fledglings, waiting for their food. // But my poor babies live in squalor / Worse than filthy piglets would. / Not to blame my children, no— / Their father bears the blame!' On the other hand, everything there is their own.

Morgunok's dream of Muravia crumbles to dust upon its first encounter with reality: 'Your life's not life, my friends, / It's only grief and pain. / I look at you and think / I must decide, can't live like you, one shouldn't.' He had to make up his mind to go to the kolkhoz. What was more, life in it was, by all standards, prosperous. It had a 'new farm, / so bright, clean-smelling', and in the livestock paddock, there were 'cows, like those at his farm', and the calves bump 'against the master's hand'; there was also a new stable, with a horse of rare beauty in it, and a young garden 'rushing to bask in sun'. This life had arisen in the 'great year'; at the time the poem was published, this was supposed to be understood not simply as history seven years in the making, but rather as a new point from which historical time would be reckoned. Against this temporal background, the future becomes boundless. Answering Morgunok's question, 'How many years will such a life last?' the kolkhoznik first says five years, then twenty, and, finally, says 'for good':

'For good, you say?'
'Forever!'

The ending of the poem, with a wedding and a boisterous feast, would become the canonical ending for kolkhoz poems (not to mention for kolkhoz novels, plays and films, as well). The abundance portrayed is emphasised redundantly: 'Maple tables stand at ready. / Good housewife, heap them high! / New harvest starts, / New weddings follow on.' The tables here are not simply covered, but are literally 'heaped high'; the 'new wedding' is also the harbinger of a new life and a 'new harvest'. Meanwhile, the table holds huge pies, 'fresh lamb', and mead, and there are 'golden, early winter apples in the garden'. The 'old men' are in contrast to these images of youth, birth, and new life. They appear in almost every chapter of Tvardovskii's poem. The old kolkhoz men at the wedding are pleased with life, and youth has returned to them. One of them, in a toast, says something about a wedding 'in my homestead / and on my land', to which an answer quickly comes: 'Authority is ours, old men! / The family all are gathered here. / We celebrate our happiness / At this, our wedding.' *My* homestead, *my* land, *our* authority, *our* happiness, and even *our* (an old man's!) wedding.

All of this brings us back to Morgunok's original dream of Muravia. At the end of the poem, the hero explains to a wanderer-pilgrim that his dream has disappeared: 'There was a land, Muravia, / And now there is no such. / It's lost, now overgrown / With grass, young grass.' Along with his dream, the 'little farm' and 'his own' land have also disappeared. Only one road remained for Morgunok—the one leading to the kolkhoz. The description of kolkhoz well-being in which Tvardovskii engages definitively derealises the peasant Utopia. The happy life has already come to the kolkhoz, and all that remains for Morgunok is to join it. The price for this virtual well-being and the 'prosperous life' promised by Stalin is the peasant dream about property and freedom. But the dreamed-of things have already been integrated into the kolkhoz paradise, where everything, as it turns out, is 'ours'.

'The Land of Muravia' was justly awarded the 'first degree' Stalin Prize. It consolidated the canon of the kolkhoz poem. Many poets of differing stripe rushed into the genre that Tvardovskii had discovered. However, even Tvardovskii would find himself more and more repulsed by it. Towards the end of his life, he would become its most steadfast opponent, and the main adepts of the Stalinist kolkhoz poem would find themselves on the opposite side of the barricades from the genre's creator.

One of Tvardovskii's most consistent epigones, and, consequently, one of his most implacable opponents, was Nikolai Gribachev. Like Isakovskii and Tvardovskii, Gribachev was also from the Smolensk Region (although he was born in the Bryansk Region and later moved to the city of Smolensk). When he chose the path trodden by his countrymen, he took advantage of the success formula they had developed. Gribachev's kolkhoz poems from the latter 1930s are similar to parts of 'The Land of Muravia', each chapter of which (be it one with glorification of the kolkhozes or with condemnations of the past, with descriptions of celebrations or of work in the fields) could be expanded into a separate poem. Gribachev maintained that his task as a poet was to 'reveal, in artistic images, the features of the communist future that have already become obvious at present in our everyday life, and to paint vivid pictures of the future as continuations of the present.'[18] And, in fact, *the fundamental collision of the kolkhoz poem is modal*: What is happening now and what people 'dream about' are both in located a sort of gray area of half-vision, and the only adequate form of conveying this half-vision is a stream of consciousness, or, more precisely, delirium.

In 'Spring in "Pobeda"', the party organiser Zernov is dying: 'Zernov as if on waves was swimming, / First to sleep and then to waking, / sleep, then waking, / sleep, then waking, / Far he swims, away, away, / Through fever, chills, and night, / He's suffered all he can, and loved, / Days and distances grow dim, / Only mem'ry links him with what's past.' His process of dying is portrayed as a process of immersion into communism: 'He dreamed a rebus, and a vision— / Or did his eyes deceive him? / To "Bolshevik", a trolley bus, / From "Victory" took the highway: / Past the school, the dam, the croplands— / It courses by like singing wind! / The girl, a brigadier, sweeps by / (I think the compact car is hers) / And can it be Somov who's meeting her?!' Somov is Zernov's assistant, whom the dying party organiser makes his successor. In a vision Zernov has, everything has been transformed: 'A dream, or real? Six ears upon a single stalk.' This is how Michurin's wheat grows now in the kolkhoz. What is more, Somov tells him, 'we grow rice in the swamps,' airplanes fly over the fields, and the machines have become electric ('Our technology / Is quiet as it works / Electricity does the plowing, / Our river makes that work'). If Zernov had only dreamed about a power station, then now everything was electrified: 'Three factories—no pipes / Cabinets, asbestos, cement. / No settlement, no city.' The dying man's reaction to what he has seen in his delirium is that communism has arrived: 'A spasm of joy catches in his throat— / So, we've really got it!'

Gribachev intensified the use of narrative, and the *raek* style that Tvardovskii and Isakovskii had used with restraint became a dominant element with Gribachev. In the poem 'Fate' (1938), he describes the difficult life of the prerevolutionary peasant. The poem had a subtitle, 'A rural tale' (*Sel'skaia povest'*), which emphasised the event-narration principle in it. (After the war, this would become a widespread genre definition: Gribachev's 'The "Bolshevik" Kolkhoz', for example, consists of 'stories in verse', each of which is a portrait or scene from the life of a million-strong kolkhoz, and in the first separate book edition had the subtitle 'Portraits of rural life';[19] Iashin's 'Alena Fomina' had the subtitle 'A tale in verse'.) The story about how fate made the younger son in a big peasant family a horse thief is told in the style of a rural peddler's story: 'Like a cart that veers down hills, / My life had gotten off the track. / Nice people have their huts and homes, / But prison's ours, and beatings.' Spending all his time with the gypsies in the market of a little town, and trafficking his stolen horses, the character laments his difficult life during the NEP (New Economic Policy) years: 'Two featherbeds I had, but sparse: / Stitched from wind, / Covered by sky, / Often drenched by rain. / The right one was a tussock, / The left one, clods of dirt.' The plot, however, runs off onto a completely Socialist Realist track. Reforging appears, but the description of it is in chant (this time, in thieves' cant): 'The girl left the boy / With shaggy hair, / But the militia / Swept him away / Into barracks in a sleepy town, / "Now, we'll teach you." / Behind the wheelbarrow, / With a mattock, / And with a saw, days on end... / Day by day, calluses grow, / His back's on fire, / Can't straighten it, / Five shirts to tatters from sweat, / The blizzards are biting, / Gnats stinging, / Day after day.' Leaving the camp, the hero understands that 'The thief's freedom is a lie.'

But it was not only the thief who was transformed at this time; it was also life beyond the camp's boundaries. Returning to his sweetheart, he expects to see the familiar picture, but sees something completely different: 'Garden. Weeds. Gate. Porch... / I looked around— / There's no porch. / Oh, my porch, my porch, / What thief dragged you off? / A hundred-metre wall's sprung up, / Not a dwelling, but a stockyard. / Through the gates a girl comes out, / Lugging buckets and singing.' The kolkhoz has transformed life, and the hero's sweetheart is already taking courses in the city. Nothing remains for him except to return to the gypsies and to horse stealing, but there, too, life has changed; there is no horse trade: 'The city's there, the square is there, / But the market? The devil took it.'

Like the gypsies in 'The Land of Muravia,' Gribachev's gypsies give up stealing horses. The Gypsy King now works as a laborer in a sawmill, and the camp has stopped wandering, since now 'the main thing for youth / Is to learn arithmetic.' Still having the stolen mare, the hero tries to sell it to the kolkhoz. But the kolkhozniks simply marvel at the self-serving man: 'Stay and put yourself on show / A sight to see for all our region / So everyone will see and know / You're not a man, you're a museum.' Everything comes to a halt for the hero when, narrowly escaping the militia, he sorrowfully lets the mare have her freedom. However, the horse does not leave, but instead follows her horse-stealing owner. He then returns her to the kolkhoz from which he stole her, in return for which the kolkhozniks ask him to join them: 'They invite him, actually: / Come on now, and settle here. / The fields give plenty, gardens more, / Just need more hands to work them all. / Stay with us! / Court a girl— / And with your food, and with your hut / You'll be full, / well-shod, / and always clothed.' Thus, yet another 'Muravian dream' has ended happily, with the 'prosperous life' just around the corner, and the hero, now a stableman for the kolkhoz, 'keeps the herds'.

Gribachev's poems are similar to traveling-show stories. The butt of 'humour' is usually the 'old men'. In 'Stepan Elagin' (1938), for example, there is no way for the 'old man embracing communism' to die, since life in the kolkhoz settlement has become extraordinarily interesting. Thus, every time that the old man is getting ready to die, he postpones his own death:

I'll die sometime, and fit the coffin,
I'll die whenever, but what if, maybe,
My grandson invents a thing,
Some like-magic new machine?

Central to the poem is a 'capricious' character, a typical *bedniak* jokester ('Stepan loved to confuse people'): All along, he has related to his home folks the delightful dreams that have, every time, become reality. He dreamed that 'like a little manor plot / All that is, is mine now,' and he supposedly became a tsar himself. After each one of these dreams, 'the whole village made fun of the jolly peasant.' But Stepan's dreams 'come true'. Once the revolution comes, his home folks call on him to 'divide his lordly land', but Stepan says that he is too old: 'I'm ready to die.' Just at the point of death, however, he relates a new 'odd' dream: he has dreamed about a 'steel bird' upon which one can 'travel through all the heights'. Just then, a plane flies into the village. Having had a flight on it, Stepan again prepares to die: 'He smokes his pipe, awaits his death. But it won't come.' Then he again 'reconsiders dying' and relates a new dream in which he saw a machine 'that cut the wheat itself, and reaped it, too. / It gathered up the sheaves itself, / Milled the kernels, too, and then / Hauled it off right to the grain bin.' And then, 'once, just at the crack of dawn, / The field-camp got a sudden shock, / When, on the combine, riding up, / Elagin's grandson came—Ivan.' The new government has caused all Stepan's dreams to come true, and Stepan decides that he doesn't want to die at all: He goes to the doctor and announces, 'I want to live!' Before our eyes is another Morgunok, who did not seek the Land of Muravia but rather lived in it, finding happiness without even leaving it. Happiness itself came to him. And on the eve of war, the kolkhoz poem came to a halt at this important point of upheaval.

War not only changed the whole structure of literature, but also dispersed poets and writers to opposite sides of the literary barricades. For some of them, after their very different debuts in the 1920s and 1930s, war seriously changed their relationship to literature and their understanding of their own places in it. Some (from Tvardovskii and Isakovskii to Erenburg and Grossman) took a much stricter and more responsible attitude towards their literary work than they had had before the war. Others (from Sholokhov and Fadeev to Surkov and Gribachev), on the other hand, went even further towards a path of political servility. These divergences were at first almost imperceptible; but the farther they went, the harder they became to reconcile. In the post-Stalin era, they escalated to the point that these writers from such different generations and of such differing degrees of talent ended up in open ideological conflict.

All of this had a most direct impact on the kolkhoz poem. This genre, by virtue of its status, became the point of concentration for the basic conflict that implicitly defined the battle in Soviet poetry in both the Stalin and post-Stalin eras—the struggle between 'avant-gardists' and 'populists'. At one extreme were Il'ia Sel'vinskii, Nikolai Aseev, and Semen Kirsanov, who swore loyalty to the traditions of Maiakovskii; at the other were the 'populist' poets, many of whom worked in the kolkhoz poem genre. For these latter, Isakovskii and Tvardovskii remained the standard.

Meanwhile, Tvardovskii himself ultimately abandoned the genre he had canonised. Immediately after the war, a poem that was in all respects definitive of the new Tvardovskii came out, his 'House by the Road' (which won a Stalin Prize for 1946). Tvardovskii had again written a poem based on rural life, but by no means was it a kolkhoz poem. It was about the past—the prewar and wartime past—not the future. Before the war, the house in the poem had 'order and coziness'. It was the world of the rural idyll: 'And good it was, at one's own table / Surrounded by one's kith and kin, / Relaxing, eating one's own bread, / And marveling at the wondrous day.' This is not a kolkhoz idyll, but a *peasant* idyll: the close and kindred circle of the family, a marvelous day, *one's own* house, *one's own* table, and *one's own* bread. The war was the past. The present was the destroyed home, the family driven away to Germany. The poem is not heroic; it is tragic (in this respect it is akin to Isakovskii's poem 'Enemies Burnt down the Family Hut,' which at the time was accused of pessimism). The reader sees a succession of gloomy scenes, the kind in which postwar literature did not indulge: files of Soviet prisoners of war, life under German occupation ('Much better, yes, / To sing of other, kinder places'). But Tvardovskii's poem is not about joy: A soldier 'came there, climbed a little hill: / The house was gone, the farm-yard, too. // And there, where fire had all consumed / The framing, posts, and all the rafters, / Lush, but somber, in the fallow field, / The nettles grew like big, bold hemp. // One could barely see / The pile of bricks and rubble, / With ashes strewn between, / And grass grown up all through it. // This mute and joyless peace / Was what the owner found. / Grieving, knotted apple trees / Swung their branches, bare, in sorrow.'

'House by the Road' is a sort of repudiation of 'The Land of Muravia', which is all the more evident since this poem unfolds in the same rural *topos*. However, instead of the largely pointless journey on which Morgunok sets out (with its attendant merriment and buffoonery), the theme of the road here has a tragic sound—both the familiar childhood road by which the House stands, and the terrible journey of sufferings imposed by the war. This journey ends with a requiem, not a feast. Instead of the rootlessness in 'The Land of Muravia', the hero of which apparently is not attached to any specific place but more like a drifter, the theme of the House (or Home) as the centre of the world (both the inner and outer worlds) is dominant in 'House by the Road': 'The dooryard just beneath the window, / Onions, plants in garden rows— / All this together made it home, / An ordered, cozy dwelling-place.' Instead of a quest for a utopian Muravia, 'House by the Road' centres on the loss of an everyday life, with a 'memory of grief' and 'the mute recollection of pain'. There is no 'little farm': Such basic concepts as suffering, memory, mothers, family, and home define the structural motifs of the poem. Finally, the buffoonery and almost outright outrageousness of 'The Land of Muravia' is traded for quite a different intonation, where melodiousness and a conversational quality are intermingled with a sense of tragedy and a new, pervasive conviction of the kind found in 'Vasilii Terkin'.

5

The kolkhoz poem undertook to make ideology '*lubok*-like'. It was both the flip side of the Stalinist aesthetic of the sublime and an integral part of this aesthetic. This *lubok* quality found its fullest expression in the 'anarchy of popular speech' in which the kolkhoz poem was immersed—literally woven from colloquial speech, picturesque expressions, turns of phrase, catch phrases, proverbs and singsong rhymes—and in the folklore that it employed, as revealed in the use of fairy tales, folk-tale motifs, legends, fables, riddles, songs and lamentations. All of this was packed into the rhymed structure that lay at the heart of folk-poetry poetics. The result is that, on the one hand, we are presented with a lively, conversational 'folk' style of speech. On the other, there is a song-like rhythm, a melodiousness (or lyricism).

Here is one of the opening scenes from 'Flag over the Village Soviet': 'The teapot droned like a bee. / Old granny sat down at the table. / She threw off her scarf. / She sat there awhile. / She glanced at his medals: / "Come from Berlin, sonny-boy? / So far off from Ryazan / Your fortunes took you! / You came by airplane, I'd be guessing?" / "Rode a little horse here, granny." / "A little horse, from so far off?! / Sonny, sure you must be joking. / Dear, what tales you're making up!" / "Check this paper, if you want. / You'll see, it says the horse was mine. / (In the war, I mean.) No joke." / "Okay, the paper must be real."' The popularity of this style can be explained by the fact that for the new Soviet urban population that came together as a result of the flood of urbanisation in the 1930s, the urban literary culture and its language were only superficially assimilated, and the (written) literary language was by no means the 'native' language of the new city dwellers. Their 'native' language was instead the spoken, conversational style speech. This was the social niche for *lubok* and *raeshnik*.

For urban culture, which took its roots from literary tradition, *lubok* was, on the contrary, not so much a style as an object to be aestheticised (suffice it to recall the works of Blok, and in particular his poem 'The Twelve'[20]), and therefore the adepts of this culture reacted quite sharply to the anarchy of *raeshnik* that was permeating poetry. Aseev, for example, in a review (entitled 'Simplicity and Dumbing Down') of 'The "Bolshevik" Kolkhoz' in *Literaturnaia gazeta* sharply criticised the poem precisely because of its mocking *raeshnik* style, holding that the entire text was made 'full of holes' by the 'vaudeville-style singsong patter.'[21] And, in fact, Gribachev's poem, which consists of a series of vignettes, is chock-full of happy, 'merry' people—the stableman, the postman Mit'ka, the fortune-teller Anfisa and various 'lads and lasses'. Between seedtime and harvest in this village, just as in *Kuban Cossacks*, there is merriment everywhere: 'The boys all run to join the dance / And fly into *prisiadka* steps.' Aseev's criticism was relevant to the entire 'populist' trend in Soviet poetry (the real incarnation of which was the kolkhoz poem in particular, with its dancing rhythm). The stylistic component of these poems stands on its own, while the content of these endless poem-conversations is absolutely irrelevant:

Po próvodu pryamómu
Iz sóbstvennogo dóma
Zvonít kolkhóznyi predsedátel'

Sekretaryú raikóma.
Zovyót k pryamómu próvodu
Po slúchayu, po póvodu,
Po khlébu i pokósu,
Po sróchnomu voprósu
Po vázhnomu, tekúshchemu,
Po délu po nasúshchnomu.

[On a direct line
From her own home
The kolkhoz chairman calls
The regional party committee secretary.
She calls to the direct line,
On the occasion, for the reason,
About bread and haying,
About an urgent question,
An important one, a current one,
About an urgent matter.]

The fact that the character Alena Fomina is talking to the regional committee secretary from her home phone (never mind that there is not even any electricity in the village!) only emphasises the importance of the conversation taking place—and the importance is not of content (since the conversation is absolutely empty in this regard) but of style. Iashin's aim here is purely formal. But seven years later, in the short story 'Levers' (one of the first works of the Khrushchev Thaw), language again becomes crucial—but in a totally different way. It is precisely through language that rank-and-file kolkhozniks, 'warm-hearted, honest people', are transformed into 'levers': The conversations before and during the party meeting reveal the explosive potential of the 'conversational form', and via an alternation of linguistic registers (from casual to formal/bureaucratic and then back again), the transformation of people into 'the Party's masses' occurs.

This only accentuates the function of language in the kolkhoz poem. We should remember that the *raeshnik* by its very nature is not so much style as stylisation, and thus it always rides an edge of style in which every disruption is fraught with a comic twist. The description of the farm in Zamiatin's poem 'Soldiers at Home', for instance, is totally in keeping with a SotsArt parody:

The sorrel horse would stamp his hooves.
The she-calves follow on his heels.
The sheep are also on his heels.

The farmyard's full of squeals and moos.
Calf's sides are surely feeling grand,
Petted by the master's hand.

This could easily be a text of Dmitrii Prigov's.

As they were the products of social stratification and alienation, *lubok* and its laughter present an adequate picture of their consumer. This is applicable to not only the quality of this *lubok* laughter but also to its very nature: As Boris Sokolov states, social alienation is expressed in a peculiar 'malevolent, satirical, or sarcastic reaction to the values of "the others"'.[22] Such was the culture of laughter among the outcasts of the suburbs who yearned for 'the better things', but who contented themselves with a substitute. Within this laughter, they restored the destroyed social harmony and found a path to self-identity through denial. As Sokolov keenly observes, *lubok* was 'one of the most vivid creations of the transitional urban culture', and it was not by chance that 'the late flowering of *lubok* coincided with the rise of "tavern civilisation"'.[23] Soviet civilisation itself was the product of this rise, and was accordingly closely tied to *lubok* culture. As Sokolov notes, *raek* 'cultivated a derisive outsider's attitude towards everything'.[24] This attitude, in turn, was the basis of a profoundly dismissive strategy (or, more precisely, a profaning, alienating strategy that bordered on mockery) with respect to life as it was derealised in Soviet art.

Dmitrii Likhachev explained that the nature of *lubok* is buffoonish humour.[25] And, in fact, Soviet *lubok* is permeated with this kind of humour. The atmosphere of buffoonery and mockery that prevails in it makes us immediately think of *raek* and the style associated with it (be it rhymed prose or the verse found in 'folk drama'). The history of Russian literature provides quite a few examples of stylisation of *lubok*—Pushkin's *Tales About a Priest and his Laborer, Balda*, Dem'ian Bednyi's satirical verses, propaganda songs, the posters made by the artists and poets of the Russian Telegraph Agency in 1919–1921, to mention a few. Purely Soviet mockery, however, is devoid of any element of satire. A classic example of the Soviet buffoon is Sholokhov's character Shchukar', an old man. The 'buffoonish old man' was one of the main characters in *raek*. A principle feature of the buffoon's mockery is that it is not satirical, which means that it is depoliticised. It might be called castrated mockery. It is no accident, then, that its practitioners are most often 'old men'.

In his poem entitled 'Farther than Far', which he published in the Thaw years but had begun writing in 1949, just at the time that the kolkhoz poem flowered, Tvardovskii with scathing irony described the structure of the already petrified canon: 'You see, it's a novel, and everything's neat: / The new construction method's shown, / The deputy's backwards, the chair's progressive, / The old man's seeing communism's wisdom. / A she and he are both advanced, / For the first time, a motor's launched, / *Partorg*, thunder, gap, slowdown, then "all hands!" / Minister's in the shop, then to the workers' ball.'

In the Eastern tradition, with its marked reverence towards old age, elders are portrayed in a compassionate, respectful way; in the Russian tradition, their portraits are mockingly unctuous. But the chief thing is that everything that becomes subject to mockery in *raek* is invariably made stupid. In the kolkhoz poem's masked theatre, the old man who is 'joining communism' is the personification of stupidity. The author's task in this boils down to finding the proper mix of this *skoromokh* tradition. The old men are always politically correct. They either talk about trifles, or they bandy about popular jokes or politically correct verdicts, as in Gribachev's poem 'Watchman', where two old men on watch at their respective kolkhozes, bored, chat by telephone 'across night and twenty versts': 'The two old men fall silent, pensive, / Smoke a little, then talk again: / "Ours'll be promoted, just you wait, / They'll take him for the district board." // "Ours are communist, too, you know. How smart our people are! …" / "Not too young? Minister, then …" / "That's okay, the young ones'll grow."' Old men are always the object of admiration mixed with some mockery. An atmosphere of *skoromokh* buffoonery surrounds them. The object of mockery is either their poor education, or their desire to understand contemporary life and speak the contemporary Soviet language that they have not completely mastered; ridiculed, too, is their miserliness and excessive sternness.

The invariable participant of all-important discussions, from family matters to kolkhoz matters, the 'old timer' is a natural philosopher. His words are themselves the fruit of 'folk wisdom'. One such old man tells the secretary of the 'Bolshevik' kolkhoz regional committee: 'We're not in the Party, but if / We could just make it plainer, / You can't tear us away from the Party, / Our heart's been with it for thirty years.' The old men's haunts are the kolkhoz head office, the field station, and, of course, the public reading room (the 'reading hut'); they are not Gogolesque peasants, but men who love to read and who yearn for knowledge. Their world is a world of idyll. The 'reading hut' is described thus: 'The reading hut through winter's cold / a comfy shelter makes: / its welcome's warmer / than evenings elsewhere.' This, too, is where the 'old timers' in 'Flag over the Village Soviet' assemble: 'Like knapweed bees a-humming, / students hunch to read their books. / With knitted brow, around the table, / old men, too—kolkhozniks—sit, / Reading *Pravda*, *Ogonëk*, / From cover to cover, not missing a line: / Indonesia, you ask, / have they forgot? / The powers of the "Axis" three? / Lord, no! / All the truth they know by heart— / word by word they've read it. / All the village's learned folk / Sit at the table in the hut.' And, in fact, 'distinguished' people do live in these poems. The old man Faddei Kuz'mich Orlov, from the 'Lightning' (*Zarnitsa*) kolkhoz, for example, in Zamiatin's poem 'The Green Shelterbelt': 'He made the fields of "Lightning" famous, / Brought new life to our old land. / He raised a special kind of wheat, / Even made the scientists stare! / Learned academics, still, / Cannot quite explain this feat… / Kuz'mich in Moscow's scholars' meeting / Gave them fodder for discussion.' Even Lysenko shook his hand and 'said he'd always dreamed of such wheat', invited him to an Academy session, listened to his presentation ('Trofim Denisych was pleased') and promised to create a 'field trials area' in the kolkhoz.

The immutable feature of any kolkhoz poem, in the final part, is a speech made by such an 'old man embracing communism' at a public meeting, like that in 'Alena Fomina': 'I may get tired, it's true, / But these old feet don't shuffle, / Old though I am. / If I'm starting / To work by the plan / I'll not be wanting to die… / I still want to tell / About those leaders of ours / 'Cause I know / They can still lead the people. / They believe in our might. / All around us there's passion for work, / In country and city alike / The hard work goes on, year after year. / Hard to believe there's such working! / You learn, yourself, / Then you teach others… / Old-timers take notions / To drowse by the fire. / But the leaders will notice, and say: / "Sure, you're tired, / but look here …" / And they'll show you such vision / That makes your heart sing. / It makes you feel mighty again! / A new battle, then, / The people are raring / To follow the leader and work. / They respect us, they do, / They believe we'll endure, / We'll plow any field that needs plowing… / Because they are just, / Because they are ours!'

The *raek* style is a product of 'professional *skoromokh* style'.[26] By stylising colloquial speech, kolkhoz *raek* simulates directness and aspires to an adequate reflection of the social behaviour that stands behind this speech. Thus, in the familial world of the kolkhoz, everything is open, country-style: The female chairman is its mother and the kolkhozniks are one big family; locks and watchmen are thought of as something alien and incomprehensible. And since everything that is incomprehensible in these poems is revealed through the speech of old men, in 'Flag over the Village Soviet' it is the old man appointed as watchman who says that he doesn't understand why his job is necessary. In a conversation with the main character, Egor, he tells the latter that he has been standing 'by this lock' for nine years, but it is still not clear why he is there: 'You?' / 'Well, yes…' / 'You're protecting…' / 'What?' / 'Goods.' / 'But from whom? / From yourself? From Mitrofan? / From Natasha Sedykh? / That is, I mean, from deceit? / That is, I mean, from *our* people? … / What can we think of ourselves, / if at home—seems to me— / we can't trust each other: / I, my family, and my family, me?' Egor can find no answer for the old watchman's questions. On the contrary, the old man himself stumps him: 'Are you guarding the granaries?' / 'Yes, the granaries.' / 'But don't you tremble with fear?' / 'No, I don't.' / 'Has there not been disaster?' / 'Never.' / 'Aren't you afraid, if a thief comes?' / 'But where would he come from, Egor?' Discussion of economic and legal subjects in a country of locks, obsessive secrecy, and epidemic theft (the latter acknowledged at the state level by a series of draconian decrees by Stalin) seems almost provocational. However, the degree of playful (indeed, buffoonish) displacement, if not to say madness, and of 'demonstrative shamelessness' and outright mockery of derealised life in the poem is such that it is not even supposed to occur to the reader in any way to fit such discussions into the context of reality.

6

The 'old-timers', with their (literally and figuratively) toothless laughter, embody senile weakness; youth, on the contrary, are full of strength. In addition, the robust energy of the 'lads and lasses' concerned with matrimonial problems is affirmed in the poems. The 'lasses' in them, therefore, are mainly brides, as in Nedogonov's poem: 'Ksenia, the bride, / Stands at the bookshelf, / clear as a sunrise, / bright as a rainbow, / a downy kerchief down her back: / And there's a tractorist, / with red calico kerchief / The one who plays the accordion. / There she stands. / You can see, in her eyes, / in the blush on her cheek, / and the lips— / she's in love. / She stands there, the picture of love: / Dubok is back from the war! / In her eyes / there are thistles of fire: / (she could burn up a boy in this fire!) / she stands, like a sunrise in stillness, / like a song / about a peddler of wares, / like a tale about spring!'

The 'lads' are all, accordingly, 'dashing'. Their main task in 'The "Bolshevik" Kolkhoz' (just as in other such poems, incidentally), besides working in the fields is, of course, to swagger for the benefit of the 'lasses': 'Come on, now, tractor driver, / That knee can stand some dancing, / In front of her, the girl that's got you, / Beat that rhythm like you *mean* it.' The 'lasses', on the other hand, are (in their free time from working in the fields) supposed to be bashful and romantically pensive and, in the presence of the inevitable symbol of romance, the bird cherry ('it wasn't the bird cherry, white, / That flitted by the window— / The boy's cigarette made that cloud...'), to lower their heads and take their sweethearts to study in town ('They beckon, with a wave of the hand, / They stroll by the river, sighing'). The moods of the 'lasses' is best expressed by the accordion: As soon as an accordion player started to play a sad song in the kolkhoz head office, 'our lasses started sadly sighing, / and all our women burst out crying,' but as soon as the accordion 'struck up a warbling song', right then and there the office walls seem to disappear and life itself turns into a song: 'The meadow sang, / As did the waving rye, / And, singing, to the field came noon.'

The rhythm of the songs in the postwar kolkhoz poem, however, changes. The songs become 'newer'. As opposed to her counterpart in the early kolkhoz romance, the 'young lady' now sets off to town herself to study, following her 'lad'—but no longer to qualify as a tractor driver, as in the 1930s, but to become an engineer: 'Put me in the rail-car, Katie, / Stations will fly by like lightning, / Come evening, I'll dash by the metro, / I'll knock on the institute's door, / I'll sit down beside him, / yes, him! / by my fellow, / I'll give him a nudge / and a sly little wink: / Honey, you shouldn't be mad, and not cross— / But I'll catch up, / I'll pass you— / Hold on!' This competition in learning, an extension of labour competition, is paraded as the 'wedding game' of the kolkhoz, ending with the same merriment: 'The locomotive took them back. / Now the kolkhoz, greeting them, / Can boast two engineers, not one, / Her fondest wish was not in vain—/ To drink, / To sing, / To dance and feast, / To tear up those expensive heels.' All of this is simply a prelude to a wedding.

The world of the kolkhoz poem is a world of natural instincts, healthy affection, and vegetative life. The people in it reproduce like the oats or the 'heifers' that they themselves raise. The harvest over, weddings begin—then children are born: 'In grooms and brides / We've added two, / As if, like wheat, / They'd sprung from earth! / Oh, it's time for kolkhoz weddings, / Yes, and kolkhoz baby parties! / There'll be dancing until morning / Under the bluish frosty moon.' In this cyclical time, the country sleeps as if in a cocoon.

Sometimes the matrimonial collision is individualised. The 'lass' and the 'lad' acquire names, and the *raeshnik* is traded for a lyrical song. The poem 'The Beautiful Mecha' tells how a girl named Tania grew up in a village before the war and how she became the leader of a small girls' work unit. Then Sergei, a soldier on leave from the war, appears. This 'lad', as it turns out, has a daydream that is narrated in an emphatically bashful way: 'The sapper had a dream within him, / nurtured, hidden almost from himself: / turns out, he's never had a special girl, / not anywhere, until this time, / no girlfriend closest to his heart, / though long he'd hoped to meet one— / before the war, and service in it, / somehow this had still escaped him. / Now his dream is ardent, eager, / maybe, now, right here at home / he will find his best beloved, / his sweetheart will be found at last. / How glad he'll be, desire fulfilled!' Then and there, Tania suddenly grows up: 'Her hair as red as autumn's maples, / the birthmark on her upturned lips… / Well, maybe she's a little swarthy, / snub-nosed more than you'd imagined— / but far beyond your wildest dreams, / her grey eyes have a brilliant light… / Tania seems him standing dumb-struck.'

Their romance is described in a pointedly asexual way: 'Embarrassed, quiet, side by side, / the first they've been so close together, / they walk abreast the narrow trail, / Tat'iana and the soldier. / Now they chance a timid word, / Then an even shyer glance.' Once they become engaged, the lovers are separated. Sergei returns to the front. Tania begins to 'wait for her intended': 'His proposal, her acceptance— / both of these seemed long ago. / Their new acquaintance, then farewell— / so new for both of them. / Now there's just a forlorn road, / the single light seen through her window. / "Seryozhenka, Seryozhenka! / There's no one in the world that's dearer! / I have no one I'd love more, / nothing is as pleasant, more familiar / than our friendship, my Seryozha, / and my girlish love for him" '.

Everything subsequent to this is similar to a stylisation of Pushkin's 'Eugene Onegin'. Tania awaits Sergei's return from the war, and the author describes this future meeting thus: 'And the girl—her name is Tania— / will dash out there to meet you.' As expected, Tania finally writes letters to her intended: 'And only Tania writes and writes, / Painstaking, writing line by line, / everything she sees and hears, / from home, to her beloved.' But she cannot write about everything: 'But Tania kept within her heart / the thing that she had learned to feel / and would not dare to write.' Thus it goes on, day after day, year after year. 'Greeting every day with love, / loving as she went to sleep, / Tania lived thus, taking note / of yet another spring gone by.' The collectively happy and lyrically romantic 'youth' is stylistically molded in differing traditions, *lubok* and literary, respectively.

7

The kolkhoz *commedia dell'arte* had a distinct thematic structure. It was defined by the very choice of characters, all having their clearly delineated thematic functions and established stylistic peculiarities. But a genre is not produced solely by coordination of the stylistic dominant, stock characters and plots. What is most interesting about Socialist Realism is the ideological fleshing-out of the plot schema.

The poem almost always began with the main character's return from war: 'I struck out walking from Berlin / in the heat that means July, / but I'll see my sweetheart's house / only when October comes' ('Flag over the Village Soviet'); 'From the dear familiar road / On his father's native soil / The invalid, returned from war, / Finally sees his wife, his home' ('Alena Fomina'); 'Past the fields and threshing barns, / On footpaths sometimes, sometimes highways, / On two legs (thank God!) he walks, / headed to his home and hearth… / The roads meander, twist and turn, / Endlessly, it seems— / But soon he'll be there!' ('Soldiers at Home'); 'The train rolled on and rattled day and night, / the sergeant, now released from service, headed home, / to which the path directly led. / And beckoning, from every side, / were wondrous deeds he knew he'd do' ('The Beautiful Mecha'). This sets the transition from wartime to peacetime (in this respect, the rejection of the road as a plot-building motif as it had been in Nekrasov and Tvardovskii, is characteristic).

The postwar poem begins with a historically 'clean slate'. It is a poem about peace, and war in it is a thing of the bygone past. This is why the arrival of the hero in the village is accompanied by an abrupt transition to 'peaceful concerns' and 'happy troubles'. The arrival is usually followed on by a meeting—sudden and happy—with the sweetheart ('Running there, his mother kicked a bucket over / and dropped the towel she'd wrapped the chicks in. / His sweetheart, though, could only cry / "Egorka!" / Grabbing him, / she nestles on his shoulder. / She trembles like a tiny bird / against his broad and sweaty chest, / and like a dew-drop on her cheek / his blue-eyed bride lets shed a tear'—'Flag over the Village Soviet') and a feast to celebrate the return: 'Pavel's house is smoky, crowded— / half the village came to eat. / They all want to see their neighbor, / hear about his time spent gone' ('Soldiers at Home').

If in 'House by the Road' the ruined house was an open wound, then the houses described in other kolkhoz poems written at the same time as Tvardovskii's have apparently been untouched by war, although the very same places under German occupation—the Smolensk, Bryansk and Orlov Regions—were being described. Miraculously, the circumstances in these other poems have unfolded totally differently. Awaiting the hero of 'House by the Road' was a picture of horrible destruction and a family cast to the four winds—children lost, a wife driven who knows where. But a family idyll awaits the heroes of postwar poems. The mother of the hero of 'Flag over the Village Soviet' (let us note that this poem came out in 1946, just as 'House by the Road' did) is not only happy about the bride, but even about the wedding: 'Since they fell in love, these two, / why should I contradict them? / Since they've stayed so true this long / I couldn't simply change their minds. / We'll respect each other and be friends.' Possible family problems were usually linked to the husband's excessive enthusiasm for his 'labor duty'. The hero's wife in 'The "Bolshevik" Kolkhoz', for example, rebukes him for always being out in the fields: 'You're always out in field and meadow, / You always pine to be outside… / But for me, it's bitter here, / Feeling like I do, abandoned… / Vanya, what I want's a baby, / A tiny little lovely baby son!' Only by inertia is the kolkhoz poem related to the poetic genres: in essence, it is rhymed prose, a narrative told in verse. But since narrative requires movement of the plot, it also requires conflict: the hero will face a meeting with a lazy fellow-countryman. The latter is at first a negative character who, of course, subsequently embarks on a path of reform: a soldier, returned from the war, who does not want to work. We learn the following about such a person in 'Spring in "Pobeda"': 'He lives by speculation, / Took up with some old woman, / and she's a merry widow. / "Work?" she asks. "Why bother! / Let the party members bend their backs, /

Let the on-time goals be up to them, / and not to you. With me / you've got your clothes and shoes, / can drink, and have me in the bed."' What can account for such a decline of yesterday's defender of the Motherland? As it turns out, 'he didn't know our policy so well / and so he made a mess of things: / Speculated, drank, and hoarded cash, / Just had bought himself a dacha. / Suddenly, there are no cards, / The huckster's business goes to hell. / They passed an act / to fix the money. / Now his money's gone, his dacha, too, / And so his lover-widow said adieu!' And although things do not disintegrate to any worse rowdy behaviour or drunken brawls, a certain glimmer of reality breaks through the kolkhoz poem through such characters.

In Gribachev's poem, everything concludes with the usual scuffle and its inevitable 'comedy': A 'speculator' who has appeared in the village gets drunk, swaggers about and picks a fight with the elderly watchman, falls down drunk in the cellar, and now lies all in bruises on the stove while the old man writes an official statement about the incident for the police; the speculator, it turns out, is his nephew. But the similar hero of 'Flag over the Village Soviet', Andrei Dubkov, is portrayed as a true social problem. Similar to other heroes of this type, Dubkov takes to drink when he returns from the war. He finds his moral right to such 'unworthy' behaviour in his military service: 'He ranted on, to please himself, / He spun a boring yarn: / "From the Germans, I defended / all the mothers, and my country, too! / So, tell me, don't I have the right— / the peasant's son Dubkov— / to have some drinks, carouse a bit, / amongst my friends and neighbors here?"'

The first step of the Party's protagonist (Shirokov), also returning from the war, is to face conflict with a drunk. Shirokov announces that Dubkov is disgracing all the front-line soldiers; the kolkhozniks call Dubkov a parasite but Shirokov a 'rabid front-line man' and a 'military lazybones': 'Why, he'd spit on all your medals, / but for you, they show the battles, / all the service that you rendered.' The question of military service was one of the most loaded issues in postwar Soviet society. Conversations about military service were not encouraged (we should recall that Victory Day became a nonworking holiday only in 1965). The official version of the war and the victory did not assume any individual 'services', just as it did not highlight individual sacrifices. This is why critics, although supposing that Dubkov might be even a 'characteristic' phenomenon, in the same stroke pointed out how 'atypical' he was: 'With the keen, attentive gaze of an artist, Nedogonov has described a phenomenon that, although it is not widespread, is nonetheless characteristic of postwar life, and has brought it into his poem.' They explained Dubkov's swaggering, however, by saying that it was 'nothing more than a consequence of intoxication and bingeing, a "forty-day revelry", nothing more than thoughtlessness, the laxity of an unstable character who has praised his own military service to high heaven, and by no means is it any depravity of his nature.' The conflict was explained as a 'contradiction between Dubkov's behaviour and the kolkhozniks' labor-conscious attitude'. Ultimately, the conflict was deemed absolutely peripheral: 'The moral atmosphere is the main thing; it is the main "hero" of the poem, and the conflict between Egor and Dubkov is only a "background".'[27]

What is most striking about the negative characters in the kolkhoz poems is their transformation: They are not 'reforged' according to the Socialist Realist schema, but instead change, unexpectedly, simply because of the 'shame' they feel before their fellow villagers. Not drunkenness, not even idleness is the crime against the community—it is individualism. Infected with it, the hero does not even need reforging because his return to collective values must not be forced or tied to external circumstances, but rather must be internal— because of 'shame'. There is nothing rational in the hero's transformation: it is unclear why he must reject the empty dissolute life or the longed-for 'villa'. Transferring the problem to a purely moral dimension removes the necessity of rationally motivating the hero's transformation, and therefore also of revealing the process of the transformation. Thus, the admonitions of the Party-minded protagonist and the (sometimes even silent) condemnation of the kolkhozniks are sufficient for a transformation.

In all its genres, postwar literature embodied one and the same idea: now is not the time for relaxing, there is no place now for postwar complacency. Its main motivation—both in the 1930s and continuing on through the war years—was mobilisational. An idyllic world and a mobilisational zeal—this oxymoronic combination defines the peculiarity of the kolkhoz poem. Labor was not simply the chief value promoted after the war: as always, it was a collective process. It is not because someone works more, or someone else less, that conflicts arise. As we have seen, the individualist, drunk or idler is condemned for not making a contribution to the common cause, whereby he not only deprives himself of his connection to the collective, but also blocks the path to his own well-being. The issue of stimuli to labor remains beyond the pale. Clearly, these stimuli are extra-economic. But they are obviously not compulsive, either (in literature, of course). The basic motifs are conscience, shame and the moral condemnation of one's neighbors. In other words, community motivation.

Problems here are solved by the commune, as it happens in 'The "Bolshevik" Kolkhoz'. Although such an unexpected circumstance does not fit into the picture of kolkhoz abundance, it surfaces that the kolkhoz has no furniture: 'Chairs were few, and sofas fewer— / Hide nor hair of them was found, / The Germans, damn them!, took them all, / and trashed them in Berlin.' But then the kolkhozniks have a meeting and decide to make their own furniture and distribute it among themselves: instead of standing about smoking, the kolkhozniks work to plane the wood. The experiment succeeds so well that even the neighboring 'Victory' kolkhoz takes up the initiative (believing this is of course no more difficult than believing that the Germans took the kolkhoz's 'sofas' away to Berlin).

In the poem 'Soldiers at Home', the one-legged soldier Frol Sedoi refuses to work in the chicken coop, and demands that the kolkhoz chairman send him to the fields: 'To tell the truth, I'm sick of it, / Hanging around the chickens. / Without real work, I'm getting rusty. / Where there's business, that's for me— / Not women's work, but men's. / I'm not an old man yet! / So, why am I among the chickens? / Don't the fields need any work? / If I've got it in me still— / I'm not the kind who needs to rest....' / Sitting on his bench (a box), / Bykov slowly filled his pipe— / But sitting down was not for Frol: / 'I'm still a front-lines man, I am! / A soldier, every person knows, / Is not the kind to loaf around. / And such a time we live in! / The country needs a lot of bread. / And here I'm miserable...' / 'Your wound will swell.' / 'No, I'm healthy!'

Without an economic dimension, this enthusiasm for labor is irrational. Tania, the leader of the girls' work unit in 'The Beautiful Mecha', faces the necessity of saving the grain that is scorching from the heat (water from the Mecha River is right there, but 'there's nothing to water the fields with'). Her team does not know what to do: 'Judging by the lasses' faces, / you'd think their best friend died.' But Tania does not despair: 'No, I can't be sad like this, / I haven't any right, / I promised Lenin something else, / when we all swore our oaths. / Comrade Stalin didn't flinch / when he told me that the foe / had waged a savage battle / on my father's house.' And then the 'battle for the harvest' begins: 'Again and again, her mother woke / to see her daughter scribbling notes.' Tania thinks only about how to 'save the harvest from disaster.' There is only one way out: they must bring forty thousand buckets of water. And so the brigade, just as at the front, achieves a 'labor feat': 'Eight little girls for ten long nights. / Their faces flushed from rushing blood, / Their ears heard hammers pounding, / Their hearts felt each and every step, / Their feet were heavy as lead... / Forty thousand buckets of water!'

The feat of a single work gang, of course, does not solve the problem: 'They hauled their loads of water, yes, / and tended their three hectares' plot. / But their small hands would prove no match / against this rampant enemy.' However, the gang's enthusiasm rallies the people to attack the 'burning winds': 'No longer just the eight of them— / People rose up all around.' But the main thing, of course, is accomplished in the Kremlin; not only the kolkhozniks, but also 'Comrade Stalin in the Kremlin / didn't sleep a wink till morning. / Night outside the windows darkened, / While cloth of green his

table covered, / and on this table lay a map / of all the Soviet fields, / and
Comrade Stalin in the Kremlin / hearkened to the hot winds howling.' But
since these strong people do not want to be 'slaves to capricious calamity', 'The
people's friend, and our best teacher, / Took up the sharpened pencil... / He
marks the Volga-Don, his long-ago invention. / Circling this, and circling
that: / Gor'kii ... Kuibyshev ... Stalingrad ... / The current, mighty, of the
hydrostation. / Millions of kilowatts. / This is all for you, my friend, / for you
and your eight girls. / The hand of Stalin sketches out / the future you and
I will see. / We just don't know about it, yet.'

Then and there, a transformation of collective labor into personal
happiness occurs. Sergei, a fiancé returning from the front, has pined for
labor. At the front, he was a combat engineer, and now he swears to his
beloved that he will 'raise the water to the fields' and give her a chance to rest:
'Like a soldier I'll go, to fix your troubles, / and machines will come with me,
too. / The beautiful Mecha I'll bring to the fields, / And let the people share
in my labor.' He repeats, like an oath: 'I love you, Tania! The water will come /
and cool our fields that are parched by the wind.' He brings the accounts to the
regional committee secretary, who turns out to be his former commissar, and
who dumbfounds him: 'We conquered fascists, you and I, / we learned and
gathered strength, my brother. / And here we'll build a waterfall, / Water
many thousand hectares, but— / It's you I want to build the dams and
stations.' In order to do this, Sergei has to go study hydraulic engineering in
the city and leave his fiancée behind in the kolkhoz. The drama begins: 'Again
we're apart. Again not together.' But then Tania understands, as her 'soul
soars', that she, too, must study. Will the kolkhoz let her go? Friends intervene:
'Seven friends, seven girls / come to see the kolkhoz chair: / "Auntie Nastya,
what's to be done? / Like a candle, Tania's fading out."' A 'family council'
(a kolkhoz managers' session) begins, at which the 'chair, a just mother' makes
a speech about love: how it is a 'wondrous force' and must be nourished; they
must let Tania go with Sergei, to the city of Elets.

The young family begins a new life there. Their family is like the
confluence of the rivers Don and Mecha, which united 'to be, together,
forever stronger / to never separate again!' In the winter, Tania is restless,
cannot sleep: she thinks constantly about a harvest luxuriating in
a countrywide 'flood': 'The waves of labor's sound / are high and burning
hot.' But then the Central Committee's February Plenum bursts forth: 'The
February Plenum booms, / like thunder in the early spring. / As if you'd
heard someone's decree, / you strain your eyes at word, / you read the
resolution through, / scarcely breathing, many times. / Like a letter from
a dear, dear friend, / that touches you within your soul, / you turn it over and
over again / in the breathless quiet of your room. / And in the paper's

dancing columns, / on a February noon in snow, / you see bright dawns and warm green lands.' Tania cannot remain in the city any longer—the village pulls at her heartstrings. She whispers to her sleeping husband, just returned from a mission: 'How can you just lie there, sleeping? / Can't you hear how bad I feel? / Not a wink of sleep I've gotten! / How could I have left the village / at a crucial time like this?' Sergei suddenly wakes up: 'Really, he had slept so little, / and his kindred soul had sensed / all her struggling, all her groaning; / he gently hugged her, squeezed her tight, / then softly whispered, "Go." ' He will build the channel for Tania's village, and will meet her at the end of it. And Tania will again wait for her husband until he arrives with the 'great water', and then, 'breathing in the calm of evening, / the smell of grass and dewy fields, / wife and husband then will start / along the mutual path they chose.' At the end, the poem turns out to be as endless as life itself: 'Our time flows like a river, / sweeping forward kindred hearts. / And our poem has no ending, / just as life will have no end.'

This temporal boundlessness of kolkhoz poem endings is by no means a sign of openness. On the contrary, the final gatherings at which victory in construction is usually celebrated and newer, more grandiose plans are confirmed, are a true apotheosis of completion and stability. All the characters talk about the future, but the fundamental emphasis is on confirmation of the inviolability of the present. As these poems draw to their close, the kolkhoz Utopia becomes petrified. It is *not* interpreted as Utopia; on the contrary, being replete with accomplishments and plans, it is interpreted as nature itself.

The past in the poems justifies the future. At the end of 'The "Bolshevik" Kolkhoz', the kolkhoz chairman talks about the way people lived before: 'The old-style plows would maim the fields / despite what science teaches; / bark was stripped to weave bast shoes; / they pounded kernels into bread, / and always went to church, / and spent their lives in stripping kindling / just to make a little fire.' But, as it turns out, up until then they had had neither electricity nor radio in the kolkhoz. What else was there to do during the long winter evenings? 'Pulling off his little jacket, / into log-like sleep he falls; / let him sleep, he's bored and crabby, / bags grown under both his eyes. / But somewhere opera's on the radio, / the waltz they play is Viennese.' But a radio is needed for something other than entertainment: one must hear the scholar-engineer's lecture 'about the element uranium'. Or, in another instance, 'The doctrine Truman's touting / is so much like a bomb. / React we must to these, / the mongerers of war!' In other words, the kolkhoz has no future without a radio and a hydroelectric station. Thus, the chairman tells the kolkhoz, 'We cannot drag our heels. / I would set the matter straight. / All Europe's watching what we do, / the rest of the world sees, too.' Needless to say, the assembly heartily supports the chairman. And in short order, no doubt, the 'Bolshevik' kolkhoz will see both its own hydroelectric station and a radio appear.

Another inevitable feature of the endings is the awarding of medals to the heroes; the medals are supposed to (in hindsight) introduce some sort of motivation for the enthusiasm that has struck the reader during the entire course of the poem. Receiving the medal for his selfless labor in the fields, the hero of the poem 'Soldiers at Home' says that this medal and a military medal are one and the same to him. When he read about his decoration in the paper, 'my hero called to mind past battles. / Remembered how he'd read, in trenches, / all about his derring-do. / These lines are much like those… / Had he really not deserved it? / Is it not the same with labor, / when he's famed for these new feats? / Yes, he is pure and not indebted / to the Fatherland for this, / nor to any, nor to life itself, / nor to his own conscience!' The price for conscience can indeed be purely symbolic.

If not everyone without exception is awarded a medal at the end, then this, as one of the characters in 'Alena Fomina' says, does not matter: 'The Motherland a hundredfold / Will recompense the peasants' labor. / If some don't have their medals yet, / It's just because the order's late.' At the end of IAshin's poem, the kolkhoz assembly is no longer discussing the construction of the power station or the radio broadcast centre, but rather the Five-Year Plan of development for the kolkhoz. Having listened to so much of this poetry of planning, even the inveterate individualist Kozlov turns over a new leaf and matures: 'How could he unhappy be / once he'd heard the new reports? / The figures gladdened him for sure, / he took them as an order given. / Fatigued he could not be, for then / He understood the hows and whys: / It seemed his heart was beaming… / That's what he'd always missed, / all these long and wasted months! / That was why they'd had to fight— / that is what the people wanted! / The plan explained in great detail, / what the country'd hankered after. / It's written there, it must be true!' And, in fact, the assembly concludes with a sort of planning song: 'The closing speech was like a song, / like a flight of fancy. / As if, suddenly, the walls / of the kolkhoz centre building / burst wide open at that instant.'

At this moment, we see the bigger picture of the happy Motherland: 'Steel is smelted far and wide. / The woodland belts of all the steppes / impress you with their wonders: / A single hectare yields ten metric tons. / You'd lose count numb'ring all the tractors. / Combines, self-propelled, / glide on boundless fields… / The river will flow backwards if we need it to; / The sun, the wind, and all of nature / To the people's beck and call are subject.' Thus the kolkhoz's Party-cell communists gathered at the meeting had only to decide: 'What to do here, in our village— / Labor's here a-plenty!— / So that communism grows apace / to every land and nation.'

8

Grigorii Kozintsev used the notion of '*raek* communism' for the first time in his diary at the very beginning of the 1950s, when he was pondering the films of Ivan Pyr'ev. He wrote that if Duhring had invented 'barracks communism', then 'Van'ka' Pyr'ev had created the *raek* variety. It was due to the latter's efforts that people again brought home the 'silly lord' from the bazaar. This reference to the poem 'Who is to Live Well in Russia?' is quite significant: In it, Nekrasov had dreamed of the time when 'they'll make the peasant understand, / That portraits are not all the same, / That each book differs from the next' and when 'the peasant brings not Bliukher / And not the silly lord— / Belinskii, Gogol'— / Home from the bazaar.' He was talking of none other than *lubok*. In a paradoxical way, Nekrasov's tradition was perfected in the kolkhoz poem—this Stalinist *lubok*—which demonstrated that *raek* communism is the only adequate stylistic form for barracks communism.

The literary roots of the kolkhoz poem lay, in the tradition of unctuously enthusiastic praise of the peasant in the poetry of nineteenth-century nationalists and Slavophiles. However, its functions were quite a bit broader: the kolkhoz poem was used to domesticate the kolkhoz Utopia, in fact reducing the kolkhoz to its real national and historical equivalent—the patriarchal commune—and thereby transforming it into a 'comfort zone'. The transformation of the 'peasant' into a 'kolkhoznik' required a transformation of the latter from an object of narrative to its subject, which led to the inevitable *lubok*-style levelling of the literary tradition, to a radical stylistic and genre reshaping of the tradition. As it became the incarnation of official Soviet populism, the kolkhoz poem as a genre was born from the hybridisation of literary tradition with *raek*; and as a political and aesthetic phenomenon, from a mishmash of two cynicisms—that of the etatists and that of *skoromokh*. In this sense, *raek* communism was not only the product of a domesticated Utopia, but was also a mockery of the very reality that was abrogated in Stalinism. When it began to speak with the voice of the 'peasant' made happy by Soviet power, the kolkhoz poem supplied perhaps the most joyous pages in the book of Soviet communism, and remained the most vivid literary monument to the kolkhoz episode in the thousand-year history of Russian slavery.

Translated by Jesse Savage.

Chapter Three

LUXURIATING IN LACK: PLENITUDE AND CONSUMING HAPPINESS IN SOVIET PAINTINGS AND POSTERS, 1930s–1953

Helena Goscilo

'Qu'ils mangent de la brioche.' ['Let them eat cake.']
— Marie-Thérèse, wife of Louis XIV[1]

'Promise, large promise, is the soul of an advertisement.'
— Samuel Johnson, 1758[2]

'All art is advertising. […] Advertising art is
truly social, collective; truly art for the masses,
it is the only such art that exists today.'
— G. F. Hartllaub, 'Art as Advertising' (1928)

Fantasy Feasts; or, The Divine Irreference of Images[3]

In a review essay published several years ago in the *London Review of Books*, Sheila Fitzpatrick, the premier historian specialising in Stalinism, declared, 'While the Soviet regime may be said to have discouraged consumerism by keeping goods scarce, it was not ideologically on the side of asceticism. On the contrary, *future* socialism was always conceived in terms of plenty; according to the regime's Socialist Realist perception of the world, the meager supply of goods in the present was only a harbinger of the abundance to come.'[4] Like the Utopia of universal egalitarian happiness, however, abundance *remained* in the ever-receding radiant future, rendering imposed asceticism an empirical reality for the overwhelming majority throughout the Soviet era. That prolonged deferral is eloquently signaled by the ubiquitous slogan *K kommunizmu!* as well as by *K izobiliiu!* ('Towards Abundance!'), the title of the introduction to the 1953 edition of *A Book of Tasty and Healthy Food/Kniga o vkusnoi i zdorovoi pishche*, and countless other instances of '*K* + x', which all invoked the Soviet rhetoric of 'en route to', 'moving towards', and similar circumlocutions that for more than six decades promised without delivering. Moreover, particularly during the puritanical evangelism of the post-Revolutionary period, the state, which unfailingly privileged the abstractness of words over tangible goods, took care to distinguish healthy Soviet values from those of both the tsarist regime and capitalist societies, with their 'decadent' tastes and overvaluation of material bounties.[5] Soviet citizenry did not live 'by bread alone' (metaphorically, at least, for during some periods, it did so literally), and therein lay its vaunted moral superiority to its Western counterpart.

That virtue sprang from the virtual, for, as Fitzpatrick acknowledges, 'The hungry 1930s' developed a 'Soviet *rhetoric* of cultured living that privileged luxury commodities like champagne, caviar and perfume, though only the last of these *came near to* reaching a mass public' [emphasis added]. The dilemma sprang not necessarily from bad faith, but, as in the grandiosely visionary, unrealised ('paper') architecture perhaps best captured by designs for the Palace of Soviets (1931–1934), from the predictable inability of the Soviet state to actualise utopian dreams of a new world order that clashed with *Realpolitik*. After years of post-Revolutionary asceticism and derogation of Western consumerism, Stalinism, as Vera Dunham originally argued on the basis of the era's popular literature, partially reinstated middle-class values. It did so selectively, however, within carefully calibrated and shifting parameters.[6] Though the early 1930s were the leanest of times—witnessing collectivisation, famine, the end of the ill-conceived first Five-Year Plan and rationing[7]—in 1934 the Party leadership condemned zealous self-denial, speciously labeling it 'self-induced pauperism'.[8] It launched concerted efforts to increase the production of consumer goods, including such luxuries as champagne and caviar, within the framework of its ambitious campaign for *kul'turnost'* ('cultured living and consumption').[9] Material rewards and the concomitant cultural *Blitzkrieg* were intended not only to ameliorate the living standards of specific groups, but also to educate them into a more civilised, modern mode of life. And though material well-being was beyond the reach of the majority, 'the possibility of a prosperous and cultured life was promised to everyone in exchange for efficient work'[10]—a message disseminated in articles, photographs, and advertisements of the thirties.

Though during the late-Tsarist era, advertising had thrived in the hands of such outstanding graphic artists as Ivan Bilibin, Viktor Vasnetsov, and

Boris Zvorykin, who designed, *inter alia*, vibrantly embellished, intricately crafted illustrations of menus for gourmet meals,[11] as an inherent feature of capitalism, advertising violated the principles of a socialist economy. During NEP, however, as Randi Cox cogently argues, three factors sanctioned agitational advertising of state-produced goods: competition with NEPmen, strengthening of relations between social classes, and the idea of consumption as an inner transformation that would further modernisation.[12] To advertise during the 1920s meant to agitate for Soviet power: 'Everything that was becoming socially, politically and economically most important for this new country was immediately picked up in the advertising.'[13] By decade's end, however, socialist ads increasingly emphasised personal pleasure over progressive ideological revision and endorsement of Soviet production.[14] Yet, despite strenuous attempts to quicken consumers' desire through public exhibitions of goods and publicity for commodities—via women's magazines, displays in 'model' store windows, and images of 'cultured' buyers—that desire was regularly frustrated owing to a dearth of commodities and to prices that exceeded the average citizen's purchasing capacity.[15]

In addition to underproduction, politicised distribution and access were decisive factors in the competitive acquisition of goods in perpetual shortage, for, as Katherine Verdery has pointed out, '[T]he whole point was *not* to sell things: the centre wanted to keep as much as possible under its control, because that was how it had redistributive power; and it wanted to give away the rest, because that was how it confirmed its legitimacy with the public.'[16] Since reward for (often putatively) meritorious contributions to the new system of centralised industrialisation was the order of the day, fine foods and luxury commodities delectated only the privileged—the political elite, the intelligentsia,[17] Stakhanovites—whereas the masses survived on a steady diet of promises.[18]

Official announcements of plenitude and happiness compensated for the widespread everyday experience of paucity. As in fetishism, enunciation camouflaged lack—a strategy epitomised in Stalin's notorious declaration of 1935, 'Life has become better! Life has become happier!' (*Zhit' stalo luchshe, zhit' stalo veselee!*) This fairy-tale formulation, which signaled a new direction to be adopted instead of a condition already attained, expanded into the song *Zhit' stalo luchshe* (1936) by Vasilii Lebedev-Kumach (lyrics) and Aleksandr Aleksandrov (music).[19] Metamorphosed into a mantra quoted by party functionaries, the media and Soviet citizens, it was cited ironically in some 'anonymous' citizens' letters to underscore the chasm yawning between claim and fact.[20] That discrepancy between circulated images and discourse reflecting Party mandates, on the one hand, and lived reality, on the other, became a cornerstone of Soviet life. As Julie Hessler succinctly sums up the situation, 'By the early 1950s, the Stalinist economy had succeeded only in proving that deprivation had been the one constant in citizens' experience for the past twenty-five years. [And...] the wartime exposure to conditions in central Europe seemed to prove that deprivation was uniquely a product of the Soviet regime'.[21]

Picture-Plenitude: Formulas and Infractions

A comparison of Soviet paintings with posters imag(in)ing food and drink from the 1930s to 1953 reveals several intriguing asymmetries, including a marked contrast in the two genres' visualisation of happy Stalinist plenitude and a disparity between Soviet poster ads and their Western counterparts.[22] Both paintings and posters depicted comestibles and beverages whose purported availability was intended to highlight the 'good life'—what Dunham calls the Big Deal—vouchsafed by the communist undertaking to create the Soviet New Man and New Woman. The campaign of *kul'turnost'*, adumbrated in the twenties and ushered in during the mid-1930s,[23] visually culminated in the *Industry of Socialism* Art Exhibition, which belatedly opened in 1939, with a subsidiary section devoted to *Food Industry*.

A brainchild of Anastas Mikoian, Commissar of Food Industries, this art exhibition in Gorky Park 'was dedicated entirely to the theme of material abundance and cultured everyday living'.[24] Paradoxically, given the exhibition's title, the methods of industrial production it highlighted, not unlike the era's painting techniques, relied on imports and Western models, modified in the transfer to an economy devoid of private ownership. During 1935–1937, so as to improve its capacity to meet the demand stimulated by official promises and various modes of advertising, the Trade Commissariat sponsored several study trips to the United States, Great Britain, Germany and Japan. Mikoian's memoirs, *Tak bylo* ('That's How It Was'), confirm the administration's eagerness to learn more efficient means of production from capitalist societies, particularly the United States. Mikoian recalls being impressed by the colossal number of standardised hamburgers sold on the streets and in kiosks, the diversity of fruit and vegetable juices, accelerated methods of making ice cream, refrigeration of fish and meat,[25] and other instances of America's miraculous ability to generate and preserve huge quantities of food and drink.[26] Not only the speed, but also the scale of American production as well as the stores—particularly Macy's, then the largest department store in the world—inspired the Soviet delegation.[27]

These pedagogical visits to the stronghold of capitalism elicited unrestrained enthusiasm and reinforced Soviet commitment to the production and visual depiction of consumer goods as an essential part of modern life, even as official speeches and reports by Mikoian negatively contrasted the crass American imperative of profit with the noble Soviet dedication to taking care of its working population.[28] For instance, in 1937 Mikoian delivered an official speech titled *Dognat' i peregnat' pishchevuiu promyshlennost' Ameriki* ('To catch up with and surpass America's food industry'), in the course of which he vowed that by 1938, trips abroad, especially to America, would be superfluous, for acquisition of the appropriate technology and the Bolshevik work ethic would enable the Soviet Union to surpass the most progressive capitalist countries (Mikoian 1941, 257). In a similar presentation, accompanied by sustained applause, he repeatedly linked the name of *velikii, rodnoi tovarishch Stalin* with *izobilie*—a catchword of the thirties (Mikoian 1941, 264–65).

Official reactions to paintings depicting food and its consumption, however, suggest the nature of the limitations—both ideological and aesthetic— imposed at various junctures upon images of consumerism. Shortly before the purges of the late thirties, which inflated rhetoric while shrinking the population, widely discussed canvasses by Il'ia Mashkov, Sergei Gerasimov and Arkadii Plastov led viewers to understand that the Soviet Union was awash in consumer goods, including fine foods, which artists could depict at their discretion. A comparison of their works with Petr Konchalovskii's *Aleksei Tolstoi Visiting the Artist* (1940–1941), however, reveals infinitely more complex circumstances, for painters and graphic artists struggled to adjust their thematic and stylistic interests to state edicts and the consequent fluctuations in approved 'artistic' criteria. The dynamic of *kul'turnost'*, Volkov maintains, accounts for transformations in the image of the enemy and of the 'good life'—transformations that ultimately defined and redefined the contemporary Soviet ideal and, consequently, the permissible in visual representation:

In 1934–1936, the first phase of *kul'turnost'*, the 'hostile elements' were dirty, badly dressed, ill-mannered, and illiterate [...] while the model heroes of the popular press were neatly dressed, clean, well-bred, and lived a joyous cultured life. In 1936–1937, as culturedness became increasingly associated with inner culture, with broad knowledge and education, those obsessed with superficial attributes and consumerism could be labeled 'petitbourgeois.' Finally, in 1937–1938 the earlier aspects of culturedness came under suspicion, and, although no one officially rejected personal hygiene and educatedness, the true virtues of Soviet Man were relegated to the sphere of consciousness and private ideological commitments. [The] official decline [of the age of *kul'turnost'*] coincided with the new motto 'To master Bolshevism!' put forward in September 1938 in connection with the publication of the *Short Course of the Communist Party*.[29]

Figure 3.1. Il'ia Mashkov, *Soviet Breads* (1936) (Volgograd Museum of Visual Arts)

This inward movement inevitably complicated the task of rendering *kul'turnost'* and its joys visible and, to some extent, explains the seemingly inexplicable responses of the establishment to paintings by various artists often trapped between official dictates and personal vision or professional abilities.

As Darra Goldstein insightfully notes, Mashkov's *Soviet Breads* (1936) makes explicit 'the connection between political power and sustenance': the apex of the political hierarchy determines who qualifies as a 'have' and a 'have not'.[30] Depicting the Soviet Union as a literal cornucopia, Mashkov's clever arrangement of various breads anticipates Vera Mukhina's renowned statue by symbolising the union of peasant and worker—the *smychka* deemed requisite for a fully productive modern society. (Fig. 3.1) Centred in the background, the standard state emblem of the hammer and sickle (plus the five-pointed star)[31] is duplicated in the batons flanking it. The latter echo the sheaves of wheat (peasant), while the round rolls in the foreground 'resemble cogs in the industrial wheel' (worker).[32] Its naturalistic style aside, the painting recalls the agitational policy of *smychka* that dominated joint advertisements of the 1920s (Cox 2006, 130). As 'the staff of life', bread evokes the quality of natural simplicity,[33] while the variety and number of breadstuffs signal wealth—of both the soil and the nation whose enthusiastic cultivation of the land yields such abundance. This triumphant display of the nation's rich harvests, of course, did not address the scarcity of other provisions or the catastrophic consequences of Stalin's policy of forcible collectivisation in the early thirties, which caused millions to die from starvation.[34] Nor did its symbolic idealisation pay heed to complaints from specific areas, usually remote from the better-supplied centre of Moscow, that bread—the minimal staple—was unavailable. Fitzpatrick cites, among other documents, a 1935 letter by a worker from Iaroslavl' complaining that he waited in line for three hours to buy bread, only to be informed by the shop assistant when he finally reached the counter that the store's supply was depleted (Fitzpatrick 1992, 220). In other words, while Mashkov's painting symbolically pinpoints the population's reliance on the state for access to goods, it also fantasizes a rosy image of plenty at a time of dearth.

Mashkov's display of Soviet profusion could hardly contrast more dramatically with Konchalovskii's portrait, done five years later, of Aleksei Tolstoi at the artist's home. Formally attired and seated alone at a cloth-covered table, a full glass in his hand, Tolstoi relishes not bread, but what by the Soviet standards of the era was a sumptuous repast—of sundry meats, smoked fish, vegetables, fruit, and wine—inaccessible to the majority of citizens as 'the hungry 30s' ended and World War II loomed on the horizon. Musya Glants speculates that Konchalovskii, an ardent admirer of Cézanne and especially Van Gogh, wished to underscore 'his subject's marvelous buoyancy' and *joie de vivre*.[35] (Fig. 3.2) Whatever his intention, the work encountered official disapproval, for it focused on the individual and his 'spiritual independence' in enjoying food that by the 1940s was deemed overly exclusionary and sophisticated for communist fare.[36] The authorities chided Konchalovskii for 'fencing himself off from the turbulence of Soviet life behind countless bouquets of flowers, piles of apples, and an *intimate little world* [emphasis added] of favorite things'.[37] Publications during the second half of the 1930s had insisted that such benefits were available to all, downplaying the policy of preferential access to commodities earned through ideological support or supernatural prowess at work. By the end of the decade, however, *kul'turnost'* depended less on cozy well-being and possessions than on self-discipline. Solitary gourmandising smacked of such undesirable elements as class distinctions and perquisites, self-indulgence, and a palate at odds with that of 'the people'. In short, as a happy consumer, Konchalovskii's Tolstoi—the author of several impeccable Socialist Realist texts—appears excessively

Figure 3.2. Petr Konchalovskii, *Aleksei Tolstoi Visiting the Artist* (1940–41) (Russian Museum, St. Petersburg)

bourgeois and exceptional, rather than typical, in the specifics of his dining pleasure.[38] A telling juxtaposition of this work with Konchalovskii's earlier *Returning from Market* (1926), which depicts four peasants in a cart but no visible goods, measures the distance between Tolstoi as the privileged beneficiary of the communist regime and Russia's traditional 'toilers of the soil,' whom Konchalovskii reportedly venerated.[39]

Whereas Konchalovskii strays from the conventions of Socialist Realism, Gerasimov and especially Plastov embrace its code in two thematic paintings that celebrate the joys of Stalinist plenitude, both titled *A Collective Farm Festival* and exhibited at the 1939 *Industry of Socialism* under the aegis of Stalin's proclamation of a happier life.[40] Though Gerasimov's *Festival* (1936–1937) was attacked by the critics Nikolai Shchekotov and Natal'ia Sokolova for its purported 'lack of finish' (that is, its cautious incorporation of Impressionist techniques), the subject matter and overall treatment render it a muted companion piece to Plastov's grandiloquent showcase of the Good Life under Stalin.[41] Gerasimov's *Festival* captures a group of collective farm workers in

Figure 3.3. Sergei Gerasimov, *A Collective Farm Festival* (1936–37) (Tretyakov Gallery, Moscow)

the sunlit countryside clustered around a table set with plates, flowers, various foods, several bottles and a carafe. (Fig. 3.3) Clearly, the happy and hospitable assembly is enjoying the fruits of collective labor on the beloved Soviet land. A male political agitator, arm raised, presumably is making a speech, for he commands the attention of most present, including a young man in the right foreground who, his back to the viewer, grips the handlebar of a bicycle. A woman in the left foreground crouches, rummaging in a basket, while another, behind her, ceremoniously carries a large, round bread or cake towards the table. Faces are smiling or rapt, eyes riveted on the speaker, but the scene emanates an atmosphere of cheerful informality: several celebrants are gazing elsewhere, the young man's bicycle and his outfit lend a degree of casualness to the festivities,[42] and the dimensions of both the table and the 'feast' are rather restrained.[43]

The heroic protagonist here is the fertile Russian land, which, stretching back towards the horizon in reverse parallel to the grassy foreground, serves to integrate the humans into a bucolic 'frame', underscoring the seamless unity of Soviets with their native soil.[44] Gerasimov was, first and foremost, a landscapist, and as Mark Bassin insightfully maintains, despite the Soviet injunction to control nature, which culminated in the 'Great Stalin Plan for the Transformation of Nature' (1940s), landscapists reared in the traditions of nineteenth-century art (and especially of the Peredvizhniki) found a means

Figure 3.4. Arkadii Plastov, *A Collective Farm Festival* (1937) (Russian Museum)

of projecting the attainment of the socialist-communist paradise through landscapes that effaced temporal distinctions by depicting a timeless pastoral idyll (Bassin passim). Gerasimov's *Collective Farm Festival* belongs to this trend, which showcases the Russian countryside and the ample rewards for those working in harmony with fecund nature. Perhaps that sense of simple, shared happiness explains why the influential Shchekotov, though faulting the painting, which he characterised as essentially a 'landscape with figures' in an impressionistic mode, for not adequately capturing the New People of Soviet agriculture, nonetheless lauded its technique (Reid 2001, 177).

Nothing underscores the comparatively modest scale of Gerasimov's festive gathering more vividly than Plastov's hyperbolic *Festival* (1937), 'a paradigm of Socialist Realism under Stalin',[45] though anomalous within the context of Plastov's oeuvre. (Fig. 3.4) Plastov portrays an earthly prelapsarian paradise, inspired and overseen by the omniscient divinity whose image benignly smiles down from the heavens upon the mortals rejoicing in their lush Eden. Their jubilation amidst natural bounties illustrates the veracity of His words—'Life has become better! Life has become happier!'—a commandment for them to live by, printed in red on the banner beneath his portrait that definitively separates his transcendent 'realm' from theirs. Stalin as Father and the 'sacred signs' that flank him—the red five-pointed star, hammer and sickle on the left, and a fluttering red flag on the right—occupy the uppermost, celestial register of the painting's composition. The remaining two-thirds consist of beaming revelers from various republics and of various ages gathered around or seated at several tables graced by samovars, bottles, carafes, and laden with fish, baked goods, eggs and colorful fruits and vegetables. Plastov's use of vibrant hues and light to irradiate the carefree, communal sharing of plenitude in the sunlit outdoors, combined with the celebrants' smiling faces and energetic gestures, animates the scene and assures viewers that the blissful communist future has arrived, thanks to Stalin. Congruent with paintings and posters of children thanking the omnipotent Leader for their happy childhood, the iconography also colludes with the official policy of glorifying (a mythical) abundance for all. In short, Plastov's 'Garden of Stalinist Delights' simultaneously engages advertising and liturgy, in both of which, as Paul Parker noted, 'the strength of the ideal can be measured by the amount of the subjection of style to iconography.'[46]

Art Versus Ad or Graphic Happiness Amid Virtual Variety

Remarkably, paintings such as Plastov's succeeded incomparably better than poster ads at conveying a terrestrial paradise teeming with assorted foods and drinks—not in industrial centres, but in the countryside—as indicative of joyous Soviet plenitude under Stalin. In doing so, canvas art fulfilled the function customarily entrusted to graphic publicity. Or, as Susan Reid nicely phrased it, 'For all but the elite, the "representation of reality in its revolutionary development" in Socialist Realist painting served, literally, as window dressing, taking the place of actual products available for purchase'.[47] Quite simply, graphic artists failed to find an adequate means of illustrating how a plethora of mouth-watering goods would guarantee universal consuming happiness.[48] Impassioned debates about advertising during the 1920s at least partially illuminate the causes of this failure, fueled by ideological contradictions and the perceived need to compromise with Western marketing practices.

A speech by Mikoian in 1936 highlighting the government's efforts to increase production while lowering prices proclaimed, 'Capitalists produce goods for the sake of profit, whereas we do so to satisfy the needs of the workers.'[49] This pronouncement echoed polemics of the 1920s, which spilled over into the thirties, about advertising's violation of socialist principles.[50] Proponents of advertising such as R. G. Driubin decried the deceptive strategies of Western advertising, deployed to galvanise 'irrational' consumption so as to offset the overproduction intrinsic to capitalist economies. They pragmatically approved, however, of advertising that purveyed information about state-produced goods to otherwise ignorant consumers.[51] Caught between the Scylla of promoting consumption and the Charybdis of ideological consistency, spokesmen for advertising resorted to a rhetoric of moralised differentiation, one that distinguished between Soviet 'rational' and Western 'irrational' commercial ads.[52] What a comparative examination of 1930s–1953 posters in their historical context reveals, however, is that Soviet poster advertising simply embraced a different sort of irrationalism.

Publicity, as John Berger contends, 'can never really afford to be about the product or opportunity it is proposing to the buyer who is not yet enjoying it. [...] Publicity is always about the future buyer.'[53] And her/his acquisition of the pertinent product provides a passport to the dream-come-true world of make-believe, whether that fantasy realm engages desire for 'love, economy, protection, pleasure, safety, wealth or what not'.[54] In other words, market images address the sphere of the ideal, allowing us to glimpse the new, happy selves into which our investment of funds will magically transfigure us—which is precisely why 'truth in advertising' is an oxymoron.[55] Writing in 1937, Paul Parker understood that persuasive ads play upon emotions, not reason, and implicitly or explicitly transmit the intimate, participatory notion that a unique 'magical quality' enables the pertinent product to best rivals in effecting such metamorphoses in the courted client.[56] What Soviet commentators called the 'irrationalism' of American ads was/is, in fact, the genre's union of excess, hyperbolic promises, and a focus displaced from the product onto the consumer, but they failed to grasp the collusion between purveyor and purchaser: Western ads are designed with the knowledge that they will be seen 'only by those interested in the product'[57] that vouchsafes an impossibly extraordinary self—a self whose glamorous aura is emanated by the consumer's surrogate within the ad.[58] Primacy of the image—whether it be romantic, lyrical, humourous or dramatic—is an axiom of advertising, for effective ads require the consumer's seduction after a single, quick glance. Whereas words cannot always create an ideal world in the buyer's imagination, a successful illustration must. And until television, posters more than other means of advertising depended on the instant legibility of the visual, which arrested the viewers' attention through colour, size, and arrangement of shapes.[59] From the outset, in the West the creation of a desirable self in a striking visual superseded details about the product.

By contrast, since 1930s Soviet advertising was inseparable from the educational agenda of *kul'turnost'*, the Soviet advertising poster forewent fantasy in favor of simple information transmitted through straightforward statements. Instead of beguiling, Soviet posters taught and preached. Their creators, during the thirties and forties, adhered all too literally and reductively to a precept articulated in an article by Vladimir Maiakovskii (1923, 57), 'To advertise is to name the item' (*Reklama—eto imia veshchi*), in which Maiakovskii forcefully argued for diversity and imagination (*raznoobrazie, vydumka*) as advertising's ammunition against competitors (*[Reklama—] eto oruzhie, porazhaiushchee konkurentsiiu*).[60] Collaborating with fellow Constructivist Alexander Rodchenko, in the 1920s Maiakovskii had generated a stream of superlative ads endorsing state products in which Rodchenko's original, dynamic images translated Maiakovskii's aggressive jingles into eye-catching equivalents that reinforced 'the message'. That balanced symbiosis between verbal and visual disappeared in Soviet posters under Stalin, for words preponderated over images.[61] In the majority of cases, Stalin-era posters were utterly mundane in conception and execution. Unlike paintings, poster ads rarely depicted reassuring or heady plenitude, as is all too evident in posters from the 1930s–1953. And, with 'the cultural revolution'[62] over, and Constructivism vilified, graphic artists retreated to the safety of an enervated representational aesthetic.

Comparatively few commercial posters appeared during these decades and even fewer have survived, the same small number issued and now reissued in book-length collections such as *The Russian Advertising Poster* (2001) and related volumes by the publishing house Kontakt-Kul'tura. Tellingly, several of the extant posters reveal a preoccupation not with consumers but with producers, store personnel, and the role of the last two in civilising the populace. For instance, Viktor Govorkov's *Kul'turno torgovat'—pochetnyi trud!* ('Cultured Selling and Buying Is Honourable Work!' 1949). (Fig. 3.5) depicts a male shop assistant behind a food-store counter weighing an *unidentified* product (!) on a scale embossed with the emblematic hammer and sickle, thereby leaving no doubt that the major 'product' here is the Soviet establishment. The drab goods displayed on the shelves behind him consist of jars with kasha, flour, macaroni, tea, and mysterious contents—all in unattractive, cheap packages. The store, the goods and the salesman are all rendered in the limited colour scheme of white, yellow, orange, brown, and dark blue. Happiness here belongs to the state employee and presumably stems from his assigned role in the government's campaign of *kul'turnost'*, artlessly signaled by the poster's title and the beret as a marker of the hygienic practices urged at the time upon the population. Devoid of any other human presence, the ad essentially tries to 'sell' an official socioeconomic initiative, one of its 'model' representatives/beneficiaries, and the state's capacity to provision stores, though the pitiful supplies on the shelves, as well as the unappetising cold meats beside the counter, hardly seem adequate to any civilising process. In all senses, the consumer is absent, and the visual unintentionally subverts the purpose of Soviet advertising, frankly acknowledged by a representative of trade writing (1936) in the journal *Sovetskaia torgovlia*: 'The Soviet Union has become a rich country and *this richness should shine with all the colors on the shelves of the shops*, in the city as well as in the village' (emphasis added).[63]

A similar poster by Galina Shubina, with the identical palette of colors, carries the same guileless message: *Obsluzhim kul'turno kazhdogo posetitelia!* ('We'll Serve Each Client in Cultured Fashion!' 1948). (Fig. 3.6) Draped in a white

Figure 3.5. Viktor Govorkov, 'To Trade Is Honourable Work' (1949) (Russian State Library)

Figure 3.6. Galina Shubina, 'We'll Serve Each Customer in Cultured Fashion!' (1948) (Russian State Library)

apron and a white kerchief—the female analogue to the male's beret—a radiant restaurant waitress carries a tray weighted down with a glass, a bottle, a huge steaming teapot (larger than her head!!), bread, sugar, two hard-boiled eggs, and two meat patties garnished with carrots and something greenish-yellow. Clearly, the focus is not the peculiarly incoherent meal (or the minimalist venue—apart from flowers on the two tables, the unnamed restaurant is a visual desert), but the sunny personnel, whose synecdochic representative stands in the foreground, looking off into the distance to the right. Given the relative space of the poster, her radically disproportionate, manifestly symbolic size dwarfs the two tables to the rear right of the poster, where another identically dressed but diminutive waitress is serving three diners. Through the window behind them, cut in half by the curtain that covers its lower portion and partly obscured by the tray in the foreground, one can detect tall buildings, trees, and smoke spiraling upward from two factory stacks—a metonym for industrial production.

Perhaps the most remarkable aspect of the poster, apart from the poverty of the spotlighted repast on the tray, is the artist's inability to integrate, in meaningful ways, the background with the cheerful 'server' in the foreground, her back turned to the only visible diners. Though the composition recalls cinema's open form (the happy waitress's gaze extends beyond the space of the poster, and the two tables in the rear represent only part of the restaurant, abruptly sliced off by the poster's right edge), the impression is of two discrete, forcibly spliced works. Manifestly inspired by the policy of *kul'turnost'* and the glorification of Soviet industry, both Shubina's and Govorkov's posters could scarcely be less effectual in capturing the imagination through techniques of consumer seduction. In a competitive market, publicity invariably insists on the unique, inestimable qualities conferred upon consumers and guaranteed by a specific brand or 'dining experience'. A society in which the state is sole owner and producer ineluctably eliminates all rhetorical comparisons with alternatives—which may partially explain why these dreary ads lack the originality and vividness of 1920s Soviet posters asserting the superiority of state-produced goods over those publicised by private enterprises.

Indeed, most advertising posters under Stalin omit the lynchpin of Western ads: a fantastically idealised image of the world to be entered by the envisioned buyer once s/he possesses the product. The 'rational' consumption advocated by Soviet ad posters not only abrogates the calculated emotional appeal requisite for a genuine market and the profit-driven competition that breeds ever escalating claims for a product, but also apparently militates against creativity in graphics. For instance, the anonymous *Goriachie moskovskie kotlety* (Hot Moscow Cutlets, 1937), a staggeringly mundane ad for the Russian version of a hamburger,[64] highlights in red the price of 50 kopeks, not the item or its buyer (again, entirely omitted), and it is difficult to imagine whom the unappetising bun with the forlorn, dark-brown blob enthroned on it could possibly entice. (Fig. 3.7) The poster is typical of the era's advertising, which subscribed to a primitive template for its design: a naturalistic image confined to the relevant product, more or less centred, with the name of the state producer/trust[65] above and basic information below, or vice versa.[66] It offered scant visual or verbal inducement. And a poster advertising margarine (1952) by E. Miniovich indicates that two decades later, some graphic artists had not abandoned this humdrum formula.

Posters featuring people largely limited themselves to an individual whose consumer-happiness expressed itself through a smile—sometimes so crudely rendered as to resemble a grimace. Children comprised a high percentage of such visuals, beaming over ice cream or, less convincingly, over a single jar of frozen fruit against a snowy background. (Fig. 3.8) On occasion, the poor quality resulted in unwittingly grotesque images, as in a 1930 poster by the prolific Aleksandr Zelenskii, which unaccountably deformed a little boy imbibing *Mors* (a fruit beverage, here in a thick, outsized glass container) into

Figure 3.7. Unknown Artist, 'Hot Moscow Cutlets' (1936–37) (Russian State Library)

Figure 3.8. Unknown Artist, 'As Fresh as in Summer' (1938) (Russian State Library)

what initially strikes the viewer as an old drunk with a contorted face nursing a hangover.[67] (Fig. 3.9) Elsewhere, anodyne mothers and daughters contemplate a solitary glass of milk (Aleksandr Pobedinskii, 1936) or smile alongside several unimaginatively arranged dishes and containers of ice cream (Pobedinskii, 1937). In other words, the very design of literalist posters in the thirties and forties, sharply contrasting with the dynamism of the 1920s (achieved through use of the diagonal, emphatic interaction among elements, and photo montage that implied a narrative), inadvertently conjured up not plenitude, but lack and lackluster staples.[68]

A few exceptions to this dispiriting rule include a 1938 poster ad by A. Miller for crabmeat,[69] in which a neatly dressed, smiling woman against an abstract background raises a piece of the Chatka crabmeat speared on a fork to her mouth. (Fig. 3.10) Though the colour combination coincides with that in the ads for 'cultured service,' and an identical darkish orange maladroitly links her lips, painted fingernails, crab and verbal text, she actually projects enjoyment as her twinkling eyes directly meet those of the viewers/potential consumers in an invitation to share her pleasure.[70] Assigned more than two-thirds of the poster's space, which exploits the diagonal, she dominates the visual, enacting the jingle in the uppermost register to her left: *Vsem poprobovat' pora by / Kak vkusny i nezhny kraby* ('It's time everyone tried/the tastiness and tenderness of crab'). Widespread in 1920s posters, the rhetoric of *vse* was especially popular in poster ads for various cigarette brands, which, indeed, were numerous and within most Soviets' buying power. Since, in the Soviet Union, crab, unlike tobacco, constituted a luxury item, the couplet evokes the dream-yearning of Western ads, even if the garish yellow of the background clashes with any intimation of transcendence.

Genuine inventiveness, nonetheless, vitalizes several extant, far-from-typical poster ads of the early 1950s. For instance, *Pokupaite morozhenoe* ('Buy Ice Cream,' 1951) by Sergei Sakharov—one of the most talented graphic artists of the period—places in an arctic environment two small penguins gazing up at a disproportionately huge penguin carrying an attractive assortment of ice cream on a tray. (Fig. 3.11) The humourously treated conceptual connection among cold, penguins, and ice cream, the implied visual parallel between penguin and a waiter in coattails, the visible choice among varieties of product, and the skillful use of colour to emphasise light and sun make for a striking advertisement. In another, similar and equally clever ad for ice cream (1954), Sakharov richly explores the cynosural power of magical feats as well as the capacity of white and various shades of blue to convey frigid temperatures: an enormous seal on a gigantic ice floe mesmerizes four miniature penguins by balancing on its nose a goblet of ice cream that in size approximates a third of its body. (Fig. 3.12) Sakharov draws

Figure 3.9. Aleksandr Zelenskii, 'Mors' (1930) (Russian State Library)

Figure 3.10. A. Miller, ad for crabmeat (1938) (Russian State Library)

Figure 3.11. Sergei Sakharov, *Buy Ice Cream* (1951) (Russian State Library)

Figure 3.12. Sergei Sakharov, *Ice Cream* (1954) (Russian State Library)

the viewer's eyes to the product not only through the conceit of a circus performance, but also through colour, for the creamy-chocolate hues of the ice cream stand out dramatically from the otherwise entirely white and blue hues of the poster. While no joyous surrogate consumer inscribes happy plenitude, fantasy-humour and a manipulation of dimensions sidestep earnest but dismal attempts to convey profusion, conjuring, instead, a magical realm of spectacle.

Few ads from the 1950s match the originality of Sakharov's,[71] though some promoting champagne evidence a degree of sophistication and unexpectedly resonate with Western paradigms. Champagne, as Fitzpatrick and Gronow observe, and Mikoian's memoirs underscore, numbered among the luxuries, earlier regarded as bourgeois, that Stalin suddenly decided to produce in sufficient quantities to keep the entire Soviet Union effervescent (champagne is an important sign of material well-being, of the good life').[72] His directive of 1936 prompted a scramble, described in the signally titled publication *Izobilie* (Abundance), which reported, 'We have to give the country 12 million bottles of champagne,' to expand champagne production at all (im)possible speed.[73] In a characteristic comparison of Soviet and foreign output, Mikoian registered that in the second half of the thirties, the USSR's single champagne plant, Abrau-Diurso, managed to produce annually only 10–20 per cent of the champagne that France generated.[74] During this full-throttle endeavor to flood Soviet cities with champagne, some segments of the population were facing starvation, and letters to authorities reflected their dire conditions: people in Stalingrad, for instance, started queuing for bread at 2:00 a.m., their ranks swelling to 600–800 by 6:00 a.m., and during the winter of 1939, stores did not carry such basic foods as cabbage, onions, and butter.[75]

Though Soviet production quickly accelerated under the third Five Year Plan (1938–1941) and according to Mikoian increased sixty-fold,[76] 'Champagne hardly became a standard household item. Nikolai Martynov's atypical advertisement for *Sovetskoe shampanskoe: luchshee vinogradnoe vino* (Soviet Champagne: The Best Grape Wine, 1952), though primarily naturalistic, effectively enveloped the sparkling wine in a nimbus of romance. (Fig. 3.13) Elegantly unfurling a spectrum of tones ranging from pale beige to lush brown, the poster balances and overlaps two images: in the lower right, an unopened bottle of champagne and a full glass emitting golden bubbles partly block the grapes and pears overflowing a glass bowl behind them; in the upper left, a pretty, soft-faced young brunette holding an identical full glass in her right, manicured hand, gazes dreamily at a distant point beyond the frame of the poster. A pervasive sense of mystery and ineffable elevation results from the hazy area between her body (shown only above the waist) and the product, suspending both in an unidentifiable, transcendental space that unites them

Figure 3.13. Nikolai Martynov, *Soviet Champagne: The Best Grape Wine* (1952) (Russian State Library)

mainly through colour and the iteration of the golden liquid in the two receptacles—the gold echoed in the pears and part of the label on the bottle. Both simple and chic, the visual eloquently speaks for the extravagant effects of Soviet champagne on the consumer, presenting the latter as attractive and refined, with a palate capable of appreciating its delights.[77]

Martynov's ad for champagne takes its cue, however cautiously, from the Western 'irrational' recourse to hyperbole and fantasy repudiated by Soviet commentators who touted the 'rationalism' of Soviet advertising. That so-called rationalism inevitably doomed the genre as a mode of selling an idealised self. Moreover, opprobrious disdain for capitalist excess conveniently ignored a more fundamental irrationality during Stalinism—that of literalist referentiality without a referent, since posters largely promoted goods in perpetual shortage and inaccessible to those whom the ads addressed. Borrowing Northrop Frye's concept of 'stupid realism' as applied to corporate advertising and political propaganda, Lears contends that both are ''official' discourses that legitimate existing structures of power'.[78] Lears's observation applies a fortiori to the Soviet Union, where in the post-NEP period the sole 'corporation' *was* the state, intent on presenting itself as the guarantor of people's happiness.

Ultimately, the utopian cast of Socialist-Realist paintings such as Plastov's proved incomparably superior at imaging the official Party line of happiness in plenitude—a never-never, fairy-tale kingdom of enunciated achievement. In contrast, the austerity and haplessness of most Soviet posters from 1930s–1953,[79] as well as their relative scarcity, unwittingly betrayed the degree to which that plenitude thrived as a theoretical ideal that never translated into concrete experience. One could reasonably claim, therefore, that whereas many posters involuntarily inscribed the diminished nature of everyday reality, some socialist-realist canvas art engaged the surreal, irrational domain of pure desire—a desire realised under Stalin only in the iconography of a Cornucopia-Utopia.

Chapter Four

TASTY AND HEALTHY: SOVIET HAPPINESS IN ONE BOOK

Gian Piero Piretto

They just now dragged themselves out of the houses in festive clothes, already having had time previously to down two or three glasses of vodka and snack on party food. Eddy-Baby knows that usually this is an 'Olivier' salad, sausages, and the customary sprats.

— Eduard Limonov, *Adolescent Savenko*

I will begin with a quotation from the radio dialogue between Petr Vail' and Aleksandr Genis. Their conversation took place on Radio Svoboda airtime in now-distant 1989. The subject of the conversation was the same book that is now the subject of my analysis: the masterpiece of Soviet culinary science, the unforgettable, incomparable and celebrated *The Book about Tasty and Healthy Food*, promoted by the USSR People's Commissar of Food Industries, Anastas Mikoian.

Genis had this to say: 'This book is an argument to the advantage of a sort of generalised Nina Andreeva, who, having become hydra-like, grows a new head every time to replace the one cut off.'[1]

Hydras heads might well 'fit' Andreeva, a fierce perestroika opponent in 1988; but they also recall many other Ninas (maids, as well as housewives) who populated communal apartments and the collective Soviet memory, with their striving to stay in line with present trends and, accordingly, to master the most vital management of Soviet cookery, or to dream about it and about abundance despite their own social level. But regrowing a hydra's *body* also means the endless innovations that arose in each new edition of this treatise. These are mainly in the text of the book's preface and in the encyclopedic articles that, in concord with all the new courses and directives of the Party and the government, were reduced, recomposed and rewritten every time, so that each new edition, coming out on schedule like clockwork, would have a new head. This head, to extend the metaphor, was arranged 'nose to nose' with the very latest party bias. Each new foreword was a refutation of the preceding one, and in each new instance, a new political accuracy and a spotless ideology made its appearance to the world.

In this article, I will focus only on a few republications from Stalin's times,[2] since in this brief space it would be impossible to encompass the evolution of the variants that appeared after 1953, much less to discuss them all in depth. The article proposes to investigate the concept of happiness as a leitmotif of this cookbook. I intend to base this on the rather well-described and studied notion of illusion/deceit as the basis of Stalinist cultural policy. In conformity with this, I will examine the issues of the strategies used, the goal of which was to reinforce the sense of the 'betterness' and 'joyousness' of life—as indeed it was prescribed in the hackneyed phrase from Stalin's speech at a Stakhanovites' congress in 1935: 'Life has become better, comrades; life has become more joyous.'

In the mid-1930s, thanks to Mikoian's efforts, a drastic reorganisation of the food processing industry was carried out, in which even the advanced methods of developed foreign countries, including capitalist ones, were used.[3] Foreign expedition teams of Soviet technological specialists were assembled with the goal of adopting foreign experience in the management of trade and agriculture for application to Soviet conditions. Meanwhile, it was naturally expected that the principles of socialism would be observed in every possible way, and even more so, that the advantages of the socialist system would be confirmed by all the innovations being introduced. The demonstration of abundance, according to this idea, was called upon to bear witness to the achievements of wise and happy management. Thanks to Mikoian's innovations (canned goods, frozen products and semi-prepared foods), it was supposed that records would be constantly broken, perfection would be achieved, and the cook would have a clear advantage according to such parameters as the time spent cooking and the ultimate quality of the results, in conformity with the norms that arose from the political and ideological discourse of the current period. This affected the processing of products, and both the preparation and consumption of food. 'Factory-made jam is completely replacing homemade. Prepared and frozen ravioli free the housewife from the lengthy bother of preparing them.'[4] (Fig. 4.1) In this respect, one can hardly forget Mikoian's notorious 1937 cutlets 'with a bun': the Big Mac *ante litteram*, the first step, in a glaring clash with Russian traditions, towards the 'fast-food-isation' of the whole country and of Soviet eating habits.

The everyday life of Soviet citizens was thoroughly ideologicalised. 'First the regime creates "a need for better life", then it satisfies it. Ideology gives way to pragmatism, fantasies of consumption to a consumption-led system of

МОСКОВСКИЙ
ОРДЕНА ЛЕНИНА
МЯСОКОМБИНАТ
им. А.И.Микояна

Сибирские
ПЕЛЬМЕНИ

Figure 4.1. Pel'meni, *Book about Tasty and Healthy Food* (1952)

industrial production.'[5] With the rise in the standard of living, a directive appeared: to orient consumers accordingly, to develop in them a socialist cultural approach to production, as is clear from a passage in the Foreword prepared by the editors of the *Food industry* newspaper: 'The continuously increasing growth of the well-being of the Soviet people makes ever newer demands on the food, fish, and meat-and-dairy industries.'[6]

The title of this treatise/textbook is more telling than anything else: the title is unchanging, unshakeable, eternal. *The Book About Tasty and Healthy Food*—a primordial pledge of stability and continuity, in spite of the lightweight subject matter (the appetite, satiety and hedonism at the table). The title of this work represents a basic symbol and a metaphor of the ideas implanted in the depths of Soviet society's collective consciousness. Tasty and healthy food, along with the parks that in those days were called 'culture and relaxation parks', was by no means a private matter and was far from a personal one. The basis of Soviet life rested on a whole series of binomials that grew out of the main and most fundamental: the private versus the public. The housewife cooked not only for her husband, son or lover, but also for her country. Messmates represented the citizens of the state to an even greater degree than one's kinfolk.

Every menu was a mini-Five-Year Plan in which the ingredients and portions were hierarchically listed depending on for how many people (messmates) the meal was designed. Guidance was given on production, with an indication of the calculated culinary processing time, and user instructions and pseudoscientific commentaries were provided. All of this was depicted in the very same bureaucratic-popularising lexicon that any other Soviet text with a political and social purpose had. One was supposed to surpass a plan at the stove, in exactly the same way that one had to in a mine, at a workstation or on a construction site. One needed only to master the inexhaustible resources that the USSR's food industry offered a person—canned goods, frozen products, and semi-prepared foods—and a miracle was supposed to happen.

Clearly, a need was felt for an encyclopedia capable of bringing into citizens' consciousness both the fact that these unusual and inexhaustible new food resources existed and cultured ways of behaving in the light of such an abundance of products—an encyclopedia that would have the goal of helping in the business of choosing (and choice is the most complicated problem that there has been up until the present, and remains an obsession for everyone who has lived through the Soviet experience).

There is yet another possibility, one that also struck Genis, of turning the metaphor in the opposite direction, although it is no less functional and convincing:

> The process of preparing food became a symbol of the transformation of life according to a wise recipe/plan. Every dish is a metaphor for the fullness and variety of life, harmonised in a painstakingly measured menu.[7]

The metaphor works in both directions, giving rise to an invariable image—the image of individual pleasure and collective exultation. This allows us, as Thomas Lahusen says, 'to study the issue of *the cuisine* of the people who lived

Figure 4.2. Cover of *Book about Tasty and Healthy Food* (1952)

in the most uncivilised of Stalinist times',[8] in the literal and metaphorical senses of the word.

The cover of this book is no less full of significance than its title. The cover is thick and solid ('monumentally political', I would say), with embossed drawings that also convey a feeling of abundance and importance. Indeed, the reliefs on the cover in and of themselves delighted the reader, promising great joy from the reading. It was not a banal binding for just any ordinary printed matter, but a signal that this book was a work of art, that it was a reliable treatise, a historical annal—that it was ultimately destined to become, as the future indeed demonstrated, a real collective *cultural monument*. (Fig. 4.2)

> The monumental, calculated to intimidate the individual and personal ... classic, for the extermination of the 'unhealthy.' All the categories of this kind of aesthetic not only express positive demands but are also instruments of struggle.[9]

All the categories of such an aesthetic are present in the *Book*. The initiative to publish this book arose from several different events of quite differing scale and nature: political, economic and cultural. As a result, this book became an important factor in ideological work: it was seen as an authoritative 'transmission

of the norm'[10] and constituted a part of the aggregate work of art
(*Gesamtkunstwerk*) that was being put together by all of Soviet culture. In 1935
and 1936, 'many of the Soviet Union's model department stores were
installed in the sumptuous buildings of prerevolutionary stores, where
administrators consciously recreated the atmosphere of luxury to match the
high-end goods that they purveyed.'[11] In 1939 the Eighteenth Congress of the
USSR Communist Party assembled. In the same year, an exhibit was put on,
devoted to the accomplishments of the food industry, in the Gorky Park of
Culture and Relaxation. The exhibit was conceived and executed as a hymn
to the abundance and consumption of goods.[12] It was a concrete and
accessible means of display, while at the same time triumphant and very
sumptuous, directly addressed to consumers. As in other measures undertaken
as well by the Soviet regime, the spectator was intensively drawn in to
combined work on the final result.

This epic that told the tale of food was one of the best examples of socialist
ideological architecture. In it, several features of Soviet ideology and culture
reach maximal expression: first, the inadmissibility of understatedness;
second, the creation of a determined will to imagine a world the belief in
which is so strong that it is often taken for reality on the basis of a
philosophical attitude. The viewer (or reader) knows that what he sees is not
real, but nevertheless he believes in this vision. Cultural, political and social
practice convince one that such a world is not subject to interpretation, and
one must simply believe in it, period, not distinguishing between the present
and the future. This is what Kirill Postoutenko defines as 'the ability of the
Soviet person to delight in aesthetic contemplation of yet uncreated objects'.[13]

For this reason, *The Book about Tasty and Healthy Food* is worth examining in
the post-postmodern stage of cultural history. A Socialist Realist text is not at
all metaphorical; it does not reflect *per omnia saecula saeculorum* one and the
same spirit of the time that gave rise to it, but rather rises above the
boundaries of history and is capable of begetting new meanings through
analysis by contemporary methods of interpretation.

The illustrations for this book, emphasising the importance of iconographic
discourse and visual culture in Socialist Realism, have within them the main
principle of a figurative text, the role of which is to illustrate the verbal series,
to expound upon it and comment on it, with no aspiration to develop anything
beyond the textual series, and having neither self-sufficiency nor individuality.
As Vladimir Papernyi observed in the context of a different art, 'If someone at
the time had invented, say, a scent generator, the culture would have eagerly
enriched its film with it as well.'[14] And not only film, we would like to add. *The
Book about Tasty and Healthy Food* lacks only a generator of scents, scents that
would in turn *illustrate* not so much the culinary recipes as the function of these

Figure 4.3. Can of green peas, *Book about Tasty and Healthy Food* (1953)

recipes in shoring up a bright future and in building communism and happiness. The appetising and tempting colour insets were focused on conveying emotional signals to the largest number of consumers possible. (Fig. 4.3) (Fig. 4.4) The book did not repeat the already well-known propagandistic formulas which were the norm in the majority of posters, films, and works of art, but it disseminated new ideas with the help of these pictures and their

Figure 4.4. Mayonnaise, *Book about Tasty and Healthy Food* (1952)

juicy victuals. One of the main principles of Socialist Realism was clearly upheld: not a simple return to the classical (naturalistic) mimetic image, but a new use of innovative imagery that had the attraction of recently invented media.[15] In the rhetoric of this type of imagery, the problem of sincerity/falsehood was simply not addressed, giving way instead to the problem of the *functionality* of the image as such. The results of distributing the *Book*, printed in several million copies, prove that this problem was fully resolved.

The kitchen as a tactical bridgehead (the kitchen itself) and at the same time as a totality of rules (for *cooking*)—harmonious, organised and strict rules, aimed at achieving 'tastiness and health'—constituted an integral part of the government's work of drawing the masses of the people into the creation (by means of this text, as well) of the main super-goal: the great *Soviet happiness*. This 'happiness' was to psychologically define the emotional well-being of citizens realising their own good fortune and their advantageous position, against the backdrop of contrast of 'Soviet prosperity and capitalist hunger'.

To create a comparative context, I think it is pertinent here to recall that among the fundamental texts of Italian gastronomy, the most famous is Pellegrino Artusi's *Science in the Kitchen and the Art of Eating Well* (*La scienza in cucina e l'arte di mangiar bene*).[16] The first edition of this book came out in 1891, and the book was reprinted at least fourteen times. Joining ranks with it was the incomparable creation of Ada Boni, *The Talisman of Happiness* (*Il talismano della felicità*): the first edition of this book was in 1929.[17]

For Artusi, in the nineteenth century (as we can see), the prerogative of the scientific approach was at the forefront (which can also be observed in the Soviet *The Book about Tasty and Healthy Food*). Let us note that the curious coexistence of the principles of science and art is highly specific to Italian culture. Both the title and the content of Artusi's book demonstrate that only the combination of a technological quality with creativity allows the Italian to perfect and ennoble cuisine. But at the end of the 1920s, in the Italy that was by then already fascist, Ada Boni, in accordance with the international trends of the time—like her Russian analogue, Elena Molokhovets,[18] whose precepts were afterwards yet again embodied (i.e., ideologically interpreted) in the *Book* that we are examining here—bestows upon her work a rather more superficial orientation, when she calls it 'a gift for young housewives'. Large printings of this tome were regularly sold out in Italy during the spring months, the traditional season for weddings. Hardly original, but true: the book was implicitly addressed to the *ancien regime* notion of the woman's role, to being 'ladylike', which equated wedded harmony with the notion of true happiness:

> Many of you, dear ladies and girls, know how to play the piano well or to sing with exquisite grace; many others have very exalted titles for upper-level studies, know the modern languages, are pleasant writers or fine painters; still others are experts at tennis or golf, or confidently guide the steering wheel of a luxurious automobile. But, alas, certainly not all of you, if you examined your consciences even a little, could claim to know how to cook two soft-boiled eggs to perfection. (Boni 1929)

Less wordy, less mellifluous, and with an embellishment, as was the custom, in the form of the ordinary cluster of abbreviations—this is how the dedication adorning the first page of the 1939 edition of *The Book about Tasty and Healthy Food* appeared:[19]

> The USSR Narkompishcheprom [Peoples' Comissariat of the Food Industry]—to the housewife.[20]

Tacked on to this, shortly following, was one of the ubiquitous quotations of Stalinist dogma, just before the 'Bouillons and Soups' section:

> We must surpass [the capitalist countries] in the area of economics, as well.... Only if we surpass the leading capitalist countries, economically speaking, can we expect that the country will be completely surfeited with the objects of consumption, that we will have an abundance of goods, and that we will have the possibility of making the transition from the first phase of communism to its second phase.[21]

Just a few more words to develop a comparative perspective, before we focus on an analysis of Stalinist/Soviet strategies and technologies—above all, about the authorship of the books on cuisine; both Artusi and Boni, exponents of quite personal concepts, stick to first person narrative. In the past, the Russian compiler of the *Guide for Young Housewives*, Elena Molokhovets, set out along those same lines. A legendary statement she made has been adduced countless times as a comic example: 'But what are you to do if guests have arrived unexpectedly? You must go down to the cellar, get a smoked ham, and then, based on that, create all sorts of culinary wonders.' But this is unfair, because this is not the main thing in Molokhovets's book: there are rather more important aspects of her work upon which one might be invited to reflect.

The authorship of the various Soviet editions of the *Book*, on the other hand, belongs to a long train of experts and consultants that replace each other (one is again reminded of the hydra). A normative, strictly regimented project was created, not an ordinary collection of recipes for preparing food. Only at the end of the foreword is it said—or rather, mumbled—that cooks and housewives participated in the work; but their participation is secondary, their contributions are anonymous and are completely edged out by the figures of the scientific and technical collaborators that specialised in different areas.

In any case, I think it necessary to dispute one truism, trying at the same time to understand from whence it came. It is commonly held that the *Book* contains culinary recipes least of all per se. It is funny that this opinion has formed despite the evidence: the majority of the pages in this book are dedicated to recipes for the preparation of food. The issue, apparently, is the kind of perception that the book was designed to promote. Fundamental importance is given to the encyclopedic sections wherein the rich resources of the socialist food industry are described. Paradoxically, despite the unassuming name 'marginal notes', these sections, from the 1960s editions onward, were rather more up-to-date and in tune with the discourse of the era than were the usual instructions—how to slice onions or to cook borshcht—which were reliably to be found in the appropriate places.

And now I would like to consider the question: Why is the word 'art' not in the title of the Soviet cookbook? Why was 'culinary expertise' not remembered? The elaborate compositions of the cooks are isolated to the obviously memorial section called 'From age-old recipes'. As if totally ignoring the problems of the real-life availability or accessibility of ingredients, as if not concerned with their price, the compilers of the *Book* nonetheless, apparently, realised that the persistent shortage of certain kinds of raw materials offered no possibility whatsoever of concocting dishes that were overly elegant or subtle.

Furthermore, the encyclopedic obsession that permeates the book did not allow for a low-stooping empirical approximation to everyday reality. How the 'everyday reality' of this era was understood is quite well known.[22] Should all the facts set forth in the *Encyclopedia Britannica* really be corroborated in every home, in every country? Or did the unrestricted sale of the *Kama Sutra* lead to the rapid and rigorous execution of all its instructions in the whole world's bedrooms? And, in particular, remembering what the times were like, it turned out that putting one's soul into complicated, elaborate cooking that required both aesthetic perfection and structural expertise would have contradicted the spirit of the moment. Art was subordinated to the aestheticisation of reality. The key concepts of Socialist Realism were the attainability of results and technical repeatability.

Memorable, too, and often studied in the scholarly literature, are such characteristic influences, peculiar to this era, as the predominance of the result over the process. In this light, the use of housewives' time in things such as complicated cooking of serious dishes that seemed by nature unrepeatable, was seen to be anti-economical and anachronistic. However, any work of Socialist Realist art was not supposed to be chiefly apparent in the original, but rather in its six million reproductions.[23] Likewise, a culinary recipe was not supposed to be conducive to the creation of a unique masterpiece, to the fruit of the hands of one and only one talented housewife. The ideal recipe was supposed to stand out for its widescale repeatability, to be in proportion to the quantity of time and rhythm of work assigned by Soviet authority, and to be in line with the assertion that 'every cook can put treasure into the culture.' This assertion[24] carries within itself the well-known but simultaneously subliminal consciousness of the fact that 'only a few specially designated top chefs were given the recipes for stardom.'[25]

The adverb 'economically' is often encountered in the book's text, but for the most part it refers, no doubt, to the expenditure of time and energy, and not to the real cost of the raw materials for cooking. The cooking processes were simplified in parallel fashion to the way in which the acceleration of everyday-life processes and the easing of women's lives were being expatiated upon, without broaching the subject of the quality of the food and the attractiveness of the dishes prepared. Indulging in the aesthetics of totalitarian kitsch, the simplification, denigration and uncritical understanding of basic problems brought a sort of simplicity into everyday life, thanks to which everyday life emotionally satisfied many people and, of no lesser importance, did not provoke particular polemics. The top-ranked goal of the signals from on high was becoming that of calling forth empathy (i.e., emotional approval) from the public: that same goal was in popular songs,[26] in film musicals and in Red Square demonstrations—completely divorced from problems of ethics. The end target was to afford 'pleasure' without belaboring it, in exactly the same way that one was not to belabor the attainment of the happiness that one was not supposed to consider critically. As Regis Debrais asserts, 'to scrutinise an experience means to organise it.' The experience in the instances we are describing came to its audience in an already organised form, along with the recipes for the kitchen.

The obligation of each housewife was not so much to prepare food according to recipes that, although partly chosen according to the principles of simplicity, were by virtue of decorum and tradition allotted space in a book like this; rather, it was to follow the practical bits of advice that were provided with illustrations of a fantasy-like design. She was finally 'permitted' to cook at home, to have lunch and dinner not only in canteens but also in her own(!) kitchen, where the incredible domestic luxury (i.e., domestic happiness) recalled the models of the most elegant restaurants or the most prestigious Stalin-era apartments.[27] On the other hand, the visual plane was arranged in parallel with that of real life: even the contents of canned goods, properly ameliorated and processed according to canon, became a luxury and an enticement. (Fig. 4.5) The pictures in the book, like the advertising and propaganda posters of the time, for the most part portrayed dishes prepared from canned goods and convenience foods. The housewife's contribution consisted mainly of choosing the products and, following right on her choices, aestheticising the food by contributing her own 'little individual touches' in accordance with the demands of the cultured life: it was suggested that she arrange the dishes and flatware in a pretty way on the table, with a little plate for butter to the side of the main plate and with a knife to spread the butter. The illustrations, genuine still lifes, included kitchen technology of the most highly developed level; the food was provided with fitting

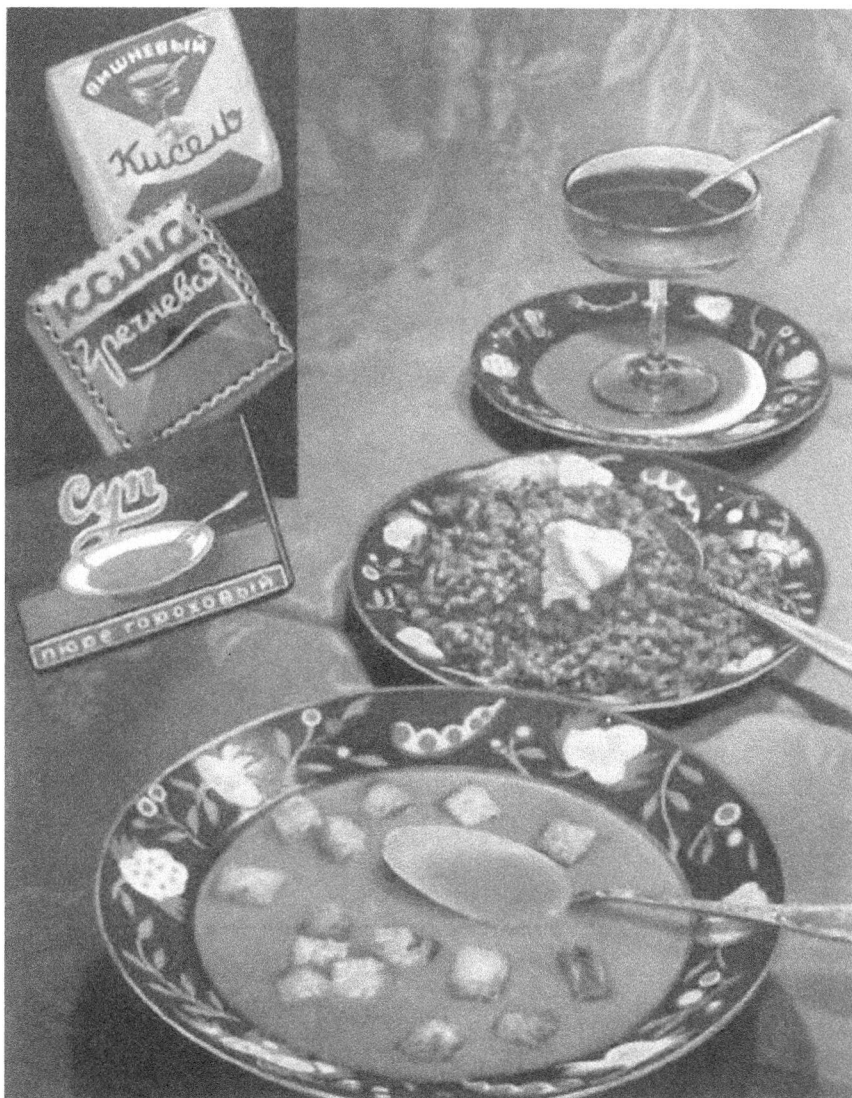

Figure 4.5. Kasha and kisel', *Book about Tasty and Healthy Food* (1953)

decorations; the layout was maintained in the spirit of complete political correctness, and so forth:

> The brand name of the product is always emphasised in the illustrations. No matter what is represented—a bottle of tomato juice, a can of compote, or a package of 'Hercules' oatmeal kasha—the label appears

in the foreground, relating in detail the bureaucratic characteristics of the product: 'Oat flakes [made by] the Order of Lenin Mikoian Moscow Food-Processing Centre.' This ploy allows *The Book about Tasty and Healthy Food* to declare its central idea: all the food in the country belonged to the state. It is because of this precisely that on the 400-some large-format pages, not once is there mention of the 'kolkhoz market'—the private sector, without which it would have been impossible to prepare even one of the dishes mentioned in the book.[28]

It is no surprise that all of this developed simultaneously to and in parallel with the most terrifying outrages of the Great Terror era. It is widely known and well studied that the purges and repressions made their own contributions, after undergoing a spectacular reshaping, to the construction of totalitarian discourse. The foreword to the *Book* is no exception:

> Despite the machinations of the enemies of the people, the Trotskyist-Bukharinist hirelings of fascism, the workers of the Soviet food industry are successfully fighting for the greatest satisfaction of the demands of laborers.[29]

The text that Mikoian dedicated to housewives during the course of the struggling campaign for culturedness and for relative rationalisation of the food industry did not in the least leave to doubt that kitchen matters had been, and continued to be, the exclusive jurisdiction of women. In Mikoian's text, yet another Stalinist cliché, 'Women are the greater force,' was reproduced; and by no means was this only in the kolhozes.

Although new processing methods and new products were aimed at the modernisation and rationalisation of work in the home, and work at home was moreover appearing in a cultured light and with unprecedented dignity, this labor nonetheless kept an obvious gender specificity in the USSR, just as it did in other countries at the time.

The prefaces to the postwar editions of the *Book* issued in 1945 and 1947 are quite interesting. Conforming to the strict, restrained tones that characterised the public oratory and all rhetoric from the moment the war began and then afterwards, the text of the prefaces changed as well, coming closer to everyday reality. Felt more strongly in them is the real situation, which, in contrast to what could be observed in the previous decade, is not pushed into the background in the name of ideological representation, in the spirit of 'revolutionary development' (which actually meant in a sugar-coated and stereotypically 'made happy' version), but rather carries both the stamp of real difficulties and traces of justifiable pride in the heroism of one's own people.

Offered now in an almost critical way, or in any case, a disembodied way, is the former leitmotif with which the first edition had been replete, concerning 'dishes made from convenience foods and all kinds of canned goods, the use of which in housekeeping significantly reduces the time wasted on preparation of food'.[30] One sees the reminder, tinged with Party-propaganda rhetoric, that 'the Party and the government ensured the complete and uninterrupted provision of the Red Army with all food products, moreover the most valuable and highly calorific products,'[31] and following right after that is a sloganish statement that was to be the trademark of this new edition of the *Book*:

> The fundamental goal of the present edition is to give the Soviet housewife a practical means of preparing food *under the conditions of economical use of a number of ingredients* [emphasis mine]; the list of dishes has been abbreviated in comparison to the one introduced in the first edition of this book.[32]

Barely two years later, the situation had changed again, and the preface was again reworked in the light of the ideological tendencies of contemporary political discourse. The preface to the 1947 edition opened with the news about the 'cancellation of cards for food and industrial goods', which was adduced as an example of the 'tireless concern' of the Party and government, and was set in boldface type in Comrade Stalin's text. The third edition of the *Book* further develops the policy in the previous variants of showing the latest innovations in science and technology and adds, at the request of numerous interested readers, a section about the rules for using heating equipment for food preparation.[33]

An extremely interesting topic in perspective is the in-depth analysis of the section about the primus stove (it is hard, however, not to immediately recall Bulgakov's scientist from *The Master and Margarita*, the cat Behemoth), about the kerosene stove and about kerosene, which now have become cult objects in the nostalgic Soviet memory[34] and have, in their own way, enriched the multilayered collection of the 'nostalgic present'.[35]

The 1952 and 1953 editions—the last that could be considered 'Stalinist'— address the lost state of *abundance*, disrupted by the war, which had never been regained. The marginal illustrations in the section that bore the name 'To abundance!' recall the iconography of the propaganda posters and films of the era, such as *Kuban Cossacks*, wherein 'glossing over the truth' and 'abundance' were mutually combined in the name of a 'Soviet' depiction of reality. Particularly impressive is the abundance in the pictures of watermelons, a product associated in the Soviet consciousness with maximal hedonism and well-being. In addition to the facets already mentioned above (the rationalisation of the process of cooking, the savings of time and energy, the use of convenience foods), these editions add interesting ideas about educating one's taste, about the appearance of new products on the market (also tied to geopolitics), and about the taken-for-granted success of these products.[36] This new overtone brings the 1930s texts up to date. The new idea was: happiness does not arise in and of itself. In other words, in 1952 and 1953 it was already necessary (or, rather, again necessary) to 'educate' the people, to instruct them how they should use the present Soviet prosperity, overcoming the moderate resistance of a few of them.[37] In the 1952 edition, the need was still felt to include the verbose observations on this subject from Mikoian himself:

> There can be two approaches, Comrade Mikoian said, to the choice of variety: a conservative adaptability to what there is and to accustomed tastes and habits, or else a revolutionary perseverance in the matter of introducing new varieties, in the teaching of new tastes.[38]

In later editions, this very same thought was now formulated impersonally:

> We must create among the populace a habit and a taste for convenience foods, for no-cooking breakfasts, concentrates, and canned goods, for all the rich and varied assortment of prepared and semi-prepared factory-made food products.[39]
>
> There is not a single person who would immediately take a liking to pickled olives. However, after trying them once or twice, people get used to the bitter-salty taste of the olives, and they begin to like them.[40]

The 'Introduction' of the 1953 edition, which was approved for publication on 4 August 1953, contained references to several meetings and plenary sessions that took place even after this date; beyond question, this edition was distanced from the previous variant, distanced without any quotations, references or open polemics whatsoever. In the lapidary 'Introduction', the authors limited themselves to announcing that the 500,000 copies printed the previous year had been sold out in an extremely short time and that the book had been 'examined and approved by the Nutrition Institute of the USSR Academy of Medical Sciences'. In the section 'To abundance!' noted above, Stalin's name was now not mentioned even a single time: it had completely disappeared, just like the quotes taken from Mikoian's speech. Instead, the words of Comrade Molotov were quoted: he had proclaimed on 8 August 1953 that the Soviet government and the Communist Party's Central Committee 'consider it necessary to significantly increase investments for the development of light industry, the food industry, and in particular the fishing industry, and for the development of agriculture'.[41] But scarcely a year before, the same pages had contained the declaration that 'In the abundance and riches of fish products, our country has no equals' (1952, 146). In the textual series that proclaimed the success of the current Five Year Plan and which contained an overview of the urgent tasks facing the country, the return of quotations from Lenin and his formula, 'the massive struggle against the petty bourgeois household, or rather, its *massive restructuring* into a large-scale socialist household'[42] is quite obvious. The accent, thus, was displaced onto the necessity of promoting industrial development, consolidating the achievements and the development of the country, preserving what had been created and fighting for the new: thus women, even on the pages of this culinary manual, were led to 'complete liberation from hard and thankless work in the kitchen'.[43] This was a return to the fervent utopianism of the 1920s, to the kind of passionate revolutionary feelings of Lenin and Aleksandra Kollontai.

The section called 'Serving the table' had in 1939 started out with self-justifying phrases:

> The few observations that we make here about serving the table are not an attempt to establish any sort of rules for so-called good form. We limit ourselves only to practical advice.[44]

In 1952, the author takes up this very same subject *in medias res*, without hesitation and further preambles. Gradually, the text acquires the character of an exhortation to children, how to behave oneself at the table—not in the kind of speech addressed to an adult audience. The illustrations and photographs depict various moments described in the text. In comparison with the actual recipes, which essentially did not change over the course of the many new editions, more and more space is taken up by lessons and sermons, and less and less by advice on how food ought to be cooked. Always remembering that 'we are born to make a fairy tale into a true story,' the authors maintain this completely fairy tale tone: I will take you by the hand, I will tell you a little fairy tale about food, I will cook for the incredible and fantastic that fills the colour illustrations:

> We will tell you the story of cheese, about its remarkable merits and most diverse variety, about its most subtle bouquet of taste and aroma.[45]

With the onset of the Khrushchev Thaw and the 1960s, the *Book* also underwent radical changes. The illustrations, texts, and composition all changed. However, these transformations could well be the topic of a totally separate study.

In conclusion, I will adduce two quotations. The first is from the 1953 edition of the *Book*:

> Under the direction of our glorious Communist Party, its Central Committee, and the Soviet government, the peoples of our immense and mighty socialist Motherland in joyous, heroic, and creative labor are erecting the majestic edifice of communism, bringing to life mankind's centuries-old dream of building a communist society, its dream about an abundant, happy, and joyous life.[46]

The second quotation (and here it seems very appropriate, again with recourse to the comparative method) is from Ada Boni's 1929 Italian cookbook. Its compiler was convinced that 'no real happiness exists where no attention is given to such an essential part of our life as food' and that 'cooking is the most cheerful of the arts and, at the same time, the most joyous of the sciences'; she bade her female readers farewell with the following words:

> Now you yourselves will be able to use the 'talisman'. Under its protection— let's say, its spell—may your happy family life go on.[47]

In fascist Italy, single women, old maids, homosexuals and bachelors could not expect happiness.

Translated by Jesse Savage.

Part Two

REALITIES

Chapter Five

'IT'S GRAND TO BE AN ORPHAN!': CRAFTING HAPPY CITIZENS IN SOVIET CHILDREN'S LITERATURE OF THE 1920s

Marina Balina

Among the most vulnerable citizens of the new Soviet state in its first decade were its children: abandoned by their families who for various reasons were not able to care for them, displaced from their homes by the Civil War, or simply lost in the constant migrations (the rural population going into big cities in search of a better life, or people leaving the cities for the villages, hoping to find food), these 'little comrades' became the first targets of the Soviet project that sought to make the 'new man'.[1] Two fictional works of Soviet children's literature—both of which confirmed the success of revolutionary rebirth—became testaments to the struggle of the street children in the early days of the Revolution: *SHKID Republic* (*Respublika SHKID*, 1926),[2] by Grigory Belykh and Leonid Panteleev; and *Pedagogical Poem* (*Pedagogicheskaia Poema*, 1933,1936),[3] by Anton Makarenko. The first, written by two former delinquents, describes the rigorous life in the school for young criminal offenders that bore Dostoevsky's name (the abbreviation SHKID comes from the Russian *shkola imeni Dostoevskogo*—'Dostoevsky School'). It was a highly romanticized picture of life in the 'republic' where self-governance and trust were integral parts of human existence, and it celebrated the freedom and creativity of its young citizens. Condemned by the literary critics of the late 1930s for its lack of 'evaluative components' in its description of characters, the novel was forgotten until it was reprinted in 1960; Grigory Poloka then adapted it for the screen in 1966. The lively and adventurous life of the SHKID Republic residents has nothing in common with that of Makarenko's work, which is a three-volume narrative that outlines his disciplining of young criminals in the Gorky colony near Kharkov. Comparing these stories, one can see how the military obedience and hard work imposed by Makarenko to 'break' his wards stands in sharp contrast to the free spirit of democracy and inventiveness promoted in the Dostoevsky School. Despite how different they are in describing the successes and failures in the process of creating new happy Soviet citizens, both these narratives attest to the existence of a certain tradition that had been established for the depiction of the complicated path of 'reforging' young criminals into productive laborers, a tradition that has its roots in the diverse and challenging body of literary texts published in the children's literature of 1920s Soviet Russia. Used occasionally today by historians of the early Soviet period for their rich factual material, these short stories, novellas and poems best reflect the utopian discourse of the nation and bear witness to the tortuous path to happiness that Soviet authorities had charted for the young audience. In this article I intend to demonstrate how the 'reforging' genre developed in children's literature, even prior to its transformation into Soviet literature for adults.

Homeless Children of the Promised Land

The notion that young Soviet citizens were destined for a happy childhood became proverbial, and it was celebrated in all forms of media throughout the years of the USSR's existence; political slogans proclaiming the happiness of the young never lost their appeal for the broad audience at home and abroad.[4] An impressive infrastructure of educational facilities was created to accommodate the needs of the 'only privileged class' in the country. 'All the best' was indeed allocated for children:[5] luxurious palaces of the former nobility were converted into Young Pioneer centres, where Soviet youth learned arts and crafts, science, and sports. From early on, the 'happiness' of Soviet youth was elevated to unquestionable mythological heights. The state promoted the creation of social structures that would not only guarantee the proper ideological upbringing but would also provide educational support, organize leisure activities and offer opportunities for the physical and intellectual development of the nation's youngest citizens.[6] Even today, many musicians, artists and scientists attribute the origins of their success to the unrestricted access they had to state-provided education and developmental opportunities.[7] Today, in the new postsocialist society, the former children of the Soviet epoch somehow forget about ideological indoctrination—which was always a vital part of the Soviet educational system—and refer to the loss of their 'privileged' childhoods in the most nostalgic terms. However, contemporary studies of the happy and secure Soviet childhood, both in the

West and in post-Soviet Russia, reveal a very complicated landscape of this 'land of happy children'.[8] As Soviet children were sent along very diverse paths on their journey toward the promised happiness, an equally diverse body of literary works was inspired—all of which reflect the complexity of the 'happy childhood'. After all, children embodied the vast potential of this new ideological experiment, serving as both its test subjects and its human 'building material'. The most eligible children for experimentation were the homeless youth that walked the streets of Soviet cities in the early 1920s. Children's literature of that period, used as both a space in which the utopian childhood image was created and as a reflection of actual experience, provides substantial evidence for the successes and failures of the Soviet experiment of human remaking.

Reminiscing about his 1920s Moscow childhood, Russian cultural historian Yurii Fedosiuk referred to a commonly seen picture of 'dirty, charcoal-black teenagers in rags' who 'scurried about the streets of the capital'.[9] These children were first identified by their contemporaries with the Russian word *bezprizorniki* (or *bezprizornye*, both meaning, roughly, 'the unsupervised'), which was later to become their enduring personal and cultural legacy. Historians specializing in the early Soviet era have come up with multiple translations (or conventional designations) for this Russian word. Western sources have often referred to them as 'homeless children', 'waifs', 'street children', and 'abandoned children', as well as describing them as 'unattended or deserted',[10] stressing the fact that these children were left alone on the streets of predominantly big cities such as Moscow and Petrograd, where they occupied city squares and railroad stations and hid in abandoned houses or slept under bridges and in sewer hatchways. Fedosiuk recalled both the fear and pity that these children evoked in Muscovites in the 1920s: 'The sad legacy of the Civil War—children left without parents, without homes and any care for them—they live their own secret lives. Nobody knows where they came from, what they eat, and where they spend the nights.'[11] The memoirist recollected the harsh winter months when local police often found the *besprizornye* frozen to death, having hidden in asphalt boilers and destroyed buildings. Frequently, these underage and lonely children would also fell prey to adult criminals who used and abused them, sending them down the road of theft and/or prostitution.[12]

British scholar Catriona Kelly provides rich factual support about the horrors of child abandonment in the early years of Soviet rule in Russia. In her comprehensive study of the Russian childhood, she states, 'The Russian Revolution and Civil War saw the problems of child abandonment, already severe in the early years of the First World War, spiral to unprecedented heights... Numbers rose out of all proportion when famine struck along the Volga in 1921–1922, reducing at least four million children to total destitution and want. Two years later, forced industrialization, followed rapidly by collectivization, added to the numbers of deserted and needy children.'[13] In his investigation of children abandoned in Russia from 1917 through the 1930s, American historian Alan M. Ball attempts to arrive at an actual number of *bespizorniki* in Russia in the 1920s, and roughly estimates that there were between four million and seven-and-a-half million such children in 1923.[14] While recognizing that a reduction in homelessness of children had been achieved—mainly through their institutionalization in various types of children's homes and colonies for juvenile delinquents—Ball nonetheless references provincial newspapers that attest to the fact that as late as 1930, '200,000 abandoned children continued to inhabit the Russian Republic alone.'[15]

The fate of these abandoned young citizens was a serious concern for Soviet officials. An attempt to provide some relief to homeless children had already been made during the short reign of the Provisional Government, when the League of Rescue for Children—one of the first and most active organizations with this mission—was established and led by the well-known political activist and journalist Ekaterina Dmitrievna Kuskova (1869–1958).[16] After the October revolution, the fate of numerous war orphans was entrusted to three different organizations: the Education Commissariat (*Narkompros*), the Health Commissariat (*Narkomzdrav*), and the Social Welfare Commissariat (*Narkomsotsbes*). The responsibilities of these commissions were often defined in very vague and frequently overlapping terms, and thus the commissariats always had opportunities to blame each other for not achieving the goal of solving the issue of children's homelessness in a timely manner. As Kelly states, 'It was equally common for the commissariats to claim that some area did not fall within their jurisdiction.'[17] As time went on, the problem of *besprizornost'* could no longer be viewed as one inherited from the Tsarist past, given the new hordes of homeless children following the first wave that was attributed to World War I; the famine of 1921–1922 alone produced almost four million orphans. Even such a prominent proponent of the new political order as Nadezhda Krupskaia—Lenin's wife, and herself an active member of the Soviet government—was forced to admit that 'the roots of *besprizornost'* are not only in the past but in the present.'[18] It was obvious that a special rescue project was needed for abandoned children, and in 1921 the infamous head of the Soviet secret police, Felix Dzerzhinsky (1877–1926), known as 'Iron Felix', joined the forces of the rescuers of the street children by creating a special Children's Commission (*Detkomissiia*). This new commission played a significant role in collecting abandoned children from the streets and placing them into newly established institutions—institutions that were far from ideal, due to scattered resources and the lack of properly trained personnel. Thus, the removal of *besprizorniki* from the streets and their conversion into future productive Soviet citizens became one of the first state-run projects that involved human transformation. And who could be better suited for such an experiment than the young and the unprotected? These children were indeed the 'Children of the State':[19] they had no family ties, and quite often they even had no knowledge of their heritage. They were a much-desired raw material, as it were, a human *tabula rasa* on which the Soviet government could write its glorious and happy future. Rightfully recognizing that *besprizornost'* could possibly take up a life of crime, the state took enormous measures to create institutions and to search for new methods that would achieve the goal of reforging street children into industrious Soviet workers. Addressing this very issue in her study of early Stalinism, Sheila Fitzpatrick states, 'The idea that men could be remade was very important in the Soviet worldview. It was associated, in the first place, with the belief that crime was a social disease, the result of a harmful environment. This was conventional wisdom in Soviet criminology in the 1920s and early 1930s.... More broadly, the idea of human remaking was part of the whole notion of transformation that was at the heart of the Soviet project.'[20]

However, before the complicated process of molding a new 'citizen' out of the lost and abandoned child could begin, important ideological issues needed to be resolved. Among these issues, the most significant was the high rate of criminality among the *besprizorniki* population. How could the men/women of the future be made from such defective human material? The initial step in resolving this process was taken during the First Moscow Conference on the Struggle with *Besprizornost'* in March 1924. The conference started with the widely recognized fact that *besprizornye* were not 'born' criminals, but rather 'socially sick' children who committed petty crimes (like theft) or even more serious offenses (like murder) because they had been forced into a life of crime by the economic conditions surrounding them. Applying—in the words of Anne Gorsuch—'the optimistic Marxism of the 1920s'[21] to the study of children, Aron Zalkind (1886–1936), one of the leading pedologists in the country, saw *besprizorniki* as victims of the environmental and social factors that led to their delinquency. Zalkind insisted that *besprizorniki* demonstrated many traits that would assist them in becoming good communists: they were independent, they already lived in communities, and they shared their belongings. Zalkind claimed: 'The communal bands of the *besprizorniki* are *closer* to the collective comradely ethic than is the "normal" morality of self-love that children from a bourgeois environment have.'[22] Thus, the paradox of the conversion of *besprizorniki* in the Soviet context lay in the fact that they were rehabilitated even *prior* to entering the Soviet institutions. Zalkind and his followers went so far as to claim that this group of children, more than any other, had a head start on other youth who had a traditional upbringing and came from traditional family backgrounds.

Among the 'advantages' of the *besprizorniki* were their lack of family, their dislike of religion, and their love of freedom, realism, and flexibility, as well as 'biological hardening' and courage. In his discussion of the workings of the 1924 conference, Allan Ball quotes a Komsomol delegate who informed his fellow delegates, 'We regard each *besprizornyi* as a child of the Revolution. If he is approached correctly, he can become an active builder of a socialist state.'[23]

Besprizorniki as Literary Characters

Referring to children's happiness as an ultimate goal of the Soviet state, Catriona Kelly affirms: 'In the Soviet era, the sense that the state—and from the mid-1930s, the leader, Stalin himself—was responsible for children's happiness, meant silence engulfed children whose experience of childhood did not fit the stereotypes of "happy childhood".'[24] Kelly mentions two groups that were denied such representation: 'the children of social pariahs such as kulaks and prisoners in labor camps' and children who were 'in young-offender institutions'.[25] However, it was precisely this second group, the delinquents, who became the most celebrated characters of children's fiction of the 1920s.[26] There could be several reasons for the emphasis on the character of young criminals at this time. The very strength and ideological importance of the 'happy childhood' message was in its *total universality*, and therefore it was not possible for the state to completely exclude this group and leave it behind; all Soviet children *ought* to be happy, regardless of their social status. The demarcation between the harsh life of underprivileged children before the revolution and the happiness of all the Soviet state's young citizens was the focus of many stories in children's journals of the 1920s.[27] Writing about the rapid conversion of *besprizorniki* and their successful integration into the new socialist order was in tune with the revolutionary promise of a better life. Another reason for the great popularity of *besprizorniki* conversion stories was their hybrid nature as works of literature. Evgeny Dobrenko, discussing Makarenko's *Pedagogical Poem*, stresses the resemblance of this narrative to that of the Bildungsroman (the long-celebrated 'novel of education' genre).[28] There is no doubt that this type of narrative strongly influenced children's stories that dealt with reforming young criminals; however, in the children's literature of the 1920s, the life story of the delinquent merged most closely not with the novel of education, but rather with the adventure story, the main character of which needs to prove himself worthy of survival.

Adventure stories were part of the early Soviet children's literature in the 1920s, and they mainly explored the theme of the Civil War of 1919–1921. Petr Blyakhin's *Little Red Devils* (*Krasnye d'iavoliata*, 1923[29]) and L. Ostroumov's *Makar the Pathfinder* (*Makar–sledopyt*, 1925[30]) topped the list of children's adventure literature of the time. It is interesting to note that the 'orphan' motif penetrated even the adventure story: it served the highly politicized message of class struggle and revenge. Thus, in Blyakhin's story, the twin brother and sister Duniashka and Mishka do not fight only for the revolutionary cause; they also fight to avenge the death of their elder brother and father who fought on the side of the Red Army. In Sergei Auslender's 'Days of Struggle' (*Dni boevye*, 1925),[31] child fighters outdo their adult counterparts in resourcefulness and are depicted as unquestionable leaders. One of Ostroumov's characters, a red-haired boy named San'ka, single-handedly saves the whole Red Army brigade by passing himself off as a White Army officer. Later, he scolds his fellow soldiers: 'You were lucky that I could pass for Eremeev [the White Army officer], otherwise the whole brigade would have been destroyed. Shame on you!'[32] Labeled as 'children's avant-gardism',[33] this literary device was highly criticized by both educators and literary critics of the time, and adventure writers were accused of diminishing the significance of the victorious Red Army's achievements.[34]

In an unexpected way, adventure was adopted as a vital element of the children's narrative for *besprizorniki* literature, and was successfully superimposed over the predominantly didactic tone. The road to the ultimate goal—to become the rightful member of the new society—turned out to be full of escapades, exciting voyages, dangerous quests and unexpected twists. After all, it was literature meant for children, and dry didacticism and straightforward propaganda would not have attracted young readers. We should also remember the diverse literary scene of the 1920s, which included private presses, among them the publishing houses Rainbow (*Raduga*), Firefly (*Svetliachok*), and Bluebird (*Siniaia Ptitsa*),[35] all of which extensively reprinted the adventure stories known to young readers from prerevolutionary times, such as those by Thomas Mayne Reid, Louis Boussenard, and Jules Verne.[36] Thus, despite the library 'cleansings' of 1923–1924 (mostly administered by Nadezhda Krupskaia, then the chair of the Central Committee on Political Education (*Glavpolitprosvet*)), when 'politically incorrect' books for children, among them adventure stories and fairy tales, were removed from the library shelves, there were other opportunities for young readers to obtain reading material that would successfully compete with the ideologically approved messages of the state press.[37]

The vast majority of stories written about *besprizorniki* in the 1920s present their main characters as daring, strong, inventive and physically fit enough to survive despite the most trying circumstances, and thus the stories themselves address the same qualities that Aron Zalkind celebrated in his evaluation of this group of children. The young protagonist in the story by Nikolai Sarkizov-Serazini, 'The Adventures of Sen'ka-Zhokh' (*Prikliucheniia Sen'ki Zhokha*, 1927),[38] is smarter than any adult character in this narrative, be it the state representative from whom he successfully escapes or the infamous NEPman store owner who is so stupid and greedy that he simply needs to be robbed in order to be taught a lesson![39] Sen'ka travels freely, does not report to anyone, and, since he is completely happy with the status quo, his life is so grand that he does not long for a family or a 'better' life in an orphanage. In the highly popular novel by Sergei Grigor'ev entitled *With the Bag after Death* (*S meshkom za smert'iu*, 1924),[40] the courageous leader of the *besprizorniki* gang is instrumental in finding and freeing an innocent girl who had been snatched by mysterious foreigners from the 1920s Moscow streets. In Aleksei Irkutov's play *Conspiracy* (*Zagovor*, 1924),[41] the character named 'Besprizornik' unravels a plot against the Young Pioneers carried out by class enemies embodied by the characters 'Young Bourgeois from the West' and the two 'NEPmen Children.' And although at the very end 'Besprizornik' is invited to join the Young Pioneers group—an invitation which he accepts—he is presented as being on equal terms with the others, and is invited to join not out of pity but rather because his bravery and correct class consciousness saved the Young Pioneers.

Summarizing the effects of these stories on their readers, the prominent Soviet scholar of children's literature Irina Lupanova stated, 'The authors are so fascinated by the descriptions of the scandalous activities of their protagonists that only on the last pages of their stories do they actually recall that the original focus of the story was supposed to have been placed on rescuing and reforming these delinquents. Thus, by changing the lives of their characters abruptly by either placing them into an orphanage or sending those to be reformed through labor to factories, writers added the reforging element to their narratives, depriving the complicated conversion process of its significance and depth.'[42] Indeed, when reading the stories by Nikolai Dmitrievskii ('Fed'ka's Life' / *Fed'kina zhizn'*, 1924)[43] or by Petr Yakovlev ('Red Forest' / *Krasnyi bor*, 1927),[44] the reader cannot find an obvious reason why the brave and risky but happy and free life of the *besprizorniki* needs to be exchanged for a monotonous institutional existence. Literary critics have brutally attacked this romantic approach to the notion of homelessness in children's literature,[45] and it was, in fact, entirely disconnected from the real situation on the streets, where the majority of young children suffered from illness and neglect. British scholar Juliane Fuerst stresses the ideological importance that this challenge held for the Soviet authorities: 'Homeless, vagrant and orphaned children who found themselves at the bottom of society were singled out as particularly potent bearers of the Soviet eschatological myth.'[46] The *besprizorniki* fiction was creating its own mythology of happiness without restrictive discipline, obedience and mandatory participation in Soviet activities. The omission of the required metamorphosis was thus undermining the very essence of the Soviet system, since a successful reforging served as the necessary proof of the moral superiority of the new society over both prerevolutionary Russia and the capitalist West. Children's writers failed to reflect upon this important ideological assignment, and new, important changes needed to be made to adjust their message to the demands of the moment. Literature for young citizens became the topic of the 1924 resolution of the Thirteenth Party Congress, which demanded outright that children's literature be created 'under the comprehensive supervision and leadership of the party' with an important goal: 'to strengthen in this literature the elements of a class-oriented, international, and industrial upbringing'.[47] Two works of fiction in particular, the novel *Captivity* (*Plen*, 1926) by Lev Gumilevskii,[48] and the story 'On the Ruins of the Count's Estate' (*Na grafskikh razvalinakh*, 1929[49]) by Arkadii Gaidar, could be viewed as essential turning points that, while preserving the adventure element of the earlier *besprizorniki* narratives, presented a crucial ideological twist in the literature for the young.

On the Road to Happiness

At the core of the plot of *Captivity* is the failed plan of the *besprizorniki* gang to steal children from the Moscow streets in order to later extract a hefty ransom from their parents. Kos'ka, the gang leader, possesses all the features of the traditional *besprizorniki* master plotter that would be recognizable to readers: he is smart and inventive, but at the same time he is depicted as a cruel cocaine user who abuses his victims as well as the rest of his own gang. The first abduction by the gang ends in disaster because their captive, Alia Chugunova, is merely the daughter of an ordinary Moscow factory worker—which thus destroys all the gang's hopes for a fast and substantial ransom. Alia, a schoolgirl and an active Pioneer, becomes a clever prisoner who carefully waits for her chance to flee; not only does she manage to escape from her captors, but she also takes with her Kos'ka's most ardent follower, a young boy nicknamed Pyliay. Pyliay appears to be completely corrupted by the stories of 'real' life that Alia shares with him as she describes her world of school, family and friends. She goes so far as to try to teach him how to read, thus demonstrating her concern for the totally neglected child. Pyliay experiences an overwhelming feeling of happiness when he is finally capable of reading a signboard above the entrance to a bakery. It is significant that the boy is seduced into embracing the new life by the possibility of obtaining knowledge, and his ability to read becomes the key element of his transformation:

Pyliay left the bakery with two loaves of bread, holding them like his most precious possession. From the porch, he looked at the street with a condescending smile. For the first time in his life, he felt connected with the huge world around him—with buildings, pavements, trams, and cabbies. He looked happily back at the signboard that had brought him closer to this previously alien and antagonistic world around him. The little tramp that left the bakery porch was changed forever, having become now a citizen of his country.[50]

While Gumilevskii does not offer his readers a story with a happy ending—since Pyliay is still left on the streets of the big city—the narrative nonetheless fulfills two very important functions. First, it places the still abstract notion of happiness outside the established world of the street children, thus connecting it with the idea of the future that awaits Pyliay in his newly obtained feeling of citizenship. Second, the story charts the path of Pyliay's conversion: it establishes the undeniable, definite coordinates of the Soviet city where he will finally be happy, and it points toward education as means of achieving a happy and productive life. The only possible way for the *besprizornik* to achieve his educational goal is to voluntarily surrender his questionable freedom in Kos'ka's gang and become a member of the Soviet 'children's home' (*detskii dom*) that will foster his desire to transform. This message was completely in tune with the massive Soviet literacy campaign of the 1920s, since it successfully superimposed a desired element of adventure on the didactic message of inevitable change. The road to happiness for Pyliay leads him directly to the doors of the Soviet orphanage.

A very different twist on the story of reintegrating a homeless child into the world of Soviet reality can be found in Arkadii Gaidar's 'On the Ruins of the Count's Estate'. Gaidar rejects the very idea of inclusiveness for underprivileged children in postrevolutionary reality. In fact, he shows how negatively predisposed the world of adults is toward the young intruder named Dergach. None of the adults in the story is concerned about the conditions in which the boy is living. The adults do not even want to try to catch the *besprizornik*, since this action would require them to take him to the city to hand him over to authorities. The only rescuers to be found in the story are children themselves, and it is their dedication and courage alone that saves Dergach from vanishing into the swamp. To fit into his story the newly found happiness that had by then become a compulsory element of *besprizorniki* narratives, Gaidar reintroduces the long-dismissed image of the family, thus revitalizing the idea of caring parents and loving children. The idea of the family being elevated to the position of a child's savior was not celebrated in the 1920s. Kelly characterizes the image of Soviet childhood during the first decade as 'often pro-child and anti-adult (or at least hostile to private adult authority as represented by parental power, which was seen as shoring up the undesirable social attitudes of the past)'.[51] The new Family Codes of 1918 and 1926 both undermined the traditional family structure, and the reintroduction of loving parents (with the concomitant idea of a possible family reunion as a happy ending to the story of an abandoned child) was almost a novelty in the children's literature of the 1920s. This turn in the plotline rather resembled the traditional prerevolutionary 'orphan tales' that were highly criticized and dismissed from the postrevolutionary children's reading lists.[52]

The story was published in 1929, during the period when Gaidar, working as a journalist in Moscow, could hardly avoid the topic of *besprizornost'*, since it was one of the most widely discussed issues in the media of the time. In his aforementioned study, Allan Ball cites aggressive slogans issued by the government at the end of the 1920s that promised 'total liquidation' of the *besprizornost'* phenomenon in Soviet culture.[53] Like Gumilevskii, Gaidar preserves in his narrative the adventure element of the plot, making it even more rigorous by highlighting the motif of a mystery that needed to be solved. A mysterious object—a photograph of the young count, the prerevolutionary owner of the estate—and the search for the lost treasure are elements that help to convert the young village boys Yashka and Val'ka into true detectives who, together with their new friend, the homeless Dergach, help to solve the counterrevolutionary conspiracy. Like many *besprizornik* characters depicted in similar stories, Dergach is the unquestioned leader of this trio: he proves himself courageous when he saves the boys' dog Wolf; Wolf is falsely accused by Yashka's revenge-seeking neighbors of killing their chickens, and has to be hidden in the ruins of an old estate. The new characteristic of this *besprizornik* hero is his sadness over the state of his own affairs. While talking to his new friends, Dergach explains how difficult the life of a waif had been for him. When Val'ka exclaims with envy, 'How lucky you are, Dergach, to have seen so many places in your life!', he receives an unexpected, bitter response: 'Well, if you were so lucky, you would howl like a wolf from sorrow.'[54] Dergach is unwilling to answer any personal questions the boys ask him, and although he shares with the boys that he had been part of a criminal gang, he never brags about his adventures. Gaidar completely destroys any glory that had been previously associated with the romantic worldview of young delinquents. Even long after Dergach has left the gang, he continues to live in fear and mistrust; the adult thief and gang leader Khriash' had promised to kill him for his disobedience, and had almost succeeded in burning the boy to death after he returned to his hiding place—the ruins of a former nobleman's estate—with another criminal, the Count. Gaidar's plot depicts the Count as the heir of the noble family to which that estate had belonged. He has come to find the family treasure that his father had hidden in the palm-tree pot prior to fleeing the country during the revolution. Yashka's father, the former gardener of the old count, has a key to this secret hiding place—a photograph showing the young count standing in the winter garden in front of the rare palm tree. All three boys are heavily involved in the hunt for the treasure, but it is the little *besprizornik* who triumphs in the end; he not only helps the authorities to arrest both criminals, but also saves the fortune for the needs of the Soviet state.

The reward for his victory is somewhat unexpected: he, the person who showed so much courage and resilience, is finally rescued from his life of crime and danger by his very own family, who had never given up hope of finding him again. Recovering from his burns at the hospital, Dergach learns the good news: 'His washed pale face was brightened by the big smile of a happy child, and, closing his eyes, he whispered happily: "How wonderful life really is!"'[55]

Here, the author's message of reforging is of a quite different nature, since instead of making his protagonist embrace happiness as a member of the big, collective Soviet family, he simply reconnects the boy to his childhood by reuniting him with his real mother and father. Gaidar's story stands out among the entire body of 1920s children's literature for precisely this subject: the regained security of family life. Less than three years later (1931), Gaidar, in his novella 'Military Secret' (*Voennaia taina*), moved away from celebrating the happiness of a single child and turned toward the promotional grandeur of the big happy childhood for *all* Soviet children. After all, as Fuerst observed, 'children were rescued from the darkness and dullness of pre- and non-socialist lives in order to build socialism, not to achieve personal happiness for their own sake.'[56]

The Redemptive Power of Self-Reliance

Achieving happiness through hard work, persistence, and above all, self-reliance was a model introduced to the Soviet readership by Aleksei Kozhevnikov (1891–1980). The lives of *besprizorniki* became more than merely literary inspiration for this writer, given the firsthand knowledge of the issue that he acquired while working at different orphanage facilities across the country. Readers of his first published work, which appeared in 1924, were appalled by his candid and even shocking depiction of the life of children on the streets. Even Lupanova, who, in her study of 1920s children's literature, praised Kozhevnikov's stories for their realism, complained about the gloomy tone of his narratives and their overall bitterness; in his works the world of adults has completely abandoned the children and cannot offer them any possible escape from their misery.[57]

In Kozhevnikov's stories, the desire for change is not inspired by the outside world surrounding the *besprizorniki*; rather, this desire is the result of their own initiative. The writer does not completely deprive his young characters of adult support, but, significantly, the support structures and adult supervision usually come into play *after* the transformation has already taken place. The only role left for adults in Kozhevnikov's stories is that of the classic 'good Samaritan'—capable of providing food and shelter, but not terribly influential in making life choices. When the sixteen-year-old thief Grigory (*Grigory Petrovich*, 1929) decides to break with his criminal past, he accomplishes it on his own, realizing that he is 'a true proletarian'. As he reasons, 'My father was a worker, and so was my mother; even my grandfather was a proletarian, so this is what my real destiny is.'[58] He decides to work as an itinerant knife sharpener, but since he lacks the necessary tools, local factory workers spend extra time helping him make them. In another story (*Alesha-Khinchin*, 1925),[59] the Russian boy Alesha and his Chinese friend Khinchin form an 'artistic' union in order to survive; they create a small show consisting of various acrobatic tricks, which they perform on the streets of Moscow. These clever and inventive children play on their ethnic differences; they synchronize their acrobatic movements to such an extent that they appear to be one person, Alesha-Khinchin, which they 'illustrate' nicely by screaming the Communist Manifesto slogan 'Proletariat of the world, unite!' in unison. The adults in the story form the willing audience whose function is simply to pay for this entertainment.

Since the children in Kozhevnikov's stories are depicted first and foremost as victims of broken families and economic disasters, his narratives could superficially support Zalkind's notion of the social and economic origins of delinquency. However, Kozhevnikov goes much further in revealing the psychological impact on the homeless children of living on the streets, and thus he demonstrates the full extent of the trauma that *besprizornost'* inflicted on a child's psyche.

In Kozhevnikov's short stories, he completely dismisses the element of adventure; instead, the stories resemble the genre of the physiological sketch, with its interest in life lived on the margins of society, its photographic accuracy and its attention to small details. Kozhevnikov's narratives are full of meticulous descriptions of his characters' clothes (or, rather, the lack thereof), their habits and even their 'techniques' for stealing. The *besprizornik*—this familiar part of a city landscape—begins to be seen in his stories as if through a magnifying glass, thus making it impossible for the reader to turn away from the horrifying conditions in which these children exist. Kozhevnikov never shared with his readers his own feelings toward the subjects of his literary inspirations; he is an objective and composed observer, and it is precisely this distance that the writer employs as his narrative device that transforms his stories into a genuine cry for help. For example, the *besprizornik* Singapur, from his story 'The Road into the Happy Land' (*Put' v schastlivuiu stranu*, 1926), looks like 'a true dandy and stands out in the crowd. On his left foot he has a red leather sandal, but for his right foot, he found a lady's velvet high-heel boot. His big straw hat has no brim; however, his coat is all buttoned up by four polished buttons with a sailor's anchor on them.'[60] The depiction is so precise that the reader can not only see this 'poster child' of the homeless, but can also easily imagine Singapur's wobbly walk as he tries to balance while wearing two different shoes. The word 'dandy', incongruous in this context, completes the horrifying picture by creating an unforgettable portrait of this child's everyday existence.

Kozhevnikov was among the very few writers who admitted the irreversible damage that homelessness inflicted on the *besprizorniki*. He challenged the Soviet belief in universal happiness for young citizens by demonstrating that, for some children, the promised entrance into the land of happy childhood may never come. Mit'ka, the protagonist of the story 'System of Closed Doors' (*Systema zakrytykh dverei*, 1929), is one of those children for whom the world of 'happy' childhood will remain forever inaccessible. Having spent his life in the summer cottages of one of the Moscow suburbs where compassionate summer guests occasionally feed him, Mit'ka is not receptive to any manifestation of human kindness, and in fact, he does not know what the point of kindness is. When he is hungry, he simply goes to other cottages and stands there, waiting for food to be given to him. The only attachment he has is to a stray dog, but rather than having a real feeling of love for the animal, Mit'ka simply appreciates the protection that the dog provides. The local teacher, Vera Grigor'evna, is concerned with Mit'ka's plight, and brings him to the city's orphanage; but he escapes, running back to his old life in the abandoned dacha. No one abused the boy in the orphanage, but, nevertheless, everything in it—sleeping in a bed, eating together with others—evokes only one reaction in the boy: a feeling of deep-seated fear of a life within closed doors. While Vera Grigor'evna tries again to 'rescue' him from his seclusion, he bitterly bites her hand while she attempts to bring him the comfort that he, in fact, did not ask for, and probably does not need. Seeing blood pouring from her wound, the screaming teacher slaps the boy's face, thus ending all attempts to salvage 'this angry wolf cub'.[61] Kozhevnikov is not afraid to admit this failure, recognizing that the scars of *besprizornost'* could not be healed with social remedies but instead required psychological intervention, which would demand greater time and effort than the Soviet system was ready to commit. Kozhevnikov's stories seriously question the universal success of rehabilitation efforts, and since they did not fit into the general mode of the quick fix of the 'homelessness liquidation' campaigns of the 1920s, they were criticized and dismissed for their overall negative and pessimistic tone.

For Kozhevnikov's characters, happiness is not to be found in the possibility of transformation and inclusion in the new society, but rather in the mere fact of their physical survival through the hardships of street life. These children are naturally good, and Kozhevnikov depicts them through the lens of martyrdom—a theme well known to Russian readers from the Orthodox Christian tradition (consider, for example, the martyrdom of Boris and Gleb).[62] Neglect, abuse, and even death from starvation are daily occurrences in the lives of his protagonists, and both state and family fail to protect them. The brutality of the conditions described in his stories undermines the very belief in the possibility of a happy childhood, which thus casts serious doubt on the validity of the Soviet project.

In the short story 'Mommy Will Be Looking for Us' (*Mamka iskat' budet*, 1925), the author describes the tragic death of two little beggars, a brother and sister abandoned by their mother at a Moscow train station. The story offers no explanation of how or why their mother disappeared; did she leave them because she was desperate and could not feed them anymore? Did she drop dead while looking for a shelter for her children? Or was she hoping that, left on the street alone without adult supervision, her children would draw the attention of the authorities? Until the very last moment, both children believe that their mother will come and rescue them. However, their tragic end—which comes when both freeze to death—creates a vivid picture of the incredible cruelty of the postrevolutionary world toward its new citizens. The story ends with a decidedly cold conclusion: 'A man walked by. He stopped for a moment next to the dead children and paused as a dark silent question mark.... And he left...'[63] Thus, the reader is left with the obvious question: Could these very children who are supposed to be the beneficiaries of the new world of universal happiness perhaps be, in fact, its first victims?

On 31 May 1935, the decree 'On Liquidation of Child Homelessness and Child Neglect', published in the main Soviet newspaper, *Pravda*, proclaimed that *besprizornost'* in the Soviet state had for the most part been 'liquidated'.[64] When the film by Nikolai Ekk with the self-explanatory title 'Road to Life' (1931) had its world release in 1933, the American educational reformer John Dewey prefaced the introduction of it to the public in the West:

Ten years ago, every traveler in Russia came back with stories of the hordes of wild children who roamed the countryside and infested the city streets. They were the orphans of soldiers killed in the war, of fathers and mothers who perished in the famine after the war. You will see a picture of the old road to life, a road of vagabondage, violence, thieving. You will also see their new road to their new life, a road constructed by a brave band of Russian teachers. After methods of repression had failed, they gathered these children together in collective homes, they taught them cooperation, useful work, healthful recreation. Against great odds they succeeded. There are today no wild children in Russia.[65]

Indeed, these 'wild' children faced institutionalization in orphanages, captivity in penal colonies for young offenders or rehabilitation and reform in various labor communes. They also effectively disappeared from the pages of children's literature. Lidiia Seifullina's novel *Criminal Offenders* (*Pravonarushiteli*, 1922), which describes the life of homeless children in the Soviet corrective institutions, and which had been part of the obligatory school reading list, was removed from the list in 1935.[66] The two stories that did survive in children's literature for the generations to follow were *SHKID Republic* and the first part of Makarenko's trilogy, *Pedagogical Poem*. Different though they were in style and in the creative approach to the subject matter, these two narratives nevertheless both promoted the rigid stance regarding the correctional power of the collective in the Soviet project of human remaking. They became the only testimonies to the struggle for survival of the most vulnerable members of the Soviet society—its youth—thus creating a one-dimensional and somewhat 'sterilized' version of the complicated path that was to lead these young characters into the 'land of happy children'.

Chapter Six

SEW YOURSELF SOVIET: THE PLEASURES OF TEXTILE IN THE MACHINE AGE

Emma Widdis

Tissue, textile and fabric provide excellent models of knowledge, excellent quasi-abstract objects, primal varieties: the world is a mass of laundry.
— Michel Serres, 'Les Voiles,' in *Les cinq sens*.

In April of 1930, the women's magazine *Zhenskii zhurnal* (Women's Journal) offered its resourceful reader instructions on how to make a 'panneau', or wall decoration. (Fig. 6.1) This sumptuous object was to be achieved by appliqué design on plain fabric, 'basic cotton, hessian or canvas'.[1] The reader of *Zhenskii zhurnal*—like that of other women's magazines of the time such as *Rabotnitsa* (Working Woman) and *Iskusstvo odevat'sia* (The Art of Dressing)—was, it is to be presumed, skilled in appliqué, for articles introducing and developing the technique and applying it to the production of all manner of useful household objects were common in editions of such magazines from the mid-1920s on.

Appliqué was just one aspect of the category known as *rukodelie* (literally, a thing made with one's hands), which appeared increasingly prominently in the female press. From 1926 until the early 1930s, each issue of *Zhenskii zhurnal* contained a one-page section with the heading '*Rukodelie*' and instructions on how to make objects for the home. In 1930, the heading was changed to the more portentous '*Remeslo i prikladnoe iskusstvo*' (Craft and Applied Arts), but the content remained essentially unchanged. Similarly, in the more obviously worker-targeted journal *Rabotnitsa*, a regular page entitled '*Novoe i prakticheskoe*' (What's New and Practical?) introduced a host of useful tips for the homemaker, and *Iskusstvo odevat'sia* (issued as a supplement to *Krasnaia panorama* in 1928 and 1929) included regular back-page columns full of such handy hints.

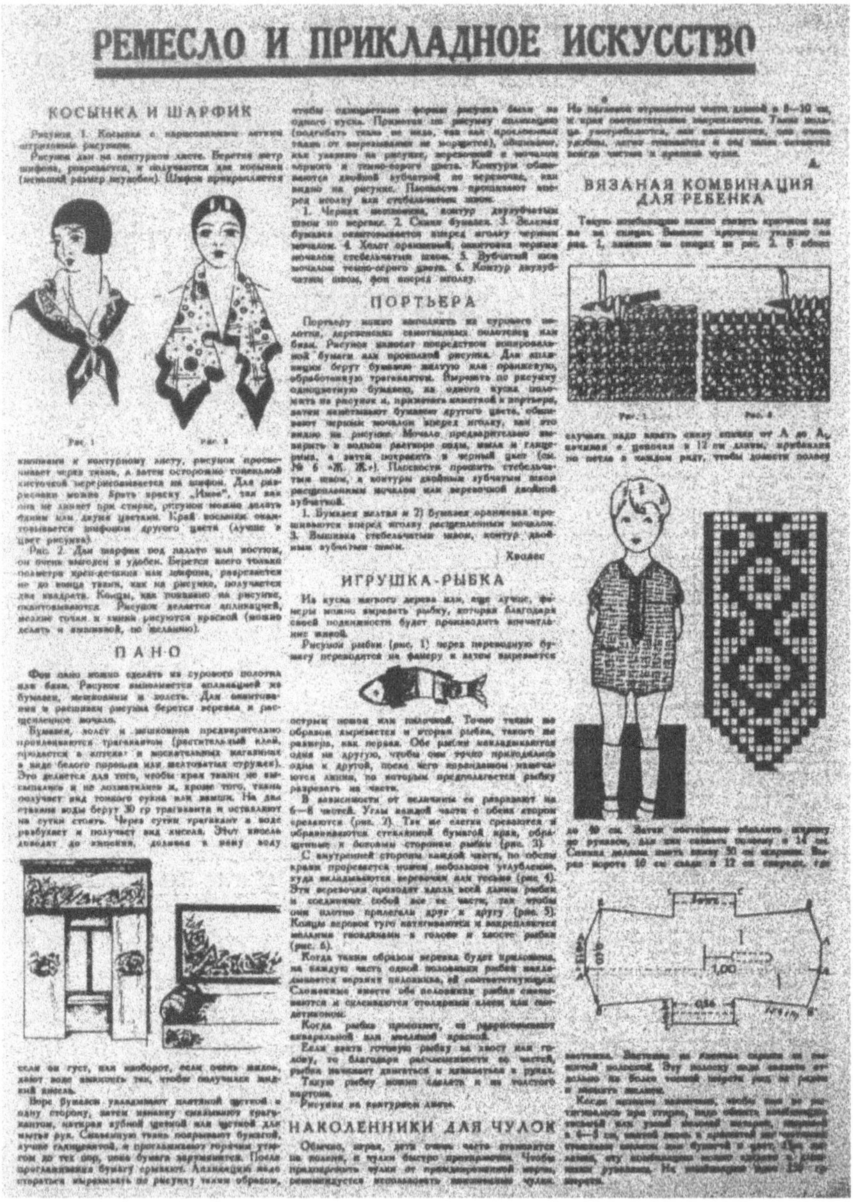

РЕМЕСЛО И ПРИКЛАДНОЕ ИСКУССТВО

КОСЫНКА И ШАРФИК

ПАНО

ПОРТЬЕРА

ИГРУШКА-РЫБКА

НАКОЛЕННИКИ ДЛЯ ЧУЛОК

ВЯЗАНАЯ КОМБИНАЦИЯ ДЛЯ РЕБЕНКА

Figure 6.1. 'Craft and Applied Arts' (with wall hanging [panneau] at bottom left) *Zhenskii zhurnal* (1930), 4.

On one level, of course, the growing importance of *rukodelie* in press of this kind was simply a straightforward response to shortage. It was a way of acquiring things that the Soviet market could not provide or—during the difficult years of the New Economic Policy, when some consumer goods were available—of obtaining articles that one could not afford. Further, this apparently officially sanctioned emphasis on the homemade can be seen as part of the validation of 'labor' that was at the heart of Soviet ideology. In contrast to the indolent consumer of bourgeois luxury, we understand, the Soviet homemaker is resourceful and self-reliant, able to use his or her *hands*. The labor carried out in factories and workshops across the nation during the day is mirrored in the home during one's free time. As such, according to this interpretation, Soviet society is not only *built*, at a macro level; it is also *made*— even homemade—at a micro one.

An alternative interpretation of the continuing presence of the 'homemade' within the emerging Soviet command economy, however, might view it rather as working against the dominant discourse. How can appliqué, of all things, be considered Soviet? What need for wall hangings in the new world? Surely the encouragement of *rukodelie*, of individual practices aimed at the creation of nonstandard objects, at the embellishment of the self or of one's personal space, worked against the collective imperative of Soviet socialism.

My principal interest in the phenomenon of *rukodelie*, however, lies not in its economic, nor even in its ideological, status, but rather in the implicit sensory experience that it offered. Making things—with one's hands—is an a priori tactile experience. Such articles were aimed not only at the satisfaction of a need; they offered luxury objects, certainly, but they also—and crucially— offered the luxury, or pleasure, of making. It is my contention that the category of 'pleasure', or more specifically 'sensory pleasure', should be considered as part of the 'happiness' equation that is the subject of this volume.

What was the role of sensory pleasure, of the tactile, within the function-led aesthetics (and economics) of the late 1920s and early 1930s?

The category of 'pleasure' adds a new dimension to the question of 'Soviet happiness'. 'Happiness', an amorphous and essentially indefinable concept, can be productively considered through scrutiny of Soviet official discourse. The term *vesel'e* (jollity) was more common in official Soviet discourse than *schast'e* (happiness). *Schast'e*, which appears to indicate a more fundamental quality of contentment, a personal sense of well-being, is to be differentiated from the *vesel'e* or *bodrost'* (merriness), to which the Soviet citizen was so often exhorted during the heady years of the mid-1930s, as Socialist Realism took hold. Jollity and merriness were shared, collectively experienced emotions, engendered—if the discourse was to be believed—by a film comedy such as Grigorii Aleksandrov's musical *Veselye rebiata* (The Happy Fellows, 1934), praised by the influential administrator Boris Shumiatskii as uniting the three crucial qualities of ideology (*ideinost'*) joy (*radost'*) and merriness (*bodrost'*), encouraging in the spectator a joyful appreciation of the Soviet world.[2] The collective ideal of *vesel'e* and *bodrost'* was represented by the open-air fêtes popular in Soviet cities throughout the 1930s, and wryly presented in Aleksandr Medvedkin's *Novaia Moskva* (New Moscow) of 1939.

The category of 'pleasure' to be considered here is distinct from either of these differing forms of 'happiness', however. A Soviet dictionary defines *udovol'stvie* (pleasure), as 'a feeling of joy, obtained from wonderful sensations or experiences'. For our purposes, 'pleasure' is rooted in sensation, in sensory experience: the pleasure of touching, of using ones hands, of texture, and of textile. Sensory experience—and, in particular, that of the proximal senses such as touch and taste—is generally seen as individual, resistant to communication. The work of anthropologists, however—and, in particular, the recent 'sensuous turn' in anthropology exemplified by the work of David Howes 2004,[3] Contance Classen 1993[4] and Paul Stoller 1997,[5] among others—suggests that this is not so. In fact, it can be argued that all of our senses are at some level socially conditioned. In the words of David Howes:

> Sensation is not just a matter of physiological response and personal experience. It is the most fundamental domain of cultural expression, the medium through which all the values and practices of society are enacted. To a greater or lesser extent, every domain of sensory experience, from the sight of a work of art to the scent of perfume to the savor of dinner, is a field of cultural elaboration.[6]

For Howes, even touch and taste operate at the border between the intimate and the shared. The 'proximal senses' act as a membrane between the personal and the social, the communicable and the incommunicable.

This emphasis on the cultural shaping of the human sensorium is important for our purposes. The Soviet project was a unique attempt to create entirely new models of human experience, to correspond to the new political order. In this respect, it is instructive to view it as an attempt to shape *sensory* experience itself—that apparently most personal and unpoliceable of realms. After all, Marx himself had said that 'the sensuous world [...] is, not a thing given direct from all eternity, remaining ever the same, but the product of industry and of the state of society...in the sense that it is a historical product.'[7] As such, the new political and social order could and should create a new 'sensuous world'. My argument is that culture, in all its forms, including the press, participated in that project to a greater or lesser extent. We may not be able to approach, in this essay, a history of Soviet touch, of the specificity of sensory experience in the Soviet context, but we can examine two key aspects of that history. *Zhenskii zhurnal* set itself the task of serving women's 'practical' needs, recognising that 'the life of the modern woman is still closely tied to the minutiae of everyday life.'[8] Examining it and other journals of the same kind, we can trace descriptions of tactile *practices* (appliqué, embroidery, etc.); further, we can examine the objects that those practices aimed to create, and what they reveal about the importance of the sensory, textural environment in which Soviet daily life took place.

The emphasis on decoration that we can trace through these women's journals has two points of interest. First, its items were homemade. Second, it was largely focused on what might be called the 'dressing' of the home. One article in *Zhenskii zhurnal*, for example, contains instructions for making a 'wall carpet'; the 'carpet' in question is, in fact, a simple hanging of appliquéd patterns onto a base fabric.[9] In September of 1928 the reader of *Iskusstvo odevat'sia* was encouraged to use her developing skills in appliqué to make a door curtain. The large floral design, cut out of colored linen or satin, was to be sewn onto the simple linen, by appliqué: 'Once you can reproduce the designs below, it is easy to make a beautiful and cheap door curtain out of unbleached linen.'[10]

Of course, in the Soviet climate of shortages, appliqué served a basic and practical function: it was a way of obtaining patterned textile when most available fabric was unprinted—linen canvas, tarpaulin, low grade woolens, or calico.[11] In *Iskusstvo odevat'sia* in May 1928, an article on appliqué provided basic instructions, informing the reader that the strength of this particular technique lay in the fact that it was both easy and cheap—beautiful effects could be achieved using mere remnants of fabric that would otherwise go to waste.[12] By applying dark blue and light green diamond shapes onto simple linen, one article instructs, and creating dark checks out of black ribbon, 'You can turn a plain, standard-supply mattress into a beautiful divan.'[13] (Fig. 6.2)

Beyond these practical features, however, the physical properties of appliqué bear further consideration. It is by definition multilayered and as such *textural*; sewing fabric shapes on top of one another to create flower designs or similar upon a plain base, the seamstress creates a fabric that is, in effect, three-dimensional—that rewards not just the eye but also the hand. Wall hangings, door curtains, sofa covers—all these appliquéd objects served to 'dress' the bare walls of mass housing, to clothe the new Soviet spaces, to enrich the sensual texture of the lived environment. In the words of Mark Wigley, interpreting the German architect and historian Gottfried Semper. 'The Interior is not defined by continuous enclosure of walls, but by the folds, twists and turns in an otherwise discontinuous ornamental surface.'[14] Appliqué—pragmatic and basic as it may appear—would have created that discontinuous surface. It was a form of textural homemaking.

The theories of Semper have been said, controversially perhaps, to have underpinned the development of much modernist architecture.[15] For Semper, building originated not with walls, but with the use of woven fabric to

Покрывало на диван или постель.

Деталь машинки (см. контурный лист рис. 2-ой).

...мые полосы исполняются из черной полотняной тесьмы. Все наставные части пришиваются петельным швом для на машине.

На контурном листе синий цвет показан крупным темным штрихом, зеленый редким, легким, а черный—сплошным черным.

Подушки на диван (рис. 6) исполняются из полотна ярких цветов. К средней дан повторяющийся рисунок, который можно исполнить аппликацией.

Вышивку на покрывале и подушках можно заменить пестрой набойкой из холста.

Такое покрывало очень удобно и практично.

Из простого пружинного матраца можно сделать красивый диван.

Фон покрывала исполняется из сурового полотна, а аппликация ромбы из темно-синего и ярко зеленого полотна, пря-

Аппликация или наложение исполняется так: все части рисунка вырезаются из материи и нашиваются петельным швом или на машине.

Figure 6.2. The cover for a sofa or a bed, *Zhenskii zhurnal* (1926), 37.

define space: 'The beginning of building coincides with the beginning of textiles.'[16] Textiles were used 'as a means of dividing the "home": the *inner life* from the *outer life*, as a formal construct of the spatial idea'.[17] The essence of architecture was therefore its 'dressing' (its covering layer), rather than its material structure. In Wigley's words, 'it is not that the fabrics are arranged in a way that provides physical shelter. Rather, their texture, their sensuous play, their textuality, like that of the languages Semper studied, opens up a space of exchange.'[18] The textural, tactile environment creates the conditions for human experience and interaction. This principle of 'dressing', understood in its widest sense, is our subject here. In its emphasis on textural covering, and its convolution of visual and tactile sensuality, Semper's work raises key questions about the material experience of Soviet daily life. What, then, of the textile dressing of the Soviet home that this phenomenon of *rukodelie* seems to imply? Here, simple anecdotal evidence—our own experiences of Soviet and late-Soviet Russia—may be instructive. Carpets on walls, curtains in restaurants, fabric shops on every street—such were the familiar signs of the Soviet domestic landscape; these were the textures and textiles within which daily life nestled.

In June of 1926, the title of an editorial article in *Zhenskii zhurnal* posed the difficult question, 'How to create domestic comfort/coziness (*uiut*)?'[19]

'An absolute absence of comfort distinguishes the great majority of our workers' apartments,' it acknowledged. How, the author asked, in the 'crowded conditions' that were the reality of Soviet housing in the mid-1920s, could domestic comfort exist? The careful balance of the article points to the complexities of sensory pleasure in the early Soviet years. On the one hand, it states unambiguously that some 'rationalisation' of the domestic environment is needed, that 'there must be no superfluous objects in the Soviet worker's home,' and that unwieldy 'old style' furnishings have no place in new socialist spaces. Despite this, however, it claims without prevarication that 'comfort is essential.' As such, the article is a kind of manifesto for the pages of the magazine itself, a call for the simple acts of *rukodelie* and homemaking that we are concerned to uncover. As another article pointed out, 'In our living conditions, with our living space, the bedroom often serves also as an office, a dining room, and a living room'; strategies of 'dressing' were needed to facilitate these daily transformations.[20]

Gottfried Semper's 'textile walls' were justified by the lexical link between the German *Wand* (wall) and *Gewand* (clothing). For him, the imperative for home decoration ('dressing', or *Bekleidung*) preceded the clothing of the body. The creation of divisions between interior and exterior space, and the softening, or embellishment, of the physical environment is, he suggests, a fundamental human imperative. In the Soviet context, we could argue, within the drive towards collectivity and visibility represented by the new society, that imperative was particularly pronounced. Enrobing and sheltering the body, at once defining and shielding the self, the fabrics of clothes and home decoration offered the vitally sensory experience of touch. They also offered forms of protection and enclosure. This emphasis on the textural environment provides a counternarrative to the often-accepted story of Russian revolutionary culture. The drive towards functionalism and efficiency, we are given to understand, worked against comfort, against the softness of pillows and eiderdowns, against extraneous ornament and towards a lived environment of maximum simplicity. The decorated home is, we are told, the petty bourgeois home, satirised in Abram Room's *Tret'ia Meshchanskaia* (*Bed and Sofa*) of 1928, as in Maiakovskii's well known propaganda poem 'O driani' (On [Domestic] Trash, 1920). At the finale of *Bed and Sofa*, we see the heroine Liudmila escape the trappings (and entrapment) of her textile-bedecked apartment, implicitly to begin a 'real' Soviet life.

Of course, any of these simplified narratives of Soviet life neglects differences of social position and wealth. It is certainly unlikely that peasants in Riazan province, for example, would have had the time or leisure to apply themselves to the creation of wall hangings, still less the access to linen and satin that some of these articles in *Zhenskii zhurnal* presume. It is clear that the magazines under consideration here are aimed at an urban population; in the case of *Zhenskii zhurnal* and *Iskusstvo odevat'sia*, moreover, it seems apparent that the actual readership was largely comprised of a moderately affluent social group, even though both journals' rhetoric suggested a readership of working women. The fact that a similar discourse of *rukodelie* is present in the worker-oriented *Delegatka* (the [Woman] Delegate), however, may indicate a more widespread aspiration to 'dress' the home and a less straightforward ideological divide between the functional and the decorative than we might expect.

An examination of cinematic interiors of the late 1920s provides support for this argument. *Bed and Sofa* itself is far more ambiguous in its presentation of domestic space than my earlier analysis might suggest. Certainly, in the early parts of the film, Liudmila is often pictured within the dominating textures and textiles of her domestic space. She is buried within pillows, for example, or caught reflected in a mirror, along with the textile pattern of a decorative scarf. And although the film's narrative certainly argues for a rejection of this domestic space, its visual impact rests in part on what the contemporary critic Bleiman described as the transformation of everyday objects into 'exotic material'.[21] In interior shots, the visual frame is densely packed with contrasting patterns and textures, and the spectator is drawn into an imaginatively sensory appreciation of Liudmila's world.

Friedrikh Ermler's 1926 film *Katka—bumazhnyi ranet* (Katka's Reinette Apples) presents a simplified opposition between petty bourgeois and workers' domestic space. The textile-bedecked, densely patterned interior in which the corrupt Sen'ka and his aspirational coquette Vera operate signifies *meshchanstvo*, its protagonists enmeshed in the trappings of the old world, prey to the allure of material possessions. In contrast, the bare room in which Katka and her baby make their home, and into which the simple-hearted hero Vad'ka is gradually assimilated, appears initially unadorned. Where Vera's mother's bed is symbolically stacked high with four feather pillows, her windows hung with vivid florals, and her wallpapered walls decorated with fans, Katka's bed is covered in a single eiderdown, with one pillow, and her walls are scarcely patterned. Within this simplified ideological opposition, however, Ermler introduces important subtlety. The overarching narrative of the film is one of homemaking; the simple workers Katka and Vad'ka gradually appropriate a corner of the urban world as their own, find their place in the new world, just as Sen'ka and Vera are increasingly excluded. And this appropriation is expressed through slight transformations in their domestic space. Vad'ka, initially alone and apparently unable to cope in society, finds shelter in Katka's world, as she takes pity on him: in a strikingly tactile image, we see him nestling within her eiderdown, his head resting on her pillow as she darns his worn clothes. Later in the film, as he adopts the role of child-minder, when Katka returns to the street to sell her apples, Vad'ka's growing ease and the increasing comfort and intimacy of his and Katka's domestic arrangement is mirrored in the film's revelation of a softer domestic environment in which texture and textile play a subtle but important role. We see a small dressing table covered by a lace cloth, a sewing basket, a covered window; alongside the swaddling of the baby, and the 'mending' of Vad'ka's clothing, these objects serve to dress Katka's simple home and to shelter their nuclear family.

Thus, although *Katka's Reinette Apples* is structured along clear ideological lines, whereby simple workers flourish and profiteers and petty bourgeoisie fall, and although Katka and Vad'ka are finally affiliated to the Soviet world via their employment in a factory, nevertheless a more ambiguous discourse on homemaking is present throughout the film and carries much of its emotional weight. The domestic space acts as a stark contrast to the frenetic urban space of NEP-era St Petersburg, in which Katka and her fellow street traders operate; its softened contours invite the spectator into a sensory understanding of the protagonists' need for *uiut*.

At its most basic level, *rukodelie* is testament to Soviet woman's desire to 'clothe' and shelter her own body, her family and her home. In addition to appliqué, 'open-work stitching' (and other forms of basic embroidery) also formed part of the ballast of skills that—with the help of her magazines and their pages of rukodelie—she would master. Simple embroidery was, in the words of one article, a good way of decorating underwear, blouses, tablecloths, etc.; it could be used to decorate such vital items as lingerie holders, for example, patterns for which appeared in *Zhenskii zhurnal* in March of 1926.

It becomes apparent that an emphasis on the decorative was common to suggestions for *rukodelie*. Are our pages of craft thus to be considered as entirely removed from the mainstream of Soviet design during the 1920s, which aimed—according to rhetoric at least—at the elimination of ornament, the creation of clean-lined clothing, furniture and housing to suit the new age of production? In fact, avant-garde discourse was characterised by a complex relationship with the idea of 'ornament'. For Russian modernists, as for their European counterparts, the elimination of the extraneous ornamentation that was seen to characterise bourgeois design was a vital first step in the creation of the new, modern aesthetic. This did not necessarily mean, however, that there was no place for the decorative in the new aesthetic. 'True' ornament, according to the German Bauhaus director Walter Gropius, was the product of the collective consciousness over a period of time. Folk ornament, that is, was entirely permissible in modern design: 'The Ornament is dead,' Gropius pronounced, 'Long live the Ornament!'[22]

In the Soviet context, recourse to folk (*narodnyi*) or 'peasant' aesthetics had particular appeal. Folk craft was an ideologically appropriate form of design, an appropriate source of inspiration for those searching for a new aesthetic for Russian textile and clothing design, and as such, appliqué and embroidery had a respectable lineage. Roginskaia, writing in *Sovetskoe iskusstvo* in 1926, for example, suggested that two key influences could and must be combined in Soviet textile design. First, she advocated the use of decorative elements drawn from the 'peasant' background (embroidery, lace, etc.); second, she suggested that they be combined with decorative elements drawn from Constructivism—geometric motifs could be appliquéd onto fabric, for example.[23]

A similar emphasis on the folk heritage is evident in articles in the artist-led fashion journal *Atel'e* (Atelier), the first and only issue of which was produced in 1923. One piece by E. Pribyl'skaia, dedicated to 'Embroidery in Contemporary Production', is, in effect, an attempt to justify a continuing role for embroidery in Russian clothing design, despite the fact that 'our life must not be overburdened with purely aesthetic objects, and with the production of things of precious but non-utilitarian purpose.'[24] Pribyl'skaia finds her justification in the folk basis of Russian embroidery: 'In folk costumes, made by the peasants themselves out of flax, hemp, wool and leather, the external working (*obraboktka*) of the material is essential.' As these rough fabrics are difficult to sew, she points out, folk techniques have recourse to externally visible and often decorative stitching, which forms part of the structure of the finished item. Her term *obrabotka* (working) is familiar in avant-garde, and especially constructivist, aesthetics. For the Constructivists, the 'processing' (or 'working') of the material is the essential human intervention into the natural, physical world. The Constructivists were explicitly concerned with the texture (*faktura*) of the materials they worked with. In clothing design, this was expressed as an ambition to 'avoid violence on the material', to make clothes that took account of the 'weight, thickness, elasticity, width and colour' of the fabric.[25] It was in these terms, via an emphasis on the tactile qualities of the material, that Pribyl'skaia framed her rehabilitation of embroidery, as a means of 'processing' the material: 'Here embroidery does not play a role of pointless decorative element; it constructs the object alongside the base material.'

It is my contention that such ideological justification of peasant craft and *rukodelie*—often linked to an emphasis on texture and 'work'—filtered down into the mainstream press, and is manifest in our lessons in appliqué and craft. Folk-style ornament was entirely acceptable, and an interest in peasant tradition is evident at all levels in Soviet clothing and textile design. In the artist-driven *Iskusstvo v bytu* (Art into Everyday Life) of 1925, for example, we see a 'Kaftan' made from two traditionally embroidered towels (*polotentsy*) from the Vladimir province, alongside a Young Pioneer suit made from what is described as 'peasant canvas'.[26] Here, it is not simply design that is appropriated, but an ethic of simplicity and economy. In similar terms, the prerevolutionary couturier

Nadezhda Lamanova, who embraced the revolution with apparent enthusiasm, transferred her prerevolutionary designs, often inspired by folk costume, to create 'ideologically-justified' shapes for the new era: 'Folk costumes are [...] work clothes, devised for hard physical work. [...] Combining the lively picturesqueness of folk costume with modern techniques of mass production, we achieve a type of clothing that responds to the needs dictated by our contemporary life.'[27] Elsewhere, in the more mainstream magazines such as *Zhenskii zhurnal* and *Iskusstvo odevat'sia*, aimed at the emerging Soviet consumer, we see similar traces of what is increasingly dubbed 'Russian style'. (Figs. 6.3 and 6.4) One interesting colour plate in *Iskusstvo odevat'sia*, for example, shows a traditional Russian scarf of floral design, worn in different ways—as a scarf, but also as a skirt, etc. (Fig. 6.5) Elsewhere, the Russian peasant shirt (*kosovorotka*) is praised for 'uniting beauty and hygiene'.[28]

A similarly complex relationship with prerevolutionary and folk precedent surrounded the issue of textile design. If appliqué and embroidery were attempts to transform plain fabrics into patterned ones, then what of attempts to produce more printed textile in the Soviet Union? In addition to the practical problems of production faced by most Soviet industry during the 1920s, textile design was fraught with ideological questions. What should Soviet fabric look like? In early Constructivist and avant-garde writings on fashion, we find an emphasis on the value of plain fabric, free of decoration, as a sign of the distinction of Soviet clothing from Western. 'Artists must take the initiative,' Nadezhda Lamanova announced, 'working to create from plain fabrics simple but beautiful garments befitting the new mode of working life.'[29] The predominance of floral motifs in existing printed fabric was viewed as a symbol of the old world, of imperial Russia's enslavement to fashions drawn directly from the West, and was to be replaced by more politically appropriate design. Textile was part of the material sphere of ideological transformation, 'entitled to play an enormous part in transforming old tastes and breaking old aesthetic habits and traditions (together with the ideological rules so deeply rooted in them) and [...] a vehicle for a new culture and a new ideology.'[30] As 'a primary necessity', it was a means of bringing propaganda into everyday life, of clothing citizens, and their homes, in the Soviet message.

By the second half of the 1920s, this ambition had assumed the most literal of forms: in 1928, at a major Exhibition of Textiles in Everyday Life, so-called 'propaganda designs' (factories, tractors, etc.) were very much in evidence.[31] In the earlier part of the decade, however, a broader variety of experiment took place, due in particular to the involvement of constructivist artists such as Liubov' Popova and Varvara Stepanova in the 'First Factory of Printed Cotton' in Moscow from 1923. During this early period, geometric

Figure 6.3. Style *à la russe*, *Iskusstvo odevat'sia* (1928)

and abstract pattern was particularly important, sometimes with symbols and patterns drawn from industrial reality (cogs, levers) or Soviet iconography (hammer and sickle, the red star). In contrast to these abstract designs, in which the 'ideological' impact aimed to be as much formal as thematic,

Figure 6.4. Style *à la russe*, *Iskusstvo odevat'sia* (1928), 2, cover

the *agittekstily* that emerged in the latter half of the decade were often more figurative in technique, reproducing factories, trains or even scenes from the Central Asian republics, in a manner which seems to owe something to the French design of Toile de Jouy. Such 'thematic textiles' were satirised

Figure 6.5. Ingenious ways with a scarf, *Iskusstvo odevat'sia* (1928), 2, 9

in *Pravda* 6 September 1933, and banned in the same year. Thereafter, the floral reappeared as the dominant design; the textile experiment had come to an end. During the 1930s, in film and magazines alike, floral summer dresses became a key signifier of the new leisure ideal in Soviet culture.

In film of the 1920s, modern textile design is rarely seen. Meanwhile, alongside the bourgeois associations that we have discussed, floral and heavily patterned textile acts as a signifier of provincial Russia, of timeless tradition. In Protazanov's *Zakroishchik iz Torzhka* (Tailor from Torzhok, 1925), for example, a provincial town and its merchant inhabitants are evoked though interiors with an excess of pattern. Melan'ia Ivanova, wealthy proprietor of the workshop where the eponymous tailor (played by the comic Igor Il'inskii) practices his craft, is pictured amidst a profusion of fabric and pattern, and a familiar excess of pillows, which cannot be attributed solely to the pragmatic demands of the profession, but which encode her, materially, as bourgeois and (harmlessly) retrograde. The tailor's escape from her amorous clutches into the innocent arms of young Katia is an escape from the suffocation of comfort. This is not to suggest, however, that he escapes into the functional simplicity of a modern domestic environment, or modern dress. The whole film, rather, is suffused with folk costume and décor, and locates its gentle comedy within an apparently timeless provincial space.

Despite the sanctioned return of floral pattern in clothing design from the 1930s on, in film of that decade an excess of pattern remained a signifier of petty bourgeois aspiration, an easy means of holding a character up to ridicule. In Konstantin Iudin's *Serdtsa chetyrykh* (Four Hearts, 1941), for example, the heroine's aspirational neighbor is shown, out of step with her age, in a parody of Parisian chic, with an excess of frills and patterned parasol that matches hat and dress. Similarly, in *Podkidysh* (Foundling, directed by Tatiana Lukashevich, 1940), the overdressed woman who attempts to abduct the eponymous runaway, and who clothes the young girl in a miniature parody of her own matching parasol and dress, is signified as absurd. Slavish attempts to emulate Parisian 'chic' act as a signifier of the Soviet version of poor taste.[32]

This rejection of the vagaries of bourgeois fashion was part of established Soviet discourse throughout the 1920s and into the 1930s. It was, moreover, common to revolutionary culture across its spheres, in Soviet Russia as elsewhere in Europe. Fashion, in this view, was a relentless slave of the 'new' for its own sake, excessively feminised (and hence dangerously sensual), unnecessarily ornamental or decorative, and linked to the domestic sphere. It was a form of 'mask' or dissimulation of the self, and as such, went against the grain of the modern celebration of the body in its natural, undecorated state. 'Let us tackle those who imitate the dandies of the Petrovka [a fashionable Moscow street] with their "latest models from abroad,"' *Komsomolskaia pravda* declared: 'Let us create new styles of hygienic, purpose-designed, beautiful clothes, made of good material, styles which will be a general guide to all young people.'[33]

Fashion might be rejected, but clothing mattered. Indeed, it was the site of some of revolutionary Russia's most innovative design experiments. From the beginning, Soviet avant-garde designers (many of whom were linked to the 'Workshop of Contemporary Dress' established on the initiative of Nadezhda Lamanova in Moscow in 1919) were well aware of the ideological power of dress. As part of the material culture of everyday life, it must be changed in line with the wholesale 'transformation of everyday life' that was the revolutionary imperative. In fashion, as in decoration, the dominant official aesthetic was officially one of functionalism: Soviet clothing would be distinguished by its rejection of ornament; its form would be determined solely by practicality, by the needs of its wearer and his or her tasks. At its most extreme, this ideal was realised in the prototype of the *prozodezhda* (production clothing), which was to provide a kind of 'uniform' of Soviet citizenship. Loose-fitting and based on geometric shapes, it would allow the human body full freedom of movement, and, in its uniformity, overcome the vagaries of fashion, gender and individualism, dressing all men and women alike: 'Today's Fashion is the Worker's Overall' ran the headline of a manifesto article by Constructivist Varvara Stepanova in 1923.[34]

In practice, of course, avant-garde fashion never achieved the wholesale transformation of everyday life to which it aspired, and had little real impact on the clothing of ordinary men and women in Soviet Russia of the 1920s. Most of these designs never went beyond the sketch; others appeared only in costumes for theatre (and, to a lesser extent, for film—Iakov Protazanov's *Aelita* of 1924 a particularly striking example). Meanwhile, real Soviet men and women were faced with a practical problem: how to dress appropriately for the new age, and, even more urgently, how to get hold of the clothes and fabrics that they needed.

The magazines that provide the material for this analysis reveal the hybrid nature of Soviet fashion, and discourse on fashion, in the second half of the 1920s and into the early 30s. In real terms, alongside these drives to standardise the Soviet aesthetic, prerevolutionary fashion remained the sought-after mode for the wealthy and the aspirational ideal for young women of all classes.[35] French magazines were available in Soviet Russia throughout the NEP years; foreign film stars such as Mary Pickford appeared in the many Western films distributed in Soviet Russia at this time, serving as models for stylish feminine beauty and dress.[36] The fashion plates in *Zhenskii zhurnal* and even *Delegatka* in 1926 differ little from those that one would see in Western equivalents of the same year, and *Zhenskii zhurnal* included regular reports on Western, and particularly Parisian, styles. *Isskustvo odevat'sia* was launched in 1928, in the same year a headline in the newspaper *Komsomolskaia pravda* posed a crucial question: 'How should we dress?'[37] What, it asked, was correct Soviet dress; what was the ideologically appropriate fashion for the new age?

In a sense, *Iskusstvo odevat'sia* represented an attempt to answer that question— or to overcome it. Its first issue contained a forward by the Commissar of Enlightenment Anatolii Lunacharskii, acknowledging that 'a certain amount of smartness and fashion (*moda*) is by no means unsuited to the proletariat.'[38] This represented a major concession to the continuing presence of 'fashion' in the popular consciousness, to the desire of Soviet people to be well dressed, and put an end to the most extreme aspirations for a specifically Soviet, purely functional, form of clothing. Costume, Lunacharskii acknowledged, is a means of self-definition: 'Nature demands that young people should play a little with their dress, to try to express their strength, their grace.'[39] Indeed, a survey carried out by *Iskusstvo odevat'sia* to mark its launch issue includes apparently 'ordinary' Russian women answering the question, 'Is it time for the worker to dress well?'. 'I welcome the publication of this magazine, which is going to help the working woman dress elegantly, modestly, and above all, cheaply!' said one Elizaveta Belugina, worker in a sweet factory.[40]

Dressing 'elegantly and cheaply' was by no means straightforward, however, even if you could navigate the ideological maze that fashion might at first appear to be. In simple terms, good clothing was hard to obtain. Thus, in our magazines, the encouragement of 'home-made,' or *rukodelie*, was not limited to the dressing of the home. In *Delegatka*, aimed expressly at the working woman, we see a growing number of articles focusing on self-made clothing, and rudimentary cut-out patterns appear as early as 1926.[41] Although less overtly practical in its general orientation, it is clear that *Iskusstvo odevat'sia* was also intended, nominally at least, to provide the wherewithal for the budding (and ambitious) amateur seamstress to fashion her own clothes according to the designs provided. Each design is accompanied by a very brief description, detailing the amount of fabric it demands.[42] Later articles were increasingly overt about their intention to encourage home dressmaking. 'A Tailor at Home', for example, aimed to 'come to the aid of those housewives who would like to make not only women's but also men's clothes themselves', and promised to give 'a series of tips and advice'.[43] Changes in fashion, the magazine claimed—in particular the rejection of the female corset and a relaxation of tailoring—had made the process of dressmaking significantly more approachable for the ordinary housewife.[44]

Like our wall hangings and sofa covers, home-made clothing in Soviet Russia was first and foremost a response to the shortage of consumer goods. It was also, however, a reaction to the growth of standardised design in mass-produced clothing, an opportunity for what Ekaterina Degot has called 'an individual escape from the standard'.[45] The successful development of the '*standart*'—factory-made clothing in 'standard' shapes and sizes for the ordinary Soviet citizen, and one of the key state-sponsored initiatives of the first Five-Year Plan—was celebrated in an exhibition in 1932 at the State History Museum in Moscow.[46] As available clothing was increasingly fixed in unchanging styles, the home-made (or home-altered or -decorated) acquired a particular appeal. It was a means of self-definition, of accentuating individuality within an increasingly standardised world. Dressing the self, like dressing the home, preceded, and to some extent defined, one's entry into the social arena. Just as rudimentary wall hangings and appliqué table clothes offered a surreptitious tactile pleasure in the home, so clothing could shelter the human body, providing it with the covering, protection—and perhaps even the correct image—needed to survive in a changing world. The 'home-made' was surely, then, a form of taking control, of managing one's self and one's environment. And it was one that was apparently sanctioned by official discourse.

This has been an essay about cloth, in its different forms, and its role in Soviet everyday life. Discovering the discreet presence of fabric in hidden corners of the Soviet interior and tracing its potential transformations, we find that alongside the official drive for pared down and functional interiors remains an urge to decorate, to 'dress' the home and the self with layers of texture and textile. This is more intriguing than a simple revelation of the emotional need for the domestic and petty bourgeois, already a well-recorded aspect of Soviet life of the 1920s and 1930s.[47] It is more than just an argument, following Boym and others, for the realm of the ordinary,[48] of everyday life, as a separate and crucial personal sphere that constantly threatened the success of the Soviet collective project. The fact that a parallel interest in the value of material texture is to be found in avant-garde aesthetics may suggest that tactile pleasure had its own important role to play. Soviet man was, according to rhetoric, to be reborn into a heightened physical apprehension of the world. That this heightened physical apprehension might be linked to the pleasures of appliqué and embroidery was, of course, far from the point. It might be suggested, however, that the ideologically sanctioned encouragement of *remeslo* and *rukodelie*, of the 'processing' of material (in this case, of textile) *by hand*, in the home, was more than just a concession to the need for material comfort. The dressing of the domestic sphere and of the self, the creation of tactile pleasure, could be justified as part of the broader ideological project. As such, the established narrative of the transition in Soviet official policy from revolutionary austerity to Stalinist 'luxury' all during the 1930s appears more complicated.[49]

It is not my intention here to claim any innate national specificity of sense experience for Soviet Russia. I hope, however, to direct our attention to the importance of the tactile, of touch, across diverse fields of the Soviet discursive field. In revealing how tactile practices are written and talked about, we can approach some understanding of the anticipated pleasure of touch. In Margaret Mead's anthropological study of 1953, a Russian respondent noted that in Russian textbooks on the senses, the sense of touch is placed first: 'The dictionary of the Russian language [...] defines the sense of touch as follows: "In reality, all five senses can be reduced to one—the sense of touch [...] It means to ascertain, to perceive, by body, hand or fingers." '[50] She points out that Russian has two verbs which translate the English 'to feel/sense:' *osiazat'*, to feel by means of touch (sensation), with an outer part of the body, is distinct from the broader *oshchushchat'*, 'to feel'. In this essay, perhaps, we have begun the long process of uncovering a history of Soviet sensation.

Chapter Seven

HAPPY HOUSEWARMING!: MOVING INTO KHRUSHCHEV-ERA APARTMENTS

Susan E. Reid

Let me begin by introducing to you Zinaida the Happy Soviet Housewife, a smiling woman in an apron, baking pies with her little girl in time for Papa to get home. This image of domestic bliss was printed in the Soviet press a day after the American National Exhibition, presenting America as a consumer paradise, opened in Moscow's Sokol'niki Park in July 1959.[1] What is Zinaida so happy about? ' "Our kitchen", she says in the caption, "is as good as the American one shown at the exhibition in Sokol'niki." ' Indeed, Zinaida's Soviet kitchen is modern and rational, if rather modest. It boasts such step-saving conveniences as wall-mounted units and a drying rack over the sink, which is fitted into a continuous worktop and has a mixer tap, indicating both hot and cold running water supplies.

Happy housewives, showing off their modern homes and dedicated to providing a happy homecoming for their hardworking husbands, are better known, in the post-war period, as the symbol of the good life on the other side of the Iron Curtain. The Happy Housewife did service in the global politics of the Cold War as an advertisement for the benefits of 'people's capitalism.'[2] She was particularly closely identified with the American dream, as represented in advertising images of suburban domestic bliss, although numerous examples may also be found in European and British publications from the 1950s.[3] Surrounded by gleaming appliances, the professional western housewife reigned over her segregated domain, keeping a serene home. Everyday, family life was constructed as a happy haven where the Enlightenment pursuit of 'Liberty and Happiness' could finally be attained through individual consumption.[4]

— Наша кухня, за-
мечает Зинаида Ми-
хайловна Ершова, не
хуже американской,
экспонируемой на вы-
ставке в Сокольниках.
   Субботний день...
Скоро муж вернется с
работы, и Зинаида Ми-
хайловна вместе с до-
черью Ирочкой спе-
шат испечь вкусные
пирожки.
Фото В. Бирюкова.

Figure 7.1. 'Our kitchen is just as good,' *Izvestiia* (July 1959)

Female obeisance to domestic hardware, epitomising commodity fetishism, was surely not an aspect of the American dream with which the Soviet Union should 'catch up and overtake'? As Soviet writer Marietta Shaginian wrote— reinvigorating the hostility of Engels, Lenin, and Kollontai towards bourgeois domesticity, and foreshadowing later socialist feminist critiques—the appliance-saturated, private American kitchen, as seen in Moscow in 1959, far from liberating women, represented a new form of bondage for them.

The countless domestic conveniences of the Americans ... anchor to woman in perpetuity her mission as 'housewife', wife, and cook. They make this role easier for her, but the very process of alleviation of individual housework, as it were, eternalizes this way of life, turning it into a profession for the woman. But we love innovations that actually emancipate women – new types of houses with public kitchens with their canteens for everyone living in the house; with laundries where vast machines wash clothes not just for one family alone.[5]

Perpetuating women's isolated labour in the home, the American kitchen— along with the version of liberty and happiness it epitomised—was not for Soviet consumption, she concluded. 'On this matter the tastes and expectations of Soviet viewers depart from those of the American exhibition organisers.'

Was not women's happiness in the land of the Soviets to be found precisely in their emancipation from the kitchen, as Shaginian indicated: in liberation from alienation, commodity fetishism and slavery to things, in the dissolution of the bourgeois, gendered segregation of public and private spheres, all of which would enable her self-realisation in productive labour and socially useful work? And yet, alongside statements such as Shaginian's and frequent admonitions that possessions must be kept in their place as 'servants not masters,' images of women as happy homemakers, acolytes of domestic appliances, and consumers of new possessions for the home were also ubiquitous in the Soviet popular press of the Thaw.[6] Indeed, during the Khrushchev era they became a vital component of the iconography of Soviet happiness and modernity, bodying forth claims that, under socialism, economic, scientific and technological progress could make the ordinary Soviet person's, and in particular, women's lives better.

The affair between women and machines was of course already well established in Soviet iconography, for example in the 1934 film *Chapaev* (dir. Georgii and Sergei Vasil'ev) and in Aleksandr Samokhvalov's painting of a monumental female *Metro Constructor with Drill* of 1937. But it was supposed to be machine guns, pneumatic drills and other ersatz phalluses that would modernise, liberate and make her a complete person. How has a domestic vacuum cleaner come to replace these potent machines, identified with the valorised realms of industrial production and military might, in her affections? (Fig 7.2) Have the image-makers been studying foreign magazines too avidly and, intent upon keeping up with their own profession, forgotten where they are? Catriona Kelly has shown the eclecticism of Soviet advice literature, whose appropriations from foreign discourses increased beginning in this period. And cutting and pasting or emulating Western magazines does appear to have played a part in the production of images of modernity and the good life. Indeed the London-based *Daily Mail's* annual *Ideal Home Book* was evidently consulted by Soviet writers, with some passages practically reproduced verbatim, while enthusiastic statements about new Soviet models

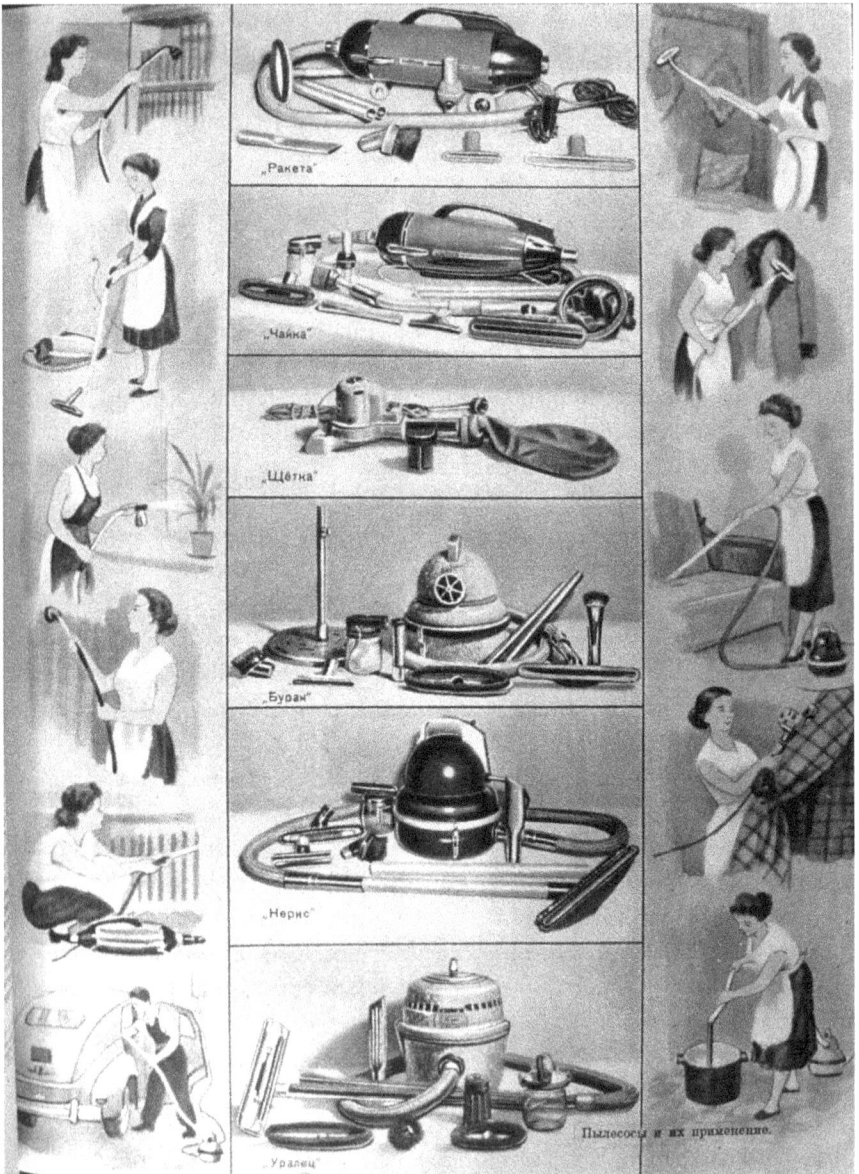

Figure 7.2. Women with vacuum cleaners, *Kratkaia entsiklopediia domashnego khoziaistva* (Moscow: Bol'shaia Sovetskaia entsiklopediia 1959)

of washing machine used the same rhetoric of 'saving women's labour and time' as did Western advertising.[7]

'Women this is for you!' ran the title of a new rubric introduced by *Ogonek* in 1960, illustrated with smiling, youthful women stepping out in the latest, Dior-inspired fashions.[8] What is this new avatar of the New Soviet Woman? In the context of Cold War peaceful competition, are we witnessing her embourgeoisement? Have consumer goods and home life become the source of modern happiness and of women's promised liberation and self-realisation? This chapter will examine Soviet representations of domestic bliss and consumption in the Khrushchev era. Visual images and discourse widely represented the family home, homemaking, and consumption for the home as a key site of happiness, Soviet style. As Vera Dunham, Julie Hessler, Sheila Fitzpatrick and others have shown, the promise and legitimisation of material pleasures was already under way by the early 1950s as part of the post-war renewal. Indeed, attention to consumer goods and the formation of the 'cultured' consumer as an aspect of Soviet civilisation began already in the second half of the 1930s.[9] But while Soviet policy makers under Stalin had accepted the idea of Soviet citizens as consumers, as Hessler has argued, '[t]hey proved unable and unwilling, however, to imagine the autonomous formation of desires that inevitably accompanied the country's emergence from survival-threatening need.'[10] The discourse that emerged in the Khrushchev era, for all that it sought to contain such desires within rational norms and was fraught with contradictions, differed from the Stalinist rhetoric of cultured consumption in that it implied an entitlement for *all* Soviet individuals – and not only Stakhanovites or VIPs – to occupy the subject position of consumer, to take on the persona in which they were hailed. If existing shortcomings of production and distribution prevented them from doing so, they would have legitimate grounds for complaint and discontent.[11] The ubiquitous discourse on the *potrebitel'* (consumer) in this period provided an identity for the 'Soviet person' as a demanding and entitled consumer.[12]

The key moment in the process by which, both discursively and in practice, the 'New Soviet Person' became a modern consumer is mass housewarming, *novosel'e:* the move to new flats not just for a few, but for millions. *Novosel'e* is, at the same time, the symbolic moment of accession to happiness in Khrushchev-era narratives. Home and home-based consumption, I want to argue, were as central to the image of Soviet modernity, progress and universal happiness as in the capitalist West, even if the nature of the domestic bliss promised was not always identical. As in the West, women were allocated a central place in this site of happiness, as its chief beneficiary and representative, and as those charged with appropriating housing and making it into 'home'.[13]

The New Soviet Person Becomes a Homemaker and Consumer[14]

' "New home: new happiness," as the folk saying goes,' began an article entitled 'Happy Housewarming' in the labour newspaper *Trud* in late 1959. It focused on a newly built five-storey apartment block into which 56 families of workers and employees of a Moscow machine-building factory had recently moved. 'Bright, cosy (*uiutnye*) rooms. A joyful, festive bustle. Human happiness takes up stable and permanent residence here.' One recipient of a new flat looks around with pride at his new home and says: 'I have often received awards for my work, but this is the very best present.'[15] His wife (as she is styled—indicating that *he*, not she, is head of household) shows the correspondent a big festive rug. 'Look at our new acquisition. And not from the shop, but from our factory bazaar. Trade union activists have given thought to us house-warmers. Thanks to them!'

This account serves to introduce several interrelated general points about the *novosel'e* genre, which we shall go on to explore. First, 'private' dwellings and consumer goods to go in them are represented as a legitimate source of pride and joy. Second, housewarming is the moment at which the Soviet person becomes a homemaker and consumer. Third, the house and lucky individuals on which the story focuses are represented not as exceptions but as 'typical'; as was customary in this genre in the late 1950s, the *Trud* article implied that it was describing a common experience in contemporary Soviet life, available to all good, hard-working citizens.[16] Even if readers had not yet been assigned a new apartment themselves, the message was, they, too, could expect this joy and could legitimately and realistically imagine themselves in the place of those whose happiness is described. For this house is one of many, this *novosel'e* one among millions. The central broadsheet *Izvestiia's* 'home and family' page (a significant innovation introduced at the time of the American National Exhibition in Moscow) announced in December 1959: 'In the current seven-year plan, millions of Soviet citizens are moving to new, well-appointed homes ... '*Novosel'e* is becoming the most common celebration genre.'[17]

The fourth point to be drawn out of *Trud's* 1959 narrative is that new apartments and consumer goods to go in them are gifts which impose an obligation of gratitude and, as such, are the cement that bonds citizens to the party–state, a relationship that is often mediated by the workplace.[18] Thus, they are a means to establish a contract between individual citizens and the state such as Vera Dunham discussed in relation to post-war living standards. But where Dunham's 'Big Deal' was a contract with only part of the population—what she designates as a Soviet middle class—this New Deal was inclusive, an 'implicit social contract between the regime and the *workers*, aimed at providing modest but steady improvements in the standard of living in exchange for labor productivity', as Victoria Bonnell notes.[19]

Many reasons can be offered for the regime's increased attention to providing housing and consumer goods for the masses. Material rewards and incentives gained in importance as the abandonment of terror made urgent the search for sources of legitimacy and of means of popular support, mobilisation and incentive. In a survey of popular opinion conducted in August–September 1960, sociologist Boris Grushin's newly founded Institute of Public Opinion gathered data on people's perceptions of whether living standards were improving and on what they deemed the most burning outstanding problems for the construction of communism. One respondent called for queues to be liquidated, for more self-service shops, and for cheap refrigerators to be provided to all families and installed in all new housing.[20] But the issue most cited was more basic: housing—overcrowding, substandard sanitary conditions, shared kitchens and bathrooms. The regime did not need to wait for Grushin's survey to know this. The problem of catastrophic living conditions was widely illuminated in the press in the mid-1950s.[21] The misery in which many people lived can be glimpsed in records of *profsoiuz* (trade union) hearings of claims for re-housing when new apartments became available. Thus a woman, her paralysed mother, and her child who had tuberculosis all lived together in a single room where the snow drove in through cracks in the walls. She had to compete for a single apartment against others in similarly dire conditions.[22] To do something about living conditions was urgent not only for regime legitimacy but also on health grounds, with tuberculosis rife. The effects of bad housing on children's health, behaviour and school performance were a matter for particular concern.[23] Workforce stability and productivity has also been cited as a reason for the prioritisation of housing in this period, but depressed *re*production rates could be as important as those of production.[24]

Moreover, we should not underestimate the ideological commitment of the Khrushchev regime, which presided over a reinvigoration of Marxist and Leninist principles. Abundance, high living standards and leisure for all were always part of the promise of communism. Khrushchev declared 'the struggle for happiness' one of the main tasks of the present day, associating this with improvement in the conditions of both spiritual and material life.[25] This position was continued after his ouster: 'Among the many blessings which socialism brings the working person,' *Kommunist* (the theoretical organ of the Communist Party Central Committee) declared a few years later in 1965, 'an important place is occupied by good, comfortable dwellings, satisfying all the requirements of hygiene and a cultured way of life'.[26] To make strides in the improvement of Soviet living standards and thereby to demonstrate the superiority of socialism over capitalism was especially urgent in the post-war global order: in the context of Cold War competition, of Soviet aspirations in the developing world, and of increasing contact and information about life abroad, both in capitalist countries and in the 'fraternal' socialist countries. It was problematic that, in regard to housing conditions and consumer goods, the Soviet Union, which was supposed to be leading other countries towards communism, showed little or no progress after forty years. As the American National Exhibition exemplified, the Cold War was not only an arms race and space race: it was also a contest of images of modernity and a competition over which system could provide the greatest happiness for the greatest number. Consumption and housing were key sites for 'peaceful competition' between the two world camps, and the projection of images of the good life was a vital weapon of global ideological warfare.[27]

If Soviet people were to be made happy, the conditions in which they dwelled had to be improved. Housing became a central pillar of the post-Stalin regime's commitment to make good on promises and raise living standards. It visibly materialised the metaphor of 'construction of communism.' The actuality of mass housing construction taking place on a vast and very visible scale in the Khrushchev era provided the material basis for an overproduction of images of happiness which became closely identified with newly built, bright, hygienic, separate apartments. In particular, the dynamic, life-changing process of moving into them was represented as a renewal and transformation not only of material surroundings but of behaviour and relations. Whether intentional or not, one product of this imagined rebirth was the new identity of Soviet homemaker-consumer. Before we go on to examine this in more detail a brief introduction to the Khrushchev-era housing campaign is required.

The Housing Construction Drive

The new homes into which people began to move *en masse* by the early sixties were the product of the intensive housing drive undertaken by the Soviet authorities in the late 1950s. Urban development and extensive housing construction was already under way by the middle of the decade, but a step change took place in the scale and style of construction after Khrushchev was confirmed in power. In 1957 an intensive programme for mass housing construction was announced which would inestimably transform the urban landscape and the quality of millions of people's lives by providing small but well-appointed apartments designed not for communal occupancy but for single, nuclear families.[28] The difference was one of scale and style, entailing a shift to industrial, modernist, *Existenzminimum* principles, expressed in

Figure 7.3. Panel building, St. Petersburg (photo by Ekaterina Gerasimova, 2004)

elevations devoid of ornament, small, low-ceilinged apartments, and a maximum height of five storeys to avoid the expense of installing lifts. (Figure 7.3.) The new blocks came to be known as *khrushchevki*. As in post-war Western Europe, where reconstruction and mass housing were also urgent priorities, modernisers in the Soviet architectural and planning establishment, vociferously supported by Khrushchev, recognised that standardisation, type plans, and prefabrication were the means to get the people housed quickly and cheaply.[29] By the Twenty-First Party Congress in January 1959, Khrushchev could make a claim which people could verify against transformations going on around them: 'Our communal ... housing construction is radically transforming the everyday life of many millions of people who receive in their new, beautiful, contemporary dwelling, central heating, a well-equipped kitchen, a gas stove, garbage chute, and hot water supply, bathroom, fitted cupboards, ... and other conveniences.'[30]

The pace and mass scale of this process of mass re-housing were unprecedented. A 1964 account noted that 'the word "housewarming" has become popular in our country'; in the almost ten years since 1956, over one hundred million persons – (almost half the entire population of the Soviet

Figure 7.4. Ivan Semenov, 'The Great Transmigration of Peoples', *Krokodil* (1964)

Union) had moved into new apartments.[31] Put another way, every day people moved into 8,500 new apartments.[32] The satirical magazine *Krokodil* humourously likened this mobility and the accompanying social upheaval to the Great Transmigration of Peoples.[33] Such claims may have been hyperbolic, but the fundamental changes in people's everyday environment and way of life constituted a social dislocation arguably more momentous for most people than such historic events as the Secret Speech.[34] The new housing regions of the Khrushchev era, notorious for having sacrificed aesthetics and monumentality to function and economy, may not generally be counted today among the monuments of world architecture, worthy of preservation orders and heritage status; on the contrary, the *khrushchevki* are widely regarded as a shameful aspect of the Soviet heritage that must be purged as quickly as possible.[35] But as one elderly woman assured me, they are 'monuments in our hearts.'[36]

Representations of Construction and Progress

As housing became a priority and a pitch on which the Khrushchev regime staked its legitimacy at home and abroad, *novosel'e* became a stock genre of Soviet image production. The move to new housing regions, usually from the centre to the periphery of cities, was accompanied by modernist images of a *tabula rasa* and joyous shock of the new. Whereas migration is usually associated with disaster and being condemned to wander forever homeless, this mass relocation was a matter not of being cast out into the wilderness but of *domesticating* the wilderness, finding a home, and settling in.[37] Nevertheless, as I will suggest towards the end, despite the rhetoric—and indeed experience—of happiness, relocation was also a traumatic process, entailing loss of familiar landmarks, certainties, communities and ways of living, and necessitating the abandonment of the material culture of the past. If any remaining material links with family history and repositories of personal memories had survived after decades of upheavals, destruction and loss they were now to be cast away on the tide of progress, left behind in the move to the radiant future.[38]

In pursuit of images of modernity to embody progress and optimism, photojournalists and artists often turned to the margins of the city. There, the process of urbanisation and modernisation was most perceptible, and the reinvigorated ideological commitment to overcoming the backwardness of rural conditions and closing the gap between countryside and city was more convincingly represented than amidst the mud tracks and tumbledown fences of the Russian village.[39] Thus, painter Petr Ossovskii, depicting a small market town (*Market Day*, 1958), suppressed signs of twentieth-century progress; but the same artist's *On the City's Edge* (1957) adopted a 'laconic' modern style to represent this locus as the front line of progress, combined with another symbol of cutting-edge modernity and speed – the racing bike.[40] The narrator of a Moscow television programme 'On the Construction Sites of Moscow' marvelled: 'There, where a year ago there was wasteland and my car got stuck, now good homes rise up and children play in playgrounds and gardens.'[41] The women workers' magazine *Rabotnitsa* also looked to transformations on the edge of the city for the embodiment of urbanisation and, more broadly, progress, thematising them as socialism's civilisation of the wasteland. It described a new apartment house located on the edge of Leningrad in an area still known as New Village: 'And all around, where once there had been the abject margins of Petersburg, where the darkness of the swamp was broken only by an occasional dim light, these new regions now rose up with their bright buildings, schools, crèches, institutes and apartment houses with young gardens and parks.' Out of the swamp had arisen the civilisation of contemporary, socialist Leningrad, bringing enlightenment to the formerly benighted margins of the city.[42]

Housing construction was well suited to provide illustrations of how socialist modernity and technological progress would directly benefit the masses. Prefabrication, mechanisation and standard planning—the thoroughgoing industrialisation of building, which Khrushchev had made mandatory in late 1954—enabled numerous buildings to be erected simultaneously and at great speed, making transformations in the urban landscape dramatically visible. The rapidity of industrialised housing construction provided a particularly vivid and photogenic image of 'the radiant future being constructed in the present day' (to paraphrase part of the definition of Socialist Realism), and was fully exploited by photojournalists, filmmakers and artists. Cranes rising over the city skyline, along with the prefabricated housing blocks mushrooming beneath them as if overnight, manifested the party-state's commitment to make fairy tales come true.

The image of mass housing construction was deployed not only in the internal, Soviet context, but also in international ones to demonstrate the Soviet Union's claim that only under socialism could advanced science and technology be fully applied to creating the best life for the greatest number of people. This was a dominant narrative of the Soviet pavilion at the first World Fair of the Cold War era, Brussels '58, inflecting the fair's umbrella theme, '*Pour un monde plus humain*,' which was expressed in Russian as '*Vse dlia cheloveka*' (Everything For Man).[43] Hovering over the displays was a monumental painting by Aleksandr Deineka, *For Peace* (1958), in which prefabricated panels are depicted being mechanically swung into place to create a new, grand and radiant city, guided by smiling workers with no more exertion than the wave of a hand. Exhibits in the Soviet pavilion included life-size models of furnished apartment interiors and stands with photographs and statistics about the reconstruction of war-damaged cities, and the construction of new mass housing regions, schools and hospitals.[44]

The Soviet Union was not alone in interpreting the 'humanist' theme of Brussels '58 in terms of housing and living standards. The World Fair served as an international forum for competing models of the new dwelling; many countries displayed their national ideals, achievements, aspirations, and models of peaceful, prosperous life, the family and gender relations in the form of model homes.[45] Throughout Europe in the post-war period, the pre-war international modernist project of making people happier and society more rational, harmonious and just by means of built space was revived, with variations. Housing become a common currency for modelling competing visions of a better future.[46] In the context of Cold War competition between the 'Two Camps' of socialism and capitalism—with their declaredly irreconcilable visions of the happy future and routes to attain it—the alternative models of modern living became highly politicised but also cross-fertilised and hybridised.

Marietta Shaginian, reporting from Brussels for Soviet readers, was rapturous about an all-electric house by Belgian architect Jacques Dupuis in the Electricity pavilion in the Belgian section. This showed how atoms could be deployed for peace, their energy put to serve domesticity, to solve all problems of the human dwelling and women's domestic labour, and to provide a life of ease and comfort.[47] Shaginian would be less enthusiastic about another state-of-the-art kitchen a year after Brussels: the fully automated Whirlpool 'Miracle' kitchen demonstrated in Moscow at the

American Exhibition at Sokol'niki in 1959, the Soviet riposte to which served as our starting point. The most notorious Cold War show home was, of course, the model family ranch house displayed at the latter exhibition. There, in the appliance-saturated, lemon yellow General Electric kitchen, Nixon and Khrushchev argued the superiority of their respective systems.[48] The grounds on which Shaginian rejected this model of electricity's miraculous power to make women happy, in the passage cited earlier, were that it presumed and perpetuated a model of women's isolated labour in the home. The Khrushchev regime had officially espoused a solution proposed by Lenin and rooted in nineteenth-century socialist, utopian and feminist thought. It promised to raise living standards while liberating women from 'kitchen slavery' by means of collective consumption and socialised servicing of everyday needs in the form of house kitchens, collective dining, and communal childcare.[49] While United States Information Agency dispatches from the American Exhibition gloated that the American kitchens shown there were set to trigger 'a minor feminine revolution' in Soviet Russia,[50] Soviet official responses such as Shaginian's contrasted the 'liberation' of women promised by 'labour saving' appliances with the opportunities for genuine freedom and self-realisation provided by socialism. As one Soviet visitor wrote in the comments book, far from a route to liberty and happiness, the American kitchen was a sophisticated gilded cage for the housewife. 'The miracle kitchen shown at the exhibition demonstrates America's last word in the field of perfecting obsolete forms of everyday living that stultify women.'[51]

Consumption, American-style, Soviet official and popular discourse around the exhibition reconfirmed, was not a path to freedom and happiness but to bondage and misery.[52] Not only did it enslave the housewife under capitalism, but also the male breadwinner. The misery wrought by the consumerist dream in the lives of ordinary Americans was indicted most compellingly by Americans themselves, the Soviet press pointed out. Arthur Miller's 1948 drama *Death of a Salesman* was currently playing in the Vakhtangov Theatre in Moscow, one of the numerous events that provided a critical frame for the American presence. There, happiness through consumption and family success – the goals pursued by Miller's salesman Willy Loman – are revealed as a chimera the pursuit of which brings tragic consequences. Dramatist Mikhail Shatrov summarised the play. Loman had everything Nixon had bragged of in the American kitchen at Sokol'niki—a car, a house, a refrigerator, a TV. He even had a son called Happy! But he mortgages his life to the American dream, their consumerist aspirations; his family's 'freedom'–from the instalment plan–is bought at the cost of his death… and of their happiness. The play ends with Loman's wife Linda realising the hollowness of this freedom: 'I made the last payment on the house today... and there'll be nobody home. [A sob rises in her throat.] 'We are free and clear. We're free... We're free... We're free...'[53]

The consumer paradise projected by the American Exhibition in Moscow was widely discredited by such exposures. The Soviet media, workplace meetings, and other forums sought to distinguish Soviet domestic bliss from the American dream of consumption, comfort and convenience and to foster a socialist, 'conscious' attitude to the home and material things; not a 'my home is my castle mentality' and consumer fetishism, but rational consumption and the accommodation of individual needs with the long term good of the collective, were the path to a fully human life.[54]

We need to be alert, however, to the contradictions and plural possibilities of this watershed moment around 1959. Notwithstanding protestations that the American dream was 'not for us,' the Soviet approach was much more complex and ambivalent than a simple rejection of the American course. The promised rise in Soviet living standards was explicitly presented in terms of 'catching up with and overtaking America'; this positioned American living standards as the benchmark.[55] While insisting that the Soviet socialist road to high living standards was premised on public services, social security, free healthcare and education, the Soviet Union also entered into direct competition on the territory marked out by the US, including the modern kitchen and mass consumer goods. The Khrushchev regime built single-family apartments with their own kitchens (admittedly quite different and certainly a lot more modest than the American home), increased production of consumer goods for individual, home-based consumption, and appropriated aspects of the iconography of the good life. The seven-year plan adopted in 1959, while promising improved services, also gave greater priority to consumer goods for individual consumption, including furniture, fabrics and wallpaper, and other necessary objects for settling into domestic space. Even though actual outputs fell short of promises, production of radios, cameras and sewing machines tripled from 1953 to 1963, as did that of furniture, while 'labour saving' appliances such as refrigerators, washing machines, and vacuum cleaners were being produced in mass quantities by 1963.[56] Household technology was represented as part of the equipment of the modern Soviet home, and the modern Soviet person—in particular the *khoziaika* (housewife)—was to be a consumer and user of technology in the home as well as in the workplace. Meanwhile, the socialised servicing of everyday life did not become an effective substitute for the 'private' labour of the individual 'housewife'.[57] Thus, as was indicated by the example with which we began, the response to the challenge of happiness, American style, was ambivalent and paradoxical. It is to this paradoxical (and indeed, for some at the time, problematic) centrality of the happy, woman-centred, nuclear family home and consumption in Soviet representations that we shall now turn.

Figure 7.5. Iurii Pimenov, *Wedding on Tomorrow Street* (collection of Tret'iakov Gallery 1962)

Novosel'e in the Separate Apartment and the Birth of the Happy Soviet Family

To represent the relation between the radiant future and the present day in which it was being constructed, Stalinist Socialist Realism had often made use of a stock structuring and symbolic motif, the shining path. It plays this role, for example, in Iurii Pimenov's painting of 1937, *New Moscow*, which aligns women's new freedoms under socialism with technological progress and urban renewal.[58] In the same artist's 1962 painting *Wedding on Tomorrow Street*, the shining path to happiness is still the organising motif, but an indicative reorientation has taken place. Instead of leading away into the distance, it now leads inwards to a new home where, according to the painting's perspectival construction, the viewer is already installed waiting for the newlyweds to arrive; the radiant future is to be lived out in the one-family flat.

Media images of the late 1950s followed the same interiorising trajectory. They 'homed in' from the structures and statistics to the interiors of apartments, following the process of new residents settling in and making the new housing into dwellings. *Novosel'e* was an important narrative device and ritual because it marked the moment when the big, public promises were experienced by individuals in their everyday, personal lives. Thus we can see the ritual of housewarming as a means to interiorise national achievements and the promise of the imminent transition to communism, to bring them 'home': that is, to render abstract statistics and promises immediate and enable the ordinary individual to grasp their implications. The mass move to new apartments was a *collective* transformation, but one that was experienced by individuals; *novosel'e* was a mass celebration that was marked not in public spaces, in the anonymous crowd, but in the relatively autonomous domain of one's own individual family apartment among chosen friends.[59] Conversely, counter to this interiorisation or privatisation, one purpose of the ubiquitous representations of moving house was to inscribe public meanings on it: to keep this private, individual experience within the sphere of public, collective values. Thus *novosel'e* was a device to link public and private, collective and individual.[60]

How to appropriate the new housing? Elsewhere in the project from which this paper is drawn I ask: what did new residents do to their new apartments to transform the given structure of housing—generic, standard built space produced by builders, architects, engineers, and other specialists—into 'home', a lived-in place invested with personal meaning?[61] Here, however, I want to turn the question around and to ask, as Daniel Miller has in his study of domestic material culture *Home Possessions*, about the effects of 'House Agency': that is, what does the house do to the new resident?[62] In the symbolic system of the Khrushchev era, what kinds of transformations is the relocation to the *khrushchevka* supposed to effect on the individual and, ultimately, on society (as the aggregate of millions of individuals undergoing this experience)? It should be emphasised that we are talking here about narrative and representations. A discussion of the actual effects and influence of the built space, plans and material fabric of the house on the individuals who moved in, on their everyday practices, experiences and attitudes must remain aside for other contexts.[63] In the remainder of this chapter I shall elaborate on how the house (comprising both the given material structure of the apartment and the public meanings and values inscribed on it in Soviet representations) does two related things in

Khrushchev-era narratives. First, it effects a life passage, in particular the consummation of conjugal relations: moving into a new one-family apartment is conflated with the arrival of a child that turns a man and woman into a family. Second, it turns the new occupant, especially the wife/mother, into a consumer.

Both effects—production of family and of consumer—are presented as exemplary already in the 1953 feuilleton in *Rabotnitsa* referred to above. It begins with the moment when a new house is unveiled. 'The new house—big, spacious, warm, four storeys high–frees itself from scaffolding. Passers-by glanced at its clean washed windows gleaming in the autumn sunshine and smiled: "there'll be a celebration here in a few days!" '[64] We then watch as the house becomes occupied and animated: arrivals, unpacking, voices, lights appear in windows. First, the charged moment of crossing the threshold (note that the emphasis is on transformation, moving in, rather than on the longue durée of dwelling). On arrival, all the new occupants 'emotionally, with a joyful and even solemn feeling, opened the nice, shiny new lock and entered the apartment'. The threshold, for Mikhail Bakhtin, is the 'chronotope of *crisis* and *break* in a life, connected with life-changing decisions and beginnings'.[65] The *Rabotnitsa* text emphasises newness, unfamiliarity, and the stillness of the new house awaiting occupation. The spacious, tasteful rooms are filled with sunlight and still smell of paint, the parquet gleams, and the snow-white bath is so enticing that some children jump in immediately, fully clothed (perhaps they had never seen a bathtub). In this way, 'New masters took possession of their rooms and apartments.' This process of appropriation extended beyond the walls of the apartment, embracing also the common open ground around it, still littered with builders' debris. Women immediately began to agree about planting flowers there and planned a sandpit for the children.[66]

Children are at the heart of this new life; the first item listed among belongings being delivered is children's beds. These youngsters, destined to become the first citizens of communism according to Khrushchev's promises, would grow up and form their tastes and dispositions in the bright, hygienic, rationally planned spaces of the new housing. The role of the family unit in Soviet society remained a matter of debate in the Thaw, especially, as we have seen, in regard to the question whether it or the collective should be the main site for the servicing of *byt* (daily life) and the upbringing of children.[67] Yet the housing programme promised single-family flats with basic conveniences to all, 'even for newly weds'.[68] The design and allocation of housing on the principle 'one family–one flat' strengthened the family unit in practice, by making it the organising principle of material structures, while the accompanying discourse, with some exceptions, focusing primarily on the individual family flat (rather than the still widespread communal apartment), also reinforced the identification of home and *byt* with the family.

The youngest couple to move in are the Sikorskiis, both workers at the Electric factory, which has built this house for its workers. 'In essence only with the move to the new house did their family life begin: they had not long been married and until this day, while waiting to receive a room, had lived apart.'[69] Only through receiving a one-family flat and crossing the threshold of their new conjugal home are the two individuals conjugated as a family. (Others worked quicker! In the 'happy housewarming' article from *Trud*, 1959, cited above regarding the acquisition of a new rug, the child has already arrived, completing the nuclear family unit which in the accompanying photograph is pictured as a stable triangle: man-wife-child.) *Rabotnitsa* continued: 'All the things which they brought and arranged were brand new, only just bought—just looking at them Lena smiled happily.'[70] The beginning of their happy conjugal life is marked not only by moving into their new home but by the acquisition of shared family possessions and the creation of domestic space. Thus the apartment that conjugates Soviet man and wife as a family also marks their rebirth as consumers and homemakers.

A New Divan: *Novosel'e* and the Birth of the Soviet Consumer

As in this account, the transformative effect of the new apartment was usually personified by a female character. Buying new things for the family home and arranging them is represented as a legitimate source of happiness, particularly for women. One tale of housewarming, however, in the satirical magazine *Krokodil*, 1958, stands out for the fact that the first person narrator and central protagonist is male. We follow the process of his domestication under the influence of comfortable furniture. In this case the answer to the question 'what does the new home do to the Soviet person?'—or more specifically, 'what does the *furniture* do?'—is that it turns him into a family man, domesticates and makes him cultured. 'Listen to what havoc a divan, for instance, can wreak on the human character', he begins.[71]

The narrator receives an apartment for his family. On moving in they find that the enterprise for which he works has installed as a housewarming gift a brand new, stylish divan of the most up-to-date construction, using plastics, which is 'good enough to send to the exhibition in Brussels'. There all the trouble starts, he says, regretting the loss of his masculine freedom to go out drinking with his mate. Instead, he gets drawn into a seemingly endless round of consumption for the home. New needs are generated by the new house and above all by the implant from the factory authorities—the divan. It makes their old furniture look shabby and dated, 'like an old cart next to a new automobile.' His wife and daughter start demanding new furniture. Then they declare that red silk lampshades are so last year and want a chandelier instead. 'They'll be wanting a piano next!' he grumbles. To make matters worse there is nowhere for him to escape to any more because the new apartment is too far from the nearest bar.[72] Instead of going drinking he is forced to take a hot shower, and then, for want of anything better to do, begins to hang curtains.

Meanwhile, the new divan reproaches him: 'You should be ashamed. They organise a new life for you, the state spares no expense on it, you live in a house like this with central heating, gas, and a bathroom! Yet you cling onto your old junk …'[73] He ends up replacing all their old furniture with new, thus modernising his entire everyday environment. And it turns out that he is not the only one to have his head turned in this way; 'the whole housing estate is out shopping. His mate also complains about what the divans they received have done to them. Instead of going drinking after work, as of old, nowadays 'you get home, straight into a hot shower, you drink something homemade, then what? You have to lead a cultured life, listen to the radio. Or read the newspaper on the divan or go to the neighbours to play *kozel*. Such an apartment makes its demands on your behaviour.' In spite of their macho resistance, the divan has made them live in a cultured way, identified here with respectable domesticity. By the end he and his mate even admit that a drink tastes better when consumed in a cultured manner at table in a domestic setting. He has to live up to the house and the divan.

The gender issues raised by this story merit more discussion than can be afforded them here. Consumption and the home are both represented as congenitally female concerns into which the male narrator is drawn in spite of himself.[74] Is this a means to signal his emasculation? Is the point a critique of the consumerism, acquisitiveness, and *meshchanstvo* (petit-bourgeois values) of the wife and daughter?[75] But no! The ironic distance placed between the reader and the narrator —the self-justifying bravado of his tale, as if told to his mates in the pub—makes clear that this domestication is a positive process to which he succumbs in spite of himself. As the reproach of the divan—representing authoritative, public values implanted in 'private' space—indicates, it is not his wife and daughter who are in the wrong with their desire to acquire new consumer goods for the home, but he in resisting it. The gift, which sets standards and imposes obligations, eventually succeeds in turning him into a home-body and a consumer.

The story is characteristic of the *novosel'e* genre in one respect that marks the essential difference between the new consumerism and the earlier identification of *kul'turnost'* (cultured-ness) with possessions. The divan accused the man of attachment to *old* things. People moving into new homes should not drag their old furniture and other domestic items with them. Instead they should make a clean break with the material culture of the past—and by

Figure 7.6. 'New homes – new furniture,' *Ogonek* (1959)

implication with its values too—and start anew, with new things. *Izvestiia* asserted the causal link in the title of a 1959 article cited above: 'New Home: New Life.'[76] Stories of *novosel'e* regularly depicted people turning up at their new homes with little more than a toothbrush. This modernist imperative of purging the past and total renewal was rationalised by reference to the low ceilings, narrow corridors and unadorned lines of the new apartments. The new housing built on rational, modern principles should not be sullied with the accumulated detritus of the past. Old, ornate, solid wood furniture would look incongruous in this new setting. It should be replaced by commensurately modern, rational furniture in the 'contemporary style'.[77]

The corollary of the mass ridding of accumulated and handed-down household items was a mass need to acquire new things. Housing policy was officially recognised as having a direct impact on the demand for consumer goods. For new homes, it was acknowledged, also required furniture, fabrics, and even household technology to equip and furnish them. 'An apartment only becomes a *home* when it is not only well planned, well organised and equipped but also well decorated,' noted the rationale for an exhibition of model interiors and prototype furniture in the new style designed for the new flats in 1961.[78] The celebration of housewarming was an occasion for giving gifts. Indeed, here practice and representation correspond. Recent interviews with tenants who moved into *khrushchevki* soon after they were built indicate that such gifts were not only transient consumables such as flowers, *tort* (gateau), or a bottle of vodka, but durables to set people up in their new homes. They might include expensive and luxury goods such as a vacuum cleaner, electric floor polisher, chandelier or crystal glassware.[79] Thus friends and relations of the lucky house-warmers also became consumers on their behalf.

Fears of Rampant Consumerism and Commodity Fetishism

The mass transformation of Soviet people into homemakers and shoppers celebrated under the rubric of *novosel'e* was not, however, unambiguously a mark of progress towards the inevitable triumph of the socialist system, and, as such, a cause for rejoicing. The shock of the new was a source of anxiety as well as of euphoria. Even official representations reflected, if obliquely, the trauma of upheaval and rupture with familiar surroundings, style, and ways. There was also ideological doubt and dissension over the legitimacy of this course to socialist modernity and happiness, combined with the intelligentsia's traditional and self-definitional disdain for material comforts and acquisitions.

Stories in the *novosel'e* genre often had the following scenario. After the joyful, carefree and sociable celebration of moving in, once the guests have left and the new tenants find themselves alone, anxiety sets in. They begin to realise the enormity of the unfamiliar tasks lying ahead in domesticating this space, making it into a cosy home, and 'living up to it'.[80] The new householder is happy and duly grateful, of course—but *not* carefree. On the contrary, she is bewildered by the decisions and choices she now has, for the first time, to face. New duties, tasks and needs followed close on the heels of the celebration of *novosel'e*: in particular, the obligation to make a cosy but at the same time *modern* home. *Uiut*—cosiness–a central concept of earlier notions of homeyness, remained vital to homemaking in the new flat. There was much discussion of how to create *uiut*, which, in spite of renewed commitment to gender equality under Khrushchev, assumed that this was primarily women's role and responsibility. Thus a mother says to her daughter when they move in: 'Lerochka, we ought to make things cosy: hang curtains and so on.'[81]

However, the concept *uiut* itself was modernised and socialised. 'It is not that *uiut* which is often accompanied by the word "philistine" ('*meshchanskii*'). Comfort, simplicity and elegance distinguish the [contemporary] interiors…'[82] Redefined in modernist terms—austere, functional and hygienic—the new cosiness was explicitly opposed to that of the bourgeois and Stalinist past.[83] The 'new-type of small scale apartment' with its unfamiliar style, plan and dimensions, along with the promised increase in the quantity and choice of consumer goods for individual and family use, was supposed to de-skill ordinary people in the art and science of everyday living. It required them to learn anew, to espouse new practices and criteria of cosiness and good housekeeping. Thus it supposedly created an urgent need for education and advice from a range of specialists on how to furnish, decorate and dwell in it. *Izvestiia's* article 'New Home: New Life' argued the need to develop the discipline of *domovodstvo*, domestic science, 'to teach how best to furnish [the new apartment] to make it more *uiutno* (cosy) to live in'. For, 'rational nutrition, knowledge of how to dress comfortably and beautifully, and how to furnish one's apartment: all this has to be taught'.[84]

Novosel'e and settling into one's new flat was a theme of much early television programming, as this new medium expanded and as ownership of television sets spread in the late 1950s and early 1960s. Broadcasts with titles such as 'For Family and Home' or 'Help for the Housewarmer' represented this as the common or 'typical' experience of the present day, presuming their viewers were either already watching from a new flat, or dreaming of receiving one soon, or at very least had friends and relatives who had already shared in this mass pleasure. Allegedly (and quite possibly in fact) in response to readers' and viewers' demand, television as well as the popular press offered women instruction on how to arrange furniture, choose elements of decoration, and find an appropriate colour scheme.[85] New consumer goods created new civic tasks and responsibilities for the housewife: they imposed the duty of rational consumption and correct choice. Advice was often a matter of informing potential consumers about goods produced (and potentially available) and how to choose; teaching them to make wise and tasteful purchases – that is, to be skilled consumers. The degree of abundance and choice available in the early 1960s was often exaggerated. According to the architect presenter of one television programme on home furnishing: 'Many of us, when we receive a new apartment, want to change the colour of the walls or put up wallpaper, all the more since now in Moscow you can get any kind of wallpaper you want. But, comrades! – in buying wallpaper it is necessary to make the correct choice of colour, pattern and texture.... [for] "everyone must become an artist in their home!" '[86] People do not passively move in, or 'consume' the apartment as a ready-made, fully finished commodity, it is assumed. Rather, they actively make the standard space into home through their purchases and aesthetic decisions. There was also some acknowledgement that choosing and arranging things for the new home was a semiotic process; it was an exercise in self-expression, whereby one could inscribe one's individuality upon the walls and plan of new apartments and make the standard architecture personally meaningful and communicative of self-image and status.[87]

Not-So-Happy-Housewarming: The 'Great Transmigration' as Regress from Modern Civilisation to Barbarism

Alongside the dominant theme of 'Happy Housewarming' there were also variations in the minor key in the genre of the 'fly in the ointment', under titles such as 'The Spoilt Housewarming' ('*Omrachennoe novosel'e*' or '*Chem ogorchen novosel*'). In such tales (and in practice) new residents' joy on moving into a newly built apartment turned rapidly to disenchantment and anger as shoddy workmanship and structural faults became apparent, as Steven Harris has explored, and as many of my informants narrate. There was much press coverage of problems with the new housing and failures of quality control. Window frames did not fit, roofs leaked, parquet squeaked, the walls had not been plastered, or the plumbing and gas were not yet installed.[88]

Some accounts inverted the theme of *novosel'e* as progress towards culture, modernity and communist consciousness. Instead of providing more up-to-date, mechanised, rational modern living, the move to new residential regions plunged new residents back into the dark ages. A cartoon from *Krokodil* ironically entitled 'Happy Housewarming!' (G. Ogorodnikov, 1966) hyperbolizes this regression to pre-modern ways of survival, showing people reduced to fetching water in buckets and cooking over campfires outside their new apartments that were supposedly fitted with all mod cons. *Un*-happiness resulting from lack of amenities and infrastructure in the new housing regions was humourously illustrated by another cartoon in *Krokodil*. A man huddles on the floor of an empty flat he is about to vacate, clinging to the telephone and weeping. The caption runs: 'Lucky fellow, he got a new apartment and he's moving!—Then why is he grieving?—He's bidding farewell to the telephone.'[89]

162 — С новосельем!
    — И вас также...

Figure 7.7. German Ogorodnikov, 'Happy 'Housewarming!' *Krokodil* (1966)

There were also more profound anxieties and ambivalence associated with Soviet people's mass transition to homemaking and consumer modernity: fears that people would try to reproduce retrograde, unhygienic, 'petit-bourgeois' forms of cosiness in their new homes, or bring their pre-modern and rural tastes with them. Above all, there were fears concerning the potential privatisation of life and rise of commodity fetishism.[90] 'The hypertrophy of interest in the individual dwelling is inclined to engender an antisocial, anticommunist mindset', warned philosopher Karl Kantor.[91] Others condemned the idea of home 'as an island where one could build one's personal (*lichnuiu*) life "as I like"'.[92] From this perspective, provision of one-family flats and the need for tenants to acquire commodities to furnish them required special measures, lest Soviet homes slide into fetishism and regressive, patriarchal relations and so come to resemble the petit-bourgeois private sphere. Kantor and other reformist publicists sought to delimit a socialist attitude towards the new, one-family apartments, and to distinguish this attitude from a philistine 'home-is-my-castle' mentality. Nevertheless, they also legitimated the principle of one-family flats and the promised new opportunities for consumption, explicitly distancing themselves in this regard from the extreme asceticism of the 1920s, when 'the struggle for the new way of life (*novyi byt*), against the old bourgeois-philistine way of life (*byt*) at times took on the form of a struggle against material comforts in everyday life, against the striving to have a separate apartment and make it comfortable (*zanimat'sia blagoustroistvom*)'.[93] But, Kantor wrote: 'No-one today would dream of accusing a person of betraying revolutionary ideals by taking an interest in how to furnish an apartment in a new building comfortably and beautifully.' Thus, one-family flats were not, in principle, counter-revolutionary, he pleaded, and concern with furnishing and decorating them was not bourgeois fetishism.

The mixture of euphoric embrace of new domestic space and its attendant new experiences with anxiety and doubt is conveyed in Daniil Granin's novel *After the Wedding* (*Posle svad'by*, 1959), as Christine Varga-Harris has pointed out.[94] Housewarming is not solely a source of unalloyed happiness; once the honeymoon period is over, it can also lead to corruption.

The novel opens with recently married Tonia's joy in the privacy of her new apartment, the couple's autonomy of action and insulation from surveillance.

> But its greatest merit was the walls. Neither the ceiling, gleaming white with a ceiling rose in the centre, nor the glossy yellow of the parquet gave so much joy as these four thick, soundproof walls. They staunchly protected from the gaze of others, allowing the occupants to jump, muck around, to say all sorts of silly things, to look one another in the eyes.[95]

Filled with a sense of their happiness and good fortune, the first thing the young couple do is to take possession of their new domain. 'Hand in hand they set off on a journey' from the corner of the room around the new flat that still creaked and smelled of its newness.[96]

The inexperienced housewife constantly has accidents in the kitchen. But she is happy! In the hostel from which they had moved she had had to do the same chores, but here it is different because the kitchen is her own sovereign domain: 'Here she lived with a feeling of irrepressible happiness in the possession of this room, the kitchen, into which no inspector was about to look, and where everything was her own. To command in the small, clean kitchen, to boil, fry, to buy, to cut scalloped semicircular napkins out of paper; she had not yet got used to all these joys.'[97] But already her enthusiasm for cutting scalloped napkins suggests—at least to readers today, familiar with Vera Dunham's analysis of 'middleclass values' in post-war Stalinist literature and public discourse—that the transformation effected in the heroine by the attainment of private space and becoming a consumer-housewife is not unambiguously commendable.[98] Is she being seduced by a petit-bourgeois desire for private property and consumer goods? Does this mark her fall from grace?

Granin traces how settling into the new apartment turns Tonia into an avid consumer. At first the newly-weds have nothing (this was common in popular experience as my interviews suggest), not even coat-hangers, and the heroine is oppressed and bewildered by the burden of needing to acquire so many things. (Furnishing and equipping the home is unquestionably her responsibility). But once she starts shopping she is seduced by the allure of commodities, turning into an enthusiastic and often irrational, spontaneous shopper.

> She accused herself of being greedy, called herself philistine, petit-bourgeois … (*meshchankoi, obyvatel'nitsei…*) Indeed she was happy in her empty, unfurnished room. She even liked her disregard for all kinds of rags. But once she got into a shop, surrounded by the gleaming newness of things, she forgot about everything, aroused by the desire to have all these beautiful things. Not for herself – for the home. She was prepared to do without food, clothes, to economise on everything. The temptation was too great, she could not restrain herself and each time bought some trifle. The unforeseen acquisitions destroyed all her accounts and plans, but she experienced an incomparable pleasure walking along the street with bags and parcels, and above all, at home when all this tumbled out onto the table.[99]

Irrationality and spontaneity traditionally had no place in the make up of the Soviet person, who was supposed to be guided by reason and consciousness. The shopaholic Tonia appears to have been corrupted by her taste of consumption-knowledge. Like Eve, she also seduces her new husband. Her shopping trips turn into something like a sexual game. Returning with her purchases concealed in their packaging she loves to tease him with the process of unwrapping her new acquisitions before him, creating a tension between concealing and revealing that borders on fetishism. Her husband Igor' even notices that she has started to smell different although he never sees her putting on perfume.

Is this the scent of corruption? What does Tonia's seduction by the Soviet consumer paradise mean? Is this a fall from grace and innocence? Or is it a new stage of Soviet modernity, socialism on a higher level?[100]

Figure 7.8. Late Stalinist domestic interior, Ethnographic Museum, Sillamae, Estonia (photo by Dmitrii Sidorov, 2004)

That Tonia might indeed be becoming petit-bourgeois is indicated when one of her parcels falls open to reveal the orange silk dome of a lampshade. (Fig. 7.8) Igor' recalls how, only the evening before, Tonia had insisted that to buy a lampshade was a luxury – they could make one themselves from coloured paper. 'But now, seeing Tonia's happy face and her eyes sparkling with laughter, he was convinced that the lampshade was indeed a good thing and it would have been impossible not to buy it.' A weak character, he is seduced and becomes an accomplice, applying his engineering expertise to hanging the lampshade so that it can be raised and lowered, to be 'totally chic!'[101]

We have already encountered the red or orange silk lampshade in the divan story as a sign of the regressive taste and attachment to old things that needed to be purged with the move to the new apartment. The changing status of such lampshades, as Dunham showed, marked changing notions of cultured living or good taste. In the Khrushchev era they became firmly identified with the regressive, philistine taste of the past – whether Stalinist or pre-revolutionary. Nevertheless, Granin is not so categorical in his judgement of Tonia's style gaffes but leaves the reader in uncertainty and confusion as to the relation between taste and socialist morality, consumption and modernity.

Conclusion

With this confusion we should end, for the contradictions will not readily resolve themselves into a conclusion. Uncertainty and disorientation were characteristic of this age of flux and transformation. As I have argued, home and home-based consumption were as central to the image of Soviet modernity, progress, and the promise of universal happiness as in the capitalist West, even if the nature of the domestic bliss promised was not always identical. Visual images and discourse widely represented the family home, homemaking, and consumption for the home as a key site and source of happiness, Soviet style. In Khrushchev-era narratives, mass housewarming is at once the symbolic moment of accession to happiness, not just for a few but for millions, and the key moment in the process by which, both discursively and in practice, the 'New Soviet Person' became a modern consumer.[102] But happiness was contradictory, especially for the new Soviet woman, torn between different models of socialist modernity and femininity. The proliferation of images and narratives predicating Tonia and Zinaida's happiness on the home and acquisition of consumer goods reconfirmed, just as Shaginian had complained about the American kitchen, women's identification with the production and reproduction of the domestic sphere. Moreover, ambivalence about the legitimacy of consumption and the nature of domesticity played out both in representations of home and in people's actual practices of furnishing and dwelling in the new flats.

Chapter Eight

WHEN WE WERE HAPPY: REMEMBERING SOVIET HOLIDAYS

Albert Baiburin and Alexandra Piir

Happiness in Russian Culture: Introductory Remarks

The specificity of the concept of happiness in Soviet culture is best understood against the background of how this concept was traditionally interpreted in Russian culture.[1] Vladimir Dahl's authoritative dictionary of the Russian language, first published in 1863, accorded two meanings to the word. The primary meaning is given as 'success, lucky chance, something unforeseen but desirable'.[2] The secondary meaning refers to 'happiness' in the sense that this word would be used in English—'bliss and the complete fulfilment of one's wishes'.[3] While a number of articles published recently have dealt with the place of *schast'e* in the Russian linguistic world-picture in terms of its 'semantic universals', so to speak,[4] these seem to have left out something of fundamental importance to the understanding of the word: what one might term the 'metaphysics of happiness' in Russian tradition.

As has often been noted, both nexuses of meaning are derived from concepts of fortune and fate, one's 'portion'. The basic morphological and semantic component of the word *schast'e* is easy to identify—*chast'* (a piece or portion of something, cf. *uchast'*, 'fate'). The prefix *s'* (съ-) with reduced vowel has been identified as originally meaning 'good, kind', which means that the whole word can be interpreted as meaning 'kind fate', 'good fortune'.[5] As recently as the nineteenth century, the words *chast'* and *schast'e* were interchangeable, as in expressions such as *svoei chasti (uchasti, schast'ya) ne minuesh'* ('you can't escape your fate'); *chas pridet i chast' (dolyu, schast'e) prineset* ('the hour will come and bring your fate'); *siden' sidit, a chast' (dolya) ego rastet* ('he's rooted to the spot but his fate is waxing'), and so on.[6]

In the late nineteenth century, A. A. Potebnya noted that according to Russian folk beliefs, 'there exists on this earth a finite quantity of happiness and unhappiness, sickness, good and evil, without there being excess in anything. If one person falls sick, that means he has been overtaken by a sickness that has quit or killed off someone else.'[7] Just so, if someone has been overtaken by good luck or happiness, then that means someone else has been overtaken by the opposite (*schast'e perekhodya zhivet*, 'good luck/happiness moves around').

From these assumptions about the fortuitous and finite nature of happiness in turn flow several other important propositions: First, there exists such a thing as 'happiness in sum', the happiness of everyone collectively; second, the 'extent' or 'quantity' of this happiness in sum is defined or fixed in advance, so to speak—its extent is non-negotiable; third, a good many sources suggest that an idiosyncratic principle of compensation or supplementation is in operation, i.e., the precise amount of happiness that has vanished in one place will reappear in another.[8] In addition, this principle applies not just to happiness / luck / fate, but to everything that can be measured. It follows logically from these principles that God does not increase the sum of human happiness, but simply regulates the way it is disposed. Consider the proverb *Bog ne gulyaet, a dobro peremeryaet* ('God does not move about/mess about, he divides and re-divides the good things of life'). He cannot increase or reduce the total quantity of happiness, but he can assign more or less to a given person. Everyone will be assigned their own portion of happiness and unhappiness. Everyone has their fate. And in turn, the idea of a variety of different manifestations of happiness/unhappiness in different individuals is, one might say, built into the basic concept of the nature of happiness. Also notable is the fact that the traditional concept of happiness placed a high value on the welfare of the group overall (if X was unhappy, the fact that Y was happy offered some consolation), and the fact that the notion of personal responsibility for happiness (as expressed in, say, recent Western advice literature about 'how to be happy', etc.) had no place at all in Russian traditional culture.

It was precisely with regard to diversification that concepts of happiness evolved over time. In other words, from the notion that there exist many different ways of being happy, developed the widespread idea that every person has his or her own individual concept of happiness. At first sight this idea seems to have empirical as well as theoretical value, but one ought to bear in mind that the totality of 'modes of happiness' within a given cultural tradition is constrained in practice. Individual concepts of happiness have to be integrated with those held by other members of society to have a general significance (in however limited a sense)—for otherwise, personal concepts of happiness would be meaningless; the phenomenon could simply not be named at all.[9]

Research on the usage of the word *schast'e* in Russian literature and journalism, carried out by S. G. Vorkachev, A. P. Zalyaleeva and others,[10] confirms that existing perceptions of happiness may be assigned to a typology (and this despite the profusion of idiosyncratic visions and representations of happiness that one finds in literature, especially poetry). Elements relevant to this typology include the localisation of happiness (whether this is seen to inhere in a person or be exogenous to him or her); the link between happiness and tranquillity on the one hand, or activity on the other; the ways by which happiness is acquired; and so on. The prevailing concepts of happiness are in turn generated by combinations of these various different elements. For instance, a formula such as *prostoe chelovecheskoe schast'e* [ordinary human happiness, roughly 'nice, normal happiness'—] assumes that happiness is located in the world at large and that people ought to value what they have, because otherwise they may only realise what it means when they have lost it. Here, happiness is associated with tranquillity, with the general order of things, with serendipity, the capacity to find delight in the ordinary: 'Happiness is everywhere. Maybe there it is: / That autumn garden back behind the shed / That pure air, pouring through the window,' as Ivan Bunin wrote in his poem 'Evening' (1909).[11] This 'epicurean' concept of happiness (as one might describe it) exists alongside a 'stoic' conception, according to which happiness is located within people themselves, in their capacity to stick to the path of virtue and not succumb to temptation, to create a state in which happiness is possible without reference to external circumstances. In the words of Pushkin's contemporary Evgeny Baratynsky, 'But the real kind of happiness / Is nowhere but in ourselves.'[12] Another very widespread notion— most famously in the poetry of Alexander Pushkin himself—is the idea that happiness simply does not exist, or that its existence is an illusion. One of Pushkin's most famous poems begins, 'There is no happiness on earth, but only peace and liberty;' another refers to happiness's 'devious shade'.[13] There are many other less-well-known concepts of happiness as well.[14] Of all the varieties of intellectual baggage associated with happiness, the most influential in the Soviet period was a high-Romantic conception that linked happiness with struggle, passion and self-immolation towards the good of a higher ideal, as in Pushkin's epistle to Alexander Chaadaev: 'My friend, have faith: she will arise / The star of captivating happiness / And on the shards of autocracy / Others will scratch our names.'[15] As these few quotations illustrate, Pushkin's own concepts of happiness were contradictory—but it was only the last, about the 'star of captivating happiness', that found its way into Soviet textbooks.[16]

Popular literature such as advice tracts also played a role in developing concepts of happiness among a wide audience. Even the titles of such publications are suggestive: *Happiness is Being Satisfied with What You Have and Knowing How to Use God's Gifts*; *Happiness and Wealth, Health and Strength: Cheap Dishes for the Lenten Table*; *Happiness in Life: Get Everyone to Love You*; *Happiness through Health*; *How to Have a Happy Family Life*; *A Happy Life Right into a Ripe Old Age—Keeping Your Nerves Healthy and Strong*.[17] Readers were being nudged in the right direction, told in the most literal way what to do so they could be happy. Here, it was concrete things—physical and moral health, the family and family values—that were held to be at the root of happiness. Such ideas also played a role in the Soviet era, though in a more muted way than Romantic notions of the 'struggle for happiness'.

Life has Become More Joyful: The Contours of the New Happiness

The various 'experiments with happiness' were carried out upon this foundation in the Soviet period. The earlier picture of an infinite variety of different levels and types of happiness was simplified and standardised as never before, while at the same time the idea of happiness as 'collective' and 'assigned' persisted. One could say that happiness was reduced to a kind of social 'common denominator' that levelled individual discrepancies in the concept of happiness, producing an enormous synthesis, a kind of 'state-sponsored view of licit happiness', as it were. Highly indicative in this sense are the final sentences of Arkady Gaidar's famous story for Soviet children, *Chuk and Gek*, first published in 1939: 'What happiness was, everyone understood for himself or herself. But at the same time everyone also knew that they had to live honest lives, to work hard and to love and cherish that huge happy land that was called the Country of the Soviets.'

The discussion in this essay will focus on the new concept of happiness that came into being in the age of high Stalinism. The concept of happiness that was framed at that point proved tenacious enough to survive de-Stalinisation into the late Soviet period—indeed, it is still relevant at the present time. One could say that the 'canons of Soviet happiness' were laid down in this era. They were propounded from above—by the Party leadership, and by the Soviet artistic establishment, or to be more accurate, by their members, writers, artists and film directors, who not only sensed the 'demands of the epoch' (what was referred to at the First Congress of Soviet Writers as 'the social command'[18]) but were prepared to respond to these and to communicate them to the Soviet masses in accessible artistic form.

At this point, several questions arise that are directly germane to the issue of how 'Stalinist happiness' was defined and to the issue of the way that definitions of happiness changed over time.

Where does happiness come from, or alternatively, who assigns happiness?

In traditional culture, the assigner of happiness, as mentioned earlier, is God. Under the Stalinist regime, God's functions were transferred to Stalin himself, who, famously modest, was pleased to occasionally allow the Party or state (or the Motherland) to figure in this role as well. As a matter of fact, 'Stalin', 'Party' and 'state' functioned as synonyms—as in expressions of gratitude such as 'Thank You, Stalin, for Our Happy Childhood!' 'Thank You, Motherland and Party!' (The reason behind the gratitude was a secondary consideration.) The full formula ('Thank You, Stalin, Motherland and Party…') supplies all three hypostases of the Leader.[19]

How is happiness achieved?

In Christian tradition, God is the regulator of happiness, and the ways of Providence are unknown to ordinary mortals. Accordingly, the process by which happiness is achieved also remains mysterious. Happiness can be the lot not just of a person who is obviously worthy of it, but also of a person who does not (in the eyes of other human beings) appear to deserve it. What is mysterious is understood in turn as fortuitous: chance is so undependable that it is perfectly possible for someone worthy to benefit; yet on the whole, the unworthy appear to benefit more often (increasing the sense that chance cannot be predicted in advance). This perception of events means that the assignation of happiness is associated as strongly with chance as it is with God (or indeed more strongly with chance: cf. the central place of this force in Russian tradition, right up to the level of personification—*ego velichestvo sluchai* (His Majesty Chance) presiding over happiness (*happy chance*)).

Of course, this situation placed in sharp focus the issue of justice in the disposal of happiness, an issue resolved by the idea of posthumous rewards for virtue. One of the most widespread views of happiness was that those who were most deserving would not receive their reward on this earth. They would, however, be admitted to bliss and glory after their lives came to an end, in compensation for what they had failed to receive in the material world. This is not to say that well-merited earthly happiness was not held to exist at all, but it was taken to be much rarer than fortuitous happiness, on the one hand, and just rewards achieved posthumously on the other.

None of these established ways of achieving happiness—by chance, or according to the will of Providence, or in the afterlife—fit the new situation, where Stalin was the new regulator of happiness. Like everything else in Soviet society, happiness was supposed to function according to a particular set of rules—the Leader's own. Happiness, therefore, had to be not a matter of chance, but of fixed principles: everyone benefiting according to their deserts. In practice, though, establishing exactly who deserved what (despite the pervasiveness of surveillance in Soviet society) proved rather too complicated and demanding. It was a good deal easier to bestow happiness on 'the Soviet people' in general. But how was happiness to be arranged in socio-economic conditions that were, to put it mildly, often less than ideal? The simple way out was to retain and foster the traditional view of happiness as a category of collective rather than individual significance, but to realise this in a way that was useful to the new society.

Whether private individuals actually were happy was a matter of indifference, so far as the Soviet government was concerned; no interest was taken in this question. Happiness acquired an absolute significance: 'universal happiness'; the happiness of all working people, of the world proletariat, of the Soviet population generally. Happiness was evoked with reference to concrete individuals only where these individuals expressed an ideal of overall significance—for instance, if a person considered himself or herself happy to 'die in the struggle for universal happiness' (this formula was extremely widespread in the Stalin era). The now widely used formula 'I wish you happiness in your private life' (as employed when wishing people a happy New Year, for example) dates from the post-Stalin era and was especially characteristic of the years under Brezhnev and later.

In general, the sphere of the personal and private was compressed, in Stalinist culture, to the absolute minimum. The entire person, emotions and all (including happiness and the reasons for this), was supposed to be on view. The proper Soviet person had nothing to hide. Only someone out of sympathy with Soviet power could possibly feel such a need. At the same time, this official view did not signify that the private sphere did, in fact, vanish completely. On the contrary—for at least some members of Soviet society (the so-called 'internal émigrés' in the intelligentsia), this sphere acquired an unprecedented symbolic importance, and people made much bigger efforts to keep it from sight than they had in previous eras.[20]

The content of universal, suprahuman happiness

Thus, it was enough for someone to be a Soviet citizen and to live in the Soviet Union to experience universal happiness. This was 'happiness by passport', so to speak. Those who enjoyed this privileged access to happiness in an overall sense were in turn able to enjoy happiness at various subsidiary levels: dying for the Motherland, or (a less elevated, but still worthy and useful version of the same fate) labouring tirelessly for the benefit of the nation. In times of peace, it was especially the latter destiny (the happiness of labour) that inspired Soviet artists and writers. In 1994, an exhibition entitled 'Agitating for Happiness' was organised at the Russian Museum in St Petersburg and displayed a range of enormous canvases commemorating the official 'social optimism' of the 1930s and 1950s: Vasily Efanov's group portrait of Stakhanovites and Soviet Wunderkinder *The Aristocrats of the Land of the Soviets*, Yury Pimenov's *Physical Culture Parade*, Alexander Gerasimov's *Hymn to October*, and so on. Such scenes of heroic life and labour were also depicted in countless posters dating from the Stalin era. It would be fair to say that calls to be happy were produced on an industrial scale.[21]

Such calls to happiness did not of course suggest that the path to bliss was open here and now. Happiness was firmly located in the future—which in turn was invariably referred to by such adjectives as 'bright' or 'happy'. Thus, Soviet happiness was a typical example of so-called 'deferred happiness'. This might, indeed, be described as the central idea of Communism as understood under Soviet power: universal happiness will arrive at some (unspecified) point later on, but for now everyone has to expend all their energy in ensuring the arrival of the bright future. In other words, it was assumed that only the descendants of those living in the Stalin era, and not these people themselves, would live in a society of peace, perfection, plenty and brotherly love. It was precisely universal happiness that would triumph in the Soviet heaven, and that meant that all previous versions of happiness (whether emerging from chance or as the reward for virtue) would simply dissolve. And happiness itself would be different; 'real', of a kind unknown before the Soviet period (which meant, by extension, that what was termed 'happiness' before the Soviet Union existed was actually not happiness at all. In the past, people had either known full well they were miserable—the case with peasants and workers— or they had been living a lie).

The Soviet Union spent more than 70 years constructing its 'bright future', but the longer the building went on, the further away the future seemed to get (in practice, if not in theory).[22] At the same time, these utopian ideals represented, for many Soviet people, their sole motivation and meaning in life. 'We aren't living too well, yes, but our children will be able to live better, and their children will be happy in the full sense of the word'—that was the conventional attitude.[23] It is no accident that in the years after the construct of inevitable happiness fell apart, many members of the older generation began feeling that life had disintegrated.[24] Once the Soviet system collapsed, people lost what had constituted the main meaning of life for them—belief that miracles could happen.

Once again, this has deep cultural roots: in Russian Orthodoxy, far more emphasis is placed on Christ's Resurrection and on the Second Coming than on the Crucifixion (in Western Christianity since the late medieval era, the opposite has been the case). One reason why the Communist view of happiness was so readily accepted is that it constituted a modulation of the accustomed belief in miraculous events. That said, according to the Leader's vision of things, happiness was supposed to descend steadily and predictably (while miraculous events are by definition unpredictable)—but then people were also used to the fact that there was a gulf between visions and their enactment.

The 'bright future' was like a monster from fable; it needed human sacrifices. Accordingly, it was essential to be ready to sacrifice oneself at a moment's notice. The idea of 'happiness through sacrifice' was not simply a motto ('we'll all die as one / in the struggle for it'), but underpinned the entire strategy for raising the growing generations. After the publication of Nikolai Ostrovsky's *How the Steel was Tempered* (the first full edition appeared in 1935), Pavka Korchagin, the book's hero, became a model for many generations of Soviet young people. There was an unvarying schema for school essays on the topic 'My Understanding of Happiness'. First you had to set down how Pavka had understood happiness (i.e., happiness is being involved in the struggle for righteousness, in which you had to lay down your strength and your life for the cause), followed by your own understanding (which, of course, was supposed to be exactly like Pavka's). Educational websites on the Internet still provide model essays on the topic 'How Pavel Korchagin Understood Happiness and How I Understand It.' One such begins thus:

> I'm happy because I have a Motherland for which I am fearlessly prepared to lay down my strength and my life… I have the strength to educate myself and to work, my hands are not tied, I can fight for my ideal, no one shall break the wings that have been given to me by my native land so that I can create and love.

And so on it goes. Finally, we get to the epilogue:

> Pavel Korchagin surrendered his youth so that I could be happy. My duty is to sacrifice all my strength so that my children are happy. That is where my happiness lies![25]

David Samoilov's 1935 diary, published as 'Diary of a Happy Boy', employs similar rhetoric. His entry of 12 October reads: 'My dearest dream is death for our country, for my ideal. I am joining the Komsomol and if war breaks out I will be the first to go to the Front, to fight till victory is ours. So what if I'm young! The children of the Paris Commune fought just like the adults did, after all!'[26]

Many have noted the following paradox: at exactly the point at which the prison camps are bursting at the seams and the largest political purge the world has ever known has just been launched, a swathe of unprecedentedly cheery film comedies appear (*The Merry Lads* (1934—the first smash hit Soviet film comedy; *Circus* (1936) and *Volga Volga* (1938)). Songs of the day—most famously, *Song of the Motherland*, the central set piece in *Circus*—were in the same vein:

A spring wind blows over the land.
Every day life grows more joyous.
No one in the world is able
To laugh and love like us!

Writing from the set of *The Merry Lads*, at Gagry on the Black Sea, the film's cameraman observed: 'The film is utter trash, you couldn't miss that for a moment, but it'll be a smash hit.' However, as the journalist Elena Kiseleva has recently noted, the film's script-writer, the dramatist Nikolai Erdman, 'was not able to enjoy the fruits of success. He was arrested in Gagry,'[27] and later was exiled to Siberia, returning to Moscow only in 1951.

We now come to the delicate, and at some level unanswerable, question of the impact of Soviet realia on happiness—not just in the sense of how far people believed in the official ideal of happiness, but of how far it was possible to believe in happiness of any kind (and even to be happy at all), given the real circumstances of Soviet life. So far as the official ethos of Soviet happiness itself was concerned, realia did not constitute a problem, since it was in any case designed to conceal these. Being happy was the civil duty of every Soviet person. It follows that, in this sense, being happy expressed loyalty to the state and to the political status quo.

The second, and far more difficult, question concerns the extent to which happiness in the ordinary sense, happiness as it would be understood in other societies, was compatible with the repressive nature of Stalinist society. In the end, only those who lived through that time can provide an answer. In her preface to David Samoilov's 1935 diary, his widow Galina Medvedeva-Samoilova (born in 1938) writes, '...happiness can come about, and it does come about in times that seem, objectively speaking, totally black, and that's one possible answer to the question often asked today: "How on earth did you live during the Terror, the War, the Period of Stagnation, and so on?" '[28] Emma Gershtein, born in 1903, recalled that the sense of disaster could sometimes increase the feeling of happiness, rather than undermining it: 'When catastrophe is imminent, you are somehow seized by a sense of happiness. For example, on the night of 22 June 1941 I had an extraordinary, blissful dream.'[29] For other historical subjects alive at this time, the sense of terror and the sense of happiness were not so much mutually reinforcing as inseparable. The high points of happiness were inextricably associated with the extremes of terror (one might compare the frequently occurring trope of the 'feast in time of plague', as found, for example, in the late poetry of Mandelstam). As Evgeny Evtushenko wrote in his poem, 'Stalinist Happiness,' people felt 'tiny joys in the face of huge disaster', and felt them more often than one might imagine.

When We Were Happy

The two types of happiness prevailing under Soviet power—the official version set out in ideology and the personal, unofficial variety—came together in an especially complex way in the *gosudarstvennyi prazdnik* (official state holiday).[30] There were, of course, other sites in Soviet culture where individual happiness was free to merge with collective happiness, but the holiday was probably the only context in which the two kinds of happiness regularly coexisted.[31] The fusion came about not simply because the state holiday had two separate parts—official (the demonstration) and unofficial (the family celebration)—but for other reasons as well. First, there was a long-standing and persistent tradition that dictated that holidays were a time during which 'collective happiness' was assigned in a different and fairer way than in ordinary life. It was customary both in cities and in the countryside, before 1917, to ask beggars into your home on religious holidays and to offer them hospitality and gifts. The idea was that these were days when everyone was supposed to enjoy their portion of happiness, and when that portion was supposed to be the same for everyone. Thus, collective happiness on such days worked on egalitarian lines. Second, during holidays everything was 'on view', 'in front of people'. This made it impossible to indulge in undeserved happiness or good fortune—it would be roughly the same as wearing a stolen medal (disgraceful and certain to be found out). At holidays, like it or not, people exposed their personal happiness to public judgement. And every holiday guaranteed everyone the chance to be happy—if only because everyone had the chance to participate in the general holiday atmosphere. Conversely, people who did not take part in the general celebrations attracted suspicion. They probably had some way of being happy by themselves, some dishonest way, some secret way. These two perceptions of the holiday—as an egalitarian event and one where a public display of propriety was essential— were to acquire a highly specific resonance under Soviet power.

The remainder of our essay examines the Soviet holiday and its links with happiness, drawing for the most part on semistructured interviews conducted with ten informants (five female, five male) now in their late 60s and 70s (dates of birth range from 1927 to 1940).[32] They come from a variety of social backgrounds—working-class, state official, military, Soviet intelligentsia.

All except one were born in Leningrad or moved there in early childhood. All of them were living in Leningrad during the period described—the postwar decades—and all received an extended education (including not just secondary, but also higher education). All later held white-collar or administrative positions, or were in the professions (that is, they were members of the intelligentsia). One of the informants is a former Party worker and 'responsible official', several others were Party members, though without holding office; one held firm anti-Soviet views from an early age (he describes himself as a former dissident). They are accordingly all representatives of the well-educated urban population, i.e., members of the social layer that was the primary target of Soviet propaganda about happiness, while Leningrad itself, the 'cradle of the Revolution', was one of the two most important centres for demonstrations in the entire Soviet Union (the other, of course, being Moscow).[33]

As many previous discussions of oral history have emphasised,[34] what people remember about events is partial and fragmentary, and strongly influenced by later experience (which here includes the festivals introduced since Soviet power collapsed, felt by many older people to be 'inauthentic'). All of these elements characterise the oral testimony cited here, too. However, the question of the 'authenticity' of this testimony in a factual sense is not of direct concern to us, since our primary aim is to establish the emotional resonance of Soviet holidays for those who participated in them, and not to catalogue 'what actually happened' at such festivals. We have, therefore, not offered commentaries on the factual accuracy or otherwise of the testimony cited, concentrating on what it reveals about informants' recollections of the past, and the role of this in their world view.

People always react to holidays in terms of everyday life; holidays are seen as both interrupting and counterpointing it. In other words, nearly everything about a holiday is unusual, as linguistic usage in Russian makes clear, opposing *budni* (ordinary days, working days) to *prazdniki* ('days of idleness'). The exceptional character of the holiday was especially clear under Soviet power; these were days on which, for a short time, the hardship of everyday life, the generally run-down and chaotic nature of workaday existence could be forgotten for a short while. This 'forgetting' also applies to the interviews; while implicitly present as a background to holidays, hardships are rarely mentioned directly, and mainly when some aspect of the holiday itself would be inexplicable without mention being made of everyday details. As for an even blacker aspect of the background to holidays—political repression—most people try not to remember this at all. Though sometimes remembered pain still makes itself felt:

Because even those families where someone had been arrested, imprisoned, or even executed, they often believed in the power structures, the idea of Communism and all that. [...] And they believed in Stalin. You see, dear? And... even if their closest relatives had been in prison, so to speak. And... and even if they'd got 'ten years without right of correspondence', and had actually been executed, if no one knew when they'd been killed. So things like that happened too. But of course there were people who understood everything, who understood everything and... kept mum, because they knew that... you couldn't say a word, and even... even a hint wasn't allowed. (H-07, PF1, woman born 1939)

The informant speaks here not about her *own* experience of repression, but about that of other people: fear is thus distanced and spoken about 'in the third person'. Recognising that 'I myself was once afraid' represents a personal taboo.

Thus, that corrosive fear, that habit of 'keeping mum', can persist even now. Highly indicative in this respect is a fragment from the oral reminiscences of a schoolteacher born in 1939, who first of all announces, 'Well, as for the political repressions, I know nothing at all about them,' and then literally a minute later comes out with the following story:

It happened on the eighth of November, on October Revolution Day. It's such a wonderful holiday. We used to love that holiday because there was such a holiday atmosphere on the streets, all that noise, the loudspeakers talking, everyone was so cheerful, singing and dancing, dancing in the streets. [...] We'd be celebrating all-out. You'd feel this sense of celebration inside. You know, we did know how to live back then, never mind what they tell you, Communists and all that, no freedom. It was like Esenin says: 'If Holy Rus' [sic] calls out to you: / "Leave Holy Rus' and live in heaven!"' / I shall say: "I need no heaven / Give me my motherland!"' Do you understand? That's how I felt from childhood onward. And I remember how those parades and those holidays, those state holidays— they made us feel so proud, such a feeling of celebration. [...] So it was the eighth of November. And Mama was doing the washing. It was the holiday, she had to do the washing. She was getting on with it. And that little girl, my little niece, little Tanya, she'd managed to wee all over herself. And my mother, well, it was really hard getting hold of material of any kind... And I'd been out in the country in forty-five, somewhere the Germans had occupied, and later the Red Army drove them away with their tails between their legs, and they turned and fled, leaving cartloads of stuff behind. And the villagers helped themselves to all that stuff. There were German parachutes in them—silk, wonderful white silk. But it had swastikas on, black swastikas. And they gave Mama some of that silk too, when she turned up to fetch me. But what on earth was she to do with it—with swastikas all over it? So she made nappies out of it! Well, what else was she to do with it? It seemed a shame to throw it away. [...] And then, that evening, it was dark already, this black maria turns up [suppressing laughter]. You understand? And they knocked at our door, and they said, 'So is that your washing hanging out in the back yard?' Mama says, 'Yes.' 'Come with us, then.' [...] We're all shaking like leaves. Because we'd heard that *when a black maria turns up, they'd take someone away you know where…*[35] [...] And then she told us, that is, she told my papa, that they'd taken her to the White… whoops, I mean the Big House on Liteinyi Prospect.[36] [...] They took her to some boss type, in his separate office, and they start asking, 'So why were you hanging out a Nazi flag on 8 November, of all days?' So then my mother, she was crying her eyes out of course, she [got the point] and said: 'What do you mean, flag? It's only a nappy… I've got a little baby… it's my grandchild, my first grandchild. Right? You can't get material for love or money. I've two other little girls to dress…' So they kept her in for quite a while. Interrogated her several times. And eventually some man there, some boss type, he said, 'All right. But please—OK, you're using it as a nappy, fair enough, but please bear in mind you can't hang things like that out on 8 November. So burn it right away or chuck it out. That rag, I mean…' [...] So it all passed off all right in the end.[37]

A kind of 'double holiday' took place: the much-loved anniversary of the Revolution coincided with a family anniversary; the day that Mama wasn't sent to prison, though she might well have been. At the same time, the informant claims to 'know nothing about' the repressions. Thus she attempts to cleanse her story about higher values (love of the Motherland, unquestioning belief in the 'bright future') of everything that might lower these ideals. She is well aware of the fact that the November holiday and the Stalinist repressions might be seen as being in some kind of contradictory relationship. Consciously or not, she sets out her own private narrative in order to stress, rather, the harmony between the two. The 'repression' motif is presented as a minor mishap by comparison with the universal expression of joy. In her own interpretation the arrest, rather than making the celebration seem hollow for her family, gave them extra reasons to celebrate the anniversary of the Great October Revolution: this was the day when Mama had been spared imprisonment by a wise 'boss type' (*nachal'nik*) for her inadvertent mistake. In a non-holiday context, repressions count as just part of 'the everyday' (*budni*).

By 'holidays', informants recalling the Stalin era (and indeed the Soviet period generally) overwhelmingly have in mind state (official) holidays, such as the anniversary of the October Revolution (7–8 November) and 1 May: 'Those festivals had status. A high status, you know what I mean. A birthday wasn't a holiday, for instance, not even a jubilee[38]—but those days had a high status.' (H-07, PF1, woman born 1939)

People do sometimes recall other holidays (23 February, 'Red/Soviet Army Day', 8 March, 'International Women's Day'), but this is much rarer.[39] One could say that there existed a 'canon' of Soviet (Stalinist) festivals, just as there did a canon of great writers (Pushkin, Tolstoy, Chekhov, Gorky), of Socialist Realist classics (*Cement, How the Steel was Tempered*), of great composers (Glinka, Mussorgsky, Tchaikovsky), and so on.

The reason why 7 November and 1 May (and in due course Victory Day[40]) were considered central was that these days witnessed the enactment of the complete holiday scenario, including parades and 'demonstrations'. In this context, the observation of a young woman born in the Brezhnev era is revealing:

Interviewer: So what holidays did your family celebrate?
Informant: Well, all the usual ones, right? New Year, birthdays, and the demonstrations, of course, that was something sacred.
Interviewer: Something sacred?
Informant: Yes, we really worshipped them. (Oxf/Lev SPb-03, PF14, woman, born 1969)[41]

It was, indeed, the demonstration that represented the essence of the state holiday, so important that the word itself (as above) could replace the word for 'holiday'.

The term 'demonstration' needs a little explanation, since it does not refer to the type of event that would be so named in Britain or America, or indeed in Russia before the October Revolution of 1917, where the term *demonstratsiya* also meant an impromptu manifestation of political protest or worker solidarity. Once the Bolsheviks established control, this type of event—briefly legal under the Provisional Government—was once again banned, and *demonstratsiya* now referred to an officially sanctioned parade, drawing on the established symbolism of the European Left (red flags, revolutionary songs, political slogans and chants), but supporting the government, rather than expressing opposition to it. In many respects, 'demonstrations' in this sense resembled less left-wing festivals than the official celebrations held for such Imperial Russian events as rulers' name days, national holidays such as the anniversary of the Emancipation of the Serfs, and one-off festivals such as victories or royal manifestoes. Just like these, Soviet festivals usually involved large-scale participation by the armed forces and took place in the presence of local dignitaries.[42] And, of course, there was also a considerable resemblance between Soviet parades and religious processions (*krestnye khody*), as the organizers of Bolshevik parades in Kazan' during the

1920s realised to their embarrassment, when members of the public began falling to their knees in front of icons of Lenin and Trotsky.[43]

'Demonstrations' were intended by Bolshevik leaders as a means of establishing and maintaining political legitimacy (in the words of David Remnick, 'parades marked the triumph of the state's persistence').[44] In contradistinction to holiday parades in Western countries for occasions such as 14 July in France, Thanksgiving Day in the US, or St Patrick's Day, there was—in theory—no division between 'parade' and 'spectators'. The crowds were, in the most literal sense, 'demonstrating' their loyalty to the system. Yet, since such loyalty was not something that could be taken wholly for granted (popular protest remained a real threat throughout the Soviet period), careful organisation was essential. Every detail—participating groups, route, slogans, portraits on view[45]—was considered in advance and set down in detailed scenarios. A heavy police presence (including plainclothes agents) ensured good public order on the day. Individual 'columns' (*kolonny*) or sections of the parade were organised by factories, institutions, and other workplaces, which made nonparticipation very difficult, since people's colleagues, superiors, and subordinates immediately took note if they were not there.[46]

In this context, the question inevitably arises of how the fact that attending *demonstratsii* was compulsory harmonised with the fact that they were supposed to be 'celebratory.' As our informants remember, the pressure that could be applied before and after *demonstratsii* (hortatory reminders that taking part was essential, sanctions applied to those who skipped them) did not in fact undermine the sense of joyful participation, the experience of the holiday itself. Sometimes, the division of the 'official' part of the festival and its reception was consciously recognised and took the form of a kind of 'defensive reaction:'

> **Informant 1:** And in the workplace back then, if you didn't turn up... well, then, you... they punished people one way or another, if they were supposed to turn up and they didn't
> **Informant 2:** You didn't get your bonus.
> **Informant 1:** So, on the one hand, you were forced to do it and so it was a kind of unpleasant duty, but on the other hand, a *demonstratsiya* was a real holiday?
> **Informant 2:** You know, dear, it was only an unpleasant duty for a small minority. Most people treated it like a real holiday.
> (H-07, PF1, Informant 1, female, born 1940; Informant 2, female, born 1939)

> **Informant 2:** It was a kind of subconscious liberation of yourself from... well, you had to live in that world, with all those conventions and rules and everything. Well, to hell with them, and if you were going to

enjoy yourself, you were going to enjoy yourself, even in those conditions. It was a holiday, why spoil things for yourself?

Informant 1: So all that [i.e., the sense that you had to go to the demonstration to avoid trouble] sort of vanished somewhere, it... just vanished. OK, it was awful, but too bad. This is a holiday. It's a holiday!

Informant 2: There just weren't any other holidays.[47]

(H-07, PF6, Informant1—woman born 1932; Informant 2—man born 1933)

The official festival scenario took for granted that people participating in *demonstratsii* were displaying their loyalty to the Soviet political order and their commitment to the dignity of labour, and the glorious results of their loyalty and commitment. The *demonstratsiya* culminated in a face-to-face meeting between the Soviet masses and members of the political hierarchy, as the columns of marchers converged on the main square of the city to line up in front of the *tribuna* (platform occupied by Party dignitaries), which in Leningrad was located in front of the Winter Palace. Given the solemnity of the outcome, strict regulation on the way to the square was inevitable. The *demonstratsiya* had a military flavour that extended not just to the vocabulary used (*sbornyi punkt*, 'assembly point', rather than 'meeting point', *marshrut dvizheniya*, 'operations route', *kolonna*, 'troop column', *stroi*, 'drill', and so on), but also to the way everything was organised (the fact that people were lined up in columns, marching along the street like soldiers on parade, and so on).

Parading in front of the *tribuna*—as an act signifying the unity of the organs of Party and state and of the Soviet people—was, in the official view of things, the culmination of the *demonstratsiya*, and of the holiday in general. But the demonstrators themselves did not see things this way. Judging by their memories, the most emotionally rich part of the holiday was the parade leading up to the arrival on the final square:

People have the banners there, everyone's cheerful. Lined up in columns. So, you see, at that point there's more relaxed socialising and jollity going on, because they're not really fully formed yet, the columns, see? It's more people sorting out for themselves where they feel comfortable and at ease. And everyone's in those small local groups, enjoying themselves. And they're singing and dancing, and generally... It really felt like a holiday, no doubt at all about it. (H-07, PF1, woman born 1940)

So while the column was stationary, you'd be amusing yourselves. People might be dancing, or singing, or having a quick drink, or telling funny stories, whatever. Well, of course, the funny stories got passed through a filter, it was self-censorship. Everyone was scared. You were always afraid. So saying something out loud with a political subtext—that was a scary thing to do and people tried to avoid it, even if they thought along those lines. But most people didn't think anything like that anyway, they were just having fun. (H-07, PF6, woman, born 1932)

At the same time, the nearer the columns got to the centre, the more people found themselves in a rigidly defined corridor with traffic moving strictly in one direction, police, army and heavy vehicles to either side. Now it was impossible either to join the procession or to move away from it:

> **Informant 2:** Every column moved along a corridor... it was fenced off by people standing there, every five metres there was a group. [....] They were marking off the corridor and keeping order—just in case.
> **Informant 1:** Keeping [order], otherwise the crowd [...]. Because everything was shut off. Even the entrances to buildings and so on. The side streets were cut off, lorries standing there.
> **Informant 2:** They moved... moved the cars and lorries around, and you couldn't get out, they wouldn't let you on the square or off the square. [....] Only if you lived there or something, then you'd have to show your passport[48]—then they'd let you in. But generally they wouldn't, not non-residents.
> **Informant 1:** It was all organised, all of it. And lots of police, some in plain clothes too.
> (H-07 PF6, Informant 1—woman, born 1932; Informant 2—man, born 1933)

Given the increasing constraints on the procession as it moved towards the main square, those who were not planning on 'demonstrating solidarity with the Soviet government' would try to drop out of the parade before it got to the 'finishing straight'. So far as they were concerned, the first part of the celebrations—meeting up with their friends and having a laugh and a chat—was over. Why bother with the 'compulsory' stuff?[49] As our informants recall, there were not many people like this before the Second World War, but afterwards, their numbers rose quite steeply:

> I'm certain that before the war [...] not coming along to the demonstration, and even more leaving without having some 'good reason' would have been... how shall I put it... well, of course no-one actually got into trouble because of that, but it was kind of 'not done', shall we say. If you'd bothered to turn up, you were supposed to stay around till

the end. Otherwise what? Say you'd got as far as the Stock Exchange, the Rostral Columns, and then you broke ranks. That looked bad. We were supposed to go in one big group. So before the War, I think, all the pre-war holidays—if people turned up, then they went as far as Palace Square [sic]. But after the War, when people's enthusiasm wasn't so great and their attitude to that holiday [had also changed], well, then quite a number of people used to slope off. (H-07, PF9, man, born 1929)

Thus, participants in *demonstratsii* were capable of adjusting even the most official section of the parades to their own tastes. It follows that earlier sections of the day were still more susceptible to 'unofficial'—emotional and sensory—responses, contributing to the sense of excitement and happiness that such occasions inspired.

A festival day would begin with unusual sounds.[50] The morning stillness would be riven by cheery 'holiday' songs pouring out of the loudspeakers rigged up on lampposts and so on down the streets:

So how did those festivals begin? What did you wake up to? [Sings]: 'It's a beautiful morning!...' Every loudspeaker in town would be bawling away, all at once. 'It's a beautiful morning, colours so tenderly...' and all that. 'The whole Soviet Union awakens at dawn. A light breeze darts...' All those fine lovely poems [with heavy irony]. Well, OK if it had been one loudspeaker, but it was the whole damn lot of them!
(H-07, PF3, man, born 1940)

The out-of-the-ordinary sound regime was the first element in the 'technology' by which the holiday mood was created. It is worth bearing in mind here that *homo sovieticus* was conditioned to be extraordinarily aware of noise. The sound of strange footsteps or a car passing at an unexpected time could convey a sense of serious political threat. The holiday racket put an end to subconscious worries of this kind and this made it relaxing; it was possible to feel safe. In addition, holidays allowed people a rare chance to make noise *themselves*—to shout, sing, play musical instruments.[51]

After the War, the holiday din was supplemented by fireworks (traditional on holidays before 1917, and revived in 1943).[52] This new noise gave people the chance to yell 'Hurrah!' after every round was fired. But even without this, sounds of all kinds proliferated. Almost everyone remembers music, song, noise of various kinds:

Informant 1: Music right away, music.
Informant 2: So you started feeling cheerful.

Informant 1: 'It's a beautiful morning…' That was the song.

Informant 2: And you felt that you had to rush along to those demonstrations…

(H-07, PF4, Informant 1, woman, born 1927; Informant 2, man, born 1929)

The brass bands were playing. All along the streets there were brass bands, the brass bands were playing. Yes. […] It was all so interesting, I'm telling you, brass bands everywhere! And music coming from the loudspeakers! Thunderous noise! No fireworks before the war, mind you. (H-07, PF8, man, born 1931)

Informant 1: And then there was music thundering everywhere, everywhere in town. All those loudspeakers were switched on, the music was bawling out of them, all these stirring marches and…

Informant 2: Songs.

Informant 1: [The March] of the Enthusiasts and so on. 'We're—the best, the very…' and all that stuff.

Interviewer: So all that also helped make a festival [atmosphere]?

Informant 1: It did help make….

Informant 2: And they broadcast it all on the square, those calls to arms.

Informant 1: …against the silence. And suddenly everyone bursts out singing! It was all worked out really well ideologically. They loaded people—like with vodka. Loaded them. Loaded them from nappy age up. (H-07, PF6, Informant 1, woman, born 1932; Informant 2, man, born 1933)

It was … music… it was all so… I've told you all the things that influenced us. Music, of course. Of course. If you turned off the music, it would just be an ordinary procession: clip-clop. (H-07, PF3, man, born 1940)

Once the unusual, but immediately identifiable, sounds of celebration had drawn people on to the street, they would be confronted by unusual sights as well:

Informant 1: It was a Soviet carnival. A flaming red,[53] Soviet carnival. People were wearing red carnations, ribbons, all that.

Informant 2: Flags hanging out. And balloons. They weren't usually for sale […] they'd be hanging there on sticks, tied to threads. Sort of bouquets of balloons. The children loved that.

Informant 1: It all seemed… seemed… how do I put this… so colourful enough back then. Ordinary days were so grey, that was the background, holidays seemed really colourful by contrast.

(H-07, PF6, Informant 1, woman, born 1932; Informant 2, man, born 1933)

This 'riot of colours' that our informants remember is often supplemented by another detail: glorious weather. In reality, the weather did not always live up to expectations (especially in November), but in retrospect, people 'retouch' it:

'And somehow it was always, I remember that well, it was always a sunny day. Always, I remember, that picture—a sunny day!' (H-07, PF3, man, born 1940)

The weather motif is also significant because people one knew as well as the streets one knew looked different on holidays. Everyone tried to dress up in new (holiday) clothes, particularly on 1 May. There is a historical reason for this: before the Revolution, Easter had been the time for new clothes, and 1 May 'New Style' and Orthodox Easter often fall close together, so that the assimilation of traditions from one festival to the other came about easily. One of the main motifs of stories about 1 May is new clothes. Reminiscences about this detail go back before the War too:

Ooh, now the First of May—that really was amazing. But they never let us, we thought it was warm enough, but Mama, I can remember it as though it were yesterday, she used to sew us little coats with shawl collars and little hats, and we'd be all dressed up, and we wanted to look our best, because the little dresses she used to make us, they were lovely as well. (H-07, PF5, woman, born 1931)[54]

Not surprisingly, memories about clothes are even more widespread with reference to the post-war era, by which time things had become a little easier in material terms:

The flags, the colours, the music, it all put you in a good mood immediately. All of it! Everyone came out, and the main thing was— everyone was wearing new clothes. New clothes! See. [...] Back then people had strict ideas about work clothes and holiday clothes. And everything nice was for holidays, for the First of May [....] now, here I'm judging by my own experience: new shoes from Skorokhod,[55] a nice new suit. Well, really everyone came out—to have a look at everyone else. What everyone had on, what new things everyone had bought... (H-07, PF3, man, born 1940)

The fact that people looked unlike they usually did, the need to 'work out who they were', created a special atmosphere. Flirting was part of this, as women are especially inclined to remember:

> You see dear, you have to remember that the population was… well, there were many more women than men. There was a bit of a shortage of men after the war. And women… well, how do I put this: they wanted to show themselves off. Sort of flirting, well, that may not be the right word even, this sort of light-hearted whatever… […] Because people were there without their families. They'd all turn up from one workplace, from a factory or whatever. And if people were singing and dancing together, someone might give you a quick cuddle, anyway, the men would pay court to you. It was a holiday, after all. They might pay court, they might even kiss you on the cheek or something. It was an essential part of life, and usually it didn't exist. Life was tough, very hard, we lived very hard in material terms, and you had no chance of that [flirting]. And there was a chance here [on big holidays]. (H-07, PF1, woman, born 1939)

Once again, it is important to remember the general context of the festivals— 'public displays of affection' were generally treated with extreme disfavour, so holidays represented a rare occasion when mild licence was in operation.

Holidays often involved celebrations at 'parks of culture and rest' as well, and it was standard in many districts for there to be a 'film show' (screens might be improvised from the blank walls on the sides of buildings or fixed up on top of trucks):

> And over at that whatsit, Kirov Palace of Culture, they'd give a film show on the street. And there'd be films on the streets here too, and in lots of other places all over Vasilievsky Island, and in other parts of the town all the more so. […] They'd show '*Chapaev*'… that was the kind of film you got back then… '*A Girl with Character*' too. Well, I can't remember them all. All those films, those patriotic films. […] And there'd be lorries on some streets, with screens on top, and they showed the film there, with projectors. They used lorries, not just walls. The lorries had big screens on top, and they had all the equipment, a projector and everything… And people crowded round. We sometimes even watched from the wrong side, from the back side of the screen. […] You see, it's transparent, right? (H-07, PF8, man, born 1931)

The Soviet holiday, like archaic rituals, was organised so that all the senses, all the channels of communication with the external world were played on to the maximum possible degree.[56] This overwhelming load meant that tactile and taste impressions also formed part of the total experience of the holiday. The impression of there being mountains of food was an important component in the celebratory atmosphere: One could say that informants recall holidays as the living embodiment of the 'abundance' promised in the key cookbook of the Stalin years (and later), *The Book of Tasty and Healthy Food*. Not everyone remembers being able to enjoy the delicacies on sale, but at the very least they could enjoy the look of them; after the hunger of the Blockade and the immediate postwar years, the food stalls evoked a particularly emotional reaction:

> **Informant:** Well, there were tables out with all these sandwiches, fruit, soda water, what else, lemonade, beer.
> **Interviewer:** Right along the street?
> **Informant:** Yes, that's right. So, on holidays the streets got turned into a, how do I put it, restaurant, let's put it like that, crudely speaking. Yes. Lots of streets, in the centre of town I mean, Bol'shoi Prospect on Vasilievsky Island, or Bol'shoi Prospect on Petrograd Side and a few other, they turned... All the places the demonstration went down, it didn't go down all the streets. On Vasilievsky, it went down Bol'shoi Prospect, mainly. And then down the [University] Embankment, and then across Palace Bridge. Whoops, I mean, first it went down S"ezdovskaya Line, and then on to the Embankment. And people gathered in different places. So there'd be this sort of unified stream from different lines, from different ones. Right. And the same in every district. Wherever there was a central street, they'd put out those tables, and all kinds of food it was hard to buy otherwise would be out there. You see, it wasn't easy getting food back then—before the war, and after. (H-07, PF8, man born 1931)

The informant here mentions 'beer' being on sale, but when it comes to hard liquor, information differs considerably. Some informants recall that people would store supplies of spirits in advance, the point being that one could not buy it on the day. The following recollection comes from the 1960s:

> True, you have to bear in mind that all the shops selling alcohol along the demonstration routes were closed. [...] All of them. I can remember that for certain, because my mate Tolya Simanovsky, he always used to say, 'Hell, that bar there's closed, would you believe it?'[57] You said it! So you had to go off somewhere, God knows, to... Detskosel'skii

Prospect to find a shop that was open.[58] But no one was going to drag off that far. So you couldn't have a drink, you see, dear?[59] (H-07, PF1, woman, born 1939)

However, other informants, recalling an earlier period, remember that the streets turned into one long line of refreshment stalls:

Informant 2: They had buffets set up on the ground floors. You'd go up to the windows and they'd pour you out a vodka, you could buy sandwiches…[60]
Informant 1: Yes, they were giving people the chance to knock back one or two. […] It wasn't a case of getting sozzled, just of raising enthusiasm and so on.
Informant 2: Yes. […] That was in forty-eight, forty-seven, right after the War. The time they did away with rationing, and all that. When there was something around to eat. (H-07, PF6, Informant 1, woman, born 1932; Informant 2, man, born 1933)

At the same time, our informants remember that people 'kept themselves in hand', as was natural enough, bearing in mind that at later stages of the *demonstratsiya* they would be right under the eye of various 'responsible people,' not to mention plainclothes policemen and KGB agents:

Informant 1: Well of course you didn't get dead drunk. Everyone was cheerful, they had a little bit to drink, but there were never any ugly scenes, I absolutely can't remember anything like that.
Informant 2: That's absolutely right. Maybe they just didn't let them out on the square if they'd had a drop too many… (H-07, PF1, Informant 1, woman, born 1940, Informant 2, woman, born 1939)

On the other hand, another informant remembers the use of alcohol as being widespread:

Informant: Lots of people were doing it [i.e., drinking].
Interviewer: Do you mean they took a bottle or two along, or was it sold right on the streets?
Informant: It was sold right there. I'm not… I couldn't say for sure whether they had vodka for sale, but there was definitely beer and wine. But probably people did take it with them, mostly. I think so, anyway. […] When I was working [at a Leningrad factory], we used to take stuff along. I used to have the right to 120 litres of ethanol a month [for work

purposes],[61] I was the head of a section. So I could easily manage to take along a couple of bottles. (H-07, PF8, man, born 1931)

To judge by what people remember, 'taking stuff along' was very common. People tried not to advertise this, which generated miracles of ingenuity:

> I remember that in the institute [...] there was this guy [...] He had this drape coat, or gabardine or something, very classy. And he deepened the pockets of the coat and he shoved something like a hot water bottle or a rubber container holding two litres [of vodka] down there, it had a stopper in the top end, yes, and a tube hanging out. And he stuck that tube through [i.e. made a hole in the coat to feed it through] and he brought it up under his collar. Like the astronauts do, yes? Then he'd squeeze it [with his elbow from outside] and take a nip from the tube. Everyone knew exactly what was going on and they'd line up by him like a petrol pump. And have their little drink. And he'd be delighted. Standing there like nothing's going on! But he's squeezing and we know he's squeezing, and we know that when he does, the vodka's flowing. If you ask me, that's when the holiday stopped being something special. (H-07, PF9, man, born 1929)

In the end, the question of whether the authorities actively encouraged the sale of spirits to get people 'warmed up' or, on the contrary, tried to stop this altogether by closing shops and bars is of marginal importance. One way or another, they were attempting to regulate alcohol consumption in a way that reflected ideological perceptions of the ideal popular festival. So much everyone can remember, even if they have now forgotten whether drinking was foisted on people or actively banned. Interesting, too, is the fact that the motif of resistance invariably crops up in one form or another: they closed the booze shops and the bars, but we found a way round that; everyone tried to get the women drunk, but I wasn't having any of it, and so on.

Music, bright colours, food and drink were all important constituents of the Soviet state holiday, but the vital core of the occasion lay somewhere else: in proxemics, the sense of communality with a multitude of brightly dressed and benevolent people on streets that would have been half-empty on ordinary days. In the late 1920s and early 1930s, Zinaida Denis'eva, a schoolteacher who had originally disliked most things about the Soviet Union, came to a rapprochement with the new culture precisely through participation in festivals.[62] Our informants are from a generation where holidays had been

familiar from birth, but nevertheless, the sense of togetherness is remembered
as very important:

> Well, I'm telling you, dear, people are kind of atomised in the ordinary
> way, yes? Everyone shut up in their own family, with this and that
> emotional concern. And when you have the chance to go out on the
> street and feel that all these people, these strangers, are feeling warm
> towards you, it's a holiday for them too… And everyone wants to be
> together and to express that sense of joy, that pleasure, all together, see
> dear? And that was really good. You felt, you felt with every pore, that it
> really was a holiday. (H-07, PF1, woman, born 1940)

People try to explain that the standard phrases about 'solidarity' actually had
meaning. As this informant continues:

> You know, strange as it may seem, the fact that they ground into us that
> it was a festival of solidarity, of communality and so on, it sank down
> inside. […] I was only a girl then. Do you see, dear? But I still felt it.
> Nobody ever said it directly. But when you got out on to the street—that
> sense of communing with other people! […] Yes-yes-yes. It's an amazing
> feeling. Because no one ever explained to me things would be like that.
> It was a sort of internal feeling. […] Right, we sort of felt, right, that…
> right… we were all together… (H-07, PF1, woman, born 1940)

This particular informant has an obvious sense of embarrassment about
the resemblance between her feelings and the official rhetoric of the day
('the triumph of solidarity', the 'unity of Party and People', 'the Soviet
people as a single community'), but she sees the holiday as an occasion when
'unity' in a real sense actually did exist. What is more, it was exactly this
sensation that, for her and others, made a state festival into a real holiday.
Of course, any holiday in any culture is meant to meld participants into
a community of members—be it a family, a village, a parish or a work
collective. Soviet state festivals gave people the chance to sense particularly
acutely their membership as part of an entire nation; awareness of common
nationality was raised to new levels, altering the quality of experience. It is not
surprising that the Stalinist motif of communing with 'the entire country' as
a special feature of major festivals survived long after 1953: 'You see, it was
this sense of communality, you feel that you're just some little person in the
midst of that great mass, of that… of that nation.' (EU Pb-01, PF-10,
woman, born 1939)

Some lines of Mayakovsky's from his narrative poem *Vladimir Il'ich Lenin* come to mind: 'I'm happy to be a small part of that vast force, / that even the tears in my eyes are everyone's.'[63] The sense of being part of a vast crowd of people not only represented the quintessence of the festival, of the holiday atmosphere in a pure sense, but also generated a kind of hierarchy of different holidays. No family festivals (birthdays, etc.) or community holidays such as New Year could compete with state holidays, since the sense of 'belongingness' was not inspired by these.

The waning of these state holidays attracted different responses from different people. Some were delighted, others distressed. But now, even those members of the older generation who took a sceptical view of Soviet festivals often feel a degree of nostalgia. It is not just the festivals that have vanished, but the sense of universal celebration, a sense that people had grown used to:

> So all that gradually vanished. And that feeling as well, the feeling that this really was a holiday. That people were united, you see, dear? Everyone has their own interests, their own view of things and their own attitude to it, you see dear? That's how it started, people being atomised. (H-07, PF1, woman, born 1940)

As we see, a kind of symbiotic interaction between the official and the personal views of happiness was characteristic for the world view of several generations of people socialised under Soviet power. For many of them, including the generation that has been represented here, the sense of separate happiness or 'private' happiness was simply not satisfying. Now Soviet festivals, which once offered the witnesses of 'glorious days' the supreme opportunity to feel personal and collective happiness at the same time, have vanished. People feel cheated. As one participant in a recent Internet forum put it: 'They've stolen a little bit of my happiness.'

Translated by Catriona Kelly.

Part Three

LOCATIONS

Chapter Nine

THE 'NEW MOSCOW' AND THE NEW 'HAPPINESS': ARCHITECTURE AS A NODAL POINT IN THE STALINIST SYSTEM OF VALUE

Katerina Clark

'Life has become better,' the Stalinist slogan of 1935 ran, 'has become gayer.' But is that really what happiness is about? All that jollity, all those 'carnivals' in Moscow's Gorky Park, and so forth, of those times did, in fact, make Soviet life 'gayer', more fun, for their brief duration; but happiness in general arguably refers to a state of longer duration, as when we say, 'He or she has a happy marriage,' or 'X is happy in their job,' etc. I would put happiness a register or two above contentment, but below bliss. Happiness is not about the ecstatic, but more about a fairly even, stable and positive state of being; perhaps about a sense of self-fulfillment.

As it happens, there has been a spate of books and articles on happiness lately, including a history of happiness.[1] The consensus: sociologists have established that although people are living better now versus a few decades ago, they are less happy. Commentators are even proposing a new version of the guns-versus-butter dilemma; governments allegedly now have to choose between greater material well-being for their citizens and greater happiness. As we look at Stalinist Russia, we can see this alternative less as a dilemma than in terms of competing aims. On the one hand, the state sought to raise the standard of living, to increase the supply of creature comforts and consumer goods. But on the other hand, it was arguably more concerned with what it saw as self-fulfillment for its citizenry. Happiness as conceived in these terms would consist of living in a higher-order society, somewhat the same conception of happiness as Socrates who, as John Lancaster put it in a recent

New Yorker article, '… made the question of happiness one of full accord between an individual and the good: to be happy was to lead a good life, one in keeping with higher patterns of being.'[2]

Balancing the demands of satisfying consumerism and attaining such higher patterns is something the Soviets never resolved. One crude example: In Ivan Pyrev's 1941 film *The Swineherd and the Shepherd*, the heroine and her *sovkhoz* (state farm) companions visit the dazzling Agricultural Exhibition in Moscow. A group decides to go to the downtown stores and buy some fabulous consumer goods, thus suggesting to the Soviet audience a higher standard of living as yet to be found only in Moscow. The heroine remains at the exhibition, drawn by that higher good, that promise of self-realisation to be found in learning to become a better pig breeder. And, of course, she gains the handsome shepherd as a reward.

I will focus here on a more serious cultural phenomenon: the rebuilding of Moscow in the 1930s.

In Soviet architecture, *the* preoccupation of the 1930s was the creation of a new 'socialist city' centred on the remodeling of Moscow. In June 1931, the Communist Party's Central Committee passed a resolution providing guidelines for the rebuilding project. Work soon began, though it was not until 1935 that a systematic plan for a 'new Moscow' was completed and on July 10 was promulgated in a joint decree of the Party's Central Committee and the government's Council of Ministers (*Sovnarkom*), 'On the General Plan for the Reconstruction of the City of Moscow.' This decree largely reiterated the same guiding principles and endorsed the same major projects as had the 1931 Resolution, but added more specifics such as target dates for completing particular projects. The Union of Soviet Architects was formed in 1932, in the wake of the formation of the Writers Union, but it did not hold its first congress until 1937. In the interim, the plans for a reconstructed new Moscow functioned as the best practical guide to what Socialist Realism might mean in architecture.

The project to rebuild Moscow continued to have high visibility, not just on the physical landscape, but on the political as well. Arkhplan was formed in 1933 as a new joint body of the Moscow Party Committee and city Soviet. Its head was Lazar Kaganovich, the First Secretary of the Moscow Party Committee, and allegedly de facto second secretary, after Stalin, of the Party itself; he was also high priest of Stalin's personality cult. And work began. The metro was dug, its stations lined with gleaming marble, its ceilings hung with chandeliers and the whole decorated with mosaics, murals, bas-reliefs and statues. Old structures were pulled down (especially those associated with religion or institutions of capitalism, but also factories and slums), roads were straightened and widened, the river embankment was clad in granite, some grandiose public buildings and hotels were erected, together with imposing apartment buildings, primarily for the new class. But the 'new Moscow' was not just an accumulation of new buildings; Arkhplan was to shape it as a total aesthetic environment.

Architecture played a central role in Stalinist political culture. While the practical advantages of reordering and modernising the capital city were no doubt a factor in launching the project for a new Moscow, the symbolic function of its 'transformation' was paramount. In 1931, even before plans were announced for reconstructing Moscow, architecture provided the dominant tropes in official speeches and *Pravda* editorials for representing the status of progress towards Communism. As such texts characteristically went, with the Revolution in 1917, the leadership had cleared away the old; during the 1920s, and particularly with industrialisation and collectivisation during the First Five-Year Plan, the state had built the 'foundation' of the new society, and now it was time to erect the socialist 'building' (*zdanie*).[3] Here, official spokesmen were drawing on the metaphoric use of architecture in *The German Ideology* (1845–1846), in which Marx and Engels used the relationship between base and superstructure as a model for the relationship between all elements of society, a model that confounded previous philosophical systems. Also, the new emphasis in Party rhetoric on 'building' signaled that the country had now gone beyond the iconoclastic phase of the cultural revolution.

Party leaders, in expanding on the Marxist trope, declared that it was time to rebuild Moscow as the 'model' for proletarians and Communists throughout the world who would be inspired to follow it. Rebuilding the capital was thus a political gesture designed not only to bring greater glory to the Bolshevik regime, but also to stand as the core of Stalin's symbolic system, and so establish a blueprint for his new sociopolitical and cultural order. From the very first, architecture and design were closely linked to other arts and cultural *cum* political practices in a coordinated structure of values centred on the city. As an example, starting in 1933, on the eve of the great revolutionary holidays of May Day and November 7, designs for the 'new Moscow' were showcased in the windows of lower Gorky Street, and citizens were expected to pay obeisance by filing past to view them.[4] When, in 1934, leading architect I. Zholtovsky's new Intourist building modeled on a Palladian palazzo was promoted as a paradigm for the new architecture, crowds marching to Red Square for the revolutionary anniversary paused en route to hail it.[5]

At the centre of Stalinist culture was a close nexus of power involving architecture, literature and the leadership. The two arts began to converge; symptomatically, two writers joined Arkhplan. But to what end?

In the 1930s, as Moscow was being rebuilt, the cliché of press accounts was 'all of Moscow is under scaffolding (*Vsia Moskva v lesakh*).' The city was presented as a chrysalis waiting for an entirely new self—a butterfly—to emerge. And emerge it did (or so people were told); in the second half of the decade a number of glossy picture albums were produced by figures like the erstwhile Constructivist Varvara Stepanova in which Moscow 'then' and 'now' faced each other across photo spreads (or in films such as Alexander Medvedkin's *Novaia Moskva* of 1938, which included similarly juxtaposed images), celebrating Moscow's transformation.[6]

The newly hatched Moscow was to be 'beautiful', a value newly held to be self-evident. As Kaganovich put it in his speech to a Jubilee plenum of the Komsomol in 1933 in a veiled attack on Constructivism:

> Many consider that a simplified and crude design [*oformlenie*] is the style of proletarian architecture. No, excuse me, but the proletariat does not only want to have housing, not only have places where they can live comfortably, but have beautiful houses. And they will make sure that their cities, their buildings and their architecture are more beautiful than in other towns of Europe and America.[7]

Avant-garde architecture, having initially proclaimed itself the 'new architecture', was now attacked as 'formalist,' 'arid' and 'soulless' for its 'aestheticisation of technology' and cult of the machine, which had allegedly crowded out 'art itself'.[8] From this environment, any whiff of modernist architecture was to be banished, and in its place arose an eclectic mix of classical, neo-classical and Renaissance styles; Gothic would emerge later.

The turn to 'beauty' meant a reaction against avant-gardism and a return to conventional tastes, but the foregrounding of the beautiful was also tied to a system that cut across discursive boundaries. It is arguably the point at which the ideological or political met the literary, the artistic and the architectural. The early 1930s were an aesthetic moment, and as such, also a utopian moment, a moment when literature, architecture and ideology came together in the one 'city' (emblematically Moscow), a moment when disparate biographies and disparate subjectivities came together in one narrative. Though it was never made explicit, in some sense a 'Marxist-Leninist aesthetics' underpinned the entire system. The system meant the aestheticisation of politics, or more accurately—since political life then was palpably messy and even bloody—the aestheticisation of meta-politics, of the model that subtended and justified practices in the political arena.

In this historical moment of state aggrandizement and consolidation of power, the beautiful was 'in'. One is reminded here of Benjamin's oft-cited pronouncement in the epilogue to 'The Work of Art in an Age of Mechanical Reproduction' (1936): 'The logical result of fascism is the introduction of aesthetics into political life.' This is the one-liner that everyone takes away from this essay, but Benjamin went on to say: 'All efforts to render politics aesthetic culminate in one thing: war' (not a surprising conclusion for one who had recently fled Nazi Germany). But he further elaborates in a point of interest for us here: 'war is beautiful because it creates new architecture, like that of the big tanks, the geometrical formation flights, the smoke spirals from burning villages, and many others …' Although Benjamin is eliding here the distinction between architecture and the architectonic, he is clearly suggesting an architectonic that has a visible manifestation (in such things as planes flying in formation) that participates in the greater reality of an architectonically organised society. In this point about the 'geometrical formation of flights' one is reminded of Cracauer's essay on the 'Mass Ornament', in which he sees much in the modern world as not merely 'geometrically' organising the technological, but also humanity itself.

Benjamin observes: '[Mankind's] … self-alienation has reached such a degree that it can experience its own destruction as an aesthetic pleasure of the first order. This is the situation of politics which Fascism is rendering aesthetic.' Later he adds: 'Communism responds by politicising art' as a necessary counteractive.[9] I would argue, however, that 'Communism', as represented in the Stalinist 1930s, featured the 'introduction of aesthetics into political life' (and vice versa), but that this 'introduction' occurred not only at the crude level of the mass ornament.

Boris Groys has argued that Stalinist culture represents a *Gesamtkunstwerk*.[10] However, his analogy with the Wagnerian ideal for opera can only take us so far. In Wagner's *Gesamtkunstwerk*, all the arts were to be integrated into a whole, but among them, music was to be dominant. Karl Schloegel and I have argued that the dominant in Stalinist culture of the 1930s was the written word, a not insignificant distinction.[11] It was the more primitive manifestations of Soviet culture in the 1930s, such as the mass parades, which, to use Kracauer's term, formed 'mass ornaments' that could more readily be compared with the *Gesamtkunstwerk*. To reinvoke Benjamin, 'politics' were palpably 'aestheticised' in this crude way, but they were also aestheticised at a more profound level.

Around 1931, the same year that architecture became a major source of metaphors for society and the plans to rebuild Moscow were announced, the aesthetic returned as a value. These developments can be seen as part of a general shift in political culture that occurred that year. In a July 1931 speech to Soviet managers, Stalin proposed a highly differentiated system of wage payment which discriminated against the unskilled worker, and a change of policy towards the old professional intelligentsia—from a policy of 'rout' to one of 'encouragement and concern'.[12] The immediate reasons for Stalin's signal speech were no doubt largely economic (the hour of reckoning for the Five-Year Plan—1932—was drawing near, and production targets had not been met). But it provided a pretext for putting the entire nexus of Five-Year Plan values up for review. Defining values of that era were reversed. The changes included a drawing away from the radical democratism of the plan years, with its emphasis on the proletariat and mass culture, to a foregrounding of the more inclusive term 'socialism'. In the cultural sector, this was accompanied by a concomitant shift from promoting proletarian culture to a call for Socialist Realism. Additional corollaries of the end to radical democratism included an emphasis on differentiation in many spheres, ranging from wages to the human, and a call for 'quality'. In terms of the symbolic geography of Soviet political culture, where the plan years had privileged the periphery (that is, both the outskirts of the cities and the far reaches of the country, which became the sites of the great industrial projects), now it was the centre, the capital, which was promoted as the nation's heart and emblem.[13] This shift meant not only that 'the periphery' (an analogue to the 'little man' of the masses celebrated in cultural revolution rhetoric) was no longer in favor, but also that a de-emphasis on industrialisation and the material was underway.

Marxist theoreticians of the 1920s had not generally used the word 'aesthetics' (*estetika*), except in commenting on Plekhanov's theories, which by then had largely been discredited. Their theoretical investigations, such as there were, were more tied to a particular branch of the arts,[14] while the avant-garde and its Formalist associates decried all mention of 'art' and 'beauty' as vapid and unscientific fetish. Starting around 1931, however, one sees a more concerted effort to elucidate a comprehensive Marxist aesthetic theory, one centred on literature, but with general principles governing all the arts.

Authoritative voices began to lament the fact that the cultural revolution's obsession with technology, statistics and immediate practical needs had crowded out the higher and more enduring values of 'ideology' and 'beauty'. Also, as we detect in Kaganovich's remarks about the proletariat wanting not just comfortable houses but beautiful ones, there was a reaction against the largely pragmatic, utilitarian and materialist approach to most fields of culture that had characterised the cultural revolution of the immediate past. 'Comfortable' apartments were what the West specialised in. In the Soviet Union, however, 'beauty' was to trump—but not banish—comfort. Culture itself became a value, and not only for its instrumentalist potential but also *in its own right*. One can see this in Stalin's own relationship to culture. In the 1930s he assigned himself the culture portfolio in the Politburo, always took care to present himself as a man of culture, and participated personally in the 1932 meeting of intellectuals that decided on Socialist Realism as the new 'method' for Soviet literature and culture. He and other leaders began to frequent the Bolshoi, the Moscow Art Theatre and the Maly Theatre, the three Moscow bastions of high culture in the performing arts.

The shift to the aesthetic potentially represents one of many ways in which Soviet culture of these years might be discussed in terms of the Enlightenment.

At that time, aesthetics returned to prominence in tracts by leading philosophers, as it did in the writings of Soviet theoreticians of the 1930s. It could be argued that one should not identify this trend with the Enlightenment because the latter occurred in a preindustrial age. But the exact meaning of 'Enlightenment' is far from fixed. As Peter Gay points out in his classic study, there were many 'Enlightenments', with different and often contradictory features. Moreover, in the 1930s the cause of industrial production that had been so central to the rhetoric of the First Five-Year Plan was increasingly played down. As an example: in 1933 cultural workers were chastised for focusing on rural and industrial production at a time when a gloriously 'new' capital was emerging before their eyes.[15]

Rebuilding Moscow was represented in Stalinist rhetoric as literally an Enlightenment project; the 'new Moscow' was to be a city of 'light.' It was also, as a feat of modernisation, aimed at increasing the well-being of residents, at bringing happiness (making people 'gayer'). But it was during the Enlightenment that 'happiness' particularly emerged as a public value. It is, for example, listed as one of the 'inalienable rights of man' ('life, liberty and the pursuit of happiness') in the United States' Declaration of Independence of 1776.

The 'happiness' of pleasurable well-being promised in a renewed Moscow was grounded in an ideologically inflected system. A useful general model for elaborating this system is explored in Terry Eagleton's book *The Ideology of the Aesthetic*. Eagleton argues that during the Enlightenment there was a palpable shift towards foregrounding the aesthetic. He sees this preeminently in the work of Kant, but also in a number of other philosophers, mostly Germans, ranging from Baumgarten and his 1750 treatise *Aesthetica* through Schiller to Hegel, allowing also that many of 'the aesthetic motifs I trace can be pursued back to the Renaissance or even to classical antiquity.'[16]

Eagleton insists that the Enlightenment return to the aesthetic must be related not only to general philosophical concerns, but also to the central ideological dilemmas of absolutist political power, or, in other words, to the very reality of Prussian Germany in which Kant (and to some extent those other philosophers) operated.[17] In treating these thinkers, he focuses on their search to elucidate the 'aesthetic' in terms of a series of interrelated problems that have not only beset philosophical inquiry, but are crucial to the relationship between the individual citizen and the state: 'freedom and legality, self determination, autonomy, particularity and universality'.[18] Such problems, it hardly bears pointing out, were no less germane in the Stalinist thirties. Eagleton argues that although the ostensible concern of these philosophers from the late eighteenth and early nineteenth centuries is the aesthetic, they address, explicitly or implicitly, such questions as: How can individual subjects with their spontaneous and even harmful impulses and desires be made to behave in a rational and coherent way; how can the state's rules be internalised to become the natural habits of its citizens; and, above all, how can one get around that old problem that if one, or an entire society, is guided by pure reason, by purely abstract principles, then actuality and particularity, the "sensible" life,[19] and even history itself 'will slip through the net of conceptual discourse to leave one grasping an empty space'.[20] How can 'reason, that most immaterial of faculties, grasp the grossly sensuous'?[21] He continues: Kant, in particular, looked to the aesthetic as 'an elusive third way between the vagaries of subjective feeling and the bloodless rigor of the understanding',[22] as 'a deft compromise between mere subjectivism on the one hand, and an excessively abstract reason on the other'.[23]

Eagleton insists that philosophers at the time of the Enlightenment were drawn to work on aesthetic issues because the aesthetic, more than the purely ethical which was relatively abstract, offered a model for relating particular to general (or universal), for integrating what Kant calls the 'egoism of taste' (i.e., of the individual subject's impulse), to a higher system:

> Within the dense welter of our material life, with all its amorphous flux, certain objects stand out in a sort of perfection dimly akin to reason, and these are known as the beautiful. A kind of *ideality* [emphasis mine] seems to inform their sensuous existence from within, rather than floating above it in some Platonic space. Because these are objects which we can agree to be beautiful, not by arguing or analyzing but just by looking and seeing, a spontaneous consensus is brought to birth within our creaturely life, bringing with it the promise that such a life, for all its apparent arbitrariness and obscurity, might indeed work in some sense very like a rational law.[24]

Eagleton is, of course, not really talking about the aesthetic per se; that is, not really exclusively about the category of beauty, but rather is using the term 'aesthetic' in a broader sense that encompasses the ethical and the political as well. It could be argued that he is refracting Kant via Marx, but his account is particularly germane for our purposes because that is what the Soviet theoreticians of the thirties effectively did, too. The Stalinist 'aesthetic' or 'beautiful' was not self-valuable or 'autonomous', but incorporated into an ideological system *as its nodal point*. The beautiful was also represented as being the 'harmonious', in effect, that which marries the subjective to the objective in concrete actuality.

In a society seeking to effect change, this new aesthetic might be seen to have its limits. Beauty conduces to pleasure or contemplation, not action or conversion. The great façades of 'new Moscow' were primarily monuments for contemplation, and, as over the course of the decade they became 'ever higher', this contemplation had to take place at an ever greater distance. Analogously, the heroes of Soviet literature, in order to provide effective models for the populace and be a spur to action, could not just project a 'kind of ideality'. Here we sense a possible limitation of Eagleton's account of the aesthetic as a heuristic model for Stalinist culture. The aesthetic is, strictly speaking, not about action but about apprehension. Yet Eagleton insists that it is 'not simply a contemplative faculty, but a whole project for the hegemonic reconstruction of subjects.'[25] This formulation was particularly relevant for the Stalinist 1930s where the aesthetic turn linked art to biography:

> The ultimate binding force of the bourgeois social order, in contrast to the coercive apparatus of absolutism, will be habits, pieties, sentiments and affections. And this is equivalent to saying that power in such an order has become *aestheticised*. It is at one with the body's spontaneous impulses, entwined with sensibility and the affections, lived out in unreflective custom. Power is now inscribed in the minutiae of subjective experience, and the fissure between abstract duty and pleasurable inclination is accordingly healed. To dissolve the law to custom, to sheer unthinkable habit, is to identify it with the human subject's own pleasurable well-being, so that to transgress that law would signify a deep self-violation. The new subject, which bestows on itself self-referentiality, a law at one with its immediate experience, finding its freedom in its necessity, is modeled on the aesthetic artifact.[26]

Stephen Kotkin's book *Magnetic Mountain* is about Magnitogorsk, the city surrounding a Soviet industrial giant that was established at the beginning of the 1930s on the bleak plains just beyond the Urals. In it he argues that under Stalin, Soviet citizens were in their daily lives and in public participating in what he calls 'Soviet civilisation'; that is, a new and comprehensive world that does not only involve a new political and economic structure, but also a new culture in the extended sense that encompasses both culture itself and the everyday way of life. Kotkin analyzes this everyday way of life as a practice structured by a narrative which generated the distinctive discourse of the new civilisation and also underwrote the new habits of association: 'The story of socialism was nearly indistinguishable from the story of people's lives, a merged personal and societal allegory of progress, social justice and overcoming adversity—in short, a fable of a new person and a new civilisation.'[27] This 'fable', a version of what others have called the 'national imaginary' or grand narrative, was inwardly assimilated. It was not merely a mental construct, but was 'performed' in myriad actions and expressions, both major and minor, which made up the civilisation. Here the aesthetic comes into play. As Eagleton has pointed out, the performative is also a defining aspect of the aesthetic: 'Judgments of taste appear to be descriptions of the world but are in fact concealed emotive utterances, performatives masquerading as constatives.'[28] In Soviet culture, actions were, in large, degree-ritualised. The 'marriage' between politics and culture, between Soviet power and would-be enlighteners from culture, was grounded in the working out, over time, of a common narrative.

Socialist Realism was, in effect, a codification of this narrative. It was originally presented as if one system, as *the* method for literature, but all the arts were expected to find equivalents (rather like, when the Writers Union was formed, the Central Committee Resolution calling for 'analogous changes' in 'other branches of the arts').[29] And it became one system. The turn to aesthetics was at the heart of a new moment in cultural evolution. In the interaction and work in tandem of specialists in the arts there evolved an aesthetic system that linked its various branches into a whole, one which crossed all their discursive boundaries. In other words, Socialist Realism was not just about heroes building power stations, or even about the wisdom of Party decrees. A Marxist–Leninist aesthetic functioned as that which linked literature and architecture and, to a lesser extent, all the other branches of the arts. Aesthetic value and political value were closely entwined. Specialists in the two leading fields, literature and architecture, began to use the same critical vocabulary, the same discursive repertoire. In architecture, this repertoire defined 'the beautiful', in literature, it identified the 'hero' as an example of anthropological 'ideality'.

Those in authority in architecture, in seeking to define what Socialist Realism might mean for that field, generally invoked classical precedents. They championed the art of the Renaissance but they also looked beyond it to the great codifiers of the beautiful in Greece. Rome was especially seen as having distilled the essence of the beautiful. Fomin, a leading architect of the 1930s, insists, in his contribution to a major debate of 1933 about the styles appropriate for Socialist Realist architecture, that architecture must have its own 'language' and that that language be the classical, arguing (somewhat Eurocentrically) that this language has been 'understood by all peoples in all cultural eras of mankind'. 'It is essential,' he continued, 'that this language be simple, laconic and [rigorous] because [architects] must be able, using few means, to say much both powerfully and convincingly.'[30]

Buildings were to 'say much, both powerfully and convincingly'. They were to be read as texts. When, in the 1930s, prominent Soviet architects declared canonical principles of classical architecture central to a 'Socialist Realist' architecture, they did not merely mean that a particular inventory of stylistic features was to be adopted. In calling for such alleged qualities of their preferred architectural styles as 'simplicity', a 'serene' exterior (*spokoinyi*) and 'a unified whole', these 'qualities' were themselves markers of an ideological and epistemological stance. Moreover, similar qualities were also required for literature.

The two dominant branches of the arts were linked in the one discursive system. Architecture defined 'beauty' in its roster of iconic qualities, while literature defined—and provided models for—the beautiful (ideal) man. The highly conventionalised account of one's life's course was, as I have argued elsewhere, an allegorical representation of the Marxist–Leninist model for historical progress.[31] Architecture cannot, per se, narrate a biography, or at any rate can do so to only a very restricted degree. The regime needed not just 'beautiful' buildings, mere shells, nor even model cities as structures of streets and amenities. It also needed a narrative about that shell to give it order, cogency and, above all, *meaning*. Thus, although the branches of the arts (especially literature and architecture) were all linked in the thirties, literature was dominant because it relates part to whole not just in an abstract way, as in architecture, but in a human narrative. Chronologically, the founding of the Writers Union and the institution of Socialist Realism postdates the project launch for the reconstruction of Moscow by almost a year; even so, literature arguably became prior to architecture.

The buildings of the 'new Moscow' were erected for citizens' specular benefit. Every detail, right down to the slightest curlicue, was to have a meaning, and as Ivan citizen moved among them, he was to enjoy aesthetic pleasure—something above the mere contentment to be experienced by his or her counterpart in the West. Citizens' happiness would come from an aesthetically ordered world, one that would be conducive to certain habits of mind and performance.

As we know, most of the 'new Moscow' was never built, but that is another story.

Chapter Ten

ANDREI PLATONOV'S *HAPPY MOSCOW*: TOLSTOI, STALIN AND THE SOVIET SELF

Philip Ross Bullock

Andrei Platonov's novel *Happy Moscow* (*Schastlivaia Moskva*) was long in the writing:[1] from 1932 his notebooks were to be filled with fitful ideas of plot and characterisation for a work that was to obsess him for several more years, and in 1933, he finished the first six chapters. What we now know as *Happy Moscow* may, in fact, have been intended as part of a longer work, *Journey from Leningrad to Moscow in 1937* (*Puteshestvie iz Leningrada v Moskvu v 1937 godu*), yet despite contracts with leading publishers, he never fulfilled his plans; in the end, only the second chapter of *Happy Moscow* was published, in the form of a short story.[2] Whether the novel's ambitious conception was ultimately beyond realisation (unlikely from the author of *Chevengur* (*Chevengur*)), whether other projects (such as *Takyr* (*Takyr*) and *Soul* (*Dzhan*), the works relating to Platonov's visits to Turkmenistan in 1934 and 1935) took priority, or whether aesthetic considerations rendered the work obsolete and even dangerous (the stories collected in the 1937 volume *The River Potudan* (*Reka Potudan'*) are altogether more deferential to Socialist Realism), by the time Platonov's son was arrested in 1938, work on the novel had been resolutely abandoned. Eventually published for the first time only in 1991,[3] *Happy Moscow* has since become one of Platonov's most commented-upon works.[4]

Its memorable title encodes a multiple set of puns, since Moscow (in Russian, a feminine noun, *Moskva*) refers both to the Soviet capital and to the novel's orphaned heroine:

> Moscow Chestnova had been in the children's home for two years. It was here that she had been given a name, a surname and even a patronymic,

since she had only the vaguest memory of her own name and early childhood. [...] So she had been given a first name in honour of Moscow, a patronymic in memory of all the Ivans who had died in battle as ordinary Red Army soldiers, and a surname in recognition of the honesty of her heart—which had not had time to become dishonest, in spite of long unhappiness.[5]

Whether any of the characters in *Happy Moscow* can be considered truly 'happy' will be discussed later. In any case, the heroine certainly has her share of luck, as the other meaning of the Russian word for happiness, *schast'e*, suggests (this term also summarizes the novel's inchoate plot). The story opens in Petrograd during 1917. The young Moscow is orphaned, and eventually is enrolled in an aeronautical school by a strange man who has taken a liking to her. Her exploits as a parachutist soon win her adulation, yet a curious accident—whilst testing a parachute, she lights a cigarette and falls to earth with a bump—leads to her dismissal. We are then introduced to another of the novel's principal characters, the surgeon Sambikin, who is operating on a boy with a rapacious tumor. Other members of the Stalinist professional elite gather at the Komsomol club, where Moscow meets Semyon Sartorius, an engineer.[6] He—like Sambikin—is attracted to the heroine. However, their fates diverge at this point, Sambikin pursuing ever-greater glory in medicine, whereas Sartorius abandons his glittering career in order to devote himself to the modest task of inventing a simple yet reliable set of scales. Moscow, too, turns her back on privilege, and takes with a decrepit reservist, Komiagin. Moscow and Sambikin are thrown briefly together. She has been working on another of Stalin's flagship projects, the construction of the Moscow metro, but after an accident, Sambikin has to amputate her wounded leg. After a brief tryst in the Caucasus, she returns to Komiagin. Sambikin and Sartorius meet once again: the former cold, rational and obsessed with humanity and history on a vast scale; the latter, reserved, modest and concerned with the intimate and day-to-day. So intense is Sartorius's ethical identification with others that he resolves to give up his own identity. He acquires a new passport—that of Ivan Gruniakhin—and finds a job in a factory kitchen. There he meets Konstantin Arapov, who has left his wife for a young French Komsomol girl, Katia, and whose elder son kills himself. Sartorius (now Gruniakhin) marries Arapov's abandoned wife, who is consumed with grief and bitterness. She beats her new husband, but he puts up no resistance. At this point, the novel breaks off.

Happy Moscow is one of Platonov's sporadic, but significant, attempts to portray the Soviet capital (earlier instances include the brief Moscow section towards the end of *Chevengur* and the short story *Doubting Makar* (*Usomnivshiisia Makar*)); moreover, it anticipates the representation of Moscow in other works of the 1930s, in which the capital city becomes a site of privilege where Soviet citizens (or at least those 'lucky' enough to belong to the political, administrative, technical and cultural elites of the time) can aspire to enjoy the pleasures and prosperity that were potentially offered by the second Five-Year Plan. For instance, Aleksandr Medvekin's 1935 film *Happiness* (*Schast'e*) culminates in a trip to the capital, a denouement that 'would seem to conform to mainstream cinema of the 1930s in which', according to Emma Widdis, 'the hero's success in the local space was frequently rewarded by recognition from the metropolis.'[7] Similarly, Iurii Pimenov's 1937 painting, *New Moscow* (*Novaia Mosvka*)—which incidentally shares its title with another Medvedkin film (withdrawn, however, in 1939)—signals the relaxed, holiday atmosphere of the city at leisure. Described by one critic as 'a hymn [...] to the reconstruction of Moscow and liberated Soviet womanhood',[8] it depicts a young woman in a floral print dress driving a soft-top car past handsomely clad Muscovites near the Bol'shoi Theatre and the Hotel Moskva. In this sense, *Happy Moscow* is a continuation of Platonov's explicit engagement with official culture and ideology in *The Foundation Pit* (*Kotlovan*) of 1929–1930, which deals with the programs for industrialisation and collectivisation that were at the heart of the first Five-Year Plan. If *The Foundation Pit* shows, however pessimistically, the violent and troublesome processes whereby socialism was to be ushered in under Stalin, *Happy Moscow* turns to the world of socialism itself, at least as it was conceived of and ostensibly delivered during the second Five-Year Plan, and particularly what Sheila Fitzpatrick refers to as 'the "three good years", 1934–36'.[9]

Appropriately, then, the title of *Happy Moscow* seems to echo Stalin's 1935 slogan 'life has become better, life has become merrier,' which stands as a summary of the values and culture of the second Five-Year Plan. Platonov illustrates the Soviet capital as it enjoys the better, merrier life ushered in by Stalin. In order to do this, he describes the lives of a group of young and successful Soviet citizens—engineers, explorers, composers, pianists—who form the social and cultural elite of the country and who are lavishly rewarded for their contribution to the development of Soviet society. The novel's sixth chapter depicts a gathering of such characters at the local Komsomol club, for whom life did appear to have become better and merrier:

> The large table had been laid for 50 people. Every half-metre there were flowers, looking pensive because of their beauty and giving off a posthumous fragrance. The wives of the designers, and the young women engineers, were dressed in the best silk of the Republic—the government liked to adorn its best people. Moscow Chestnova was wearing her tea-rose dress, which weighed only ten grams and had been sewn with such skill that even the pulsing of her blood vessels was revealed by the rippling of the silk.

All the men, even the untidy Sambikin and the shaggy, melancholic
Vechkin, had come in suits that were simple but expensive, made from the
finest material; to dress badly and in slovenly fashion would have been to
reproach with poverty the country that had nourished everyone present and
dressed them with her choicest goods, herself thriving on their youthful
strength and drive, on their talent and labour.[10]

There can be no doubt that *Happy Moscow* can be read as a poignant reaction
to the second Five-Year Plan, which, for proletarian idealists such as Platonov,
amounted to a tacit return to the detested New Economic Policy and even to
the bourgeois values of the Imperial past.

Yet happiness had always been a key work in Platonov's ideologically loaded
vocabulary; indeed, to borrow a term proposed elsewhere by Eric Naiman,
happiness is one of Platonov's key 'lexical heroes'.[11] In *Happy Moscow* there are
some 59 references to 'happiness' (counting occurrences of *schast'e, schastlivyi,*
etc.), and only 11 references to 'unhappiness' or 'misfortune' (*neschast'e, neschastnyi,*
etc.). This constitutes the most intensely focused use of the word 'happiness' in
all Platonov; the novel *Chevengur*, for instance, contains 93 references to
'happiness' and 21 to 'unhappiness', although, as a work around six times the
length of *Happy Moscow*, the density of references is correspondingly lower.
By comparison, *The Foundation Pit*—slightly longer than *Happy Moscow*—refers to
'happiness' and 'unhappiness' 49 and 6 times, respectively. And in 'The River
Potudan', a short story published the year after work on *Happy Moscow* was
abandoned, Platonov continues his enquiry into human emotions, with 13
references to happiness and only one to unhappiness.

Happy Moscow comes at an important juncture in Platonov's developing
attitude to happiness and its sources. To trace the author's changing use of the
word 'happiness' is to map philologically, as it were, his subtly evolving
philosophy. In *The Foundation Pit*, for instance, happiness frequently has a
literal, concrete quality, functioning as one of the materialised metaphors that
Joseph Brodsky identified as being central to Platonov's prose style: 'It can
safely be said about this writer that his every sentence drives the Russian
language into a semantic dead end or, more precisely, reveals a proclivity for
dead ends, a blind-alley mentality in the language itself.'[12] Consider, for
instance, the following examples, all from *The Foundation Pit*:

Happiness will come from materialism [...] not from meaning.[13]
    Although they possessed the meaning of life, which is as good as
eternal happiness, their faces were glum and thin, and the nearest they
had got to the peace of life was exhaustion.[14]

'Sadness is nothing, comrade Kozlov,' he said. 'It just means that our class can sense the whole world. In any case happiness is still a long way away… And happiness just leads to shame.'[15]

History says happiness is inevitable.[16]

Day and night alike, everything seemed so murky and pointless that he even began to doubt the happiness of the future—something he had always imagined as a deep blue summer, lit up by a motionless sun.[17]

By the time of *The Potudan River*, however, happiness has noticeably changed register. It no longer has a political, ideological or philosophical function; rather, its tenor has become personal and intimate, although it still retains a strikingly literal quality, typical of Platonov's writing throughout his career:

The younger people were mostly laughing, looking closely into each other's faces, animated and trustful, as if on the eve of eternal happiness.[18]

And so they were friends, patiently, almost all the long winter, tormented by anticipation of their approaching future happiness.[19]

The most poignant evocation of happiness occurs in the story's very final lines, when the reluctant hero submits to domestic life with his wife: 'I've got used to being happy with you now.'[20] It seems, then, that in calling his book *Andrei Platonov in Search of Happiness* (*Andrei Platonov v poiskakh schast'ia*), Mikhail Geller long ago isolated the evident importance of this question.[21]

I would like to suggest here, though, that the title of *Happy Moscow* encodes a specific and unexpected intertextual reference, namely to the famous opening line of Lev Tolstoi's *Anna Karenina*: 'All happy families are alike but an unhappy family is unhappy after its own fashion.'[22] After all, Stalin's slogan was not uttered until 1 December 1935, late in the composition of *Happy Moscow*. In his notebooks, Platonov had referred to the novel by name since early 1933,[23] and in any case, Stalin referred to life becoming 'merrier' (*veselei*) not 'happier' (*schastlivei*), a far from insignificant difference. Platonov's indebtedness to the literature of the past is well-established: the influence of Dostoevskii has been examined in detail;[24] Chekhov[25] and Pushkin play a particularly important role in Platonov's works of the late 1930s;[26] whereas certain stories from the 1920s clearly betray the influence of Leskov and Saltykov-Shchedrin.[27] Of course, the influence of Fedorov is well accepted,[28] as is that of Freud,[29] with allusions to Dante forming a more surprising element in the composition of *The Foundation Pit*.[30] *Journey from Leningrad to Moscow in 1937*, the putative title of the longer work of which *Happy Moscow* may have been a part, refers explicitly to Radishchev's attack on the evils of Tsarist Russia (published clandestinely in 1790), raising the possibility that Platonov's narrative was designed to unmask what he perceived as failings in the Stalinist system.

Tolstoi, though, has barely been proposed as a figure who may have influenced Platonov, let alone in the specific, intertextual manner I am proposing here.[31] Matters are little helped by the discovery that Tolstoi, along with other writers, hardly figures in Platonov's notebooks.[32] However, the realisation of the significance of *Anna Karenina* for an understanding of *Happy Moscow*—initially based on the congruence of Tolstoi's opening *bon mot* with Platonov's title—allows us to see how Soviet 'happiness' is read through the prism of a famous nineteenth-century tract on the search for human self-fulfillment and self-understanding. Moreover, a number of parallels in plot and character, when taken cumulatively, further suggest a profound ideological and artistic engagement on Platonov's part with the legacy of Tolstoi, and illuminate aspects of both the composition and interpretation of *Happy Moscow*.

There should, in fact, be little surprise to discover the number of correspondences between the two novels. After all, when writing about Soviet happiness under Stalin, why should Platonov's attention not have turned to that *locus classicus* of Russian thought on happiness and the fate of man? Conversely, once Platonov had chosen to make a woman the central figure of his novel—a device unusual enough for him—the philosophical baggage of the Russian novel, so often borne by the dilemmas of a woman and the men who surround her, was sure to follow. Consider, for example, the titles of both novels, which refer to heroines around whom many of the most important events are structured, yet who are often strangely absent. In each case, the fate of an individual woman stands at the centre of a novel that paints a portrait of an entire era. Moreover, Platonov picks up on one of the most remarkable aspects of *Anna Karenina*, its foregrounding of the female body (and not only the heroine's). For instance, the opening of Part 2 of *Anna Karenina* sees Kitty Shcherbatskaia physically examined by a celebrated doctor, much to the shame of both the patient and her family. This anticipates the near-fatal birth of Anna's daughter (Part 4, chapters 17–19), which makes the heroine the frequent and passive object of masculine observation. Anna's beauty, captured so well in a number of portraits in the novel, is tragically inverted at the moment of her suicide at the end of Part 7 when her broken body is bequeathed for all to see:

> [Vronskii] had rushed like one distraught into the railway shed and seen her mangled body, still warm with recent life, stretched out on a table shamelessly exposed to the gaze of all. The head, which had escaped hurt, with its heavy plaits and curls about the temples, was thrown back, and the lovely face with its half-open red lips had frozen into a strange expression—pitiful on the lips and horrible in the fixed open eyes[.][33]

In *Happy Moscow*, Platonov echoes such scenes, most notably when Sambikin carries out his search for the human soul in the bowels of a young dead woman (Chapter 8), and then when he operates on the wounded Moscow after her accident on the metro (Chapter 11):

> Sambikin examined her leg. Blood was coming out under pressure, and slightly foaming; the bone was shattered along its whole length and all kinds of filth were embedded in the wound. But the surrounding intact body looked gentle and tanned, and the curves of late innocence were so fresh and full that this worker surely deserved immortality; even the strong smell of sweat given off by her skin brought with it a charm, an excitement of life, that made one think of bread and of wide expanses of grass.[34]

Such scenes demonstrate Platonov's indebtedness to the 'physiological strain' in Soviet literature, 'the celebration of flesh, blood, love, death, sex' that Aleksandr Voronskii had traced back to Tolstoi in the 1920s.[35] Likewise, Dmitrii Merezhkovskii's celebrated description of Tolstoi as 'the seer of the flesh' maps onto Platonov's materialist vision of human corporeality.

But does the heroine of *Happy Moscow* have any further claim to be considered a modern incarnation of Anna Karenina? Natal'ia Kornienko has compared Moscow both to the *Mona Lisa* and to Nabokov's Lolita,[36] but the comparison with Anna Karenina is closer and more dynamic. Both women have a flagrant erotic power which captivates the men they encounter, although the context in which they display this power differs in each novel: the social constraints placed upon Tolstoi's heroine are replaced by Soviet concepts of free marriage and sexual liberalism. More profoundly, Platonov borrows from Tolstoi not only the character of the erotically powerful heroine, but also the plot device of the love triangle, more familiar in nineteenth-century literature generally, where it is employed to present both the strengths and failings of competing world views. Specific examples in *Anna Karenina* would be not only the conflict between Karenin, Anna and Vronskii that is at the heart of the novel, but also the tense relations between Vronskii, Kitty and Levin that mirror, albeit in happier form, Anna's dilemma, as well as the anxieties provoked in both Kitty and Levin by Levin's temporary infatuation with Anna (Part 7, chapters 9–11). Platonov distils these multifarious relationships into the single triangle at the heart of *Happy Moscow*, that between the two most articulate heroes—Sambikin and Sartorius—both of whom fall in love with the heroine, this emotional juxtaposition matching their different ideological positions.

Platonov's title reveals a further Tolstoyan influence, that of the contrast between town and country. It is instructive that *Happy Moscow* is Platonov's only major urban narrative—he otherwise prefers the steppe, the countryside, the village or the liminal space of the suburban settlement. The tension between urban and non-urban settings had already been anticipated in *Chevengur*, written between 1926 and 1929, and which contains a brief but crucial Muscovite digression towards the end of the novel. Tellingly, the word 'happiness' occurs more frequently in this section of *Chevengur* than anywhere else (fifteen times in just seventeen pages), and its heroine Sof'ia Aleksandrovna has been described by Mikhail Geller as 'the only character in the novel to know happiness'.[37] In both *Chevengur* and *Happy Moscow*, as in *Anna Karenina*, cities are associated with the machinery of power and the deceptive charms of society and pleasure—all of them false promises of happiness—against which is set the true search for meaning in life which takes place in the rural, or at least the non-urban, environment. In *Anna Karenina*, for instance, Moscow is referred to as 'our corrupt Babylon',[38] and later on Levin confesses that 'living for so long in Moscow with nothing to do but eat, drink, and gossip was beginning to demoralise him.'[39] An exchange wryly recorded in Platonov's notebooks suggests just how closely he shared Levin's aversion to the consequences of life in the city:

'In Moscow and New York there's only noise, fumes, danger to life, hysteria, neurosis...'
  Atabaev's wife: 'Ah, how marvellous! That's where life is really wonderful!'
  (In love with *The Moscow Evening News*, she even peruses the advertisements)...[40]

Platonov overheard this exchange whilst travelling through Turkmenistan in 1934; such a setting would have reinforced his awareness of the distance between the centre and the periphery and heightened his indignation at the idea of the Soviet capital resembling the American metropolis. *Happy Moscow* is, admittedly, less obviously concerned with the countryside than *Anna Karenina* (or even *Chevengur*, for that matter). It is, however, full of incidental, yet telling, references to the world beyond Moscow, and most notably to the collective farms that provide the city with its evident luxury.

One might also seek other, more specific parallels. If *Anna Karenina* does in fact function as a productive intertext, then the Komsomol feast cited earlier can be read as a version of the sumptuous meal that Levin shares with Oblonskii near the very beginning of Tolstoi's novel (Part 1, chapters 10–11)—and, what is more, with similar effect on the reader. Komiagin, Moscow's final, decrepit lover, is a military reservist, a role that invests him with bathetic features both of Vronskii's first, failed military career, and of his subsequent self-destructive heroism in the Serbian campaign. Anna and Vronskii's Italian sojourn in Part 5 of *Anna Karenina* is translated into the brief romantic trip that Sambikin and Moscow take to a Black Sea resort near the Caucasus. Such examples—which can seem without motive in the fragmentary narrative of *Happy Moscow*—take on a sudden significance if read as echoes of *Anna Karenina*. Moreover, as a 'strong' writer,[41] Platonov did not merely borrow, but rewrote, and indeed parodied, to use the language of the Russian formalists. As the above examples suggest, there is certainly much that is parodic about *Happy Moscow*, both of Tolstoi on the one hand and of Stalinist culture on the other. In this regard, one of the most adroit fusions of the Tolstoyan intertext with the Stalinist social context is Moscow's accident when working on the construction of the Moscow metro, which invests the tragedy of Anna Karenina's suicide with a profound sense of modernist irony.

Platonov's *Happy Moscow* contains, then, a series of close intertextual borrowings from Tolstoi's *Anna Karenina*, as well as a number of less tightly argued parallels and general points of contact, which derive from a certain similarity in the two writers' world views, and take on significance in the greater intertextual scheme at work in the later novel. *Anna Karenina* is certainly not the only influence on *Happy Moscow*; nor can every element in Tolstoi be carried over into Platonov's appropriation of the earlier novel. Furthermore, my insistence on the intertextual relevance of *Anna Karenina* for *Happy Moscow* is in part creatively speculative, an act of preposterous reading designed to force open a troublesome and challenging text.[42]

Yet the structural and thematic parallels between *Anna Karenina* and *Happy Moscow* take on overwhelming significance when seen in the context of the Stalinist 1930s. On the aesthetic level, *Happy Moscow*—when read through *Anna Karenina*—becomes a meditation on literary realism, not least because, despite the numerous similarities between the two novels, Tolstoi's realism is one thing that Platonov so ostentatiously eschews. Tolstoi had been a model for Soviet writers from the mid-1920s—in his notebooks, Platonov himself referred to 'Tolstoi and his Fadeevs'.[43] As a novel started in the year that artistic factions were dissolved and centralised artistic unions set up, and which was written as Socialist Realism was being debated both in public and private, *Happy Moscow* forms an invaluable commentary on the development of that particular literary discourse. Paradoxically, Platonov explores—at the very moment when literary modernism came under attack—the possibilities of that modernism in a more extreme manner than ever before. Thus, *Happy Moscow* constitutes a commentary not only on Socialist Realism, but on literary style as mediated through the contested legacy of Tolstoi and the classical tradition more generally. It is as if Platonov objects to straightforward attempts to transplant the literary legacy of the past into a very different age; he calls on us to reread Tolstoi for ourselves, provoked by the experience of reading his (Platonov's) idiosyncratic vision of the older writer. If, in the 1930s, artists were being called on to learn from the classics, then Platonov would prove just how idiosyncratic such an apprenticeship could be, as he dealt with the found material of the time as creatively as he had ever done.

Yet *Happy Moscow* is not just a novel about style; its aesthetic ambitions enfold an intensely ethical core. If *Happy Moscow* is structured around the very word 'happiness', treating it almost as a self-conscious literary device, then it is equally concerned with the nature of happiness itself, in terms both of the Stalinist happiness promised by the second Five-Year Plan, and of a deeper philosophical enquiry into human existence. Ever an attentive reader, Platonov has noticed the centrality of happiness to *Anna Karenina*, not just as Tolstoi facetiously puts it in the novel's opening sentence, but as it runs obsessively through every encounter, every exchange, every relationship in the novel.

The ethical yearning that runs through *Happy Moscow* is most violently experienced by one character, who in his striving and uncertainties, is as classically Tolstoyan as he is classically Platonovian; when read in the shadow of *Anna Karenina*, Sartorious comes across as a Soviet embodiment of Tolstoi's *alter ego*, Konstantin Levin. Uneasy in societies from which they ultimately withdraw, both men search for some kind of overarching meaning in life, and learn to find it in unexpected ways. Moreover, both novels appear to dwell on their eponymous heroines, while ultimately sacrificing these women in favor of a narrative centred on the growth of a different, yet complementary, male character. These heroes are palpably and autobiographically close to their respective authors; their crises are narrated with omnisciently authoritative intensity that brings their attitudes and personalities more acutely before the reader than those of any other character. At the very start of *Anna Karenina*, Oblonskii's claim, 'the whole aim of civilisation is to make everything a source of enjoyment,'[44] leaves Levin uneasy at his friend's easy-going conscience and sybaritic nature. The statement resonates throughout the rest of the novel and serves as a standard against which the behaviour of all the other characters in the novel will be measured and, indeed, implicitly judged. The rhetorical question posed by Oblonskii (for that is surely what it is, placed by Tolstoi in the mouth of one his creations) is one which applies to *Happy Moscow* too; Sartorius grows uneasy with the privilege and luxury around him, and begins to question the cost of the enjoyment offered to and expected of him as a member of the Soviet elite. As Platonov himself remarked in his notebooks, 'Happiness, "life," is yet more terrible than sorrow.'[45]

When, at the end of the novel, Sartorius observes the suffering provoked when Konstantin Arabov abandons his wife for the lithesome Katia Bessonet-Favor, he questions Arabov's mistress about the price of happiness in a scene that distills all of his previous doubt and anxiety:

'You've heard of the golden rule of mechanics. Some people have thought they can use this rule to cheat the whole of nature, the whole of life. Kostya Arabov wanted to obtain with you, or from you—how can I put it?—some kind of free gold. And he did find a little.'

'A little—yes,' Katya agreed.

'But how much? Not more than a gram. And to achieve equilibrium it was necessary to weigh down the other end of the lever with a whole ton of the graveyard earth that now lies on top of his son and crushes him.'[46]

This exchange echoes one of Levin and Oblonskii's later encounters, in which the light-hearted adulterer gaily puts the other side of the argument, defending the philosophy behind his amorous infidelities:

> 'You don't admit, I know, that one may like a roll when one's ration of bread is there for one—to your mind it is a crime; but I don't count life without love,' he said […]. 'It can't be helped: I was born that way. And besides, it does do little harm to anyone else but gives so much pleasure to oneself…'[47]

Oblonskii may believe his intrigues cause little harm, but Levin suspects otherwise, and the reader too is in no doubt of Dolly's suffering. Similarly, Arabov and Bessonet believe that there will be no price to pay for their selfishness, whereas Sartorius gives voice to their otherwise absent conscience which ought to tell them that happiness cannot be bought at the price of someone else's pain. Furthermore, the allusion to Archimedes' lever—a typically Platonovian borrowing from the world of mathematics to clarify a human and moral predicament—seems to render explicit the content of a clichéd and throwaway comment made by Oblonskii, again during his dinner with Levin: 'Yes, my boy, women are the pivot the world turns on.'[48] In each case, the narrative device of marital infidelity unfolds into a broader metaphysical speculation about the nature of human happiness.

The flight from society and its selfish attitude to happiness is the path taken by both Levin and Sartorius. Moreover, this flight is not merely a negative act of departure in which the hero moves away from a situation which provokes uneasy reflection; it also involves the embrace of alternative forms of self-realisation which are held to be truer precisely because they are altruistic. Thus, when Sartorius gives up a prestigious career as an engineer, he turns his skills instead to inventing a simple yet reliable set of scales for use on collective farms. This echoes Levin's attempts at agricultural improvement on his estate; Soviet collectivisation is read through the experience of agrarian reform in post-emancipation Imperial Russia.

Yet, even a more modest and less celebrated form of practical engagement fails to bring satisfaction to the nervous heroes. The first half of *Happy Moscow*'s eighth chapter portrays Sartorius's apparently rewarding work on his improved scales; the second half, however, deals with a troubling encounter with the surgeon Sambikin, who is searching for the secret of human history in the digestive tracts of human corpses:

> 'And now [...] we shall see the general reason for life.'
>
> Sambikin opened up the fatty envelope of the stomach, and then guided his knife down the intestine, revealing its contents: inside lay an unbroken column of food that had not yet been assimilated, but soon this food came to an end and the intestine was empty. Sambikin went slowly down the section of emptiness and reached the beginning of the excrement, where he came to a stop.
>
> 'You see!' said Sambikin, opening more widely the slit down the empty section between the food and excrement. 'This emptiness in the intestines sucks all humanity into itself and is the moving force of world history. This is the soul—have a sniff!'[49]

Unsurprisingly, Sartorius remains dissatisfied with such grandiloquent philosophising. For him, Sambikin's scientific hubris only serves to highlight the failure of his ambitious and teleological historiography, tinged with more than a little metaphysical speculation. Sartorius leaves, saddened by this realisation:

> He was distressed by the sorrow and poverty of life, distressed that life was so helpless that it needed almost constant illusions in order to distract itself from a consciousness of its true situation. Even Sambikin was seeking illusions in his ideas and discoveries—he too was carried away by the complexity and great essence the world possessed in his imagination. But Sartorius could see that the world consisted primarily of destitute matter, which it was almost impossible to love but essential to understand.[50]

Sartorius's predicament follows Levin's dissatisfaction with a world view shaped by materialism and rationalism (as represented by his studies of agriculture and economics), as well his later alienation from a more idealist school of philosophy, as suggested by his reading of 'Plato, Spinoza, Kant, Schelling, Hegel, and Schopenhauer'.[51] In both cases, any philosophical system is necessarily unequal to the challenges of life as it really is.

For both men, philosophical despair is also matched by waning confidence in the possibility of large-scale social action. As Levin observes:

> Formerly [...], whenever he had tried to do anything for the general good, for the good of humanity, for Russia, for the province, for the village as a whole, he had observed that the idea of it had been pleasant, but the

activity it entailed had always been incoherent. There had never been full conviction of its absolute necessity, and the work itself, from at first appearing so great, had grown less and less, till it vanished into nothing.[52]

However, as the passage continues, Levin's life is not devoid of meaning, as his former activities have been replaced by another form of commitment:

> But now, since his marriage, when he had begun to confine himself more and more to living for himself, though he no longer found any delight at the thought of the work he was doing, he felt confident of its usefulness, saw that it succeeded far better than in the old days, and that it was always growing instead of getting smaller.[53]

Marriage here functions as the final stage in the heroes' search for moral and personal fulfillment, coming as it does after failed attempts at integration within privileged society, then displaced involvement with the aims of that society, and lastly in philosophical enquiry. Like Levin, Sartorius marries, willingly submitting himself to the discipline of contingency and intimacy. Both men learn to embrace domesticity, having sought—and failed to find— truth elsewhere. Moreover, in both cases, marriage is portrayed neither as the stereotypical happy end, the fulfillment of the erotic trajectory of much nineteenth-century fiction ('Reader, I married him'); neither is it a simple and convenient refuge from the public, the political and the ideological; rather marriage is seen as a tense and difficult act of confinement and renunciation of the self. In the case of Sartorius, this loss of selfhood is literally the case, since, in a further synthesis of an ethics learnt from Tolstoi with elements of contemporary Soviet reality, Sartorius acquires a new passport not, as happened in the 1930s, in order to conceal the unsuitability of his past and deny his class origins,[54] but precisely to reject the advantages available to him as a member of the Stalinist elite. His subsequent marriage merely finalizes this ethics of inversion.

Sartorius's decision to renounce recognition and freedom for the self-imposed limitations of marriage makes *Happy Moscow* the first in a series of works (most notably *The River Potudan* and *The Return* (*Vozvrashchenie*)) in which the burden of the hero's salvation falls on the nobility and superiority of a woman. This alignment with a characteristic feature of the Russian classical tradition (here facilitated through the intertext of *Anna Karenina*) is, however, far from complacent. In Tolstoi, Levin's marriage functions as a sign of personal and national salvation, and for all his hesitancy, Levin seems ultimately happy. For Platonov's hero, however, marriage is no easy refuge or source of contentment; in a frank and startling departure from Tolstoi,

Sartorius's wife—the bitter and doleful Matryona Filippovna Cheburkova—is as deliberately unlike Kitty Shcherbatskaia as can be imagined. It is as if Platonov shares a widely felt dissatisfaction with the probability of Levin's journey, the verisimilitude of his relationship with Kitty and the depth and durability of his hard-won faith. The rows which only serve to strengthen the bond between Kitty and Levin—'Their quarrels, too, afforded them both disenchantment and new enchantment'[55]—are translated by Platonov into something altogether more profoundly miserable:

> As a rule, Cheburkova did not allow her husband to go anywhere except to work, and she would keep an eye on the clock: would he be back home on time? She did not believe in official meetings, and she would begin weeping and cursing, saying that her second husband was a scoundrel too and that he was betraying her. If her husband still came in late, Matryona Filippovna would open the door and set about him, using an old felt boot, a coat rail together with its clothes, a flue from what had once been a samovar, a shoe off her own foot, or any immediate thing she could lay her hands on—anything to exhaust her own irritation and unhappiness. During such moment Grunyakhin [i.e., Sartorius's new identity] would look at Matryona Filippovna with surprise, while she cried pathetically—because one grief had simply turned into another, and had not disappeared completely. Grunyakhin, who had seen much of life, was not especially upset at being treated like this.[56]

In his stoic sadness, Sartorius seems to hark back to the restless and even suicidal aspects of Levin's character. Moreover, Platonov here superimposes onto the prototype of Kitty and Levin's happy marriage the wretched suffering of Anna and Vronskii as their relationship disintegrates into jealousy and recrimination, thereby heightening Sartorius's self-imposed retreat into suffering, and, in turn, both confusing and consolidating the relevance of the Tolstoyan intertext.

By stressing the unhappiness in the strange marriage of Semyon Sartorius/ Ivan Gruniakhin and Matryona Cheburkova, Platonov astutely reveals a facet of Tolstoi that is provisionally overlaid at the end of *Anna Karenina*: its intimation of sadness. Angela Livingstone—not, admittedly, in a discussion of Anna Karenina, but of *Childhood*—makes the following observation: 'In Tolstoi, as in Platonov, sadness must always inscribe itself into daily life.'[57] The presence of sadness and the acceptance of daily life figure heavily at the end of *Happy Moscow* and have their roots in Platonov's engagement with Tolstoi. Tolstoi extricates Platonov from the personal despair and creative dead end he had potentially found himself in by the early 1930s, forced to be loyal to both his own utopianism and to the new-found utopianism of Stalin's

Five-Year Plans, yet full of doubts about both. *Happy Moscow* comes at a point in Platonov's career when he revisits his previous commitment to the common cause, considering, instead, a more personal, intimate form of goodness, if not happiness. In this context, *Anna Karenina* functions, in Catriona Kelly's apt description, as a 'novelized conduct book,'[58] a self-help guide for the writer at a personal and professional crossroads.

Platonov's unsuspected affinity with Tolstoi is no mere historical equivocation or a retreat into the safety of the literature of the past. Rather, it forms a prism for enquiring precisely into the present; the implications of this for Platonov's relationship to Stalin's rule should be clear enough. Platonov, like his proximate hero Sartorius, seeks happiness not in the vanished past or the unobtainable future, but in the unbearable present. Stalin's declaration that 'life has become better, life has become merrier' left vast areas of human misery unaccounted for and unresolved. Platonov willingly and self-consciously embraces such misery, as revealed by the 23 recurrences of the novel's other 'lexical hero', *toska*— 'sadness', 'melancholy' or 'ennui'. Merriment, on the other hand, is a mendacious façade, a moral deception, and a dangerously synonymous deceit.

Chapter Eleven

'BUT WHERE IS YOUR HAPPINESS, ALEVTINA IVANOVNA?': NEW DEBATES ABOUT HAPPINESS IN THE SOVIET FILMS OF 1956

Julian Graffy

The Russian Cinematic Search for Happiness

The search for happiness in Russian film began before the birth of the Soviet Union. Pre-Revolutionary Russian filmmakers were preoccupied with the theme, notably the preeminent Russian director Evgenii Bauer. His characters sought happiness in conventional worldly success in films such as *Child of the Big City* (*Ditia bol'shogo goroda*, 1914), but also in ecstatic delusion and self-sacrifice in two films whose titles make explicit reference to happiness, *The Happiness of Eternal Night* (*Schast'e vechnoi nochi*, 1915) and his late masterpiece *In Pursuit of Happiness* (*Za schast'em*, 1917).

The search continued after the Revolution. One of the most daring and inventive films of the Soviet 1930s bears the one word title *Happiness* (*Schast'e*). Made in 1934 by Aleksandr Medvedkin, it tells in allegorical form the tale of the Russian peasant's doomed struggle for happiness. Such is Medvedkin's sense of irony that the film did not attract official approval. Far more consonant with the ideological imperatives of the time was the representation of happiness in the musicals of Grigorii Aleksandrov and Ivan Pyr'ev, in which happiness is encapsulated in songs that are still sung today. In Aleksandrov's first musical, *The Jolly Fellows* (*Veselye rebiata*, 1934), for example, the heroine Aniuta sings:

Сердце в груди
Бьется, как птица.

И хочешь знать, что ждет впереди,
И хочется счастья добиться.
(The heart in my breast
Beats like a bird.
And you want to know what lies ahead
And you want to get happiness.)

Happiness for Aniuta is performing at the Bol'shoi Theatre and the love of Kostia Potekhin, a collective farm shepherd turned jazz-band conductor (for such transformations are possible in the Soviet Union). In similar fashion, much of the intrigue of Aleksandrov's next film, *Circus* (*Tsirk*, 1934), is concerned with the American heroine's search, comically expressed in her broken Russian but ultimately successful, to 'find happiness in the USSR', a happiness also achieved through career success and the love of a good man. Though the setting is different in Pyr'ev's variations on this theme (in which the provincial collective farm replaces the metropolis), the formula is essentially the same.

The fact that happiness is such a universal aspiration makes its voluntary renunciation, in another group of Soviet films of the period, all the more emotionally potent. Soviet war films of the Stalinist period, whether set in the Civil War or in World War II, include a recurrent trope of the postponement or sacrifice of happiness to a noble cause. In the Civil War film *Chapaev* (1934, directed by Georgii and Sergei Vasil'ev), the young Red fighters Pet'ka and Anka eschew any mention of their mutual attraction. Though Chapaev himself speaks of the future happiness that awaits them, his words are closely followed by Pet'ka's heroic death in battle. Fifteen years later, in the Second World War film *The Fall of Berlin* (*Padenie Berlina*, 1949, directed by Mikhail Chiaureli), the hero and heroine, Alesha and Natasha, are just about to declare their love when German troops invade. They immediately forget all thoughts of personal fulfillment and are reunited only four years later, at the end of a war in which both have shown exemplary courage.

Failure to reach this exacting standard of personal morality is harshly punished in the war films of the time. *Wait for Me* (*Zhdi menia*, 1943), directed by Aleksandr Stolper and Boris Ivanov and taken from a famous play by Konstantin Simonov, explicitly contrasts the behaviour of two women, the heroine Liza and her friend Sonia. The plane that their airmen husbands are flying is shot down and the men are presumed lost, though their bodies are not found. Sonia cannot bear the prolonged isolation, uncertainty and sadness, so she takes up with a new lover, puts on a new dress and goes out dancing. To Liza's implied rebuke she responds, 'Let Andrei send me to the devil if he comes back.' He returns, of course, though badly wounded, and she is punished for her decision to privilege personal happiness by being doomed to arrive too late at his deathbed to secure his forgiveness. Liza, who, by contrast, steadfastly waits and waits, is eventually rewarded by the safe return of her husband and the chance to speak the film's famous last words: 'My God, what a long time you were away' (*Bozhe moi, kak dolgo tebia ne bylo*). The pervasiveness of such plots led Soviet film critics of the period to the following conclusion:

> In the cinema, mutual love and happiness figure as the top mark for exemplary behaviour and assiduousness. The duty of the examiners is to hand out the right marks.[1]

Further evidence that the question of happiness remained a central preoccupation of Soviet filmmakers is provided by the largest single-volume catalogue of Soviet films, the *Domashniaia sinemateka* (Home Cinémathèque), which contains a list of the words that are used most frequently in the titles of Soviet and Russian films. This establishes that the word happiness (*schast'e*) occurs in the titles of 61 films made in the Soviet Union or Russia between 1918 and 1996, putting it in fourth place behind love (*liubov'*, 221 times), life (*zhizn'*, 75 times), and day (*den'*, 69 times) and just ahead of person (*chelovek*, 59 times) and night (*noch'*, 50 times).[2] The films that include the word in the title are, of course, merely a fraction of the number for which the subject of happiness is a central concern.

The Films of 1956

Within this vast amount of material, it may be timely to take a snapshot of the treatment of the theme of happiness in the Soviet films of 1956. The Thaw era (approximately the dozen years following the death of Stalin) is currently being closely scrutinised in the context of the fiftieth anniversary of Nikita Khrushchev's Secret Speech, which partially unmasked Stalin, and the period is conventionally seen as one of both societal and cinematic innovation. Looking at a small number of films made or released in this year may shed light on a stage in the evolution of the treatment of this perennial subject, and may expose the contradictions inherent in periods of historical change. Thaw-period films are, moreover, marked by a strong urge to represent life *as it is* and to give lessons on how to live it. Petr Vail' starts his 1996 essay on the treatment of daily life (*byt*) in Soviet films with the words:

> The semantic richness of Soviet cinema of the 1940s–1960s is so high that wish as you may to look at these films simply as 'cinema', you cannot do it. Every time it's a model of life [...] Of course the message of

Stalinist and Thaw cinema was mutually opposed, but what is much more important is that the requirement to provide a message was doubted by no one. And what is even more important for me as a viewer is that this crucially important task was resolved on the surface of the screen with touching simplicity and expressiveness.[3]

Films About the Revolution and the Civil War

The films I have chosen to concentrate on here have official production dates of 1955 or 1956 and were released on Soviet screens in 1956.[4] They are all films about young people whose 'search for happiness' is perhaps more urgent than that of their elders. Most of them are set in the present, but the cinema of the Khrushchev period also paid much attention to the revolutionary past. I shall start by looking at films about the attitudes and behaviour of young people during the birth years of the Soviet state as imagined from four decades later, when film studios were instructed to make films to mark the fortieth anniversary of the Russian Revolution.

They Were the First (*Oni byli pervymi*), directed by Iurii Egorov and released on 15 May 1956, is set in Petrograd and devoted to the heroic efforts to defend the city against White forces by a group of young workers who are among the first members of the Komsomol, the Young Communist League, which was founded at the First All-Russian Congress of the Unions of Worker and Peasant Youth on 29 October 1918. In its predictable story of the political radicalisation of young proletarians, *They Were the First* is reminiscent of Grigorii Kozintsev and Leonid Trauberg's classic 1934 film on the same theme, *The Youth of Maksim* (*Iunost' Maksima*), and its plot draws heavily upon *Chapaev*. It opens with a song, 'Beyond the Factory Gates' (*Za fabrichnoi zastavoi*), which allegorically predicts its plot by telling of a seventeen-year-old lad in 1918 who is too shy to tell his first love of his feelings for her. He then goes off to fight for the workers' cause and is cut down by an enemy sabre. The song's final stanza makes a conventional connection between the personal and the political:

Парню очень хотелось
Счастье здесь увидать.
За рабочее дело
Он ушел воевать.

(The lad really wanted
To see happiness here.
For the workers' cause
He went off to fight.)

Stepan (*Stepa*), the young worker hero of the film, who will later himself sing this song, is radicalised by the events of 1918, joins the Komsomol and prepares to go away to fight. Though it is obvious to all his friends that he loves Glafira (*Glasha*), and she loves him, Stepan insists that love is just 'prejudice'. When Glasha confides her feelings to an old worker, Uncle Andrei, he suggests that she drop a hint to Stepan, since that is what 'we men' need, but Glasha demurs. An extended conversation between them provides evidence that some films of 1956 were still presenting the search for personal happiness in a completely traditional way.

> 'No, Uncle Andrei. I have my own dream. I want to go into battle with Stepa!'
> 'What battle?'
> 'The usual one, with the Whites. Bullets whistling, shells exploding, our red banner unfurled, and we are going forward, all our Komsomol brigade… wind, snow, snowstorm, and Stepa and I are at the front. We'll destroy the Whites in that battle, and Stepa will come up to me and say, I've fallen in love with you, Glafira, for your bravery. That's when I'll tell him…'

Soon after this, the young men are sent to fight the Whites. On the train taking them to the Front, they sing the song with which the film began. As a young woman, Glasha has not been allowed to go, but she stows away, riding on the roof of the train. When Stepa finds her she exclaims, 'What, everyone's off to the Front and I stay at home?'

When winter comes, the young people capture a White Armored Train, but in the ensuing battle Glasha is shot. She dies in Stepa's arms, too soon for him to tell her that he loves her. Love has again been sacrificed to the cause. Stepa's only recourse is to continue to fight in her memory; in the film's final scene he meets Lenin at the Third Congress of the Komsomol.

The most innovative film of 1956 about the fate of young people during the Civil War and their intense but paradoxical ideas about love and happiness is Grigorii Chukhrai's *The Forty First* (*Sorok pervyi*), released on 15 October. In its staging of the clash between the forces of duty and love, it is instructive to compare it with two similar films of the period: Aleksandr Alov and Vladimir Naumov's *Pavel Korchagin*, released on 29 January 1957, which, like *The Forty First*, was taken from a famous novel and had already been filmed during the Stalin period; and Iulii Raizman's *The Communist* (*Kommunist*), made in 1957. Pavel Korchagin renounces the love that he feels for Rita Ustinovich because, as he explains to her, the revolutionary has no right to personal happiness in a period of revolutionary struggle. They shake hands and part. By the time he realizes his mistake, she has married someone else.

On the other hand, Vasilii Gubanov, the eponymous hero of *The Communist*, refuses to renounce his love for the married Aniuta Fokina. Indeed, it leads him to ask a Party official, 'How will things be under Communism with regard to love?' The official replies that he must 'overcome himself'. Gubanov refuses to do so and Aniuta bears his child, for which they (and the film) are heavily criticised. Gubanov goes on to give his life in the Revolutionary cause, which, of course, helps to redeem him, but this film explicitly finds Gubanov's (flawed) humanity in his *combination* of revolutionary duty and the pursuit of personal happiness.

In the context of these two films, *The Forty First* would seem, by its conclusion, to stand on the Korchagin side of duty and renunciation. At the end of the film, the Red sniper Mariutka shoots the White Lieutenant Govorukha-Otrok, despite having fallen in love with him, just as she had done in Boris Lavrenev's story and Iakov Protazanov's 1926 film, and he becomes her forty-first victim.

But what is interesting about this remake, partly, of course, in consequence of its being a sound film, but partly as a measure of its Thaw sensibility, is that personal happiness as an alternative to revolutionary duty is discussed at length in the film and also found to have its claims. As Petr Vail' and Aleksandr Genis write in their book about the Soviet Union of the 1960s, in the art of this period:

> The single and adequate basis for love became the presence of strong and sincere emotion. This is where the novelty lay: in loving someone not for some quality, but simply because you love them (*prosto tak*).[5]

Just before the film's conclusion, Govorukha-Otrok admits that the time that the storm on the Aral Sea has unexpectedly delivered to them has provided the 'fullest days' of his life, and that he has merged with nature, felt a part of it, and rejoiced in this closeness. These words are too high-flown for Mariutka. 'You speak like a learned man,' she tells him, 'I'll put it simply. I am happy' (*Schastlivaia ia*).

Despite all this, when the Lieutenant suggests that perhaps they should stay there forever, Mariutka retorts that this is not a time to sit around, and remembers her revolutionary duty. Yet even the final scene of revolutionary retribution is represented in the probing spirit of the Thaw. In the words of A. Usmanova, writing about the phenomenon of the remake in Russian cinema:

> But if at the end of the 1920s the ending of the film was imbued with the ideology of class warfare—Mariutka's hand did not tremble and pressed the trigger of the rifle when her beloved attempted to escape—

in the new version, filmed at the end of the 1950s [sic, JG], the ending turned out to be more ambiguous: the heroes of the 'new wave' cinema turn out not to be prepared to provide a politically correct answer to the question of 'who you should and who you should not love.'[6]

Films Set in the Present

My attention in the rest of this article will be devoted to some of the large number of films made in 1955–1956 about contemporary young people and their 'lessons in life,' to borrow the title of another film of the period, Iulii Raizman's *A Lesson in Life* (*Urok zhizni*, 1955). In a recent article about the youth culture of these years, Juliane Fürst says that the three aspects of the behaviour of young people which caused most alarm in 1956 were hooliganism, *stiliazhnichestvo* (how they dressed) and their potential reaction to Khrushchev's Secret Speech, which many of them had been encouraged to discuss (an experience which, it was feared, might lead to their loss of faith in the competence of the Komsomol).[7] There is direct evidence of this in a memoir entitled *The Year 1956* by the literary scholar Marietta Chudakova. It describes being present when the speech was read to students of Moscow State University in the spring of that year, and contains this memorable phrase: 'I entered the auditorium as one person, and left it as another.'[8] Needless to say, none of these three areas of concern is directly reflected in the films under discussion. Rather, they look at the moral dilemmas thrown up by the characters' ordinary lives and, in most cases, offer their protagonists, and their viewers, a relatively conventional 'recipe for happiness'. The films that I shall now discuss contain a number of recurring tropes: finishing school or study, making a career choice, leaving home and setting up in a new place, making a journey to a new life, getting married and/or having your first child, discovering your ordinariness and coping with it, and so on, and the presentation of these experiences is always ethically loaded. From film to film, material well-being is represented as an obstacle to happiness. If your parents are well connected and successful and try to pull strings for you in your choice of career or place of study, if you live in their large flat in the centre of Moscow or Leningrad, you are more likely to behave badly—and therefore less likely to be happy. A journey from the periphery to Moscow *may* bring you happiness, but a journey in the opposite direction is more likely to do so (scenes of family and friends seeing off characters at a railway station are a staple of these films), since it will lead you to discover value in the unspoiled hinterland of the country. You should make your own happiness; neither your interfering mother nor any Komsomol official—who is likely to be indifferent or incompetent—can make decisions for you.

Films Set on Collective Farms

Some of the films of the period about young people cling to the simple Pyr'ev collective farm-musical model. Ivan Lukinskii's *The Soldier Ivan Brovkin* (*Soldat Ivan Brovkin*, 1955), released on 9 September 1955, is a colour film in the style and tradition of the major postwar examples of the genre, such as Pyr'ev's *Kuban Cossacks* (*Kubanskie kazaki*, 1949) and Iulii Raizman's *The Chevalier of the Golden Star* (*Kavaler zolotoi zvezdy*, 1950). It has lots of songs, and it structures the search for happiness in absolutely conventional terms: discovering the joy of efficient work for the collective, becoming a model combine-harvester driver, and finding true love. The love problems are caused by two girls loving the same boy and vice versa, and there are no evil characters. The unsuccessful lover is just an 'intellectual bookkeeper', saddled with a profession which makes him ill-placed to win hearts. In a device that goes back to the 1930s musicals of Aleksandrov (and from him to the prose of Nikolai Gogol'), his very name, Samokhvalov (self-praiser), provides further indication of the way the plot will be resolved. This is clearly far from the model of Thaw innovation, but, perhaps not coincidentally, it was a huge popular success and was Soviet box office champion in 1955. A further indication of its popularity is a scene near the start of Vladimir Men'shov's 1979 film *Moscow Doesn't Believe in Tears* (*Moskva slezam ne verit*), set in the time of the release of *The Soldier Ivan Brovkin*. The young heroines of Men'shov's film are seen standing excitedly outside a cinema showing a 'Week of French Films'. But their excitement is caused not by the hitherto inaccessible foreign films, nor by the visiting French stars, who mean nothing to them, but rather by Leonid Kharitonov, Lukinskii's Brovkin. The critic Irina Shilova, who was born in 1937 and so grew up with these films, records her maturation as a viewer in her 1993 book *...i moe kino*, which is a wonderful guide to the films of the period and the evolution of popular taste. She reminds us that even in these years of supposed experiment and change it was conventional films that won the biggest audience.[9]

The same model is used by Andrei Frolov in his *The Guest from the Kuban* (*Gost's Kubani*, 1955), released on 6 February 1956. This is another colour film that combines bringing in the harvest with a love story, and the plot involves explicit invocation of *Kuban Cossacks*. The inexperienced hero Nikolai Vorobtsov drives a combine–harvester, and the film contains a song with the line, 'If a fellow is interesting, that means the fellow is a combine driver' (*Esli paren' interesnyi, znachit paren' kombainer*). Vorobtsov has to do double norms in order to compete with the legendary Gorban', a 'distinguished combine–harvester driver' (*znatnyi kombainer*) from the Kuban', who turns out to be a woman. At the same time, he falls in love with Nastia, and the ups and downs of their love story run in parallel with the work on the farm right through the film. When Nastia's friend Dus'ka falls for Vorobtsov, her own temporarily spurned collective-farmer lover Min'ka declaims Pushkin's famous poem of jilted love *Ia vas liubil* (I loved you) to her—just as a similar unlikely taste for the works of Russia's greatest poet was displayed by the collective farmers of *Kuban Cossacks*.

The old model still applied in 1958 when Lukinskii took his popular accident-prone hero out east in *Ivan Brovkin in the Virgin Lands* (*Ivan Brovkin na tseline*), which combines the collective farm film with the construction film in a plot based on the building of the new *Komsomol* State Farm and houses for its workers on the Orenburg steppe. This film explicitly looks backwards, both through a flashback sequence set in the 1930s and through its Komsomol songs, 'Komsomol Members of the 30s' (*Komsomol'tsy 30-kh*) and 'On Difficult Paths' (*Na trudnykh dorogakh*), the latter of which speaks of happiness in these terms:

Веди же, счастливая юность моя,
В заветные дали родные.
И там, где пройдем, там возникнут моря,
Сады зашумят молодые

(So lead, my happy youth,
Into the cherished and dear distance.
And there, where we pass, there seas will rise,
There young gardens will start to rustle.)

Ivan Brovkin in the Virgin Lands was the second-largest-grossing film of 1959.

By contrast, one of the most innovative and thoughtful treatments of the question of happiness is in another film set on a collective farm, Mikhail Shveitser's *Alien Kin* (*Chuzhaia rodnia*), made at Lenfil'm Studios in 1955 and released on 16 January 1956. This is taken from Vladimir Tendriakov's story *Ne ko dvoru* (Not Wanted), and tells the story of Fedia, the leader of a brigade of tractor drivers, who comes to the *Novyi put'* (New Path) collective farm to marry Stesha, the daughter of the Riashkin family, who are conservative, religious (and therefore alien) and obsessive hoarders of all sorts of junk. Here, too, the engagement with the question of what is needed to make a person happy is direct, expressed through the words of the film's narrator near the start of the film. After the marriage of the young couple, Stesha breaks a plate in traditional manner *na schast'e* (for happiness). The narrator responds:

Yes, happiness. No war. Peaceful work. A rich harvest. Happiness of this kind is uniformly dear to everyone. It is general. But under every roof

Figure 11.1. *Alien Kin* (courtesy *Iskusstvo kino* archives)

there also lives personal, small happiness of your own, a happiness which
is no less dear. A loving wife, a comfortable home, caring parents. A man
needs all of this. Without this, life is not full.

So happiness, explicitly, from the start of the film, in addition to having
a shared, civic dimension, is seen also to depend upon personal factors.
Though set on a collective farm, *Alien Kin* in fact takes scant interest in work,
finding all the causes of its characters' happiness or woe in their personal
circumstances, which in itself was considered to be an innovation. (Fig. 11.1)
The clash of values between Fedia and Stesha's parents is so great that he
repeatedly tries to get her to leave them and move into a single room with
him, but despite being pregnant, she refuses, and eventually he moves back to
the workers' hostel. At this point Stesha remembers her lapsed Komsomol
membership and goes to the Regional Committee of the Komsomol to get
them to intervene and force her husband to return to her. Gladysheva, the
Komsomol Secretary, insists upon issuing a 'strong reprimand' (*strogii vygovor*)
to Fedia, but the other young people present declare that this would be wrong,
and a young teacher tells her that she 'wants to do everything according to
formulae,' whereas life is not like that.

Eventually, in the maternity hospital, Fedia persuades Stesha that 'after all, our happiness depends on you and me.' This is followed by a joyous scene of their move into new accommodation, with all their young friends helping them out.[10] The film ends with the deserted parents still stubbornly counting and sorting their possessions. The voiceover commentary on the characters' behaviour has proceeded throughout the film. It culminates in words addressed to Stesha's parents that reiterate the link between the film's plot and the question of where happiness lies.

> The trunk is full, full. The house has accumulated a lot of goods. But where is your happiness, Alevtina Ivanovna, Silantii Petrovich?

The camera then cuts from this exemplary miserabilism to the smiling faces of the young couple and the film ends with the words, 'Yes, let's wish them happiness' (*Da, pozhelaem im schast'e*).

Films About Urban Young People

The other films from 1956 that I shall look at are about urban young people: El'dar Riazanov's *Carnival Night (Karnaval'naia noch')*, released on 29 December 1956; Viktor Eisymont's *In Good Time! (V dobryi chas!)*, released on 11 February 1956; Leonid Lukov's *Different Fates (Raznye sud'by)*, released on 21 September 1956; Nadezhda Kosheverova's *The Honeymoon (Medovyi mesiats)*, released on 10 December 1956; Vasilii Ordynskii's *A Person is Born (Chelovek rodilsia)*, released on 5 November 1956 and finally, Feliks Mironer and Marlen Khutsiev's *Spring on Zarechnaia Street (Vesna na Zarechnoi ulitse)*, released on 26 November 1956. It is a further sign of the continuing didacticism of Thaw period films that so many of these films have bluntly 'meaningful' titles.

The most famous and popular of them, but also the least probing, is *Carnival Night*, set in the period leading up to New Year's Eve, which is eagerly anticipated among young workers preparing a New Year's ball at a young people's club. It pits the old—the bureaucrat Ogurtsov (Gherkin), played by Igor' Il'inskii—against the young and the new. Ogurtsov condemns himself both through his words ('There is an instruction to celebrate the New Year with merriment,' or 'I don't like joking myself, and I shan't let others do so') and through his plans for the occasion, a formal address followed by a forty minute lecture on the theme of 'Is There Life on Mars?' A key weapon which the young people and the film use in this battle over leisure time (a battle that was raging in those years) is, as the title suggests, carnival mockery. At the end of the film, Ogurtsov complains that he does not like 'unhealthy laughter', but

Figure 11.2. *In Good Time!* (courtesy *Iskusstvo kino* archives)

it is precisely laughter that is liberating and healing in the film, along with songs and music, performed by the formerly suppressed and disbanded jazz band of Eddie Rosner, of which Ogurtsov naturally also disapproves. The main force for change, however, is the independent spirit of the young people. As the heroine Lena says, they will sort things out for themselves: 'What are we, children, to go and make complaints? We have to find our own way out of the situation.' Though the words which Lena speaks to end the film, 'Happy New Year! I wish us all New Happiness!' (*S novym godom! S novym schast'em!*) are entirely conventional, they are also consistent with the idea that young people have a new way of looking at the world and a new understanding of what constitutes happiness.

Viktor Eisymont's *In Good Time!* is taken from a play by Viktor Rozov and contrasts the behaviour and desires of two cousins. (Fig. 11.2) Alesha is a Siberian orphan who comes to Moscow at the start of the film to try to get a place to study at the Timiriazev Academy. His cousin, Andrei (played by Leonid Kharitonov and therefore never without charm) lives with his parents in their grand flat, suffers from ennui (*toska*) and does not want to study anywhere. His elder brother Arkadii is an unsuccessful actor who feels angry, irritable and disappointed by love, and therefore bullies his girlfriend, Masha. An accident has forced Masha to give up her dream of being a concert pianist, but she accepts what life throws at her and is therefore, as she tells Arkadii, 'much more happy than you are' (*gorazdo bolee schastliva, chem ty*). Alesha's aunt is appalled at the thought of her nephew taking up space in her flat. (Her description of what all its various rooms are used for recalls the justification which Professor Preobrazhenskii gives to the House Committee for retaining all seven rooms in his flat in Mikhail Bulgakov's 1925 novella *The Heart of a Dog* (*Sobach'e serdtse*)). She divides her time between complaining of the bad influence she fears that Alesha will exert upon Andrei, and pulling strings to get her feckless son into some place of further education, eventually singing him the praises of the Fish Institute. Neither young man actually wins a place to study; Andrei does not even take the exams. Alesha, the sincere and honest provincial, wins the love of the girl whom the immature Andrei pines for. But he also offers a positive model for Andrei (and a lesson for his possessive and fearful mother) by saying that he will return to Siberia to work and to study as an external student. Andrei decides to go with him. Throughout the film Andrei has wondered about what do with his life, but now he has decided to go to work and realizes that what is important is not 'who I'll be, but what kind of person I'll be' (not *kem ia budu, a kakim ia budu*). His father tells him to go off and grow up, and the journey to Moscow from the start of the film is reversed. The film ends with his twice-repeated words to Andrei's mother, 'Let him search!' So happiness, once again, lies in work, honesty and acceptance of life's difficulties, and is more likely to be found in the simple pleasures of Siberia than in a grand Moscow flat.

The very title of Leonid Lukov's *Different Fates* suggests that it, too, will work through comparison and contrast. (Fig. 11.3) This is the story of the different life choices of four young people, Tania, Fedia, Stepa and Sonia, all of whom have just left school in Leningrad—the film begins with their graduation party. The choices that face them, and in particular the main figures, Tania and Stepa, revolve around career (whether to study or to start to work), around place (whether to stay in Leningrad or to leave for Novosibirsk), and, of course, around love. Like her namesake Tat'iana Sergeevna from *Spring on Zarechnaia Street*, another 1956 film to be discussed below, Tania is presented with the choice faced by Kuz'mina, the heroine of Grigorii Kozintsev and Leonid Trauberg's 1931 film *Alone* (*Odna*). But unlike those two schoolteacher heroines (who leave and profit from it), she opts to remain in the metropolis. Though she loves the dynamic Stepa, she is more concerned with continuing to live in Leningrad, where, like Alesha's aunt and uncle in *In Good Time!* her parents occupy a grand flat, so she chooses to marry the weak and malleable Fedia. The filmmakers helpfully signpost the folly of her choice in the surnames of the characters—she is Ogneva (Woman of Fire), Fedia is Morozov (Man of Frost).

Figure 11.3. *Different Fates* (courtesy *Iskusstvo kino* archives)

Stepa, by contrast, decides to work rather than study, and to attend classes in the evenings. His choice of labour (*trud*) is also significant in the context of these films. In the words of Dmitrii Bykov,

> Labour—and the harder the better—was called upon to bring Soviet man joy, and that is not as stupid as it seems at first glance. […] The main task of all Soviet art, and of cinema art above all—was to demonstrate that joy can also be brought by an activity which has been imposed as an unavoidable duty. More than that: it was precisely the unavoidability of the process which was intended to provoke joy—delight at merging with a certain collective body and collective deed. Here too there is an element of good sense, since it is precisely labour which, more than anything else, lets you achieve that collective merging which for a certain time really is capable of saving you from existential loneliness. Labour was a patented remedy against reflection, a panacea against excessive musing, and in this sense it carries out its role in an exemplary way in all Soviet films.[11]

Bykov goes on to suggest that in time the situation alters:

> Everything changes in the 1950s and 1960s, when it seems to become possible to admit that labour can be arduous, and that 'a certain part'

of the population does not want to get up every morning as soon as the factory whistle blows. It goes without saying that this part of the population is for the time being still represented as negative characters.[12]

Tania is a striking example of this. It is through the prism of work versus idleness that she is contrasted with all the other main characters. She despises Fedia for having to work as a chauffeur in order to finance her expensive tastes. But when she divorces him (and takes up with an older married man) Fedia qualifies as an engineer. Sonia, on the other hand, follows Stepa to practical work in Novosibirsk where he finally realizes that he loves her, and the young couple are married. Another young woman, Vera, travels in the other direction, from Novosibirsk to St Petersburg to train as a doctor (and to fall in love with Fedia). So work brings personal happiness, and laziness does not. In fact, laziness brings unhappiness to everyone around Tania—her parents, her husband, her aged lover Roshchin and his wife.

In contrast to the equivalent character in *In Good Time!*, the central figure of *Different Fates* is not able or ready to change and is fated to be cast as a melodramatic, incorrigible villain. It is something of an innovation that the film has a negative heroine. It is also interesting that her attempts to invoke the help of Soviet officialdom only contribute to her negative status. Oleg Kharkhordin has suggested that the Khrushchev period saw a big expansion of the readiness of Soviet society to assess and comment on individual behaviour, and specifically, an increase in the use of Comrades' Courts, both as a way of admonishing people to live righteously and as a means of increasing social control and pressure.[13] There *are* Comrades' Courts in the films of the period—there is a light-hearted one in *The Soldier Ivan Brovkin*, which immediately turns Vania into a model worker. But where the phenomenon is treated more seriously, it is found to be clumsy and intrusive. In *Alien Kin*, the recourse to punishment on the part of the Komsomol Secretary is unhelpful and resented. Here, in *Different Fates*, when Tania brings an action against Fedia at a comradely court of the Komsomol at the Institute at which they are studying, the Komsomol chairman is very unhappy about delving into personal lives. Tania's fellow students take Fedia's side, and she herself is called 'rubbish' (*drian'*), a word which will be repeated by her honourable father. She will also be rejected by Fedia, and called a 'terrible predator' by her lover, Roshchin. Like *In Good Time!*, the film ends with a scene of departure at a railway station. Fedia, too, is leaving for Novosibirsk, and Tania has realised his qualities too late. 'It's all your fault...' (*Vinovata ty odna...*), he tells her, 'we are different people' (*My raznye liudi*). Lukov's film is still working through stereotypes, with Tania remaining villainous and blind to the end. This may be psychologically primitive, but it affords viewers the pleasure of a melodramatic ending. Contemptuous of Vera and of Fedia's love for her, Tania tells her long-suffering mother: 'I don't understand what he found in her.' (*Ne ponimaiu, chto on v nei nashel?*) 'Probably a human being' (*Naverno cheloveka*), is her mother's sad reply, to which Tania retorts: 'But what about me?' (*A ia?*)

Many of the themes of *Different Fates* are repeated in Nadezhda Kosheverova's lyrical comedy *The Honeymoon*. The young heroine of the film, Liudmila Odintsova, lives with her father and aunt in a luxurious Leningrad flat, complete with maidservant. She has just qualified as a doctor but is horrified at the prospect of being sent to work somewhere in the hinterland, so she asks her father to pull strings and help her avoid this unthinkable fate. Though he swears that he will not do so, he allows himself to be weighed down by her insistence, only to be thwarted by Liuda's formidable aunt, herself a surgeon, who began her own career in the provinces and believes that everyone else should, as well. Like Olga Ivanovna, the heroine of Chekhov's story 'The Grasshopper' (*Poprygun'ia*), Liuda is surrounded by men, with whom she flirts enthusiastically, but she decides to marry a man whom she does not love, the solid construction engineer Aleksei Rybal'chenko, since she thinks that this will enable her to stay in Leningrad as the wife of someone employed in the city. Everything goes according to plan until her new husband shocks her by announcing that he has accepted a post as chief engineer on a Siberian construction site. Though initially Liuda refuses to go with him and demands a divorce, she is shamed into accepting the vacant post of doctor in the same settlement.

Since the house that is being built for them is not ready, the couple begin their married life billeted on a barge. When it seems impossible for them to get along together, Aleksei, like Fedia in *Alien Kin*, moves out into a hostel. This unorthodox approach to married life and Liuda's squeamishness about local conditions are viewed with a mixture of amusement and disapproval by the inhabitants of the settlement. The local Komsomol Secretary tells Aleksei that their behaviour is 'not Soviet' and, under the 'pressure of society', he moves back onto the barge. And though the couple continue to squabble, gradually Liuda, who had initially lost confidence even in her capabilities as a doctor, begins to find a niche. She learns to admire the toughness of the local workers, especially the women, and decides to use her influence to improve their working conditions. She gets the workers' dining room cleaned up and makes sure that the menu is improved. She also persuades the head of the construction site to turn the impressive new house that is being built for her and Aleksei into a nursery for the workers' children.

Eventually and predictably (for this is a comedy), the couple are reconciled. Unlike Tania in *Different Fates* (and Chekhov's Olga Ivanovna) Liuda has recognised her husband's qualities in time and she tells him she no longer

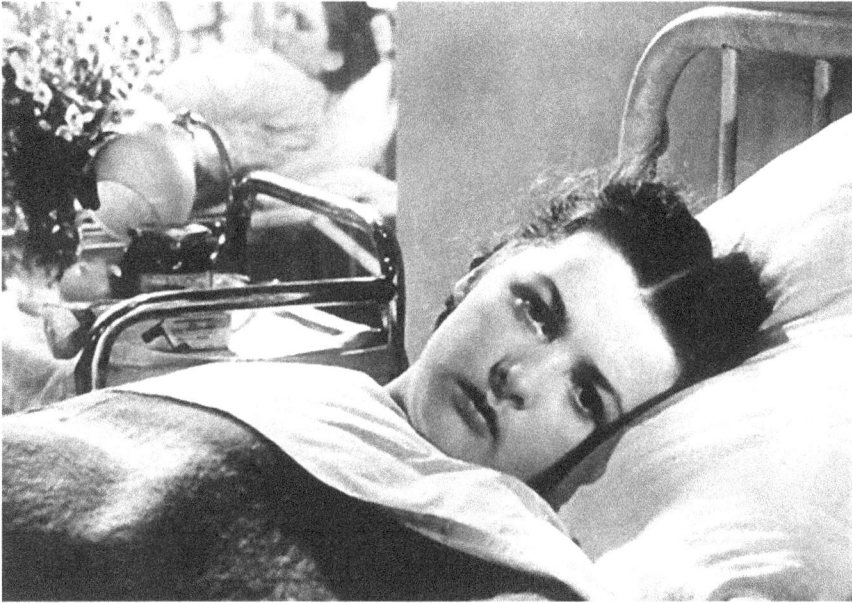

Figure 11.4. *A Person is Born* (courtesy *Iskusstvo kino* archives)

wants a divorce. Aleksei, meanwhile, is full of admiration for his wife, who has 'become a person'. The formula that commitment to hard work and the good of others will be rewarded by personal happiness is once again in evidence.

Aleksei's portentous words to Liuda are echoed in the very title of another variant on the theme, Vasilii Ordynskii's *A Person is Born*.[14] (Fig. 11.4) This film begins in a maternity hospital where the heroine, Nadia, has just given birth, but unlike the other women, she has no husband to visit her. From the flashback which follows we learn that Nadia, like Alesha in *In Good Time!* is a provincial who had come to Moscow with great hopes of studying and of achieving something 'out of the ordinary' (*neobyknovennoe*). Alas, she fails her entrance exam and falls in with the socially well-placed 'born and bred Muscovite' Vitalii, who seduces her and, when she becomes pregnant, insists that she have an abortion with the words 'I have a tame doctor' (*I vrach svoi chelovek*). So Nadia leaves him and attempts to bring up her child in Moscow alone.

The record of a discussion of an early version of Leonid Agranovich's script for the film at the Artistic Council of Mosfilm Studios on 15 February 1955 has recently been published. The film dramatist and Deputy Editor of Mosfilm Studios, Boris Dobrodeev, recognised that the story 'poses a series of moral questions, topical questions, which the cinema must respond to'.[15] The film dramatist Mikhail Papava spoke of the 'stunning impression' that Italian

Neo-Realist films had made on Soviet young people, an impression impossible without 'widescreen grief', and complained of the absence of 'widescreen grief' from Soviet cinema.[16] The director Grigorii Roshal' insisted, 'It is a very important theme (one of the general themes of life) and it has remained untouched to such a degree that now it is essential.'[17]

Nevertheless, there were more and more demands for changes to the script. In Agranovich's words:

> I rewrote the script of *A Person is Born* eight if not ten times, bringing it to a point of complete absurdity. The film would get launched and then closed down, directors got changed. And then young Ordynskii got to work on this hopeless case. With the 'patronage' of Pyr'ev, we return to the first version.[18]

This version, read and approved by Pyr'ev, who had been Director of Mosfilm Studios since October 1954, went in its turn for discussion at the studio's Artistic Council. Here the filmmakers were accused of making things up and of 'slander of reality'. It was only because Pyr'ev was prepared to ignore all this criticism that the film got started at all.[19]

What sustains Nadia in *A Person is Born* is the kindness of strangers, in particular a student, Gleb, whom she meets in the street and who is instrumental in finding her somewhere to stay (significantly located in the semirural outskirts of the city). She finds a job as a bus conductor and also hires an old woman to help her look after her son, but she is unable to respond to Gleb's love. When problems arise for her at work, the Komsomol cannot help her and she leaves it, since, in her view, it is not interested in the concerns of a nursing mother.

An interesting innovation here is the choice of a heroine who, in modern terms, would be said to be living with depression, though there is no medicalisation of her condition in the film. She is very tough with Gleb and tells him, 'I don't know how to get on with people. I don't believe in happiness' (*Ladit' s liud'mi ne umeiu. Ne veriu v schast'e*). Late in the film Vitalii's father discovers where she lives and comes to try to persuade her to go back to Vitalii, or at least to accept some money. Hearing of how she has been treated he slaps Vitalii's face and calls him a scoundrel. It is this encounter that makes it possible for Nadia to accept Gleb's love and, in an interesting reversal of the usual ending, she refuses his offer of a move to the provinces, telling him that he alone is all she needs. *A Person is Born*, with dual meaning in its title, is one of the most interesting and least formulaic treatments of the theme of happiness in the films of this year, both in choosing far less privileged, more 'ordinary' characters as its protagonists, and in giving a much more gritty

Figure 11.5. *Spring on Zarechnaia Street* (courtesy *Iskusstvo kino* archives)

description of societal problems. Its solution remains, however, to seek happiness through hard work and, afterwards, through personal fulfillment.

I turn finally to Feliks Mironer and Marlen Khutsiev's *Spring on Zarechnaia Street*. (Fig. 11.5) The film opens with the heroine, Tat'iana Sergeevna Levchenko, arriving in a small and nondescript industrial town fresh from her graduation in Moscow and preparing to take up her first job, teaching in an evening school for workers. Tania is the embodiment of Soviet values, an enthusiastic and committed pedagogue who lives for Russian culture and wishes to transmit the joy it gives her to the young workers who have not yet been lucky enough to encounter it. Alas, her strategy for inculcating a love of Russian literature is a clumsy and alienating mixture of the rote learning of Pushkin and writing dictations from Griboedov's play *Woe from Wit*.

Tania is explicitly contrasted with a local young woman, Zina, in whose mother's house she first rents a room. Zina and her mother are the incarnation of provincial Soviet philistinism, concerned only with money, pleasure and making a good marriage match. The confrontation with Zina is mainly expressed through their rivalry over the affections of the young steelworker and reluctant nightschool student Sasha Savchenko. At the start of the film, Zina confidently expects to marry this local hero, but he is increasingly drawn to his teacher. Not that the prim Tania is able to respond, harshly rejecting his clumsy advances and telling him that he is drunk. When Sasha, deciding that he can perhaps win her affection by proving to be a good student, comes round to ask for extra instruction, she is of course ready to help him, but asks him first to wait while she listens to Rachmaninoff's Second Piano Concerto, which is about to be played for her on a radio request programme. As Tania listens to the music, her face bathed in radiant light, Sasha becomes ever more embarrassed and eventually he leaves, unnoticed. Whereas in David Lean's 1945 film *Brief Encounter*, the same Rachmaninoff piano concerto had orchestrated genuine and mature feeling in the doomed love affair between the characters played by Celia Johnson and Trevor Howard, Tania's enthusiasm for it paradoxically signifies her inexperience and fear of emotion.

The further development of the story is predictable enough: as winter turns into spring, so iced-over Tania gradually thaws. She had thought that she was happy and contented—but a visit to her students' workplace convinces her that she is not, and that fulfillment through work is not enough. A sign of her acceptance of the simple values of this place is her decision to stay there and to move into her own new apartment. In this she is helped by all the friends she has made, in a scene that echoes the similar scene in *Alien Kin*. At the end of the film, with delicate understatement, Tania and Sasha, both of whom have grown in human terms through exposure to the other's values, seem poised on the verge of true happiness.

Spring on Zarechnaia Street, then, concerns itself with the same issues and sets up confrontations similar to those in the other films that I have discussed, but unlike, for example, *A Person is Born!* and especially *Different Fates*, it does not cast its characters irrevocably into the camps of heroes and villains. It allows its heroine to change, and it also reveals this personification of Soviet values to be lacking in humanity. The film's plot offers a more complex equation—it is not just a model of ways to behave with a formula for happiness attached—and it is open-ended. Amusingly, however, there is indirect evidence that audiences were frustrated by this incompletion—they wanted to be certain that the story of these attractive and personable young people had ended happily. In a scene at a teachers' reunion in Veniamin Dorman's 1964 film *An Easy Life* (*Legkaia zhizn'*) a character is introduced as Tania Levchenko. She is played by Nina Ivanova, who played Tania Levchenko in *Spring on Zarechnaia Street*. And she puts an end to the anxiety of a generation of sentimental Soviet viewers by replying: 'My name is now Savchenko' (*Ia teper' Savchenko*).

We see that the debate about happiness in the 1956 Soviet films about young people was pervasive, and it often involved direct use of the word itself. In general, it stuck to the established Soviet formula that happiness came from fulfillment both at work and in personal life. The tropes it used to discuss happiness were either the opposition between 'bad' and 'good' characters, or the journey to understanding (often involving physical travel) of someone who was well-intentioned but deluded. Some of the treatments of the subject were superficial and predictable (though that was often the cause of their popularity), but the most ambitious and thoughtful among them give evidence of a real shift towards concentrating the search for happiness in the personal, a search that encapsulated the hopes of Thaw culture. In this respect, they brought insight both to the discussion of eternal human dilemmas and to the representation of a generation with new and different desires.

Chapter Twelve

EASY ON THE HEART; OR, 'STRENGTH THROUGH JOY'*

Maya Turovskaya

Glance, stare, really *see*!

In fact, the logocentric era (in any case, as far as the transmission of news is concerned) waned long before the advent of the period that we now call the 'audiovisual' age. From the moment that Daguerre and Niépce observed the effect of a ray of light on silver, mankind (without yet realising it) began to prefer image over text. Newspapers still had priority, but illustrated journals, according to the authoritative evidence of Jean-Louis Servan-Schreiber, had already learned to make use of two advantages: their news could reach 'the sticks' via the traveling salesman's baggage and, even more, they could make 'national advertising coverage' a reality.[1]

The illustrated journals of the times when the transmission of news over distance was still in an infantile state in fact fulfilled the role of the future small screen and were its direct predecessors. They delivered viewable news to the home and made it a part of familial and societal customs.

Our topic is a comparison of two 1930s journals: the Soviet *Ogonek* ('Little Fire') and the German *Berliner Illustrierte Zeitung* ('*BIZ*'). This will be a comparison on a basic thematic level, although this is not the only possible approach, and maybe not even the most interesting.

The Soviet–German parallels of this time are not at all coincidental nor speculative. In his very important and well-researched monograph, *The Sickle and the Ruble: Conservative Modernisation in the USSR*, the sociologist and demographer Anatoly Vishnevskii observes:

> Both geographically and historically, Russia was closer to Germany than to other countries of the world that had been gradually drifting towards modernisation … particularly in the similarity of their visions of an ideal

future. Their visions were not identical, but were in fact similar...
Modernisation was not understood in this in its full complexity, as a
many-sided and profound restructuring of the whole social body, but
rather was becoming almost a synonym simply for an industrial and
technological progress that could be combined with the preservation of
social conservatism.'[2]

A multidimensional analysis—social, economic, and demographic—leads the
author to conclude that both countries on the eastern edge of Europe have a
'catch up' type of development. This is due to their common complex as regards
'the West'. In this light, the Soviet-model socialist Utopia and the German
(National Socialist) one both cease to be instances of 'falling out of history' (as it
often seems), and instead become completely natural, logical developments. The
polarity of slogans turns out to be a less essential component of these totalitarian
regimes than the practices they shared.

In fact, the 1920s and 1930s were a time of rather widespread totalitarian
experimentation (according to Hannah Arendt). It was just at this time that
Russia happened to complete its 'great leap'—in the most conservative,
irrational, and agonising form. Lingering in the mind as a collection of garish
emblems and terminology, this era nonetheless remains a sphinx. Somewhere
among the system of symbols, the statistics, and Socialist Realism there lies
nonetheless a *terra incognita* of everyday existence. The illustrated journal, of
course, presents this everyday existence in a rather ideologicalised form—be
it in a 'bourgeois' fashion, or a 'socialist' one—but the shifting substance of
everyday life can never be completely formalised. Alongside its obvious meaning,
a photograph often has a latent component for which time functions as a no
worse developer than chemicals. The weeklies' orientation towards the masses
and their obvious slant towards 'leisure' (not to mention their entertainment
purpose) make them less politicised and more for 'the common man' in
comparison with the dailies.

The evolution of these publications was quite different. *Ogonek* (founded in
1900) was at the beginning of the 1930s published on poor-quality newsprint
paper; but it bore some imprint of avant-garde influence. Its photographers,
with varying degrees of valor, went through the crucible of Rodchenko's bold
innovations; their massive production still maintains this level. As the 'empire'
style advanced, the photography settled down a bit and became more illustrative
and 'Socialist Realist'; the layout became less montage-style.

BIZ, on the contrary, was a completely bourgeois publication, on good paper.
It was founded in 1890 by the publisher Ullstein, on the cusp of the Weimar era.
Its photographs were more conservative, but diluted by the American reportage
photographic style. The advent of Nazism would in turn give the journal

a change of clothes, imposing subject matter and stylistics on it, à la Riefenstahl. With time, the structure and character of both journals grew similar, 'Agitation for happiness' ran the show, and the same symbolic themes (aviation, the Arctic, the 1937 Paris Exposition) cropped up in both. Despite this, both publications did not lose their competitiveness; the favorite enemy is constantly held up within their sights.

The Bourgeois and the Antibourgeois Journal

The year 1930 was pivotal for both the Soviet Union and for Germany. After the New York Stock Exchange crash (October 29, 1929), the Great Depression began, which was particularly devastating for the Weimar Republic, already aggravated by the consequences of the Versailles Treaty. On September 14, 1930, the National Socialists won their first victory in the Reichstag elections.

The second Stalinist 'revolution' (collectivisation) had basically been completed, and Stalin's Five Year Plans were at hand, as well as the urbanisation that caused the exodus from countryside to city. The consequences of this 'time bomb' were for the moment indiscernible; it seemed that industrialisation could change the country in a very short time.

Understandably, each journal at this time found itself facing different tasks and different audiences.

BIZ was an entertainment journal and, for as long as it could, closed its eyes to the social upheavals. It kept politics to a minimum (although Hitler ended up in one picture—in issue No. 25, 1930, 1146—as a witness to legal proceedings), and focused on stars from sports, film and theatre (Max Schmelling, the transplanted-to-Hollywood Marlena Dietrich, Charles Lindbergh), and royal pageants and weddings, including the most exotic. Sensation is the constant engine for mass media, although it still remains a function of the narrative, and photography endeavors to soothe the reader; the sensational layout of the postwar journals had yet to be created.

The German and Soviet journals were of interest to different people. *BIZ* was a journal about and for the city. The class-restricted crowd scenes of *Ogonek* were still primarily rural; its pages presented the face of a peasant country at the moment of its exodus into the city.

At the cusp of the decade, *Ogonek* was far less an entertainment publication than was *BIZ*. It was not ashamed of its agitprop function, and its forte was to catch life 'unawares.' The proportion of photography in it was higher, and the layout more montage-like than in the German journal. For the time being, it was still trying to 'refashion' life (to use Mayakovsky's word), not to 'celebrate' it.

Rodchenko, the ideologue and mentor of revolutionary photography, linked the destruction of the old-style photograph to the destruction of the old world, and the consolidation of the new photography to the struggle 'for a photographic language to depict the Soviet theme'; he was searching for the photographic angles from which people had 'still not grown accustomed to seeing' the world. He was attentive to the 'signature' of each reporter, trying to overcome the inertia of some and trying to teach others. Even after Rodchenko was pronounced a formalist, his 'agitation for the facts [and] for reportage' was still evident on the pages of *Ogonek*.[3] Rodchenko's approach helped to make visible the shift that the country was experiencing.

Consider, for example, the famous photograph called 'They go to build Moscow'. We see 'leaver' peasants (*otkhodniki*, those who left the villages for the labor force), who have just come off the train; tomorrow they will have to become industrial workers and take the newest technologies imported from the West into their own hands, but they still have not taken off their bast shoes, and they are bringing their saws—their whole 'industrial' past—with them. The caption is imperative: 'Providing … a qualified work force … is one of the bottlenecks… Industrial construction should be, and must be fully equipped with a work-force' (1930, no. 11, 7). This photograph explains, far more clearly than any possible statistics could, the kind of bottleneck in which the 'pile-up of plans' would find itself. The word 'qualified' comes across in obvious, glaring contradiction to the photograph.

The five-year period that forgot to take the 'human factor' into account looks, in *Ogonek's* pages, like the expected 'military' period. Consider the headline, 'FROM THE FRONT OF THE FIVE-YEAR PLAN. Situation Report.' Under it is a photograph in which the entrance of Elektrozavod is visible, dramatically modeled in the shape of a tank with a cannon. Then there is the article entitled 'Workers' correspondents have observed lack of planning, slovenliness, and sabotage in the transformer shop' (1930, no. 26, 3). Also mentioned is a profit-damaging welder, who wanted not labor enthusiasm, but rather to be paid more; he was driven off the job in disgrace. There was a 'gap' (one of the favorite words of the era) at the 'Red Pathfinder' metal plant, which the 'opportunistic management' had permitted to happen. Here is yet another text: 'The American "contraptions" line up. They are silent, because there is no practiced hand to get them moving. There is no master's eye that would caution them against endless breakdowns. No sooner do we train a worker than he flies off to a different factory where they pay more… To battle for the liquidation of the gap!' (1930, no. 28, 8).

People stand 'queued up' for hours in the canteen, but despite this, 'on the provisions front' a 'new form of workers' provisions' arose by popular demand (*na volne obshchestvennosti*): 'closed distributors' for food products (1930, no. 30, 3).[4] In the photograph of the distributor's booth one can discern a tiny placard urging both the seller and the buyer to be mutually polite.

Looking through sets of the journal, which became a 'wall newspaper' for all of the Soviet Union, one can follow step by step how, in the mutual movement of the 'higher-ups' and the 'lower-downs' towards each other, a model of the 'mobilisational' Soviet economy arises: 'distribution' instead of trade, and a search for 'saboteurs' and 'enemies of the people' instead of a concern about workers' qualifications. The journal published a dramatic two-page montage from the 'Industrial Party' trial: 'The proletariat of the Soviet country tries the counterrevolutionaries'; the speech of State Prosecutor Krylenko (extra large), the reading of the sentence by the ever-present Vyshinskii (large), and the inevitable wide-angle pictures (with indistinguishable individuals) of workers' meetings (1930, no. 35, 8–9). The 'international section' of *Ogonek*, still influential in those years, offers proof of 'class struggle': the huge meeting of unemployed persons at the Busch Circus in Berlin, the *Schutzpolizei* encircling the cinema that was showing an undesirable film by Remarque (1930, no. 36, p.11).

BIZ regards its eastern neighbor with mixed feelings of expectations and misgivings. A miscellany strikes its lens: a huge new building in Khar'kov (the twin to the House on the Wharf, no. 5, 166), the destruction of the Church of Christ the Savior (no. 7, 244), an everyday scene from a correctional 'colony' for the general population, the Lenin monument from a Pudovkin film. Alongside European beauties, Russian women are also represented—athletic, with cropped hair. Sometimes an *Ogonek* photograph is 'quoted': *Ogonek*'s 'Cleansing in the Supreme Soviet of the National Economy: The working class investigates' (1930, no. 8, 6), which demonstrates righteous proletarian vigilance, receives a new caption in the German journal: 'The face of the ruling class' (*BIZ*, 1930, no. 16, 666). And at that moment, the latent meaning of the same photo comes to the foreground: the frightening, almost monumental brutality of that 'face'.

Intermezzo

What sets the two journals apart more than anything is the advertising. This can be seen in the details, but, according to Servan-Schreiber, the always problematic and reprehensible connection between an illustrated journal and advertising has a systemic nature, and not only a practical one (being the source of financing). Servan-Schreiber considers even the origin of this type of publication to be a 'Michurinist' hybridisation of the catalogs (sent by mail) of outer garments and of literary serials.[5] Entertainment and trade are the coordinates of the genre.

In the bourgeois *BIZ*, this genotype is comprehensively manifested. Advertising and novels with sequels and hand-drawn illustrations make up its backbone. Reportage photography (often American) is not the guest on its pages, but is still not quite the master of the house, either. The very existence of advertising in *Ogonek* can seem surprising. As NEP waned, advertising could serve as an aid to financing, but not as a source of it. With shortages and the distribution system, there were few of the sorts of things that might have been advertised. The free commerce of goods or services receded further and further into the shadows.

Among the many shortages, there was also a shortage of space—in any and all Soviet publications. Thus *Ogonek* shows little advertising in either volume or variety; it is small, with no photography at its disposal. One might assume (in the spirit of the 'Freudian' version of our times) that quasi-erotic objects that had become taboo are marginalised into advertisements; among them are, for example, treatments for impotence and baldness, certain English beds, pearls for women and the TEZhE Soviet perfumes (their advertising, more likely, was also the result of the energy of Polina Zhemchuzhina—Molotov's wife, and the director of TEZhE).[6] One might also assume a social function: in a society knocked off all its foundations, a maniacal advertising of all sorts of 'teach-yourself books' arises (let us recall Nikolai Erdman's play *The Suicide*). Other printed works are advertised as well, sometimes remarkably interesting ones, like the unique library of memoirs published by the Society of Political Convicts. However, the journal's advertising does not create any sort of integral image—neither an image of a balding impotent man, nor a reader of the memoirs, nor a pimply-faced young fan of adventure magazines, nor a powdered NEP-lady. It 'survives' at the periphery of the collective image of a peasant country dashing towards modernisation.

BIZ, on the other hand, offers an image of the reader, in particular the female reader, and, what is more, in all her material components, beginning with the Felina corset and ending with the DKW motorcycle. She is offered Alpina watches, footwear from Hess, Tack, and Dorndorf, Bleyle dresses, Elbeo socks, Palmolive soap, and Coty powder. Among the creams, Mouson and Nivea take the lead. Marlene Dietrich and Leni Riefenstahl advertise Ponds. Advertising does not let Knorr soups be forgotten, and so on and so forth. In the same way, the woman figures in the German journal as a 'sex object' (as we would say now), in the aura of the 'lady's happiness' industry, which constitutes a not insignificant field in any developed country.

In the Soviet publication, the subject of women's dreams—not of beauty contests, to be sure, but rather of tractors—is the cult object of the early 1930s. Equal rights for women occupied one of the higher positions in the 'list of benefits' of Soviet power; women realised this in the most difficult 'men's' professions. The woman figures as a 'labor unit' (as Kollontai put it) in *Ogonek*, while labor in the Soviet Union was primarily physical work.

Meanwhile, it is not only the half-dressed photographic models in undergarments who accentuate the extent of the gap in the way of life between that of the Western and the Soviet person; much more telling are the ordinary painted advertisements of the Siemens vacuum cleaner: the small connected pictures (like those bordering the 'main figure' on an icon) portray an almost complete assemblage of the everyday gadgets (other than vacuum cleaners) that we are still using today. But in *Ogonek*, after yet another ten years had passed, the things that became objects of discussion—not even of advertising—were brooms and teapots, and the novelty was the slow kerosene stove. This means that Germany would enter into the period of dictatorship as an already developed industrial country with a European standard of living, while in the Soviet Union, urbanisation had just barely begun, and everyday life was assumed to be collectivised: 'The city [Magnitogorsk] is being planned on the basis of complete collectivisation of the cultural-educational and everyday life of all laborers.'[7]

Nevertheless, a popular journal, even a bourgeois one, could not ignore the depression that had set in. Around 1932, the women appearing on the pages of *BIZ* were no longer concerned about Felina undergarments, but rather a dish of soup (1932, no. 3, 61); the reader is shown entire camps of makeshift shelters (1932, no. 4, 89), masses of parked bicycles and unemployed people waiting at labor registry offices (1932, no. 23, 757) (which became the prototypes for the 'proletarian films' of Phil Jutzi and Slatan Dudow–Bertolt Brecht). The unemployed would form the ranks of the 'volunteer' labor conscription (1932, no. 14, 411). (The Third Reich did not invent this, but rather borrowed it from an existing practice, just as the Bolsheviks did with 'closed distributors'. Politics bursts onto the pages, no longer in the respectable guise of conferences or of the voyages of the aging Hindenburg, but in the crowd scenes from the election campaigns. History takes on the role of the montage editor: going back-to-back in one layout are both a proletarian meeting with Ernst Thälmann, and a Nazi march with Hitler (1932, no. 10, 270–273). This is both the apogee and the epilogue of bourgeois objectivity: even Roosevelt is photographed, in his family circle (a stormy election campaign was also underway in America). The eastern neighbor also remains at the centre of attention for the journal, the more so since the Soviet Union is the only country escaping a crisis. Stalin, young and still not yet well understood, agreed to pose for a German reporter in the Kremlin (1932, no. 19, 595); there is a portrait of Nadezhda Allilueva as well (among other highly placed wives); both photographs were unknown in Russia.

The year 1932 would pass in *Ogonek* under the motto, 'Everyone with their own hands, from their own materials, with their own machines'; socialism in one country was preparing for the regime of self-sufficiency. The journal is filled with 'portraits' of things (even a special supplement with this heading is issued). Here one could find sundries (like paper clips or tacks) or objects for the home (cameras and watches, record players and telephones), but 'heavy industry' predominates—the 'Pioneer-1' printing press, tractors and generators, locomotives and planes. On this subject, Vishnevsky wrote, 'The central link in the Bolsheviks' modernisation strategy was the accelerated transformation of the country from an agrarian one into an industrial one... This is how the rhythm of pumping resources out of consumption and into accumulation was set... The mass consumer in the USSR had no influence on the development of macroeconomic proportions, and this led to the suppression of reconnection to the economic system.'[8]

Coming down from the level of macroeconomics to that of the mass-oriented journal, it must be said that the difference between the most ordinary advertisement and the All-Union Agricultural Exhibition was exactly the same as that between the concepts of 'commerce' and 'provisioning'. No matter how much Siemens might offer for sale, the shortage-ridden existence of the 'kommunalka' did no less to enable the preservation of the serf mentality than ideology did. Despite enduring the crises of urbanisation, the new city dweller failed to win the greatest prize: personal independence.

In 1932, Roosevelt and his New Deal took the victory in the US elections. In 1933, victory in the German elections—with the obvious connivance of Comintern—was won by Hitler. As a result, the popular journal took on a new guise and was 'workerized'. Appearing among the portraits of the Führer, with all sorts of symbols of distinction and emblems (e.g., painted First of May posters) was a proud Aryan worker (1934, no. 17, 579), as well as a worker and a capitalist together supporting the German economy (1934, no. 12, 375). Thus far, wartime propaganda is featured only in Trommler and Oberst cigarette advertisements, with corresponding illustrations.

Meanwhile, Russia in *Ogonek* was gradually losing its peasant face. Appearing alongside the tractors and industrial photographs were young prize-winning musicians (among them, the future great pianist Emil Gilels), the halls of the Lenin Library, and the Culture and Relaxation Park. Stalin's 'cult of personality', which had begun two years previously, was becoming just as commonplace as that of the Hitler cult on the pages of *BIZ*...

A Duel of Dictatorships

It is impossible in a small article, of course, to even graze the surface of the whole corpus of the two publications' themes: in the German journal, the growth of antisemitic propaganda advances, and the militarisation of the economy and later the expansion of Germany into neighboring countries are both reflected; in the Soviet publication, the sublimation of the 'besieged camp' ideology progresses, as does the propaganda of the achievements of socialism 'in one country.' We will only dwell on certain significant years (1937, 1939, and 1941) and certain significant themes.

As the 1930s drew to a close, *Ogonek* became more 'respectable' and the paper it was printed on a bit better; on the other hand, the montage quality and the keen documentary nature of its photography began to decline; the zeal for reportage from the construction site and the ardor of the all-union wall newspaper also went away. The journal moved away from its 'peasant' mass appeal in the direction of a Soviet 'bourgeoisness'—also simple-minded, however. Replacing its former militant internationalism, it devoted its attention to the culture and life of its own republics, which were 'national in form' (although 'socialist in content').

For its own part, *BIZ* grew a bit slimmer due to lost advertising, archived its bourgeois objectivity, and became Nazified, saving the worker-and-peasant rhetoric only for anniversaries. The successes of the Four-Year Plan (the parallel to Soviet Five-Year Plans), however, were aimed towards the future. Shortages forced Germany to exploit the production of 'substitute products' (ie - chemicals) that still comprise the basis of contemporary industry.

If the Soviet journal cultivates the 'friendship of nations', then the Nazi publication cultivates the 'friendship of the leaders of nations'. Ceremonial party-mindedness or party-minded ceremony becomes the focus of the themes and style of the German publication; represented in it are the opulent visit to Germany by the Italian *duce* and coverage of the Spanish *caudillo* (the portrait of the Führer, meanwhile, is clearly seen in the background). Stalin took note of the German use of dapper uniforms and, after the war, would introduce this in the USSR. But for the time being, he was impressed by an 'image' for the outside world that corresponded to the aphorism of Henri Barbusse: 'with the face of a worker, the head of a scholar, and in the clothing of a simple soldier'.

At the same time that the Soviet publication was growing ever more isolated within the boundary of 'one-sixth of the world', the German publication was growing more commercial and trying to satisfy the universal curiosity of its buyers. As it had previously, *BIZ* did not disdain exotica from faraway places, nor the chronicle of high society (like the coronation of the English heir), nor the oddities of worldwide fashion, nor the American reportage photograph. In this respect, it was trying to hold on to its entertainment potential as well as its level of Europeanness. There was perhaps more Hollywood in it than in German film studios.

The percentage of photography in *BIZ* was gradually increasing, and *Ogonek* was using graphics more than it had previously. But the war theme was sounding ever louder, both from underneath the luster of the pictures of the Nazis' fourth anniversary, as well as in the multipaged collages in *Ogonek* that celebrated the twentieth year of the Russian Revolution. The progressive convergence somewhat recalls Kipling's tale, 'The Beginning of the Armadillos'.

The most 'symmetrical' theme of the two publications was, of course, the theme of the leader and the people. In both regimes, 'cult' by this time was ceasing to be a metaphor: its rituals were shaping a general type of quasi-religion.

A small notice in *Ogonek* in 1937, about a minor subject, is replete with superlatives:

> On December 20th in the Great Kremlin Palace, in the presence of *the great* leader of the peoples, comrade Stalin, and of his *renowned* companions-in-arms, the All-Union Conference of the Wives of Red Army Officers ... was opened. In the hall where the *best* representatives ... of the people had ratified Stalin's *great* Constitution, our female warrior friends, ... the *outstanding* women of our *glorious* Red Army, assembled. In the speeches ... the *remarkable* profile of the women emerges, the women who love their country *immensely* and who know how to combine their concern for the family with *great* public work, and who are ready at any moment to take their place beside their husbands for the defence of the USSR. (1937, no. 1, 4. Emphases mine.)

In the issue of *BIZ* devoted to the Nazi anniversary, the Führer is glorified in photographs and in text—in all his supposed hypostases:

> The people's chancellor has dignified German work. The friend of youth has guaranteed Germany a future. The lance corporal of the World War has strengthened the German defenses. A man from the people has created a community of the German people. The creator of the German State has shaped the face of Germany. The warrior of the World War has battled need. The peasant's grandson is leading us out of the food crisis. (1937, no. 4, 98–101)

This is reminiscent of Stalin—the friend of children, the scholar, and so forth. However, what most draws the attention is the predominance of the 'German' epithet. If one adds to this the bravura-laden comment to a photograph of Mussolini, 'A blacksmith's son is forging imperialism' (1937, no. 37, 1347), then the archetype of the people's leader—a god on earth—can be considered full-blown.

Against the backdrop of this single archetype in the photographic representation of both leaders, we notice differences of both a historical and a personality-related nature.

The figure of the Führer occupies a substantial portion of the visual series in *BIZ*. Hitler posed a lot for photographers, and was glad to do so—among workers, among Hitler Youth, in the foreground of military and party parades and processions; but the journal also did not skimp on reportage shots— whether the leader was giving the usual speech, visiting an art exhibit, or meeting with *Il Duce*. The Führer, it must be said, did not disdain cinematic shots—he was a constant and leading figure of all the national mass media.

By contrast, 'the great Stalin,' ever-present in the verbal series of *Ogonek*, was rather sparingly represented iconographically, and more often by the official portrait or the outline at the mausoleum. Reportage photographs (at that same conference of Red Army women, for example) were tightly controlled, as were cinematic shots.

We could offer several explanations for this. Possibly Stalin, being short and pockmarked, was less intoxicated by his own outer appearance and oratory skill than was Hitler. Hitler, the 'drummer of revolution,' was a forerunner of television careerists, of what we now call a 'public policymaker'. Not without reason did he take declamation lessons and work out his poses in front of a mirror. Knowing the value of an 'image', he was a diligent 'image maker' for himself.

Also not without reason, Stalin called himself a 'bureaucrat' and chose the role of the Politburo's 'gray eminence', preferring that others elevate him to the rank of 'leader of the peoples'. This is partially explainable historically: Hitler was the founding father, but Stalin was merely the 'incarnation' of Lenin, whose cult he always upheld, even when he, in fact, edged it out with his own. Hitler eagerly harked back to his own 'peasant roots', but who would have dared in 1937 to write that Stalin was 'the son of a Georgian shoemaker'? He traced his lineage directly from Il'ich and was 'the Lenin of today'. But the archetype of 'the leader's youth' in artists' representations was common to both leaders.

Of course, much depended on the difference in the characters of Stalin and Hitler, but on the deeper levels, the differences in their images were tied to the peculiarities of the local mind-sets of their peoples. Still, Germany was a developed European country, while Russia, even in its spurt of modernisation, had still not abandoned its patriarchal nature. Like Dostoevsky's Great Inquisitor, Stalin preferred miracles, secrecy, and authority over public policy (in which he differed, by the way, from Trotsky), and the image of 'father of the peoples' over that of national messiah. Owing to the logocentrism of Russian culture, Stalin's image was shaped from words: he was surrounded by a cloud of constant epithets. As a result, the shaping of the 'cults' in the two countries by illustrated periodicals was not identical— despite their symmetry.

This symmetry can be observed both in the theme of youth (Hitler's steely youth in *Mein Kampf* and that of the Soviet ideal of youth in the novel *How the Steel Was Forged*) and in the theme of childhood. The Young Pioneers in *Ogonek* and the Hitler Youth in *BIZ* wear identical neckties (the difference in colour was undetectable in a black-and-white photograph) and are fulfilling their 'happy childhood': the German children are fencing, or sitting in front of a map ('Adolf Hitler, student' in 1937, no. 2, 1172–1173); the Moscow schoolchildren are building model aircraft, or collecting radio receivers. Experiments in the electricity laboratory bring Stalin's glowing silhouette to life ('Central Children's Technical Station,' 1937, no. 8, 14–15). But the children, within the framework of each of the ideological myths that they are illustrating, derive obvious satisfaction from the role that both dictatorships confer on their own 'next shift'. Still excluded from the pretty pictures are Jewish children, the children of 'the enemies of the people', the 'moments of hate' and all of the organised persecution for which both regimes were so mirror-image similar.

The theme of the 'hero', as well as that of the 'enemy' (closely connected to the former), shows structural similarity across the two publications, yet also reveals a substantial difference. Let us remember that in the USSR, 1937 was the peak of the 'Great Terror'. In *Ogonek*, however, this was reflected only in an implied, indirect fashion, just like the trials of the saboteurs on the threshold of the 1930s, which were still being illustrated reportage fashion. The famous 1937 trials, with their famous defendants, do not make it into the shots shown in the masses' journal (although they are recorded on film, as was the trial of the participants in the attempt on Hitler's life). Maybe it was thought that the faces of the former leaders did not interest anyone, or, on the other hand, that they were capable of arousing undesirable feelings. The verbal series of this time (see, for example, the page 1 article in *Ogonek* no. 4, 1937, 'Enemy caught red-handed') can offer the most absurd information: Karl Radek and Grigory Sokolnikov, for example, on Trotsky's orders, had held negotiations with Hess and promised to give Ukraine to Germany and Primor'e to Japan; Georgy Pyatakov was accused of plotting terrorist acts against Stalin. It is not even the absurdity of the accusations that is important, but rather the rhetoric of hate, which eliminates any kind of content: 'Traffickers in the blood of the motherland and of the people, murderers and oppressors of the workers, spies and saboteurs, and Trotskyist fiends, have sunk to such a level of baseness in their black, treacherous schemes and activities, the likes of which history had never known before.' All of these unsubstantiated invectives were corroborated by a completely random photograph: 'Workers of the Red-Banner sheet-rolling shop in the "Hammer and Sickle" factory vote for the execution of the contemptible bandit-terrorists' (1937, no. 4, back cover). The photograph shows a sea of hands. The lowering faces in the foreground are devoid of even the emotions that made the snapshots of the 1939 'purge' broader than their subject. Conversely, *Ogonek* no. 34 opens with a heroic portrait of People's Commissar Nikolay Yezhov (who was, as is well known, short of stature) and the 'Tale of the Hero Yezhov' by *akyn* (improvisational poet-singer) Dzhambul Dzhabaev.

Thus, the model for coverage of the trials had been set: the visual 'figure of silence' had a profound meaning.

It is well known that in the Soviet Union, an Orwellian continous rewriting of history was practiced, a guided excision of pictures of the 'enemies of the people'. Even in my liberal elementary school (No. 10, named after Fridtjof Nansen), the students were ordered to paste over the portrait of the legendary marshal Vasilii Konstantinovich Bliukher (who had quite recently headed the tribunal for the 'Case of the Trotskyist Anti-Soviet Military Organisation') in their history textbooks. The attitude towards the 'enemy without' also changed constantly. Portraits of Hitler long served as a model for the ever-present caricaturists—Boris Efimov and the *Kukryniksy* (Mikhail Kupriianov, Porfirii Krylov, and Nikolai Sokolov—*Ed.*). But my search in *Ogonek* for photoreportage about the 1939 pact between the Soviet Union and Germany was in vain: as it turned out, the corresponding issue was left out altogether and combined with the following one (1939, no. 21–22). And on the cover of *Ogonek* no. 24, omitting the unpopular handshakes, we can see the joyous meeting of Soviet troops in Western Belarusia.

The strategy of *BIZ* at this point was completely opposite. The cover of number 35, hot on the heels of events, features a photograph of the Ribbentrop-Stalin handshake (Stalin's friendly smile would have been exactly the kind of superfluous information that the Soviet viewer could have done without), and the journal also provided comprehensive 'Berlin–Moscow' photoreportage (1939, no. 35, 148–9), even portraying the English public's (Downing Street's) reaction to the Soviet–German pact.

BIZ did not hesitate, either, with respect to the 'portrait of the enemy'. When antisemitism emerged from the shadows in 1939, it immediately spilled onto the pages of this popular publication. Chosen most often were photographs were dull, ugly, or haggard Jewish faces, which were supposed to repulse the reader (later on, this same kind of propagandistic strategy would be applied to Soviet prisoners of war). But the faces of the French antifascist volunteers in the journal's photographs could have become the prototypes for Jean-Pierre Leo or Jean-Louis Trintignant—the stars of the 'new wave'. The caption alone directs the emotions in the appropriate direction: 'A group of especially typical representatives of the Jewish race eagerly poses for the photographers.' But the big four-page report from the Warsaw ghetto (1941, no. 30, 790–3), as well as, one might add, the photograph taken from a high point of Warsaw destroyed to its foundations (1939, no. 45, 1731), could easily serve as a document for the Nuremberg trials.

The diametrically opposed strategies of the totalitarian regimes at this point allows us to advance several hypotheses. In the Soviet journal's 'figures passed over in silence', the usual pragmatic hypocrisy of the regime is of course quite plain, but we must also consider the differences in the mentalities of the two peoples. The image is, after all, a bigger thing than text: it influences feelings and more easily shapes prejudices. Nazism invoked the irrational rejection of 'the other' (Jews) or an irrational feeling of the triumph of the victor (Warsaw). It was not afraid of the possible ambiguity of interpretation. On the other hand, the logocentrism of Soviet culture feared emotional fluidity. On delicate issues, it preferred the definiteness of the word ('traffickers of the motherland', 'Trotskyist monsters', and the like). It was no accident that music was a minion of Hitler's, but was an object of Stalin's suspicion. In the Soviet Union, in turn, verbal formulas attained the irrationality of an incantation designed to change reality.

It goes without saying that, in damning its 'enemies', mass culture needed not only a leader cult but also a 'hero' figure (a role played by, for example, the sons in the Socialist Realist model of the 'big family').[9]

A cult of heroes that are taken not from literature but 'from life' is the feature of Soviet culture that Sovietology (both the western and dissident varieties) has made most difficult to understand. The TV era, with its passion for 'stars', could become a commentary to this cult, but the Soviet type of 'stars', in the light of subsequent exaggerated mythologisation, has its own specifics.

The main Soviet art—literature—never did succeed in creating the ideal image that the state required, except in the case of Pavka Korchagin. *Ogonek* in 1937 (no. 1, 9) marked the death of Nikolay Ostrovsky—with a photograph, an obituary and a poem. But still, the metaphor 'triumph of a heroic life' is more applicable to the author than to his character.

Popular culture began to create for itself the heroes that it needed, in order to later reconscript them into literature. According to Hans Günther, the figures of the pilots and polar explorers were not a Soviet peculiarity. Aviation and the Arctic, as was the case later with outer space, at that time filled the vacant space of the 'journey into the unknown'. But for the 'one-sixth of the world', with its almost nonexistent roads, long-distance flights and the problematic 'North Sea Route', they were also an economic and transportation necessity. It is no surprise, then, that *BIZ* had only drawings of tents on the ice ('The Dream of Science: A North Pole Station', in 1937, no. 15, 513), while in *Ogonek*, there were feature stories with Papanin's actual floating station depicted ('Wintering at the Pole', in 1937, no. 14, 20–1). The close-up portrait of the famous Shmidt (Otto Iul'evich Shmidt—famous Arctic explorer, awarded a Hero of the Soviet Union medal in

1937 for his leadership in the 'Cheluskin' expedition—*Ed.*)—with a picturesque beard, and in a hat with earflaps—graces the cover of *Ogonek* No. 15.

Dramatic foreshortened 'portraits' of aircraft, as well as the theme of aviation in the future war (and even of women in aviation), occupied a substantial amount of space in both publications; they were topics for essays, predictions and photographs. It was quite another matter that the Nazi journal needed the steely face of the pilot at the helm as a symbol, and that this face became the trademark of the German chronicle of wartime. In the Soviet journal, the image of the pilot was personalised, heroicised and glorified in the 1930s, especially in the year of the 'Great Terror'.

A Parenthetical Novella

At this point I will allow myself a digression, since I have had occasion to personally meet the 'heroes' of those times. In the 1970s, Yuri Khaniutin and I made a picture for Mosfilm about Petr Aleinikov, a cult actor of the 1930s. In conjunction with this, we interviewed the most iconic figures of the 1930s—Papanin, Gromov, and Stakhanov—in order to have a look at the real side of the exploits for which they were renowned and to find out 'what it really was like'. Here I will use the evidence that was recounted orally to us, and not the published texts that, like our film, went through the censors' filters.

The most legendary of the 'Stalin falcons' was Valery Chkalov. In 1937, he completed the first nonstop flight over the North Pole to the American continent, and his portrait graced the cover of *Ogonek* no. 18. A month later, the flight was repeated—and surpassed—by the team of Mikhail Gromov, who followed the course westward without deviating and landed in the Los Angeles area (see no. 26). The very fact that this event was repeated might suggest the 'custom made' nature of this 'exploit', and that it was 'invented' by Stalin. But we should recognise that in the 1930s, the repercussions of revolutionary explosion were still audible; such echoes always bring terror, even as they raise the creative potential of a nation. The people of the 1930s were still rich in initiative and audacity.

The initiative for the second flight was in fact Gromov's; he was a highly professional prerevolutionary-model test pilot. Gromov told us that once he (and his team) had thought through the idea of the flight and had laid a course, he understood that permission for such an adventure could only come 'from the very top', and he did not have such access. On the other hand, it was well known that Stalin favored Chkalov; accordingly, Gromov suggested to his team the idea of a twin flight. This tactic succeeded: Chkalov agreed, and permission for the twin flight was actually granted. But when he arrived at the airfield,

Gromov discovered that only Chkalov's ANT was 'at the ready', and that he would have to follow in a separate plane, with Chkalov given a head start. As opposed to the first team, which landed in the Vancouver area, the team of Gromov, Sergey Danilin and Andrey Yumashev maintained the course, speed and timetable of the flight precisely (the high quality of which even *BIZ* noted)—and received the prestigious Delyavo medal as a consolation prize. The photographs of the ritual meeting of the fliers' retinue in Los Angeles differ little from the Moscow pictures, except that the pilots are sitting on the back seat of an open car. We asked Gromov what this had been like, to be a hero at that time: how did he feel? He replied, 'This is what I felt—it was either win all or lose all. Anything could have happened—both the flight and getting arrested. We were lucky.' Incidentally, the handsome Yumashev was offered the lead in a feature film about a pilot, and a further three-year contract in Hollywood. Of course, the 'Stalin falcon' could not even dream of doing that; the most he could do was to make an amateur film about his stay in America and good-naturedly talk about this in *Ogonek*.

We might also adduce the similar story of Ivan Papanin, about the intrigues and the strategic moves he had to make in order to organise his drift station—and he was on 'the way up'. The point is that the Soviet government, the Party and Comrade Stalin (at least personally) were not the inventors or even the designers of these 'exploits', as it has often seemed in later legends (which I would call a 'secondary cult' with a minus sign). On the contrary, promoting an audacious idea required acquaintances, connections, tenacity and finagling, not to mention success. The power hierarchy knew how to expropriate any success to its own advantage, to co-opt it; in this regard, Stalin was reminiscent of Hoffman's Little Zaches. Lindbergh was glorified as Lindbergh, but Chkalov and Gromov as 'Stalin's falcons'.

More broadly, we might say that if Stalinism was ahead of its time in anything, it was in ideological 'marketing' of itself. It imagined Soviet society as an ideally governed structure, which it never was. (Nazism, by the way, achieved more in this respect, thanks to German accuracy and punctuality.) And the popular journal was just the right agent for that kind of ideological marketing.

Issue no. 4 of *Ogonek* for 1937 opens with an almost symbolic photograph: a young worker is holding a globe—one might say he is holding the world. The subject, however, is prosaic: Stakhanov is taking a geography exam for admission to the Industrial Academy. The myth of Stakhanov and the Stakhanovites is the strangest of the 'heroic' myths, one that many have attempted to explain. Bernice Rosenthal, for example, has written, 'Literature and art glorified the Stakhanovites, whose feats were the result of staging.'[10] For the Western consciousness, the Stakhanovite movement is quite inconceivable, and is modelled after the 'misrepresentations' of Brezhnev's times. But in the native encyclopedic biographical dictionary of Konstantin Zalesskii, *The Stalin Empire*, one can read, 'According to the reminiscences of the people who worked alongside S[takhanov] (who had garnered the support of Party organizers), his system for work came to be that several people would work at his side, providing him help and offloading the coal, which made it possible for S. to set records exceeding reasonable proportions.'[11] Why a peasant farmhand who had come to the mines as a driver, and not even a Party member, could get such support and help, remains unexplained. Thus, it is quite impossible to explain the phenomenon of the Stakhanovite movement about which all the mass media clamored from 1935 onward.

We had the opportunity to film Stakhanov from his mine with that same Party organiser, who in fact was the originator of the idea of the 'feat' and the father of the 'Stakhanovite movement'. We also talked to the 'distinguished female Stakhanovite', Tat'iana Fedorova, who had long since worked in the managerial system of the Moscow Metro Construction Project. The 'enigma' of Stakhanov was explained to us by the Party organiser, who had taken upon himself the role of mentor for the future 'hero'—in full accord with the Socialist Realist canon. The fact was that this fellow from the countryside, who had no miners' roots, as he himself said, 'knew the vein', like 'dowsers' for wells do. He did not simply 'gobble up coal', but rather sensed how to find the right place to strike with the pick so that the whole seam would come tumbling down. Of course, while he was doing this, he was given help, and someone to haul away the coal. The quick-witted Party organiser understood how to take advantage of this natural gift; he took the initiative into his own hands and in deep secrecy began to prepare a 'record' that, in fact, turned out to be fantasy: Stakhanov exceeded the norm by 350 per cent. Thus he became the 'ringleader of the movement', which brought him to the ranks of the 'heroes'.

It goes without saying that not all the Stakhanovites were distinguished by a divine gift, but the system that had come together with the beginning of 'industrialisation' provided definite opportunities for clever and ambitious people from the new working class. First, this time coincided with the rotation of the cadres of the old Party elites connected to the Revolution. Second, after the 'unmasking of the bourgeois *spetsy*', industrialisation lost the criteria of quality and profitability; thus, in the various 'gaps' and 'rush jobs', there remained possibilities to substantially raise productivity, not to mention the organisation of labor. Finally, the Stakhanov movement (both strikes and 'socialist competition') substituted for the stimulus of competition that had been eliminated from the monopolistic economy. The Stakhanovites became the 'working-class aristocracy' that was by no means specific to the USSR; the only thing unique about it was its glorification as the agent of the 'feat'.

The 'role of the individual' does not have a substantial place in Sovietology. Among the Stakhanovites were different people who experienced 'promotion' in different ways (their official statements and biographies retained the features of a hagiography). The one who suffered most from this was the 'founder' himself, who was not psychologically prepared for an academic or management career. Fedorova told us what a 'headache' Stakhanov was for the 'other' Stakhanovites at all the forums and conferences: raising hell in the new Moscow Hotel, disappearing, having too much to drink, so that they had to dash out somewhere and bail him out, and the like. He did not fit in among the new businesslike working-class elite, but no one quite dared to send the bearer of 'the name' back home. Strange as it might seem, the fate of this Soviet symbol, smiling from innumerable photographs, is comparable to the fates of Western 'stars' who could not endure the burden of fame. Stakhanov, whom we were able to film, was an enormous, sad human ruin. In a way, he became a victim of the Stalin era—the embodiment of the inhumanity of its 'proletarian humanism' and of its slow, lumbering 'modernisation'.

At that same time in *BIZ* (1937, no. 10, 306), Willy Sarbach, the inventor of the famous highway interchange called the 'cloverleaf', was mentioned but not made famous, just as indeed other potential 'heroes of labor' were not made famous. The preference was to carve the ideal Aryan in marble, like Josef Thorak and Arno Breker did, but to draw, poster-style, in the mass-oriented journal. Appearing as 'heroes' were Hermann Göring (with Il Duce and a lion cub, on the cover of no. 40) or Baldur von Schirach (with two children, on the cover of no. 18 for 1937), since there was only one 'leader'. The model of the 'big family' and its 'sons' did not work in a society that was far less traditional and patriarchal than the Soviet Union.

What remained the most asymmetric between the two journals were the stereotypes of women. If the 'heroes'—of race or class, made of marble or coming from documentary—did in fact coincide structurally, expressing the idea of the superiority of the ideology in question, then women's roles as there appeared in the two journals continued to differ as they had before. The woman for Nazism—within the bounds of the new 'masculine', militarised regime— was, above all, the potential mother of a soldier, but also a sexual object, with all of the accompanying industry of fashion. Nonetheless, the tasks of propaganda did not squeeze out the entertainment function of the journal; it remained commercial and 'bourgeois' (just as it did in German filmmaking).

Women in Soviet culture, as before, served as 'work units'. Even with its 'leisure' accent, *Ogonek* remained a predominantly didactic publication. The journal was always politically correct with respect to women's equality; its figurative symbols were the male and female Komsomolian challenging the heights in Serafima Ryangina's picture 'Higher and Higher!' (1937, no. 32, cover) and Vera Mukhina's famous 'Working Man and Kolkhoz Woman' (1937, no. 18, 12). The picture featuring ranks of 'svelte women's legs' was not captioned 'Girls' but rather 'The Parade of Athletes' (1939, no. 20–21, back cover). The very same subject—a pair of female acrobats—in *Ogonek* means a female machine gunner and a standard-bearer on a motorcycle (1939, no. 16, back cover), but in *BIZ*, it is called 'Ballet on the Moto-Roller' (1939, no. 8, cover). An April 1st photo-joke became the 'hit' of 1937 *BIZ*—a young lady in a perky little hat with plumets, with the hat breaking into two pieces (1937, no. 13, cover); many European journals reproduced it. But the most famous *Ogonek* photograph was of the same Stakhanovite, Fedorova, that we met wearing a respectable 'managerial' suit made of fine woolen fabric—with a chisel hammer in the Moscow Metro construction pit.

Intermezzo

The advertising in both journals changed, but, as before, marked the difference in the level and way of life. *BIZ* got noticeably thinner, and cigarette advertisements gave way to actual military manoeuvres. The 'women's industry' became poorer, and practical devices were improved. Leisure and travel receded into the background, under the leadership of the 'Kraft durch Freude' organisation. Everyday electrical devices were improved; on the other hand, Servan-Schreiber's postulate about the backbone of novels and of advertising suffered some shrinkage and weight loss. Party rhetoric reshaped the journal, and propaganda, although not totally squeezing out entertainments, had a significant competitive edge over them, although the novelties of world fashion, the curiosities of international high life, and film and sports sensations did not disappear from its pages.

In *Ogonek*, advertising changed more noticeably. The 'birthmarks' of NEP, set in huge type, disappeared. Advertising became predominantly graphic, state-oriented and even targeted—a real offer of goods and services. Reflected in it was Stalin's famous saying, 'Life has become better, life has become more fun.' There was even a corresponding expression for the mid-1930s: 'neo-NEP.'[12] Distribution did not disappear anywhere, but elements of state commerce and goods of one kind or another (albeit not high-demand ones) appeared. The attitude towards everyday life changed. The journal reflects a time of not only 'processes' and target overshooting, but also of a Culture and Relaxation Park, the 'Indposhiv' Studio, Western-style dancing to record players, 'diet' magazines and Intourist hotels—a sort of Soviet ragtime. The *Ogonek* advertising is a self-portrait of this time of internal disruptions and yawning gaps.

Together, the country marked the one hundredth anniversary of Pushkin's death, and the 'Red October' candy factory offered selections of candies 'in an interesting form'—'Pushkin's Tales,' 'Pushkin Five-Volumer', and 'Old Man Krylov's Little House'. The elegant picture of a restaurant was painted into the shape of a train: the railway employees advertised lunchrooms and restaurant dining cars. The All-Union Textile-Making Trade organisation (with a woman depicted in a checked outfit) offered natural fabrics, as well as 'snapshots of the latest fashions in Leningrad, Moscow, Paris, London, Vienna, and New York'. The All-Union Jewellers' Trade organisation (picturing a Baccarat vase, cameos, cigarette cases and tableware) announced that 'the prices for ... have been substantially reduced,' and also offered 'a great selection of antiquarian/artistic articles'. The All-Union Fur Organisation made a show of its 'great selection of squirrel-fur coats' and also promised a 'price reduction'.

The journal on the whole began to include more illustrations, but the hand-drawn nature of the advertisements revealed yet another yawning gap. As opposed to *BIZ*, where the 'women's industry' (from corsets to bras) was predominantly advertised via models in photographs, the advertisement of 'luxuries' in the Soviet journal was anonymous, not personified, faceless: the woman in the fur coat is hand drawn. Even if ideology permitted fur coats and antiques, the mindset of the common people did not appreciate them.

In the popular comedic film *A Girl with Character* (with the Soviet bombshell Valentina Serova), a simplistic plot about a girl named Varia from a fur farm in the Far East revolves around a wily paradox. The heroine sets off to Moscow to seek justice against her boss, who is interfering with the proper way of raising silver foxes (their fur was all the rage in world fashion at the time). In the capital, Varia has to become a saleswoman and at the same time the store's model for furs. She has a hard time, however, wrapping her Komsomol thinking around the idea of 'furs' as a commodity. Instead of modelling the fashions, she entices a whole group of girls to go to the Far East (there really was a 'Khetagurova girls movement').[13] It is hard to imagine Varia posing for fur advertisements. The idea of 'the product' and the idea of 'consumption' were not connected in the society's consciousness except by the Marxist cause-and-effect connection. And at this point, the asymmetry between the two journals reached its height.

It would be very interesting to examine in the two publications, in a parallel fashion, not only the heroic themes, but also the everyday ones—as well as the themes in art and science, where the reader could find quite a bit of interest. *Ogonek* described, for example, experiments 'about resuscitation of an organism', showing the system for artificially feeding 'an isolated dog's head' (with a graphic) and a photograph of the 'resuscitated dog' (1937, no. 16/17, 26). *BIZ* exhibited 'the most powerful setup in the world for splitting atoms' (1937, no. 23, 834). But this would require too much space.

With respect to several events, the themes of the two journals overlapped. The Spanish war (which became a preliminary run-through for World War II) and the famous Paris Exhibition of 1937 were examples.

All in all, the reporting on the civil war in Spain from different sides of the front could provide an approximate first picture of the future great war. The early photographs of the victims of the 'carpet bombings' of the German Condor Legion in *Ogonek*, captioned 'Fascism is death' (1937, no. 29/30), are the beginning of the endless catalogue of martyrs assembled in Nuremberg. The evacuation of children from Bilbao, soldiers at their positions and off-duty... anti-Fascism united, perhaps for the first time, the self-awareness of Soviet society with the West (the popular front). We did not learn about the shady side of the 'help' given by the Stalinist emissaries (who were more concerned with destroying the Trotskyist faction than with anything else) until the Thaw—the 'figure of silence'—had done its work.

BIZ would show 'Red Madrid' as the 'City of Poverty' (1937, no. 30, 1096–97), a constant motif for defaming the enemy; but also printed the victorious communiqués and, as always, included a portrait of the local 'leader'—Franco.

The organizers of the Paris Exposition, we must suppose, quite deliberately provided face-to-face pavilion spots for the Soviet Union and Nazi Germany. There was not only a spatial metaphor in this, but also, possibly, a subconscious hope for the clash of the two regimes. Accordingly, both dictatorships tried to express themselves symbolically, and did this through Freudian emblems. The Nazi pavilion, with its crowning imperial eagle, has the look of a phallic symbol; the Soviet one serves as a horizontally oriented base for Mukhina's 'Working Man and Kolkhoz Woman'. In the perspective from which this famous structure was photographed for *BIZ* (1937, no. 22, 790), one can detect in Mukhina a hint of the flying silhouette of the Winged Victory of Samothrace. In contrast, the Socialist Realism of the hammer and sickle is accented by the angular perspective of *Ogonek* (1937, no. 18, 12–13). The pavilion is shot in closeup, so no German eagle can be seen. And even the overall panorama of the exposition is composed in such a way that the confrontation of the two pavilions remains outside the frame of the shot (the famous 'figure silently overlooked' of the 'unpleasant' subject). The German journal returns to this *piquant* point, this time showing a 'triangle' from the Italian side of the pavilion and noting that it is just these three silhouettes that comprise the characteristic peculiarity of the exhibit as a whole. The Nazi graphic artist makes a drawn postscript to this: the wearied worker and female kolkhoznik have taken a load off their feet to rest, but the eagle has not even noticed this invitation of theirs (1937, no. 39, 1420–1). Jean Effel (François Lejeune), incidentally, makes his own comment on this: the eagle has also perched for the night in his nest, not to mention that the fascist horseman and his horse also have settled down for a snooze.[14] Thus the dictatorships connected themselves through their own symbolism.

Ogonek would imprudently start the year 1941 with a humourous drawing of the infant New Year descending in horror by parachute onto the ruins of the old Europe (1941, no. 1, inside cover). In No. 5, it would print the essay 'In Paris', with the cynical subtitle 'Impressions of the German Newspapers' Correspondents'. There would be reports from the European fronts as well, of course, but this mass-oriented journal would be surprisingly tied up in the everyday life at home. Whole pages, even covers, would be devoted to 'portraits' of teakettles and brooms, sleds, scissors and children's bicycles—all the things in which 1932 had taken such pride. But the slogans would not be as optimistic as they had been: 'Increase the production of mass-consumption goods twofold and threefold,' or 'Are you getting good service?' The old ills—shortages and the low quality of goods—would make themselves known just as they had before. A photograph of the dining car, which had once served as the model for hand-drawn advertisements, would turn out to be the reproach of the disappointing reality of the State Organisation for Feeding the Population. Alongside the 'good' things, snapshots of the 'bad' ones would appear—the 'wall of shame' of consumer goods, so to speak. Criticism of advertising of services would transition into criticism of advertising itself, which totally failed to correspond to the 'truth of life'. If we take the masses' journal to be a cross section—not a time slice, of course, but maybe a fraction of the emotions of the times—then we must suppose that the Soviet Everyman was, on the eve of the fateful date of 21 June, wrapped up in himself, in his own everyday problems, or at best concerned with the Stalin Prize winners or the smelting of pig iron and steel. The poster of the soldier under banners and emblems which appeared in *BIZ* in 1941 (no. 10, 'Victory in the West') had already appeared in *Ogonek* in the twentieth anniversary year of 1937. True, the German journal in this fateful year (for Germany, as well), was brimming with war topics.

Ogonek countered the *Drang nach Osten* with the text of a Molotov address—without even a picture of Molotov—and an anti-Nazi caricature on the cover. *BIZ*, as always, would resort to a defamation tactic (portraits of Russian *Untermenschen*); a snapshot of the impassable Russian road in which a German tank had mired could have become a warning to the Third Reich, but it did not. Then the time of war propaganda begins.

Born at the crossroads of the advertising catalogue and the novel with a sequel, the mass-oriented illustrated journal, no matter how its structure changed under the conditions of dictatorships, remained the same thing that it had been: a novel with a sequel about the life of society—and an advertisement of its way of life. Its documentary quality, despite any ideological contrasts, is just as unquestionable and just as conventional.

The duel of the journals of both 'base' dictatorships reveals, even more obviously than art does, both parallels and differences. Parallels include the creation of images of the living gods of quasi-religions; the heroic rhetoric that kept pace with the growth of militarisation; the cult of iron (the industrial landscape, planes and tanks); and the body cult (its youth, health, and strength, with the connotations of that same iron). Also parallel are the predominance of pageantry over reportage in the pictures, of 'beauty' over expressiveness; the monumental qualities of the layout (accompanying the advertisements); and the resort to the sublimating function of the graphics (ie - posters).

At the same time, the historically developed difference of traditions and of the level and mode of life are more obvious in the illustrated periodicals than in art. Russia chose the 'Prussian path'; Germany veered far off the road of 'industrial and technical progress,' and, no matter what its 'vision of the ideal future' might have been, the real life of its population was bourgeois in a European way. The Soviet economy, trying to 'catch up', but at the same time monopolised by the state, could not offer anything similar.

At the end of the great war to the death, when Soviet soldiers would advance onto German territory, the young officers brought up to feel the superiority of socialism would experience a sort of culture shock. Wristwatches and penknives, ballpoint pens and ladies' silk underwear, cosmetics and motorcycles, not to mention automobiles, would strike their imagination forever as a vision of a different way of life. *The Woman of My Dreams*, the film with Marika Rökk taken home as booty, would become a phenomenon of Soviet cinema and self-awareness.

This is in life. But the chronotopes of both journals are comparable, ideologically synchronic, but historically asymmetrical.

The propaganda in *BIZ*, beginning with the image of the Führer, is visualised, aggressive and arranged by topic (in time, but not in space). Its rhetoric is potentially like television's, targeted from the industrial age towards the information age. Regardless of the defeat in the war (the Reich came 998 years short of its thousand years), the racist Utopia was incompatible with this exactitude of the informational field.

Ogonek (starting with the patriarchal Stalinist myth) lived in an age that was not only logocentric, but indeed almost folkloric: both the leader and the enemy have their set of permanent epithets. Its layout is more hieroglyphical, and if it is montage-style, then it is so in a spatial sense. The everyday archaism of the Soviet chronotope—a sort of awkwardness, the primitiveness of its 'modernisation' compounded with the echo of the Avant-Garde in photography—makes its world visually more interesting and more charming (archaism is always more photogenic than bourgeois style). Didacticism and leaving things unsaid are also features of a patriarchal rhetoric that does not trust the ambiguity of the photograph and prefers to terrorise with the word and to suppress the unpleasant image. 'Hypocrisy' is a word that ought to be brought into the Stalinist canon, not for the purposes of a moral category but of a term. The great leftist Utopia takes root best of all in patriarchal soil, but modernisation, even of the most conservative kind, will sooner or later bring it down from within.

If ideology is the conscience of the mass media, then its strategy belongs to the subconscience of tradition and culture. Both journals demonstrate the two different stages of 'catch-up development,' multiplied by geographic and cultural coefficients. This is what makes them similar, but also profoundly different.

Translated by Jesse Savage.

NOTES

Introduction

1 Sheila Fitzpatrick. *Stalin's Peasants: Resistance and Survival in the Russian Village after Collectivization.* (New York: Oxford UP 1994), 262.
2 Joseph Stalin. *Voprosy leninizma.* 11th ed. (Moscow: Partizdat 1946), 507–513.

Chapter One: A Joyful Soviet Childhood: Licensed Happiness for Little Ones

N=Nedelya
PP=Pionerskaya Pravda

1 This paper is based on research supported by the Leverhulme Trust under grant no. F/08736/A, 'Childhood in Russia, 1890–1991: A Social and Cultural History.' The interviews cited below, coded 'Oxf/Lev,' were part of the work carried out for this project. Material has been recorded in St Petersburg (coded 'SPb.'), Moscow ('M'), Perm' ('P'), Taganrog ('T'), and in villages in Leningrad and Novgorod provinces. The code also includes a date ('03', '04', etc.), an identifier specifying the number and side of the cassette ('PF1A', etc.), and a page number referring to the written transcript. The interviews in St Petersburg were carried out by Aleksandra Piir, in Moscow by Yuliya Rybina and Ekaterina Shumilova, in Perm' by Svetlana Sirotinina, in Taganrog by Yury Ryzhov and Lyubov' Terekhova, and in village sites by Oksana Filicheva and Ekaterina Mel'nikova (2004) and by Oksana Filicheva and Veronika Makarova (2005). My thanks to all of them, and to Albert Baiburin, European University, St Petersburg, and to Vitaly Bezrogov, Russian Academy of Education, Moscow, for their help. For more information on the project, and extracts from interviews, see http://www.mod-langs.ox.ac.uk/russian/childhood (accessed 19 March 2009).
2 Anna A. Zaliznyak, I. B. Levontina, A. D. Shmelev, *Klyuchevye idei russkoi iazykovoi kartiny mira* (Moscow: Iazyki slavianskoi kul'tury 2005), 167.
3 L. N. Tolstoi, *Sobranie sochinenii v 20 tomakh,* vol. 3 (Moscow: Khudozhestvennaia literatura 1961), 284.
4 Ibid., 169.
5 See e.g., 'V izbe zazhitochnogo kolkhoznika Bogdanova,' *Pionerskaia pravda* 10 April 1934, 3.
6 See Albert Baiburin and Alexandra Piir, 'When We Were Happy' in this volume.

7   Tolstoi. *Sobranie*, 243. Andrei Platonov's *Dzhan* (1934) contains a closely similar passage: 'He lay down on his bed and unexpectedly fell asleep—with that sense of sudden bodily delight [*schast'e*] you only feel in youth.' *Izbrannye proizvedeniya* (Moscow: Ekonomika 1983), 397.

8   'Schastlivoe detstvo rebiat bol'shevitskoi strany,' *Pionerskaya pravda* [henceforth *PP*] 20 January 1934, 20; 'My deti schastlivoi strany,' *PP* 24 January 1934, 8; 'Prazdnik radostnoi molodezhi,' *PP* 4 September 1934, 2; 'Samym schastlivym detiam v mire,' *PP* 1 May 1935, 1; 'Radosti net kontsa,' *PP* 30 June 1935, 1; and many other such articles.

9   *Svetlyi, radostnyi, veselyi, / Den' nad gorodom vstaet, / Zdravstvui, osen'! Zdravstvui, shkola! / Zdravstvui, uchebnyi god!* The poem loses only a little in translation. It is credited to *detkor* (child correspondent) A. Alyanchev, of Tula (see 'Schastlivym detiam nashei strany,' *PP* 2 September 1935, 1).

10   The earliest version of the slogan seems to have appeared in *PP* 28 September 1935, page 2, in a story called 'Detskii tramvai v Shakhtakh, Azovo-Chernomorskii krai'. On the children's tram in question appears: *Spasibo tebe velikii Stalin za schastlivuiu, radostnuiu zhizn'* (Thank You, Great Stalin, for a Happy and Joyous Life). By the end of the year, however, the slogan had stabilised as *...za schastlivoe detstvo*. On October 23, 1935, *PP* printed a full-page splash on page 3, to mark the newspaper's tenth anniversary, under the banner headline, *Thank You, Comrade Stalin, for a Happy, Joyful Childhood!* A 1936 example of the slogan (this time without 'joyful') appears as the front cover of the magazine *Kolkhoznye rebiata* for October. 'Happiness' was also more widely used generally in Stalinist culture than 'joy,' though the following loyal Stalinist definition of the latter term in D. K. Ushakov's thoroughly ideologised defining dictionary, published in the late 1930s, is an exception: 'The faces of those taking part in the demonstration on Red Square are always full of joy at the sight of the Party leaders with Comrade Stalin, the leader of the nations, at their head. A sharp overwhelming joy always gripped them.' D. N. Ushakov (ed.). *Tolkovyi slovar' russkogo iazyka* (Moscow: Gosudarstvennoe izdatel'stvo 1939), 1110. However, the explanation for this is that the volume P-R appeared in the year of Stalin's sixtieth birthday, making a jubilee tribute to him appropriate.

11   *PP* 28 June 1935, 1.

12   The first version of Mikhail Krasev's 1953 opera about Pavlik Morozov had the title 'In the Cause of Justice and Happiness' (*Za pravdu, za schast'e*): see http://www.te06.mnogosmenka.ru/te060218/te060246.htm (accessed 18 September 2007).

13   *PP* 22 November 1934, 1.

14   I. Aisberg, 'Malen'kie khoziaeva bol'shogo doma,' *Nashi dostizheniia*, 10 (1934), 115.

15   Kornei Chukovsky's first publication of the text appeared in 'Pust' vsegda budet solntse!,' *Literatura i zhizn*, 14 December 1960. For the text of the song, see *Kul'turno-prosvetitel'skaia rabota*, 9 (1962), 50.

16   The last gasp of the old collective ethos was the campaign to set up *internaty*, boarding schools, between 1956 and 1964. Originally envisaged as an admirable destination for all children, such schools were from the mid-1960s the destination of children in special circumstances: traditional 'orphanages' (*detskie doma*) were replaced by 'boarding schools,' where children went back to their parents on weekends, and children of Soviet officials who worked abroad, or children living in sparsely populated areas where settlements were few and far between, were also accommodated in such schools. (See Catriona Kelly, *Children's World: Growing Up in Russia, 1890–1991* (New Haven: Yale University Press 2007), ch. 4, ch. 12; on critiques of institutions, see ibid., ch. 4, and Catriona Kelly, 'Sovetskii soiuz—rai dlia detei?' (paper presented at 'L'URSS: un paradis perdu?,' Université de Paris-IV, Sorbonne, Paris, 15 November 2006). Russian version available

online at http://rggu.com/article.html?id=58601 (accessed 19 March 2009). English version forthcoming in F. Conte (ed.), *L'URSS: un paradis perdu* (Paris, 2009).

17 In fact, the Soviet ideal of childhood happiness was in signal respects different from the Christian idea of paradise: see Kelly, 'Sovetskii soiuz—rai dlia detei?'.

18 Mikhail Zhvanetsky, 'Detskii sad,' *God za godom*. (Leningrad: Eks libris 1991), 437. For an academic discussion on these lines, see Evgeny Dobrenko, 'Totalitarnaia kul'tura i mir detstva,' *Wiener Slawistischer Almanach*, 29 (1992).

19 M. Rakhmanova, 'My sami ikh kalechim,' *Nedelya* [henceforth *N*] 43 (1989), 8. For earlier shock reports on infant mortality, see e.g., 'Malen'kie deti—bol'shie zaboty,' *N* 7 (1987), 16–17; Yu. Rakhval'sky, 'Otvechat' za svoe zdorov'e' and 'Lozh' ne vo spasenie,' *N* 15 (1987), 18; 'O malyshe i professional'nom urovne vracha,' *N* 33 (1987), 33; V. N. Mudrak, 'Dlia zdorov'ia malyshei' *N* 2 (1988), 2; and especially, 'Okno v mir statistiki,' *N* 44 (1988), 12–13, and 'Puteshestvie za initsiativoi,' *N* 44 (1988), 18.

20 S. K. Zhuravlev and A. K. Sokolov, "Schastlivoe detstvo", *Sotsial'naia istoriia: ezhegodnik* 1997 (Moscow: Rosspen 1998), 159–203.

21 David Samoilov, 'Dnevnik schastlivogo mal'chika,' *Znamya* 8 (1999). See also http://magazines.russ.ru/znamia/1999/8/samoilov.html (accessed 19 March 2009).

22 Oxf/Lev V-04 PF12A, 5: male b. 1928, village, Tver' province, father mechanic, mother factory worker (later housewife), moved to settlement, Leningrad province after War (date not known), graduated from seven-year school. Interviewed Leningrad province, August 2004.

23 Oxf/Lev T-04 PF8A, 25: female, born 1970, Penza, mother house painter, father systems controller (*puskonaladchik*); trained at a conservatory, music teacher. Interviewed Taganrog, December 2004.

24 Oxf/Lev P-05 PF5A, 16: male, b. 1973, Perm'. Parents both factory workers and recent migrants from the countryside; secondary education, manual worker. Interviewed Perm', August 2005.

25 Yuri Slezkine has asserted (*The Jewish Century* (Princeton: Princeton University Press 2004), 257) that 'happy childhood' in the Soviet period was particularly likely in Jewish families: 'More of Hodl's children than just about anybody else's had the proverbial Soviet "happy childhoods."' But this is a moot point; while literary sources might suggest this was correct, oral history gives a rather more ambiguous picture. The offsetting of poverty and a sense of happiness is characteristic of informants recollecting working-class childhoods in other countries as well. Ruth Simmons, an African-American academic who is now President of Brown College, recalled in an interview with John Crace in *The Guardian*, Education section, 3 October 2006, 11, that life had been intimidating in Grapeland, Texas, but that 'things looked up after the family moved to Houston when she was seven.' 'The neighborhood was shabby, there were bars on every corner, and crime and alcoholism was part of the daily routine,' she says. 'And yet I was blissfully happy. People bothered to insist I went to school, and I loved it. There was a calm and order that was missing from elsewhere in my life.'

26 Collection of Vitaly Bezrogov. My thanks to Vitaly Bezrogov for making this text available to me. (See drafts of chapter 5, 75 of typed transcript, page 4 of handwritten text.).

27 Oxf/Lev P-05 PF29B, 18; on discipline, see PF29A, 14; on washing, see ibid.,16–17; on the dried pea treatment, ibid., 2. For similar reminiscences, see Oxf/Lev SPb-05 PF67–68: this informant, female b. 1951 and in an orphanage (boarding school) from age ten, remembered that the children were made to do heavy housework, such as polishing floors, as a punishment (PF67A, 12), and that they had no gloves in winter

(PF68A, 34), but that life had generally been OK (PF67A, 1); Oxf/Lev SPb-05 PF69A, 3 (female informant, b. Leningrad 1951; in orphanage from age 10; secondary education; agent for trade firm; divorced, two children), also emphasizes the positive.

28 Oxf/Lev V-04 PF9A, 5: female, b. 1923, Chelyabinsk province.

29 Oxf/Lev P-05 PF12A, 1: female, b. 1960, small town, Perm' province, mother worked in kindergarten and then as cook in canteen, father lathe operator, secondary technical education. Interviewed Perm', August 2005.

30 Oxf/Lev V-04 PF5A 2: female, b. 1938, Leningrad, father union official (died 1942), mother housewife (later agricultural worker), evacuated as small child to village in Vologda province, lived in settlement, Leningrad province from c. 1945, graduated from ten-year school.

31 CKQ-Ox-03 PF6A, 2: female, b. 1931, Leningrad, father commander in army, mother did not work, higher education.

32 Oxf/Lev SPb-04 PF47A, 3: female, b. 1967, Leningrad, in orphanage from age seven, now works as an orphanage supervisor.

33 Oxf/Lev SPb-02 PF 1A, 4: female, b. 1937, Leningrad, in orphanage from age 5, secondary education, worked as secretary in academic institute.

34 A very striking example of this pattern is found in a poem written by the young Kursk writer Mikhail Doroshin, then in his mid-twenties, entitled 'Perekrestok schastlivykh dorog' (At the Crossing of Happy Roads), which describes how a young man, gone to the bad, suddenly finds himself in the cozy, delightful, and happy world of... the labor camp. Having wondered where to find happiness—perhaps in someone else's pocket?—the lyric hero finds himself, in the camp, sleeping on clean straw for the first time in his life and feeling 'at home' there. (Mikhail Doroshin and, Nikolai Korneev, Perekrestok schastlivykh dorog (Kursk: Kurskaia pravda 1935, 10–12). By a cruel irony of fate, Doroshin was himself arrested in 1937; it is not recorded how his idealistic views of the Soviet penal system stood up to the test of first-hand experience.

35 Oxf/Lev M-04 PF 22A, 1: female, b. Yaroslavl, 1951, parents manual workers, specialised secondary education, accountancy clerk.

36 Oxf/Lev V-04 PF1A, 1: female, b. 1932, village, Mordovia, Mordvin background (but gave up speaking the language after moved to Russia), parents kolkhoz workers, moved to settlement, Leningrad province 1946, primary education (three years).

37 See e.g. Oxf/Lev V-04 PF2B, 16: female, b. 1927, village, Novgorod province, father carpenter, mother kolkhoz worker, moved to settlement, Leningrad province, as young woman (date unknown), attended but did not complete seven-year school.

38 Oxf/Lev P-05 PF23A, 7: female, b. 1977, Perm'. Mother, laboratory technician in factory, father, driver; parents separated when informant was aged three, trained as teacher, now works in arts education. Interviewed Perm', August 2005.

39 See Catriona Kelly, 'Den' rozhdeniia, prazdnik detstva: Celebrating Children's Birthdays in Twentieth-Century Russia,' in G. A. Levinton and N. B. Vakhtin (eds.), AB-60. Sbornik k shestidesiatiletiiu A. K. Baiburina (St Petersburg: Evropeiskii Dom 2007), 264–77. On children and Soviet holidays generally, see Catriona Kelly and Svetlana Sirotinina, '"I Didn't Understand, But It Was Funny": Late Soviet Festivals and their Impact on Children', Forum for Anthropology and Culture 5 (2009), forthcoming.

40 The informant presumably means at the station: paying a guard a small bribe to make sure that a package was safely conveyed and delivered at the other end was a standard way of getting bulky items transported in the late Soviet era.

41 Soviet Army Day (now known as Defenders of the Motherland Day), which is treated as a kind of generic men's day to go with International Women's Day (8 March).

42 Oxf/Lev SPb-03 PF 28B, p. 18: male, b. Leningrad 1972. Single mother was factory worker, uncompleted tertiary education—expelled from institute after fight, manual worker.

43 Cf. the publication of many dozens of brochures on Soviet holidays: see, e.g., G. Gerodnik, *Dorogami novykh traditsii* (Moscow: Politicheskaia literatura 1964); E. Lisavtsev, *Novye sovetskie traditsii* (Moscow: Sovetskaia Rossiia 1966); Yu. N. El'chenko, *Novomu cheloveku—novye obriady* (Moscow: Politicheskaia literatura 1976); I. I. Fursin, *Obriadnost' i ee mesto v sotsialisticheskom obraze zhizni* (Moscow: Znanie 1977). A Western secondary survey of this material is Christel Lane, *The Rites of Rulers: Ritual in Industrial Society: The Soviet Case* (Cambridge: Cambridge University Press 1981).

44 Oxf/Lev P-05 PF12A, 4: female, b. 1960. Small town, Perm' province; mother worked in kindergarten and then as cook in canteen; father, lathe operator, secondary technical education, furniture technologist. Interviewed Perm', 2005.

45 Oxf/Lev SPb-03 PF 17A, 2: male, b. Leningrad 1960. Father, factory worker (did not live with family); mother, clerk in factory, grandmother (lived with family), teacher in vocational education; works in arts administration.

46 This is particularly vividly described in Oxf/Lev WQ1 GM, 3. On indignation inspired by being made to stand in the corner, see CKQ-0x-03 PF12.

47 See Kelly, *Children's World*, chapter 11; Alexandra Piir, 'What is a Courtyard For,' *Forum for Anthropology and Culture* 4 (2007), 311–45; Mariya Osorina, *Sekretnyi mir detei (v prostranstve mira vzroslykh)* (St Petersburg: Piter 1999).

48 See, e.g., I. Medvedeva, T. Shishova, 'Novoe vremya—novye deti?,' *Oktyabr'* 2 (1997), 132.

Chapter Two: Utopian Naturalism: The Epic Poem of Kolkhoz Happiness

1 See Iurii Lotman, 'Kanonicheskoe iskusstvo kak informatsionnyi paradoks,' *Izbrannye stat'i v 3-kh tomakh* (Tallin: Aleksandra 1992), T. 1.; Lotman, 'O soderzhanii i strukture poniatiia "khudozhestvennaia literatura",' *Izbrannye stat'i v 3-kh tomakh* (Tallin: Aleksandra 1992), T. 1.; Lotman, 'Massovaia literatura kak istoriko-kul'turnaia problema,' *Izbrannye stat'i v 3-kh tomakh* (Tallin: Aleksandra 1993), T. 3.

2 Boris M. Sokolov, *Khudozhestvennyi iazyk russkogo lubka* (Moscow : RGGU 1999), 154.

3 Ibid., 31.

4 Ibid., 154.

5 See Evgeny Dobrenko, *Formovka sovetskogo pisatelia: Sotsial'nye i esteticheskie istoki sovetskoi literaturnoi kul'tury* (St. Petersburg: Akademicheskii proekt 1999).

6 Kornei Chukovskii, *Masterstvo Nekrasova* (Moscow : GIKhL 1955), 639.

7 Ibid., 643–44.

8 Ibid., 646.

9 Ibid., 646–47.

10 Quoted in Chukovskii, *Masterstvo Nekrasova*, 647.

11 Chukovskii, *Masterstvo Nekrasova*, 648–49.

12 Iosif Brodskii was one of the first to pay attention to Platonov's connection to Zabolotskii, when he wrote in the foreword to *Kotlovan*: 'I would say that the only one close to Platonov in language was Nikolai Zabolotskii in the period of [his book of verse] *Stolbtsy*'.

13 Viacheslav Zavalishin, 'Posle Bunina,' *Novoe Russkoe Slovo*, Vol. XLI (25 April 1954), 8. My thanks to Igor' Loshchilov, who pointed out Zavalishin's article to me.

14 Oleg Kovalov, 'Sovetskii lubok,' *Iskusstvo kino*, No. 2 (1993), 79.

15 Ibid.

16 Ibid., 80.

17 In the poem, a nickname of Eremei, Erema (pronounced yi-RYO-ma), is frequently used, to better fit the rhythm and 'casual' style.

18 Nikolai Gribachev, 'Cherty budushchego v poezii,' *Kul'tura i zhizn'* Mar. 28 (1950), 2.

19 Nikolai Gribachev, *Stikhi* (Smolensk), 1948. Critic Boris Privalov wrote, 'As in a precious mosaic, by piling gem against gem, the artist creates a picture.' Privalov, *Nikolai Gribachev: Kritiko-biograficheskii ocherk* (Moscow: Sovetskaia Rossiia 1962), 61.

20 See Iurii Lotman, 'Blok i narodnaia kul'tura goroda,' *Izbrannye stat'i v 3-kh tomakh* (Tallin: Aleksandra 1993), T. 3.

21 Nikolai Aseev, 'Prostota i prostiachestvo,' *Literaturnaia gazeta* 22 October 1947.

22 Sokolov, 168.

23 Ibid., 172.

24 Ibid.

25 D. S. Likhachev, A. M. Panchenko, and M. V. Ponyrko, *Smekh v Drevnei Rusi* (Leningrad: Nauka 1984), 21.

26 See Sokolov, 129; V. Adrianova-Peretz, *Ocherki po istorii russkoi satiricheskoi literatury XVII veka*, 259; L. I. Timofeev, *Ocherki teorii i istorii russkogo stikha* (Moscow: GIKhL 1958), 196; L. S. Sheptaev, 'Russkii raeshnik XVII v.', *Uchenye zapiski LGPI* (Leningrad: Kaf. rus. lit-ry 1949), T. 87: 26.

27 K. Pozdniaev, *Utverzhdenie: Aleksei Nedogonov i ego stikhi* (Moscow: Sovremennik 1937), 191, 195, 197, 201.

Chapter Three: Luxuriating in Lack: Plenitude and Consuming Happiness in Soviet Paintings and Posters, 1930s–1953

1 The statement has been misattributed to Marie Antoinette.

2 Quoted in Paul Parker, 'The Modern Style in American Advertising,' *Parnassus* 9/4 (April 1937), 21.

3 Jean Baudrillard, *Simulacra and Simulation*. Trans. Sheila Faria Glaser, (Ann Arbor: Michigan University Press 1994), 3.

4 Sheila Fitzpatrick, 'The Good Old Days,' *London Review of Books* 25 (9 October 2003), 19, emphasis added HG.

5 Julie Hessler justly notes, 'In the 1920s, an interest in material possessions was portrayed in official publications as a sign of bourgeois decadence, a deviation from the ascetic values of the socialist revolution' (Hessler, 'Cultured Trade: The Stalinist turn towards consumerism,' in *Stalinism: New Directions*. ed. Sheila Fitzpatrick (London & New York: Routledge 2000), 183). Lev Tolstoi's tirelessly iterated denunciation—in his later fiction, journalism, and pronouncements—of the morally corruptive effects of superfluous possessions and goods in civilised societies laid an unacknowledged basis for Soviet criticism of Western self-indulgence, which, moreover, exploited workers who never shared the luxuries produced by their labor.

6 Vera S. Dunham, *In Stalin's Time: Middleclass Values in Soviet Fiction* (Durham & London: Duke University Press 1990). While amplifying Dunham's thesis, more recent scholarship (Cox, Fitzgerald, Hessler, Volkov) has provided persuasive evidence that this shift occurred

not during the postwar years, as she proposed, but in the mid-1930s. Indeed, Cox adduces copious evidence that consumerist attitudes of various stripes enjoyed official approval in the 1920s.

7 Hessler offers the acute insight that the rationing periods of 1917–1924, 1928–1934, and 1939–1947 'served as the crucible of consumer culture in Stalin's Russia' (183). See her dissertation, 'Culture of Shortages: A Social History of Soviet Trade' (PhD dissertation, University of Chicago, 1996), chapter 3.

8 Jukka Gronow, *Caviar with Champagne: Common Luxury and the Ideals of the Good Life in Stalin's Russia* (Oxford & New York: Berg 2003), 9.

9 Volkov provides an incisive commentary on the nature of *kul'turnost'*, which became programmatic in 1935, but, as he notes, fluctuated in its specifics from year to year. Vadim Volkov, 'The Concept of *Kul'turnost'*: Notes on the Stalinist civilizing process,' in *Stalinism: New Directions*. ed. Sheila Fitzpatrick (London & New York: Routledge 2000), 226.

10 Volkov, 216.

11 See the gorgeous, vivid examples in Elena Chernevich, Mikhail Anikst, Nina Baburina. *Russian Graphic Design 1880–1917.* (New York: Abbeville Press 1990).

12 Randi Cox, ''NEP without Nepmen!': Soviet Advertising and the Transition to Socialism,' in *Everyday Life in Early Soviet Russia: Taking the Revolution Inside*. eds. Christina Kiaer & Eric Naiman, (Bloomington & Indianapolis: Indiana University Press 2006), 126.

13 Elena Chernevich, 'Introduction,' in *Soviet Commercial Design of the Twenties*. M. Anikst (ed.). (New York: Abbeville Press 1987), 31. The new Soviet designers, primarily Constructivists, 'used simple typefaces, pure geometric forms and clear structures. They created that gaudy, totally undecorated and genuinely agitational style of typography and graphic design which was come to be identified with the Soviet Union in the twenties, and which contrasted sharply with the decorativeness of the styles that preceded it' (Ibid.). A brief glance at Soviet ads for beer, as compared to those of Ivan Bilibin during the late-Tsarist era, instantly drives home the point of Soviet minimalism in ads.

14 As Hessler points out, the 1927 publication of the *Commodity Encyclopedia*—'the first major reference book on goods under the Soviet regime'—manifested a clear preference for producers' over consumer commodities. The Thaw reversed that priority in its nine-volume series, *Commodity Dictionary*, published from 1956 to 1961 (182). Hessler astutely calls the latter 'a belated answer to NEP-era criticisms that socialist trade functionaries did not know how to sell' (183).

15 Hessler, 'Cultured Trade', 196–97.

16 Katherine Verdery, *What Was Socialism, and What Comes Next?* (Princeton: Princeton University Press 1996), 26.

17 For a concise differentiation between the 'old (formerly bourgeois) Russian intelligentsia' and the new 'Soviet intelligentsia,' see Sheila Fitzpatrick, *The Cultural Front: Power and Culture in Revolutionary Russia* (Ithaca: Cornell University Press, 1992), 218–19.

18 On the topic of 'model' workers and 'model' stores, see Hessler 197–200.

19 For the lyrics, see *Mass Culture in Soviet Russia,* James von Geldern and Richard Stites (eds.), (Bloomington & Indianapolis, Indiana University Press 1995), 237–38.

20 Hessler, 'Cultured Trade', 208. Regarding the ubiquity of the slogan, see Sheila Fitzpatrick, *Everyday Stalinism: Ordinary Life in Extraordinary Times: Soviet Russia in the 1930s,* (Oxford: Oxford University Press 1999), 90.

21 Hessler, 'Cultured Trade', 203.

22 Culture's dedicated efforts to unite the Soviet Union against the Nazis after Hitler invaded the Soviet Union, obviously, established different priorities for the years 1941–1945.

23 On many aspects of this campaign, see Fitzpatrick 1992 and 2000; Hessler; Volkov; and Lewis Siegelbaum, ' 'Dear Comrade, You Ask What We Need:' Socialist paternalism and Soviet rural 'notables' in the mid-1930s,' in *Stalinism: New Directions. Rewriting Histories*, ed. Sheila Fitzpatrick, (London: Routledge 2000), 231–57.

24 On the plans for, and various facets of, the Exhibition, see this excellent article to which I am indebted: Susan Reid, 'Socialist Realism in the Stalinist Terror: The *Industry of Socialism* Art Exhibition, 1935–41 *The Russian Review* 60 (April 2001), 174.

25 Anastas Ivanovich Mikoian, *Tak bylo. Razmyshleniia o minuvshem* (Moscow: Vagrius 1999), 305–8.

26 For a list of the places he visited and the discoveries he made, see Mikoian 305.

27 Regarding the Soviet visitors' hyperbolic reaction to Macy's, see Hessler 192–93.

28 Anastas Ivanovich Mikoian, *Pishchevaia industriia sovetskogo soiuza* (Moscow: Pishchepromizdat 1941), passim.

29 Volkov, 226–27.

30 Darra Goldstein, 'Domestic Porkbarreling in Nineteenth-Century Russia, or Who Holds the Keys to the Larder?' In *Russia*Women*Culture*, eds. Helena Goscilo and Beth Holmgren, (Bloomington & Indianapolis: Indiana University Press 1996), 125–51. Mashkov was a master of still lifes, a subject that, though grudgingly acceptable by the regime in the 1930s, hardly conveyed the purported dynamism of a progressive in the making; he tended to avoid ideological painting. The irreproachable symbolic value of this painting, with its state emblems and transparent hierarchy, however, compensates for its generic stasis.

31 Just as the five-pointed star embodies the union of all workers in the five continents, the hammer and sickle signifies the union of worker and peasant. Both emblems, ordered by Lenin and approved in June 1918, figured prominently in the graphic culture of the early Soviet period. See Chernevich, 90.

32 Goldstein, 146.

33 Paintings and sculptures of bread or corn and wheat proliferated during the thirties and forties: David Shterenberg's still life *Bread*, Vera Mukhina's group sculpture by the same title, Aleksandr Bubnov's and Tat'iana Iablonskaia's *Corn* (1948, 1949) number among the best-known works.

34 Viewed by some commentators as engineered genocide, the collectivisation campaign coincided with the persecution of Ukrainian intellectuals (1932–1934), and suggests Stalin's desire to wipe out or diminish a sense of Ukrainian identity. See Andrew Gregorovich, 'Black Famine in Ukraine 1932–33: A Struggle for Existence,' *FORUM: A Ukrainian Review* 24 (1974), available: http://www.infoukes.com/history/famine/gregorovich/ (accessed 23 November 2007). On the 1929–1931 famine in the Soviet Union, see Robert Conquest, *The Harvest of Sorrow: Soviet Collectivization and the Terror-Famine* (Oxford: Oxford University Press 1986).

35 As Reid points out, whereas in 1933 'impressionism and Russian 'Cézannism' were admitted, with reservations as legitimate sources for the 'Soviet style,' ' by the mid-1930s, critics 'declared impressionism the beginning of bourgeois art's decline into subjectivism and formalism, the influence of which must be expunged from Soviet art' (2001, 159). By the end of the 1930s, however, impressionism was sufficiently rehabilitated for an exhibition of French landscape painting to have taken place at the State Museum of Modern Western Art (1939), stimulating a laudatory article on Cézanne (Reid, 178).

36 On individualism, see Matthew Cullerne Bown, *Socialist Realist Painting*, (New Haven & London: Yale University Press 1998), 127.

37 *Food in Russian History and Culture*, ed. Musya Glants and Joyce Toomre (Bloomington & Indianapolis: Indiana University Press 1997), 222.

38 On the role of 'typicalness' in Socialist Realist art, see Bown 166–70.
39 Bown, 71. Konchalovskii's still lifes—a genre acceptable, if not particularly valued, during this period—were admired, and one of them was shown at the *Industry of Socialism* Art Exhibition.
40 Susan Reid, 'All Stalin's Women: Gender and Power in Soviet Art of the 1930s,' *Slavic Review* 57, 1 (Spring 1998), 142.
41 Bown cites Gerasimov's statement that it was 'the task of Soviet artists to carry out an evolution in painterly culture, using impressionism; the influence of this movement on our vision is an accomplished fact' (Bown 192, quoting *Krasnaia niva* 1923, no.17, 13). As Bown observes, the impressionist emphasis on surface violated the Socialist Realist concern with 'essence' (Bown 192 [quoting *Krasnaia niva* 1923, no.17, 13], 194).
42 Mark Bassin rightly notes that the bicycle here replaces the tractor or combine harvester as the customary Socialist Realist image of the mechanisation of the countryside (Mark Bassin, 'The Greening of Utopia: Nature, Social Vision, and Landscape Art in Stalinist Russia,' in *Architectures of Russian Identity: 1500 to the Present,* James Cracraft and Daniel Rowland (eds.), (Ithaca and London: Cornell University Press 2003), 162. Yet the bicycle also signals healthy physical engagement in sport, which constituted another sphere of political competition with the West. On the ideology of sport in the Soviet Union, see Irina Makoveeva, 'Soviet Sports as a Cultural Phenomenon: Body and/or Intellect,' *Studies in Slavic Cultures* III (2002), 9–32.
43 Bassin's hyperbolic claim that 'the table is lavishly decked' ignores the smallness of the table and the glassware that takes up much of the surface space (163).
44 Yet that soil, as Bassin contends and as countless literary texts bemoan, sooner proved a challenge in its inhospitable bleakness (151).
45 Bown, 156.
46 Parker, 21.
47 Reid, 146–67.
48 For a more comprehensive treatment of Soviet commercial ads for the full spectrum of consumer goods from 1928–1956, see Randi Cox, 'All This Can Be Yours!: Soviet Commercial Advertising and the Social Construction of Space, 1928–1956,' in *The Landscape of Stalinism: The Art and Ideology of Soviet Space*, Evgeny Dobrenko and Eric Naiman (eds.), (Seattle & London: University of Washington Press 2003), 125–62. Her evaluation of ads during this period is appreciably more positive than mine, probably because her article focuses on items other than food and drink—advertised, moreover, not only in posters. Cosmetics, for instance, seemed to stimulate more creative and colorful images in various visual genres.
49 *Kapitalisty proizvodiat tovary radi pribylei, a my—dlia udovletvoreniia potrebnostei trudiashchikhsia* (Mikoian 1941, 159). The orientation and the tone of the articles, speeches, and reports collected in this volume differ substantially from those in his memoirs, published much later. Whereas the retrospective nature of the latter permits Mikoian to describe various initiatives and frustrations regarding goods (and other matters) in a relatively measured manner, and occasionally to note Stalin's mistakes, the items in the 1941 publication laud Stalin at every turn, repeatedly praise Stakhanovites, exhort audiences to ever greater feats of production, and justify official decisions about supplies, prices, and so forth. The propagandistic nature of these 'performances' is evident in such manifestly dishonest statements as Mikoian's claim at the second session of the Central Committee on Industry's (TsIK) seventh meeting (*sozyv*) in 1936: 'All the major difficulties in the internal development of our country have been successfully eliminated by us' (*Vse glavnye trudnosti vnutrennego razvitiia nashei strany nami uspeshno*

likvidirovany) (111). Here Mikoian unabashedly mimics the example of Stalin, whose every major speech from 1931 on, as Julie Hessler has noted, 'contained some mendacious reference to the increasing well-being of Soviet citizens, as well as rosy projections into the prosperous socialist future' (185).

50 Volia Nikolaevich Liakhov, *Sovetskii reklamnyi plakat i reklamnaia grafika 1933–1973* (Moscow: Sovetskii khudozhnik 1977), 10.

51 Cox, 131.

52 They preferred, however, either exhibitions of material goods or write-ups of such 'model' grocery stores as the luxurious Tsarist-era Eliseev emporia in Moscow and St. Petersburg, with their impressively palatial, chandeliered Art Nouveau interiors preserved and renovated; though, true to Soviet fashion, their names had been replaced by numbers.

53 John Berger, *Ways of Seeing* (London: BBC and Penguin 1972), 132.

54 Parker, 22.

55 For a survey of how advertising images in Russian glossy magazines peddled dreams in the early post-Soviet period, see Helena Goscilo, 'Style and S(t)imulation: Popular Magazines, or the Aestheticisation of Postsoviet Russia,' *Russian Culture of the 1990s: Studies in 20th Century Literature* 24, 1 (Winter 2000), 15–50. Evgenii Dobrenko investigates Soviet advertising as located between art and propaganda, in the process citing examples from literature that verbally advertised Stalinist abundance. Evgenii Dobrenko, *Politekonomiia sotsrealizma* (Moscow: Novoe literaturnoe obozrenie 2007), 400–26.

56 Parker, 21–2.

57 Parker, 20.

58 Alan Gowans believes that 'advertising by irrational association is a logical development from compulsive symbols, but in essence involves a much more complicated mental process' (9). No such processes structured Soviet advertising posters during Stalinism, which favored a mundane transmission of basic information about the product. If, as Gowans asserts, 'the implications of psychological hard sell are all totalitarian,' then capitalist totalitarianism in advertising could hardly contrast more with advertising in a political totalitarian state (10). Alan Gowans, *The Unchanging Arts: New Forms for the Traditional Functions of Art in Society* (Philadelphia: Lippincott 1971).

59 Parker, 22, 20.

60 'Advertising is a weapon that routs the competition.' See Maiakovskii's 'Agitation and Advertising' (Vladimir Maiakovskii, 'Agitatsiia i reklama,' in *Polnoe sobranie sochinenii v 13-i tt.* Vol. 12 (Moscow: Gosizkhudlit 1959), 57–8) and the error-ridden brief remarks by Aleksei Tarkhanov, which, astoundingly, collapse the graphics of the 1920s and 1930s into one. Maiakovskii's brief article commends Europe's grasp of advertising, adducing an example from Germany (58).

61 Hessler, 197.

62 Sheila Fitzpatrick, *Cultural revolution in Russia, 1928–1931* (Bloomington: Indiana University Press 1984).

63 Cited in Gronow, 83.

64 Presumably, this ad followed Mikoian's trip to the United States and his realisation that mass-produced hamburgers sold on the streets were an enormous convenience— a revelation to be repeated in January 1990, when the first McDonald's opened on Moscow's central Pushkin Square and attracted 30,000 customers, soon becoming the busiest branch of the McDonald's chain in the world. See Erin E. Arvedlund, 'McDonald's Commands a Real Estate Empire in Russia,' *New York Times*, March 15, 2005.

65 All unwieldy, the names changed from *Mossel'prom* to *Narkompishcheprom*, etc.—none of them, of course, paralleling the Western pattern of short, snappy, memorable acronyms.

66 See, for instance, Izrail' Bograd's anemic poster ad for *pel'meni*.

67 Compare this unsuccessful ad with his less naturalistic ads of the 1920s, especially for cigarettes.

68 If one accepts Jackson Lears's idea that '[t]he courtship of art and advertising has been clouded by distrust and only fitfully consummated' (Jackson Lears, 'Uneasy Courtship: Modern Art and Modern Understanding,' *American Quarterly*, 39, 1 (Spring 1987), 135), as one surely must, then the Soviet twenties instantiate that rare consummation.

69 Elsewhere, however, Miller adhered to the stereotypical model, as in his ads for ice cream.

70 Needless to say, that eye contact lacks even a hint of the sexual solicitation ubiquitous in contemporary print and TV advertisements.

71 In fact, that holds true for some of Sakharov's other ads, such as the naturalistic, wintry *Svezhezamorozhennye plody i iagody* (Freshly Frozen Fruits and Berries, 1954).

72 Gronow, 17. According to Mikoian, he dissuaded Stalin from concentrating solely on the sweeter variety that was his own preference (1999, 313).

73 Gronow, 19.

74 Mikoian 1999, 312. Mikoian boasts that both Anthony Eden and Winston Churchill praised Soviet bubbly, of which they subsequently received several cases (1999, 315).

75 Gronow, 122. Gronow cites letters quoted in the thoroughly documented study by Elena Osokina, *Za fasadom 'stakinskogo izobiliia'. Raspredelenie i rynok v snabzhenii maseleniia v gody industrializatsii, 1927–1941* (Moscow: Rosspen, 1998).

76 Mikoian lists the dates of the plan as 1937–1941 (1999, 313).

77 Whether female workers on collective farms could identify in their imaginations with the idealised image of femininity here as a possible future self remains a question, of course.

78 Lears, 136.

79 Liakhov also maintains that as soon as Maiakovskii, Rodchenko, Anton Lavinskii, and Aleksei Levin stopped working in this sphere, 'the originality of the Soviet advertisement graphic dwindled' (9).

Chapter Four: Tasty and Healthy: Soviet Happiness in One Book

1 Alexander Genis, 'Poverkh bar'erov.' Radio Svoboda, 6-1-1989. http://www.svoboda.org/programs/OTB/2003/OBT.061703.asp

2 In this essay, I will cite the 1939, 1945, 1947, 1952, and 1953 editions of the *Book about Tasty and Healthy Food*. I would like to take this opportunity to thank Andrea Lena Corritore for her valuable assistance locating several source works.

3 Jukka Gronow, *Caviar with Champagne: Common Luxury and the Ideals of the Good Life in Stalin's Russia* (Oxford-New York: Berg 2004).

4 *Kniga o vkusnoi i zdorovoi pishche* (Moscow: Pishchepromizdat 1952).

5 Catriona Kelly, *Refining Russia: Advice Literature, Polite Culture, and Gender from Catherine to Yeltsin* (Oxford: Oxford University Press 2001).

6 *Kniga o vkusnoi i zdorovoi pishche* (Moscow: Pishchepromizdat 1939).

7 Genis.

8 Thomas Lahusen, 'Kak zhizn' chitaet knigu: massovaia kul'tura i diskurs chitatelia v pozdnem sotsrealizme,' in *Sotsrealisticheskii kanon*, eds. Evgeny Dobrenko and Hans Guenther, (St Peterburg: Akademicheskii proekt 2000), 609–24.

9 Hans Guenther, 'Totalitarnoe gosudarstvo kak sintez iskusstv,' in *Sotsrealisticheskii kanon*, 7–15.

10 Typical in this respect are the ideas expressed in the Mayak radio broadcast about *The Book about Tasty and Healthy Food* on January 19, 2006, in which Grigorii Zaslavskii and Irina Kaspe participated, available http://www.radiomayak.ru/schedules/69/25634-audio.html

11 Julie Hessler, 'Cultured Trade. The Stalinist Turn Towards Consumerism,' in *Stalinism. New Directions*, ed. Sheila Fitzpatrick, (London: Routledge 2000), 182–209.

12 Guenther, 9.

13 Kirill Postoutenko, 'Istoricheskii optimizm kak modus stalinskoi kul'tury,' in *Sotsrealisticheskii kanon*, 481–91.

14 Vladimir Papernyi, *Kul'tura Dva* (Moscow: NLO 1996.)

15 Boris Groys, 'Utopian Mass Culture,' in Boris Groys and Max Hollein (eds.), *Traumfabrik Kommunismus; Dream Factory Communism: The Visual Culture of the Stalin Era*, (Ostfildern: Hatje Cantz 2003), 26.

16 Pellegrino, Artusi, *Science in the Kitchen and the Art of Eating Well* (Toronto: University of Toronto Press 2003).

17 Ada Boni, *Il talismano della felicità* (Roma: Colombo 1929).

18 Elena Molokhovets, *Classic Russian Cooking: Elena Molokhovets' 'A Gift to Young Housewives'*, trans. Joyce Toomre (Bloomington: Indiana University Press 1998).

19 *The Book about Tasty and Healthy Food* was not the first and last cookbook to be published in the Soviet Union, but it was, and still is, the flagship of this flotilla, and as such, an unshakeable symbol of the Stalinist regime. This is discussed in Rothestein (Halina and Robert Rothestein, 'The Beginning of Soviet Culinary Art,' in *Food in Russian History and Culture*, eds. Musya Glants and Joyce Toomre (Bloomington and Indianapolis: Indiana University Press 1997), 177–94), which is, incidentally, not without its errors. See also Kelly 2001.

20 *Kniga o vkusnoi i zdorovoi pishche*, 1939, title page.

21 Ibid., 15.

22 Evgeny Dobrenko, 'Sotsrealisticheskii mimesis ili 'zhizn' v ee revolutsionnom razvitii,' in *Sotsrealisticheskii kanon*, 459–71.

23 Katerina Dëgot', 'Die Kollektivierung der Moderne: The Collectivization of Modernism,' in *Traumfabrik Kommunismus: The Visual Culture of the Stalin Era*, eds. Boris Groys and Max Hollein (Ostfildern: Hatje Cantz 2003), 85–105.

24 '[A] newsreel on Moscow's Central Department Store highlighted upper-class shoppers, but it was above all Stakhanovites who came to represent the 'citizen-consumer' in Stalinist depictions of the prosperous life' (Hessler, 198).

25 Svetlana Boym, *Common Places. Mythologies of Everyday Life in Russia* (Cambridge, Mass: Cambridge University Press 1994), 200.

26 Gian Piero Piretto, 'Suggestioni e batticuori: ideologia e politica staliniana in forma di canzoni,' *Itinera. Rivista di Filosofia e Teoria delle Arti e della letteratura*, http://filosofia.dipafilo.unimi.it/itinera/mat/saggi/?ssectitle=Saggi&authorid=pirettogp&docid=suggestioni&format=html

27 I would like to thank here the journalists Tat'iana Livchenko and Anna Zafesova, who both discussed this issue with me.

28 Peter Vail and Alexander Genis. 'Kolobok. Sekrety sovetskoi kukhni.' Radio Svoboda,29-1-2004. http://www.svoboda.org/ll/cult/1004/ll.102904-3.asp

29 *Kniga o vkusnoi i zdorovoi pishche*, 1939, 11.

30 *Kniga o vkusnoi i zdorovoi pishche*, 1945, 3.

31 Ibid.

32 *Kniga o vkusnoi i zdorovoi pishche*, 1939, 4.

33 *Kniga o vkusnoi i zdorovoi pishche*, 1947, 4.

34 Daniil Granin, *Kerogaz i vse drugie. Leningradskii katalog.* (Moscow: Tsentrpoligraf 2003).

35 Natal'ia Ivanova, *Nostal'iashchee. Sobranie nabliudenii.* (Moscow: Raduga 2002).

36 I would like to adduce here the example of crabs, which in the 1930s were an ordinary food, advertised in order to promote their consumption, but by the early 1950s had become an elitist delicacy, and were now obviously 'scarce goods'.

37 See also Kelly, 2001, especially chapters four and five.

38 *Kniga o vkusnoi i zdorovoi pishche*, 1952, 16.

39 *Kniga o vkusnoi i zdorovoi pishche*, 1954, 17.

40 Ibid., 75.

41 *Kniga o vkusnoi i zdorovoi pishche*, 1953, 6.

42 Ibid., 10.

43 Ibid., 11.

44 *Kniga o vkusnoi i zdorovoi pishche*, 1939, 19.

45 *Kniga o vkusnoi i zdorovoi pishche*, 1952, 73.

46 *Kniga j vkusnoi i zdorovoi pishche*, 1953, 15.

47 Boni, 11.

Chapter Five: 'It's Grand to be An Orphan!': Crafting Happy Citizens in Soviet Children's Literature of the 1920s

I would like to thank the National Endowment for the Humanities Collaborative Humanities Research program, the American Councils for International Education, and the National Council for Eurasian and East European Research for the opportunity to research this subject in the libraries of Moscow, St. Petersburg, and Perm'. I would like to offer special thanks to Jesse Savage, Scott Sheridan, Lauren Nelson, and Mark Lipovetsky for their numerous recommendations and suggestions during the work on this article.

1 The quote used in the title is taken from *Adventures of Mottel the Cantor's Son* by Sholem Aleichem, translated by Tamara Kahana (New York: Henry Schuman, Inc. 1953), 3.

2 Belykh, Grigory, Panteleev, Leonid. *Respublika SHKID* (Moscow: Detskaia literatura 1960).

3 Anton Semenovich Makarenko, *Izbrannye pedagogicheskie sochineniia, kniga pervaia* (Moscow: APN RSFSR 1948). The English translation, entitled The *Road to Life*, Stephen Garry, trans., vol. I, Stanley Nott, London,1936.

4 On this subject, see various sources that deal with the Soviet state's policies regarding childhood: Anne. E. Gorsuch, *Youth in Revolutionary Russia: Enthusiasts, Bohemians, Delinquents* (Bloomington: Indiana University Press 2000); Judith Harwin, *Children of the Russian State: 1917–95* (Aldershot: Avebury 1996); James Bowen, *Soviet Education: Anton Makarenko and the Years of Experiment* (Madison: University of Wisconsin Press 1965); Allan M. Ball, *And Now My Soul Is Hardened: Abandoned Children in Soviet Russia, 1918–1930* (Berkeley: University of California Press 1994.) The most recent and comprehensive study of Soviet childhood is that of Catriona Kelly in *Children's World: Growing up in Russia, 1890–1991* (New Haven: Yale University Press 2007). In Russia, Vitaly Bezrogov (RGGU) has also done interesting studies on Soviet childhood. For information see the site http://childcult.rsuh.ru (date accessed: December 15, 2008).

5 This phrase is usually attributed to Lenin. In her recollections of a meeting with Lenin in November 1917, the director of the preschool department of the Education Commissariat, D. A. Lazurkina, quoted the following sentiment that the first leader of the Soviet state expressed: 'Keep in mind that all the best we have belongs to the children!' However, this sentence was missing in the first version of her memoirs, so it is difficult to establish the authenticity of this statement. See *Slovar' sovremennykh tsitat*, ed. K. V. Dushenko (Moscow: Eksmo 2007), 215.

6 See Catriona Kelly, 'Shaping the "Future Race": Regulating the Daily Life of Children in Early Soviet Russia', in *Everyday Life in Early Soviet Russia: Taking the Revolution Inside*, eds. Christina Kiaer and Eric Naiman, (Bloomington: Indiana University Press 2006), 256–81.

7 On this subject see, for example, memoirs published in the series *Moi dvadtsatyi vek* (My Twentieth Century) established in 1995 by the Vagrius Publishing House. The actors Veniamin Smekhov (*Teatr moei pamiati / Theater of My Memory, 1995*) and Lev Durov (*Smeshnaia grustnaia zhizn' / This Funny Sad Life*, 2008), and the poet Andrei Voznesensky (*Na virtual'nom vetru / On the Virtual Wind*, 1998), for example, all speak of their childhood experiences at the creative facilities for Soviet children with the greatest of admiration.

8 At the end of his play *Zolotoi kliuchik* (*The Golden Key*, 1938), Aleksei Tolstoy's fairy tale characters identify the USSR to their children's audiences as the *strana schastlivykh detei* ('land of happy children'). See Catriona Kelly's article in this volume on the origins of the 'happy childhood' formula in the 1930s.

9 Iurii A. Fedosiuk, *'Utro krasit nezhnym svetom...': Vospominaniia o Moskve 1930–1930x godov*. (Moscow: FLINTA 2004), 39.

10 On this subject see Gorsuch (150); Ball (XI); Kelly (194); and Juliane Fuerst, 'Between Salvation and Liquidation: Homeless and Vagrant Children and the Reconstruction of Soviet Society', *Slavonic and East European Review* 86:2 (2008), 231–58.

11 Fedosiuk, 39.

12 See Ball (44–60) and Kelly (205–6).

13 Kelly, 193.

14 Ball, 16.

15 Ibid.

16 Kozlov, V. A. *Istoriia Otechestva: liudi, idei, resheniia. Ocherki istorii sovetskogo gosudarstva*. (Moscow: Politizdat 1991), 117–9.

17 Kelly, 197.

18 Quoted in Ball, 12.

19 I have borrowed this term from Catriona Kelly, who identifies as such the institutionalized orphaned children (253–7).

20 Sheila Fitzpatrick, *Everyday Stalinism: Ordinary Life in Extraordinary Times: Soviet Russia in the 1930s* (Oxford: Oxford University Press 1999), 73.

21 Gorsuch, 159.

22 Quoted in Gosuch, 160. On Zalkind and his work with *besprizorniki*, see Gorsuch, 158–61, and Ball, 127–41.

23 Ball, 129.

24 Kelly, 6.

25 Ibid.

26 Irina Petrovna Lupanova, *Polveka. Sovetskaia detskaia literatura, 1917–1967* (Moscow: Detskaia literatura 1969), 64–81.

27 See Lidiia Feliksovna Kon, *Sovetskaia detskaia literatura, 1917–1929* (Moscow: Prosveshchenie 1960), 51–76, and Evgeniia Oskarovna Putilova, *Istoriia kritiki sovetskoi detskoi literatury, 1929–1936* (Leningrad: LGPI 1975), 11–25.

28 Evgeny Dobrenko, *Politekonomiia sotrealizma* (Moscow: Novoe literaturnoe obozrenie 2007), 182–6.

29 Petr Bliakhin, *Krasnye d'iavoliata* (Baku: 'Bakinskii rabochii' 1923).

30 Lev Ostroumov, *Makar-sledopyt* (Moscow-Leningrad: GIZ 1925).

31 Sergei Auslender, *Dni boevye* (Moscow-Leningrad: GIZ 1925).

32 Ostroumov, 15.

33 On the subject of 'children's avant-gardism' see Lupanova, 48–50.

34 See Putilova, *Ocherki po istorii kritiki sovetskoi detskoi literatury, 1917–1941* (Moscow: Detskaia literatura 1982), 40–1.

35 For an overview of the 1920s publications see Marina Balina, 'Creativity through Restraint: The Beginnings of Soviet Children's Literature,' in *Russian Children's Literature and Culture*, ed. Marina Balina and Larissa Rudova, (London: Routledge 2008), 1–19.

36 On children's literature in translation see Evgeny Pavlovich Brandis, *Ot Ezopa do Dzhanni Rodari* (Moscow: Detskaia literatura 1980).

37 See Evgeny Dobrenko, *Formovka sovetskogo chitatelia* (St. Peterburg: Akademicheskii proekt 1997), 173.

38 N. Sarkisov-Serazini, *Sen'ka—zhokh* (Moscow: ZIF 1927).

39 The NEP (New Economic Policy) was introduced by Vladimir Lenin at the Tenth Party Congress in March 1921 as a temporary measure to stimulate economic recovery in Soviet Russia after years of civil war. This policy allowed for private initiative by loosening governmental control over trade and manufacturing industries. The word 'NEPman,' however, was used in Soviet everyday culture as a derogatory term, to label an entrepreneur who would profit from the work of others.

40 Sergei Grigor'ev, *S meshkom za smert'iu* (Moscow-Leningrad: ZIF 1924).

41 Aleksei Irkutov, *Zagovor* (Moscow: GIZ 1924).

42 Lupanova, 65.

43 N. Dmitrievskii, *Fed'kina zhizn'* (Sverdlovsk 1924).

44 Petr Yakovlev, *Krasnyi bor* (Moscow: GIZ 1927).

45 See L. Kon, 221.

46 Fuerst, 235.

47 See the collection *O partiinoi i sovetskoi pechati* (Moscow: Politprosvet 1954), 294.

48 Lev Gumilevskii, *Plen* (Kharkov: Proletarii 1929).

49 Arkadii Gaidar, *Sobranie sochinenii*, t. 4 (Moscow: Detskaia literatura 1965), 183–259.

50 Gumilevskii, 70.

51 Kelly, 76.

52 On the Soviet attitude toward the pre-revolutionary treatment of the 'orphan' theme, see Lupanova , 64–71.

53 Ball, 193.

54 Gaidar, 210.

55 Ibid., 256.

56 Fuerst, 236.

57 Lupanova, 67.

58 Kozhevnikov, Aleksei. *Shpana*. (Moscow: GIZ 1929), 31.

59 Kozhevnikov, Aleksei. *Vokzal'niki*. (Moscow-Leningrad: ZIF 1925), 26.

60 Kozhevnikov, Aleksei. *Put' v schastlivuiu stranu*. (Moscow-Leningrad: Molodaia gvardiia 1926), 46.
61 Kozhevnikov, *Shpana*, 319.
62 On the martyrdom of Boris and Gleb see Serge A. Zenkovsky, ed., *Medieval Russia's Epics, Chronicles, and Tales* (New York: Meridian 1974,) 101–5.
63 Kozhevnikov, Aleksei, *Mamka iskat' budet* (Sverdlovsk: Uralkniga 1925), 10.
64 Ball, 194.
65 Quoted in Bowen, 5.
66 On the reception of Belykh and Panteleev's novel see the editorial on 'Dorevolutsionnaia i sovetskaia shkola v detskoi literature' in *Detskaia literatura* 12 (1935), 6.

Chapter Six: Sew Yourself Soviet: The Pleasures of Textile in the Machine Age

1 'Remeslo i prikladnoe iskusstvo,' *Zhenskii zhurnal*, 4 (1930), 4.
2 B. Shumiatskii, 'Trudneishii zhanr osvoen', *Kino*, 16 December 1934, 2. See also F. Ermler, 'Kartina raduetsia,' *Kino*, 16 December 1934, 2.
3 David Howes, *Sensual Relations: Engaging the Senses in Culture and Social Theory* (Ann Arbor: Michigan University Press 2004).
4 Constance Classen, *Worlds of Sense: Exploring the Senses in History and Across Cultures* (London: Routledge 1993).
5 Paul Stoller, *Sensuous Scholarship* (Philadelphia: University of Pennsylvania Press 1997).
6 Howes, xi.
7 Karl Marx and Friedrich Engels, *The German Ideology*, trans. and ed. R. Pascal (New York: International Publishers 1947), 35.
8 'Zadachi zhenskogo zhurnala,' *Zhenskii zhurnal*, 4 (1926), 1.
9 'Rukodelie,' *Zhenskii zhurnal*, 4 (1926), 24.
10 'Port'era iz kholsta,' *Iskusstvo odevat'sia*, 9 (1928), 16.
11 Tat'iana Konstantinovna Strizhenova, *Iz istorii sovetskogo kostiuma* (Moscow: Sovetskii khudozhnik 1972), 15.
12 'Vyshivka aplikatsiei,' *Iskusstvo odevat'sia*, 5 (1928), 14.
13 'Pokryvalo na divan ili postel,' *Zhenskii zhurnal*, 4 (1926), 37.
14 Mark Wigley, *White Walls, Designer Dresses: The Fashioning of Modern Architecture* (Cambridge, MA: MIT Press 2001), 11.
15 Wigley.
16 Gottfried Semper, *Style in the Technical and Tectonic Arts; or, Practical Aesthetics*, trans. H. F. Mallgrave and M. Robinson (Los Angeles: Getty Research Institute 2004), 247.
17 Ibid., 248.
18 Wigley, 11.
19 'Kak sozdaetsia domashnyi uiut?,' *Zhenskii zhurnal*, 6 (1926), 13.
20 'Ugolok khoziaiki,' *Zhenskii zhurnal*, 9 (1926), 13.
21 M. Iampolskii, 'Byt kak material 'Pestrota i sliakost' Rossii' in *Iazyk—Telo—Sluchai: kinematograf i poiski smysla* (Moscow: Novoe literaturnoe obozrenie 2004), 198–209.
22 Cited in Wigley, 110.
23 E. Roginskaia, Problemy kostiuma) *Sovetskoe iskusstvo*, 7 (1927), 63–7.
24 E. Pribyl'skaia, 'Vyshivka v nastoiashchem proizvodstve,' *Atel'e*, 1 (1923), 7.
25 Aleksandra Ekster, 'V konstruktivnoi odezhde,' *Atel'e*, 1 (1923), 4.

26 *Iskusstvo v bytu: v tablitsakh,* ed. Vera Mukhina and Nadezhda Lamanova (Moscow: Izvestiia TsIK SSSR 1925), 19.

27 N. Lamanova, 'Russkaia moda,' *Krasnaia niva,* 30 (1923), 32.

28 Nikolai Aleksandrovich Semashko, 'Gigiena kostiuma,' *Iskusstvo odevat'sia,* 3 (1928), 1.

29 Lamanova, 1920, cited in Strizhenova, *Iz istorii sovetskogo kostiuma,* 17.

30 A. Fedorov-Davydov, 'An Introduction to the First Soviet Exhibition of National Textiles,' in *Revolutionary Costume: Soviet Clothing and Textiles of the 1920s,* eds. Lydia Zaletova, Fabio Ciofi degli Atti and others (New York: Rizzoli 1989).

31 *Revolutionary Costume.*

32 D. Bartlett, 'Let Them Wear Beige: The Petit-bourgeois World of Official Soviet Dress,' *Fashion Theory,* 8 (2004), 127–64.

33 *Komsomolskaia Pravda,* 30 June 1928.

34 Stepanova, V. (Varst), 'Kostium sevogniashnego dnia—prozodezhda.' *LEF,* 2 (1923), 65–8.

35 Anne E. Gorsuch, 'Moscow Chic: Silk Stockings and Soviet Youth,' in *The Human Tradition in Modern Russia,* ed. W. B. Husband, (Delaware: SR Books 2000), 64–76.

36 Vlad Korolevich, *Zhenshchina v. kino* (Moscow: Teakinopechat' 1928) offers a systematic account of female film stars, Western and Russian, according to different models of femininity. For information regarding the popularity of Western films in Soviet Russia of the 1920s, see Denise Youngblood, *Movies for the Masses: Popular Cinema and Soviet Society in the 1920s* (Cambridge: Cambridge University Press 1992).

37 *Komsomolskaia Pravda,* 30 June 1928.

38 Anatolii Vasilievich Lunacharskii, 'Svoevremenno li podumat' rabochemy ob iskusstve odevat'sia,' *Iskusstvo odevatsia* 1 (1928), 1.

39 Ibid.

40 *Iskusstvo odevat'sia* 1 (1928), 6.

41 *Delegatka: zhurnal rabotnits i krest'ianok,* 7 (1927), 17.

42 These were designed for making at home, or to be copied by a professional seamstress. It is interesting to note that the profession of dressmaking was legalised only on 27 March 1936: Sheila Fitzpatrick *Everyday Stalinism: Ordinary Life in Extraordinary Times: Soviet Russia in the 1930s* (Oxford: Oxford University Press 1999), 44. A. Vasiliev, *Russkaia moda, 150 let v fotografityakh* (Moscow: Slovo 2004), however, claims that there were some 204 tailor's workshops (for women) in Moscow between 1923 and 1932. Note that properly fitted off-the-peg clothing did not reach the Soviet Union until late 1930s, so home-tailoring gave the ordinary man or woman a much better change of clothing that would fit.

43 'Portnoi doma,' *Iskusstvo odevat'sia,* 9 (1928), 15.

44 'Portnikha na domu,' *Iskusstvo odevat'sia,* 10 (1928), 1.

45 Ekaterina Degot, 'Ot tovara k tovarishchu: k estetike nerynochnogo predmeta,' in *Pamiat' tela: nizhnee bel'e sovetskoi epokhi: katalog vystavki,* eds. Ekaterina Degot and Iuliia Demidenko (Moscow: 2000), 8–19 (13).

46 T. Strizhenova, 'Textiles and Soviet Fashion in the Twenties,' in Zaletova et al (1987), 6.

47 Vera Dunham, *In Stalin's time: Middle Class Values in Soviet Fiction* (Cambridge: Cambridge University Press 1976).

48 Svetlana Boym, *Common Places: Mythologies of Everyday Life in Russia* (Cambridge, MA: Harvard University Press 1994).

49 Jukka Gronow, *Caviar with Champagne. Common Luxury and Ideals of Good Life in Stalin's Russia* (Oxford: Berg Publishers 2003).

50 Margaret Mead and Rhoda Budendey Metraux, *The Study of Culture at a Distance* (Chicago: Chicago University Press 1953), 162.

Chapter Seven: Happy Housewarming!: Moving into Khrushchev-Era Apartments

1 *Izvestiia* (26 July 1959). For the American context of the exhibition and 'kitchen debate', see Elaine Tyler May, *Homeward Bound: American Families in the Cold War Era* (New York: Basic Books 1988), 16–20 and chapter 7; Karal Ann Marling, *As Seen on TV: The Visual Culture of Everyday Life in the 1950s* (Cambridge, MA: Harvard University Press 1994), 252; Walter L. Hixson, *Parting the Curtain: Propaganda, Culture and the Cold War, 1945–1961* (Basingstoke: Macmillan 1997), chapters 6, 7. The Soviet response to representations of happy housewives and modern domesticity at the American Exhibition in Moscow is discussed in more detail in Susan E. Reid, ' "Our Kitchen is Just as Good": Soviet Responses to the American Kitchen,' in *Cold War Kitchen: Americanization, Technology, and European Users*, ed. Ruth Oldenziel and Karin Zachmann (Cambridge, MA: MIT 2009), 83–112. I am indebted to the Leverhulme Trust for the Research Fellowship 'Everyday Aesthetics in the Modern Soviet Flat'.

2 May, *Homeward Bound*; Cynthia Lee Henthorn, 'The Emblematic Kitchen: Labor-Saving Technology as National Propaganda, the United States, 1939–1959,' *Knowledge and Society* 12 (2000): 153–87; Henthorn, 'Commercial Fallout: The Image of Progress and the Feminine Consumer from World War II to the Atomic Age, 1942–1962,' in *The Writing on the Cloud: American Culture Confronts the Atomic Bomb*, ed. Alison Scott and Christopher Geist (Lanham: University Press of America 1997), 24–44.

3 See the 1956 and 1957 editions of the *Daily Mail Ideal Home Book* (London: Associated Newspapers 1956, 1957). See also Marling, *As Seen*; Tyler May, *Homeward Bound*; Sue Ellen Hoy, *Chasing Dirt: The American Pursuit of Cleanliness* (New York, Oxford: Oxford University Press 1995).

4 For a present-day example see responses to the online American Photographers' Gallery invitation to documentary photographers to capture the contemporary meanings of Thomas Jefferson's phrase 'the pursuit of happiness'. According to one contributor, April Saul, who chose to focus 'on one of the most elemental meanings of the pursuit of happiness: the everyday life of a family,' the pursuit of happiness is 'having a roof over your head, raising your kids, making it from one day to the next, and trying to be reasonably happy'. Photographers' Gallery http://www.pbs.org/jefferson/frame4.htm last accessed 2 August 2006.

5 Marietta Shaginian, 'Razmyshleniia na amerikanskoi vystavke,' *Izvestiia* (23 August 1959). For collective services as the socialist solution see V. I. Lenin, 'Velikii pochin. (O geroizme rabochikh v tylu),' *Polnoe sobranie sochinenii*, 5th ed. (Moscow: Politicheskaia literatura 1970) vol. 39, 24; S. Strumilin, 'Rabochii byt i kommunizm,' *Novyi mir*, no. 7 (1960), 203–20.

6 Iu. Filipovich, 'Veshchi—ne khoziaeva, a slugi!' *Izvestiia* (11 July 1959), 4.

7 Compare George Mansell, 'Kitchen Commentary,' *Daily Mail Ideal Home Book, 1957* (London: Associated Newspapers 1957), 131; 'Oblegchaet trud, sberegaet vremia,' *Ogonek*, no. 27 (3 July 1960); I. Luchkova and A. Sikachev, 'Sushchestvuet li nauka o zhil'e?' *Nauka i zhizn'*, no. 10 (1964), 25; R. Chakovskaia, 'Dlia domashnego khoziaistva,' *Sovetskaia zhenshchina*, no. 1 (1954), 44–5; I. Tsyganov, 'Est' takaia mashina,' *Izvestiia* (2 August 1959), 6. On the myth of labour-saving technology see Ruth Schwartz Cowan, *More Work for Mother*, 2nd ed. (1983; London: Free Association Books 1989); and, in the Soviet context, Alix Holt, 'Domestic Labour and Soviet Society,' in *Home, School and Leisure in the Soviet Union*, ed. J. Brine, M. Perrie, and A. Sutton (London: George Allen & Unwin 1980), 29–31. Compare on the role of images of consumption in constructing gender and national identity in divided Germany: Erica Carter, *How German is She? Postwar West*

German Reconstruction and the Consuming Woman (Ann Arbor: University of Michigan Press 1997); Jennifer Loehlin, *From Rugs to Riches: Housework, Consumption and Modernity in Germany* (Oxford: Berg 1999).

8 'Zhenshchiny, eto dlia vas!' *Ogonek*, no. 24 (12 June 1960).

9 Vera S. Dunham, *In Stalin's Time: Middleclass Values in Soviet Fiction* (Cambridge, Eng.: Cambridge University Press 1976); Julie Hessler, 'Cultured Trade: the Stalinist Turn towards Consumerism,' in *Stalinism: New Directions*, ed. Sheila Fitzpatrick (London: Routledge 2000), 182–209; Julie Hessler, *A Social History of Soviet Trade: Trade Policy, Retail Practice, and Consumption, 1917–1953* (Princeton: Princeton University Press 2004); Sheila Fitzpatrick, 'Becoming Cultured: Socialist Realism and the Representation of Privilege and Taste,' in Fitzpatrick, *The Cultural Front: Power and Culture in Revolutionary Russia* (Ithaca: Cornell University Press 1992), 216–37; Lewis Siegelbaum, *Stakhanovism and the Politics of Productivity in the USSR, 1935–1941* (Cambridge, Eng.: Cambridge University Press 1988), 223–36; Svetlana Boym, *Common Places: Mythologies of Everyday Life in Russia* (Cambridge, MA: Harvard University Press 1994); David Hoffmann, *Stalinist Values: The Cultural Norms of Soviet Modernity, 1917–1941* (Ithaca: Cornell University Press 2003), 118–45; Catriona Kelly, *Refining Russia: Advice Literature, Polite Culture, and Gender from Catherine to Yeltsin* (Oxford: Oxford University Press 2001); and Jukka Gronow, *Caviar with Champagne: Common Luxury and the Ideals of the Good Life in Stalin's Russia* (Oxford: Berg 2003).

10 Hessler, *Social History*, 328.

11 I argue this more fully in Susan E. Reid, 'Khrushchev Modern: Agency and Modernization in the Soviet Home,' *Cahiers du Monde russe* 47, no. 1–2 (Jan–June 2006), 227–68.

12 Studies of Soviet/Soviet-type consumption and consumer society after Stalin include: Ibid.; Marshall I. Goldman, 'More for the Common Man? Living Standards and Consumer Goods,' *Problems of Communism* 9, no. 5 (Sep.–Oct. 1960), 32–41; M.-E. Ruban, 'Private Consumption in the USSR: Changes in the Assortment of Goods 1940–1959,' *Soviet Studies* 13, no. 3 (1962), 237–54; Jan S. Prybyla, 'The Soviet Consumer in Khrushchev's Russia,' *Russian Review* 20, no. 3 (July 1961), 194–205; Jane Shapiro, 'Soviet Consumer Policy in the 1970s: Plan and Performance,' in *Soviet Politics in the Brezhnev Era*, ed. Donald R. Kelley (New York: Praeger Publishers 1980), 104–28; Jane Zavisca, 'Consumer Inequalities and Regime Legitimacy in Late Soviet and Post-Soviet Russia' (PhD diss., University of California, Berkeley 2004); Stephan Merl, 'Sowjetisierung in der Welt des Konsums,' in *Amerikanisierung und Sowjetisierung in Deutschland 1945–1970*, ed. Konrad Jarausch and Hannes Siegrist (Frankfurt am Main: Campus 1997), 167–94; Stephan Merl, 'Staat und Konsum in der Zentralverwaltungswirtschaft: Rußland und die ostmitteleuropäischen Länder,' in *Europäische Konsumgeschichte: zur Gesellschafts-und Kulturgeschichte des Konsums, 18.–20. Jahrhundert*, ed. Hannes Siegrist, Hartmut Kaelble, Jürgen Kocka (Frankfurt am Main: Campus 1997), 205–41.

13 For detail see Susan Reid 'Women in the Home,' in *Women in the Khrushchev Era*, eds. M. Ilič, S. Reid and L. Attwood (Houndmills: Palgrave 2004), 149–76.

14 The section heading refers to John Bushnell's 'The "New Soviet Man" Turns Pessimist,' in *The Soviet Union Since Stalin*, ed. Stephen Cohen, Alexander Rabinowitch and Robert Sharlet (Bloomington: Indiana University Press 1980), 179–99.

15 'Schastlivoe novosel'e,' *Trud* (7 November 1959).

16 Ibid. The article emphasised that alongside the apartment block on which it focused, other similar buildings were rising that would soon also see their own housewarmings.

17 M. Nikol'skii, 'Novyi dom–novyi byt,' *Izvestiia* (19 December 1959).

18 Marcel Mauss, *The Gift: Forms and Functions of Exchange in Archaic Societies*, trans. Ian Cunnison (London: Cohen and West 1954).

19 Dunham, *In Stalin's Time*, 13; V. E. Bonnell, 'The Remaking of Homo Sovieticus during the Thaw,' commentary presented at conference 'The Thaw: Soviet Society and Culture during the 1950s and 1960s,' University of California, Berkeley, 15 May 2005, 4 (emphasis added). See also Richard Sheldon and Terry Thompson, eds., *Soviet Society and Culture: Essays in Honor of Vera S. Dunham* (Boulder, Co.: Westview Press 1988).

20 B. A. Grushin, *Chetyre zhizni Rossii: V zerkale oprosov obshchestvennogo mneniia. Epokha Khrushcheva* (Moscow: Progress-Traditsiia 2001), especially chapter 2, 'Dinamika i problemy urovnia zhizni naseleniia.'

21 N. I. Andreeva, 'Gigienicheskaia otsenka novogo zhilishchnogo stroitel'stva v Moskve (period 1947–1951 gg.),' *Gigiena i sanitariia*, no. 6 (1956), 23–4; 'Iz pisem chitatelei "Pravdy". Stroit' doma deshevo, bystro i prochno,' *Pravda* (8 August 1956), 2; A. Balanovich, 'Pretenzii k proektirovshchikam i stroiteliam,' *Zhilishchno-kommunal'noe khoziaistvo*, no. 5 (1956), 10. Indeed, it was openly discussed already in the mid-1940s. Timothy Sosnovy, *The Housing Problem in the Soviet Union* (New York: Research Program on the USSR 1954), 114–15.

22 For some, 'living space' amounted to no more than a hostel bed (*'koika-mesto'*), while many lived in conditions unfit for human habitation. In cases considered for rehousing in new apartment blocks, tuberculosis was frequently cited. Tsentral'nyi arkhiv goroda Moskvy (TsAGM), f. 62 (Moskovskii gorodskoi sovnarkhoz), op. 15, d. 267 (Perepiska o zhiloi ploshchadi i zaselenii doma v Nov. Cheremushkakh kvartal 23 korpus 8, 1964; TsAGM, f. 62, op. 15, d. 266 (Perepiska s Upravleniem ucheta i raspredeleniia zhiloi ploshchadi Mossoveta i zaiavki na dopolnitel'nuiu zhiluiu ploshchad', 1964).

23 Compare Donald Filtzer, 'Standard of Living Versus Quality of Life: Struggling with the Urban Environment in Russia During the Early Years of Post-war Reconstruction,' in *Late Stalinist Russia: Society Between Reconstruction and Development*, ed. Juliane Fürst (London: Routledge 2006), 81–102.

24 On high labour turnover resulting from poor housing conditions as the primary reason for changes in housing legislation: Sosnovy, *Housing Problem*, 146; Timothy Sosnovy, 'The Soviet Housing Situation Today,' *Soviet Studies* 11, no. 1 (July 1959), 13.

25 N. S. Khrushchev, 'K novym uspekham literatury i iskusstva,' *Kommunist*, no. 7 (May 1961), 3.

26 'Sovetskim liudiam—blagoustroennye zhilishcha,' *Kommunist* no. 6 (April 1965), 41. The Third Party Programme adopted in 1961 stated: 'The CPSU sets the historically important task of achieving in the Soviet Union a living standard higher than that of any of the capitalist countries.' Grey Hodnett, ed., *Resolutions and Decisions of the Communist Party of the Soviet Union*, vol. 4: *The Khrushchev Years 1953–1964* (Toronto: University of Toronto Press 1974), 228–34; Jerome M. Gilison, *The Soviet Image of Utopia* (Baltimore, Md.: Johns Hopkins University Press 1975).

27 For more detailed discussion see Reid, ' "Our Kitchen is Just as Good" ,' 83–112; and Reid, 'Cold War in the Kitchen,' *Slavic Review* 1, no. 2 (2002), 211–52. The issue was not only to persuade Soviet citizens to keep faith, but also to convince those in decolonising countries that to align themselves with the Soviet block was the path to rapid progress and development.

28 Postanovlenie Tsentral'nogo Komiteta KPSS i Soveta Ministrov SSSR, 'O razvitii zhilishchnogo stroitel'stva v SSSR,' *Sobranie postanovlenii Pravitel'stva Rossiiskoi Sovetskoi Federatsii Sotsialisticheskikh Respublik*, Moscow 31 July 1957 (Moscow: Gosiurizdat 1960), article 102, 332–48. On the one-family apartment see Steven Harris, 'Moving to the Separate Apartment: Building, Distributing, Furnishing, and Living in Urban Housing in Soviet Russia, 1950s–1960s' (PhD diss. University of Chicago 2003).

The intensive housing drive is directly associated with Khrushchev's ascendancy. Although Khrushchev had denounced architectural excess and called for industrial construction methods as early as 1954, decisive action on the housing crisis waited till after the 'antiparty group' had been defeated, following within a month of their defeat amidst accusations that they had neglected the essential needs and interests of the broad masses. Alfred DiMaio, Jr., *Soviet Urban Housing: Problems and Policies* (New York: Praeger 1974), 17–9; N. Lebina, 'Zhil'e: kommunizm v otdel'noi kvartire,' in N. Lebina and A. Chistikov, *Obyvatel' i reformy: kartiny povsednevnoi zhizni gorozhan* (St Petersburg: Dmitrii Bulanin 2003), 175.

29 N. S. Khrushchev, *O shirokom vnedrenii industrial'nykh metodov, uluchshenii kachestva, i snizhenii stoimosti stroitel'stva: rech' na Vsesoiuznom soveshchanii stroitelei, arkhitektorov i rabotnikov promyshlennosti stroitel'nykh materialov, stroitel'nogo i dorozhnogo mashinostroeniia, proektnykh i nauchno-issledovatel'skikh organizatsii, 7 dekabria 1954 g.* (Moscow: Politizdat 1955). In the United Kingdom, for example, concern with slum clearance and homelessness was reflected and popularised in the 1966 BBC television drama *Cathy Come Home* (dir. Ken Loach).

30 N. S. Khrushchev, *O kontrol'nykh tsifrakh razvitiia narodnogo khoziaistva SSSR na 1959–1965 gody* (Moscow: Politizdat 1959), 59–63; L. Abramenko, L. Tormozova, eds, *Besedy o domashnem khoziaistve* (Moscow: Molodaia gvardiia 1959), 3. Our focus here, like that of the contemporary media, is on the brand new housing regions, but new construction was accompanied by an extensive programme of modernisation and renovation of the existing housing stock, including the installation of mains plumbing, gas and central heating and inside toilets and bathrooms.

31 K. Zhukov, 'Tekhnicheskaia estetika i oborudovanie kvartir,' *Tekhnicheskaia estetika*, no. 2 (1964), 1. In line with the 7-year plan (1959–1965), 75 million Soviet people, nearly a third of the population, were expected to celebrate *novosel'e* in 6 years. I. Shutov, 'Novosel'e,' *Zhilishchno-kommunal'noe khoziaistvo*, no. 10 (1963), 7–8; N. Kuleshov, '15 millionov kvartir,' *Sovetskaia zhenshchina* no. 9 (1961), 20–3. See Gregory D. Andrusz, *Housing and Urban Development in the USSR* (London: Macmillan 1984), 178, table 7.5.

32 Kuleshov, 15 millionov kvartir, 20–3.

33 I. Semenov, 'Velikoe pereselenie narodov,' *Krokodil*, no. 22 (10 August 1964), 8–9.

34 This is also argued by Steven E. Harris, '"I Know all the Secrets of my Neighbors": the Quest for Privacy in the Era of the Separate Apartment,' in *Borders of Socialism*, ed. Lewis Siegelbaum (Houndmills: Palgrave 2006), 171.

35 Vadim Movchaniuk, 'Reshaetsia sud'ba "khrushchevok": v interesakh grazhdan,' and Mikhail Shvarts, '"Krushchevki" eshche postoiat,' *Etazhi*, no. 2 (1 March 1998). My thanks to Ekaterina Gerasimova for bringing this discussion to my attention, and to Mikhail Shvarts for discussing the options for dealing with *khrushchevki* with me, St Petersburg 2005.

36 St Petersburg, April 2005.

37 The motif of movement out into the wilderness, and of cultivating, settling and making a home there, was established as part of the mythology of the 1950s in the context of the Virgin Lands campaign. Its iconography emphasised a fresh start and new birth, settling, putting down roots, domestication of the wilderness, and starting a family. Nature's fertility was paralleled by human fecundity in paintings and sketches of mothers with babies at their breast in the open air, appropriating the Italian Renaissance iconography of the Virgin in the Meadows, as in the work of Irina Vitman, *On New Land*, 1954. See S. Reid, 'Destalinization and the Remodernization of Soviet Art' (PhD diss., University of Pennsylvania 1996), chap. 3; A. Kamenskii, 'Tema i obraz,' *Iskusstvo*, no. 2 (1955), 11–9; Michaela Pohl, 'Women and Girls in the Virgin Lands,' in *Women in the Khrushchev Era*, eds. Ilic, Reid and Attwood, 52–74; and, regarding the youth novel of the Thaw:

Katerina Clark, *The Soviet Novel: History as Ritual*, 2nd ed. (1981; Chicago and London: University of Chicago Press 1985), 22–30.

38 The material repositories of memory might be reduced to the portable and concealable form of a small treasure box. Discussions with Tat'iana Nazarenko and Nataliia Vinokurova.

39 On some critics' complaints about a prevalence of 'dismal scenes of tumbledown barns, abandoned ponds and broken fences' in contemporary painting in the mid-1950s, see S. Reid, 'The Soviet Art World in the Early Thaw,' *Third Text* 20, no. 2 (March 2000), 161–75.

40 Ossovskii painted a second, even more starkly abstracted and modernist version in 1967.

41 'Na stroikakh Moskvy,' TV script, 25.01.63, Gosudarstvennyi arkhiv Rossiiskoi Federatsii (GARF), f. 6903 (Gosteleradio), op. 26, d. 449, no. 4588.

42 Irina Golovan, 'V novom dome,' *Rabotnitsa*, no. 5 (1953), 8. Radiance was frequently associated with the modernist city in international modernist discourse, notably Le Corbusier's 'Ville radieuse'. But radiance, *svetlost'*, was also a defining characteristic of Socialist Realist architecture whereby it represented the construction of the radiant future. Catherine Cooke, 'Beauty as a Route to "the Radiant Future",' *Journal of Design History* 10, no. 2 (1997), 137–60.

43 Thus in Soviet representations, the theme of the World Fair as a whole was coopted and conflated with the 'great idea of communism'. 'Everything in the name of man, for the good of man' became the slogan of the Twenty-Second Party Congress at which the new Party Programme was ratified. For the identification of this promise with improvement of living standards and housing in particular see, for example, T. Druzhinina, 'Vse dlia sovetskogo cheloveka,' *Rabotnitsa*, no. 11 (1958), 21–2; M. Vershinin, 'Dlia blaga cheloveka,' *Zhilishchno-kommunal'noe khoziaistvo*, no. 4 (1962), 6–7. On Brussels '58 see Robert Haddow, *Pavilions of Plenty: Exhibiting American Culture Abroad in the 1950s* (Washington DC: Smithsonian Institution Press 1997), chapter 4. The fair's Director General, Baron Moens de Fernig, instructed participants that 'each nation should demonstrate its own conception of happiness and of the paths to attaining it.' The Soviet organisers wanted to emphasise above all the right to labour, 'But do western people understand that labour is the main element of happiness?' They decided therefore that it was necessary not only to demonstrate the rights Soviet people had, but to show how they live, 'what Soviet power has given to man'. GARF f. 9470, op. 1, d. 9.

44 GARF f. 9518, op. 1, d. 588; d. 589; Photo album of Soviet Pavilion at Brussels '58: (Rossiiskii gosudarstvennyi arkhiv ekonomii (RGAE), f. 635, op. 1, d. 369: l. 15; GARF f. 9470, op.1, d. 9.

45 Rika Devos and Mil de Kooning, *L'architecture moderne a l'expo 58* (Brussels: Dexia: Fonds Mercator 2006); and Fredie Floré and Mil de Kooning, 'The Representation of Modern Domesticity in the Belgian Section of the Brussels World's Fair of 1958,' in *Journal of Design History* 16, no. 4 (2003), 319–40. I am indebted to Rika Devos, Fredie Floré and students in the Department of Architecture, University of Ghent, for stimulating and informative discussions about the model homes at Brussels '58, and to Rika Devos for her help in the archive of the Brussels World Fair, Brussels, before its transfer to the Belgian National Archives.

46 See Raphaelle Saint-Pierre, 'Happiness in French Houses of the Fifties,' in *Constructed Happiness: Domestic Environment in the Cold War Era*, ed. Mart Kalm and Ingrid Ruudi (Tallinn: Estonian Academy of Arts 2005), 130–43.

47 Floré and de Kooning, 'Representation of Modern Domesticity,' 334–5; M. Shaginian, *Zarubezhnye pis'ma* (Moscow: Sovetskii pisatel' 1964), 80–1.

48 See May, *Homeward Bound*, 16–20 and 162–8; Oldenziel and Zachmann, *Cold War Kitchen*; Greg Castillo, 'Domesticating the Cold War: Household Consumption as Propaganda in Marshall Plan Germany,' *Journal of Contemporary History*, 40, no. 2 (2005), 261–88.

49 CPSU Central Committee and Council of Ministers Resolution, 'O merakh po uluchsheniiu bytovogo obsluzhivaniia naseleniia,' *Sobranie postanovlenie pravitel'stva SSSR* (Moscow: Upravlenie delami Soveta ministrov SSSR, 1959), article 30, 86–91. The new Party Programme in 1961 promised that the need for service establishments would be fully met within years, and free public dining would be provided at workplaces by the 1970s. Hodnett, *Resolutions and Decisions*, 232.

50 National Archival Record Administration (NARA), Washington DC, RG 306, entry 1050, box 7 (report of contact with guides at American National Exhibition; and report of geographer Kostanick); G. Zimmerman and B. Lerner, 'What the Russians Will See,' *Look* (21 July 1959) 4.

51 S. Yatsenko, construction engineer, 19 August 1959. NARA RG 306, entry 1043, box 11. Throughout Europe, attitudes to the consumerist dream were often ambivalent. As Karin Zachmann, Ruth Oldenziel and others have noted of European reception of American technology and efficiency ideals, the global conquest of the American-type kitchen was not a foregone conclusion in 1959. Karin Zachmann, 'A Socialist Consumption Junction,' *Technology and Culture*, 43, no. 1 (2002). But compare Victoria de Grazia, *Irresistible Empire: America's Advance through Twentieth-Century Europe* (Cambridge, Mass.: The Belknap Press of Harvard University Press 2005).

52 For popular responses see Susan E. Reid, 'Who Will Beat Whom? Soviet Popular Reception of the American National Exhibition in Moscow, 1959,' *Kritika* 9, no. 4 (Fall 2008), 855–904; Reid, ' "Our Kitchen is Just as Good",' 83–112. For a critique of the wide identification of prosperity with happiness see the conclusion of social psychologist David Myers: 'Our becoming better off over the last 30 years has not been accompanied by one iota of increased happiness and life satisfaction.' London: Wellcome Trust, http://www.wellcome.ac.uk/en/imagine/inspire_happiness.shtml (accessed 02 August2006).

53 M. Shatrov, 'Razmyshleniia o vystavke,' *Trud* (31 July 1959); Arthur Miller, *Death of a Salesman* (1949; repr., New York: Penguin 1963), 112. The 1959 production was by the Leningrad Pushkin Theatre.

54 M. Chereiskaia, 'Zametki o khoroshem vkuse,' in *Podruga,* ed. R. Saltanova and N. Kolchinskaia (Moscow: Molodaia gvardiia 1959), 220–34; Filipovich, 'Veshchi – ne khoziaeva, a slugi!'; B. Brodskii, 'Novyi byt i kamufliazh meshchanstva,' *Dekorativnoe iskusstvo SSSR*, no. 8 (1963), 24; K. Kantor, 'Chelovek i zhilishche,' *Iskusstvo i byt*, no. 1 (1963), 26–48; K. Makarov, 'Zhizn' trebuet,' *Smena*, no. 4 (1961), 28–30. In addition to the print media, television programmes and exhibitions sought to shape citizens' taste in home decorating.

55 This long-standing battle cry was made into a promise and a date set for its attainment by Khrushchev in a speech to agricultural workers, Leningrad, 1957, and reaffirmed at the Twenty-first Party Congress in January 1959, and in Khrushchev's speech for the opening of the American exhibition in Moscow, 'My peregonim Ameriku! Rech' Pred'sedatelia soveta Ministrov SSSR N. S. Khrushcheva pri otkrytii vystavki Soedinennykh shtatov Ameriki v Moskve,' *Trud* (25 July1959).

56 Khrushchev, *O kontrol'nykh tsifrakh*, 28–9, 59–63; CPSU Central Committee and Council of Ministers Resolution, 'O merakh po uvelicheniiu proizvodstva, rasshireniiu assortimenta i uluchsheniiu kachestva tovarov kul'turno-bytovogo naznacheniia i khoziastvennogo obikhoda,' October 1959, in *Sobranie postanovleniia pravitel'stva SSSR*

(Moscow: Gosiurizdat 1959); 'Dobrotnye, krasivye veshchi – v nash byt! *Izvestiia*, (16 October 1959); Zavisca, 'Consumer Inequalities'.

57 Economic priorities and organisational factors combined with questions of quality and the resistance of traditional concepts of good housekeeping. Mervyn Matthews found lower-income women more likely to launder at home, probably because the expense services seemed unwarranted when expense compared to the unpaid labour of the housewife. M. Matthews, *Class and Society in Soviet Russia* (London: Allen Lane: Penguin Press 1972), 104; Lebina and Chistikov, *Obyvatel' i reformy*, 189 and 238; Sosnovy, *Housing Problem*, 146.

58 On the shining path motif in visual art see A. I. Morozov, *Konets utopii* (Moscow: Galart, 1995), 123.

59 As Katerina Clark notes, drawing on Van Gennep and Victor Turner, rituals are concerned with transformations and their role is to personalise abstract meanings, making them specific and comprehensible. Clark, *Soviet Novel*, 9. On the need to mark ceremonially the collective process of occupying a new house by the invention of new, Soviet mass housewarming rituals, see Shutov, 'Novosel'e,' 7–8.

60 On the contentious private sphere in Soviet society see Vladimir Shlapentokh, *The Public and Private Life of the Soviet People* (New York: Oxford University Press 1989); Lewis H. Siegelbaum, ed., *Borders of Socialism: Private Spheres of Soviet Russia* (Basingstoke: Palgrave 2006); Deborah Field, *Private Life and Communist Morality in Khrushchev's Russia* (New York: Peter Lang 2007).

61 Reid, "The Meaning of Home," in *Borders*, ed. Siegelbaum, 145–70.

62 Daniel Miller, ed., *Home Possessions: Material Culture Behind Closed Doors* (Oxford: Berg 2001), 4.

63 This is the focus of interviews conducted under my research project "Everyday Aesthetics in the Modern Soviet Flat" supported by the Leverhulme Trust.

64 Golovan, "V novom dome," 7.

65 Mikhail Bakhtin, 'Forms of Time and of the Chronotope in the Novel,' in *The Dialogic Imagination*, ed. M. Holquist (Austin: University of Texas Press 1981), 248. For Yuri Lotman, the threshold is the 'hottest spot for semioticising processes'. Yuri M. Lotman, 'The Notion of Boundary,' in *The Universe of the Mind* (London: I. B. Tauris 1990), 131–32. In Slavic folklore and traditional popular ritual practices, there are many customs and taboos associated with the threshold, some of which are maintained to this day such as the taboo on shaking hands over the threshold. Thresholds are also intensely ritualised in other cultures. See Céline Rosselin, 'The Ins and Outs of the Hall' in *At Home: An Anthropology of Domestic Space*, ed. Irene Cieraad (Syracuse, N.Y.: Syracuse University Press 1999), 53–9.

66 Golovan, 'V novom dome,' 7–8.

67 Strumilin, 'Rabochii byt i kommunizm,' 203–20; D. P. Gorskii, 'Sem'ia v sotsialisticheskom obshchestve,' in *Sotsial'nye problemy zhilishcha*, ed. A. Kharchev (Leningrad: LENZNIEL 1969), 68–73. After some wavering, Khrushchev unequivocally espoused the pro-family position at the Twenty-second Party Congress in 1961. See *Pravda* (19 October 1961); Gail Warshovsky Lapidus, *Women in Soviet Society: Equality, Development, and Social Change* (Berkeley: University of California Press 1978), 232; Deborah A. Field, 'Mothers and Fathers and the Problem of Selfishness in the Khrushchev Period,' in *Women in the Khrushchev Era*, eds. Ilič, Reid and Attwood, 96–113.

68 'The universal transition to type building with economical apartments for single-family occupancy has radically improved conditions of life of new residents. If in buildings of the old type only 30 per cent of families received separate flats and the rest were accommodated in communal apartments, then in the houses of new type 90 or more

per cent are under [single] family occupancy.' 'Sovetskim liudiam–blagoustroennye zhilishcha,' 41.

69 Golovan, 'V novom dome,' 8. At the same time as the promise was made to provide newly weds with separate apartments, in the late 1950s, wedding ceremonies were among a number of new life-cycle rituals introduced by party and Komsomol officials. Field, *Private Life*, 99–101.

70 Golovan, 'V novom dome,' 8.

71 M. Edel', 'Divan,' *Krokodil*, no. 12 (30 April 1958), 12.

72 There were frequent references to the failure to plan amenities for the new housing regions, or to construct them in time for people moving in, for example a Moscow Television broadcast, 'Na stroikakh Moskvy,' 7 January 1963. Script in GARF, f. 6903, op. 2, d. 449.

73 Edel', 'Divan,' 12.

74 Gender aspects are examined in Reid, 'Cold War in the Kitchen'; and Reid, 'Women in the Home,' in *Women in the Khrushchev Era*, 149–76.

75 The same term used to refer to the old junk—'*staraia rukhliad*'—is used about material possessions that should be left behind on moving into the new apartment in anther story in *Krokodil*, Varvara Karbovskaia, 'Simochka,' *Krokodil*, no. 19 (10 July 1958), 5. Here, their rejection and the demand to replace them with new things is cast negatively, associated with regressive values such as female snobbery, acquisitiveness, and 'keeping up with the Joneses'. This points to the continuing ambivalence concerning consumerism, especially when, as in 'Simochka', it is taken to excess and driven by wrong motives such as covetousness, ostentation and social status.

76 Nikol'skii, 'Novyi dom—novyi byt' ['New Home: New Life]. See also L. Novogrudskii, '…My khotim, chtoby v novykh domakh novoiu stala zhizn´!' *Trud* (12 July 1961).

77 For example: N. Svetlova, 'Tvoi dom,' *Ogonek*, no. 3 (1959), 14–6; E. M. Torshilova, 'Byt i nekotorye sotsial´no-psikhologicheskie kharakteristiki sovremennogo zhilogo inter´era,' in *Sotsial´nye issledovaniia*, vyp. 7: *Metodologicheskie problemy issledovaniia byta*, ed. A. G. Kharchev and Z. A. Iankova (Moscow: Nauka, 1971), 143; I. Abramskii, A. Krylov, M. Sokolov, 'Staroe v novom,' *Krokodil*, no. 9 (30 March 1959), 1–2; Blair Ruble, 'From Khrushcheby to Korobki,' in *Russian Housing in the Modern Age: Design and Social History*, ed. William C. Brumfield and Blair A. Ruble (Cambridge, Eng.: Cambridge University Press 1993), 245; Victor Buchli, *An Archaeology of Socialism* (Oxford: Berg 1999), 56–62. In practice, even if people had any significant accumulation of old furniture, which many did not, they often found it difficult to transport, and then impossible to get it through the door and narrow entrance.

78 Rossiiskii gosudarstvennyi arkhiv literatury i iskusstva (RGALI), f. 2329, op. 4, d. 1388 (exhibition 'Iskusstvo—v byt!').

79 Interviews for 'Everyday Aesthetics in the Modern Soviet Flat,' 2004–07, St Petersburg, Kovdor, Kazan.

80 Edel', 'Divan,' 12.

81 Ibid, 12; Golovan', 'V novom dome,' 7; Nikol'skii, 'Novyi dom—novyi byt'. Compare Chereiskaia, 'Zametki o khoroshem vkuse,' 220; A. Gol´dshtein, 'Chto takoe uiut,' *Rabotnitsa*, no. 1 (1959): 30; I. Voeikova, 'Uiut—v prostote,' *Rabotnitsa*, no. 10 (1964): 30–1; Iu. V. Sharov, G. G. Poliachek, *Vkus nado vospityvat´. (Besedy dlia molodezhi)* (Novosibirsk: Novosibirskoe knizhnzoe izdatel´stvo, 1960), 72–3; Buchli, *Archaeology of Socialism*, 56–62. Specific male roles in homemaking were sometimes addressed: 'Esli ty novosel', *Zhilishchno-kommunal´noe khoziaistvo*, no. 3 (1962), 32; A. Lapin, 'Malen'kie zaboty bol'shogo novosel'ia,' *Izvestiia* (14 November 1959).

82 I. Odintsova, 'Veshchi v nashem bytu,' *Sovetskaia torgovlia*, no. 7 (1961): 51; 'Mechta vashei prababushki,' *Krokodil*, no. 31 (10 November 1959), 14.

83 Voeikova, 'Uiut – v prostote,' 30–1; Gol'dshtein, 'Chto takoe uiut,' 30; K. Makarov, 'Zhizn' trebuet,' *Smena*, no. 4 (1961): 28–30; N. Voronov, 'Ob iskusstve, meshchanstve i mode,' *Sem'ia i shkola*, no. 3 (1962): 14–6; Sharov, Poliachek, *Vkus nado vospityvat'*, 72–3.

84 Nikol'skii, 'Novyi dom—novyi byt'.

85 V. V. Rybitskii, 'Dlia doma, dlia sem'i. V pomoshch' novoselam,' 5 January 1963 (television script in GARF, f. 6903, op. 2, d. 449). I am indebted to Kristin Roth-Ey for alerting me to the prevalence of the advice on homemaking in television programming as reflected in scripts held in GARF. See also B. Merzhanov, K. Sorokin, *Eto nuzhno novoselam* (Moscow: Ekonomika 1966); 'Esli ty novosel'; and regular features such as *Izvestiia*'s 'For Home and Family' page, which included Lapin, 'Malen'kie zaboty bol'shogo novosel'ia'. The period saw a significant increase in the publication of domestic advice literature, including a two-volume household encyclopaedia, *Kratkaia entsiklopediia domashnego khoziaistva* (Moscow: Bol'shaia sovetskaia entsiklopediia 1959). See also Deborah A. Field, 'Communist Morality and Meanings of Private Life in Post-Stalinist Russia, 1953–1964' (Ph.D. diss., University of Michigan 1996), 41.

86 Rybitskii, 'Dlia doma, dlia sem'i.'

87 G. Liubimova, 'Ratsional'noe oborudovanie kvartir,' *Dekorativnoe iskusstvo SSSR*, no. 6 (1964), 15–6; Irina Voeikova, 'Vasha kvartira,' *Rabotnitsa*, no. 9 (1962), 30; O. Baiar and R. Blashkevich, *Kvartira i ee ubranstvo* (Moscow: Stroiizdat 1962); Lynne Attwood, 'Housing in the Khrushchev Era,' in *Women in the Khrushchev Era*, 189; Torshilova, 'Byt i nekotorye sotsial'no-psikhologicheskie kharakteristiki,' 137–44.

88 M. Akolupin, 'Chem ogorchen novosel'e,' *Trud* (28 December 1960); A. Kondratiuk et al, 'Omrachennoe novosel'e,' *Trud* (28 November 1962); M. Moisiuk, 'Pokhititeli radosti,' *Trud* (10 May 1962). This was a stock theme of *Krokodil*, e.g. I. Chernykh, G. Dubovitskii, G. Kirpichevskii, 'U moikh podshefnykh neuiutnoe novosel'e,' *Krokodil*, no. 19 (10 July 1959), 3; 'Univermag,' *Krokodil*, no. 2 (20 January 1958), 6–7. For example, the last of these begins: 'When you look around—well, your heart can only rejoice! How many happy housewarmings here and there! How many people move day by day into new, well-appointed houses! But wait… It turns out that even in regard to such an absolutely pleasing context one often has to recall the old saying … about the tar in the ointment.' See also Harris, 'Moving to the Separate Apartment,' 341–91; Harris, ' "I Know all the Secrets",' 179.

89 *Krokodil* (10 October 1960)

90 For example, Filipovich, 'Veshchi—ne khoziaeva, a slugi!'; Karbovskaia, 'Simochka,' 5. That a tendency to privatisation emerged, beginning in this period, has been asserted most unequivocally by Shlapentokh, *Public and Private Life*.

91 Cited by Iu. Gerchuk, 'S tochki zreniia shestidesiatnika,' *Dekorativnoe iskusstvo SSSR*, no. 7 (1991), 9; K. Kantor, 'Veshchi i sotsial'nye otnosheniia,' in K. M. Kantor, *Krasota i pol'za* (Moscow: Iskusstvo 1967), 228 ff.

92 Brodskii, 'Novyi byt,' 24.

93 K. M. Kantor, 'Chelovek i zhilishche,' *Iskusstvo i byt*, no. 1 (1963), 29–30.

94 Daniil Granin, *Posle svad'by: roman* (Leningrad: Sovetskii pisatel' 1959). Christine Varga-Harris discusses Granin's novel in her dissertation chapter 2, 'Homemaking: Keeping Appearances and Petticoat Rule,' presented at conference 'The Thaw,' Berkeley, May 2005. I am indebted to Dr Varga-Harris for bringing Granin's treatment of this subject to my attention.

95 Granin, *Posle svad'by*, 5. This was rather idealised, of course, given the inadequate soundproofing in *khrushchevki*. See Harris, ' "I Know all the Secrets," ' 171–90. Granin may have had a late Stalin-era building in mind since it still had ceiling moldings.

96 Granin, *Posle svad'by*, 5.

97 Ibid, 9.

98 Dunham, *In Stalin's Time*.

99 Granin, *Posle svad'by*, 8.

100 It was orthodoxy that a rise in the national economy determined increased consumer demand. In the rest of the novel Tonia is redeemed by being removed far from Moscow and coming to terms with tough conditions and challenges. On the motif of 'Far from Moscow' in Khrushchev-era novels where Moscow is associated with corruption or moral torpor, see Clark, *Soviet Novel*, 227.

101 Granin *Posle svad'by*, 9.

102 For later developments see James Millar, 'The Little Deal: Brezhnev's Contribution to Acquisitive Socialism,' *Slavic Review* 44, no. 4 (Winter 1985), 694–706.

Chapter Eight: When We Were Happy: Remembering Soviet Holidays

1 This article is largely based on specially conducted interviews carried out by Alexandra Piir in St. Petersburg during January and February 2007. These interviews are cited with the prefix 'H[oliday]-07.' On the methodology and selection of informants, see further below. We also cite two other interviews, both conducted by Alexandra Piir as part of work for other projects. The interview with the prefix 'EU-SPb01' forms part of a project on the city courtyard in Leningrad being carried out for Alexandra Piir's candidate dissertation, while the interview prefixed 'Oxf/Lev' was part of a project on the history of childhood sponsored by the Leverhulme Trust under Grant No. F/08736/A ('Childhood in Russia: A Social and Cultural History:' see www.mod-langs. ox.ac.uk/russian/childhood, accessed 19 March 2009). The authors would like to thank Catriona Kelly for her translation, and also for many helpful editorial suggestions and supplementations. [The title of the original, *schast'e po prazdnikam*, is difficult to render adequately in English. The phrase *po prazdnikam* means something that happens rarely, close to 'once in a blue moon,' so that there is an implied pun: people were happy on holidays, but therefore also weren't happen very often. There is so far as I know no phrase in English that will capture the full significance. –Trans.]

2 Vladimir Dal', *Tolkovyi slovar' zhivogo velikorusskogo yazyka*. T. 3 (Moscow: Progress 1994).

3 There is an etymological link between these two concepts in English, too—cf. the terms 'happen,' 'happenstance,' 'happy go lucky'—but of a 'buried,' rather than obvious, kind. [The word 'fortunate' (rather Latinate in English) captures the two senses of the Russian term. Cf. German *Gluck/glücklich*, French *bonheur/heureux*, etc. –Trans.]

4 S. G. Vorkachev, 'Kontsept schast'ya: ponyatiinyi i obraznyi komponenty,' *Izvestiya Rossiiskoi Akademii nauk. Seriya literatura i yazyka*. Vol. 60, No. 6 (2001), 47–58; A. Zalyaleeva, 'Kontsept "schast'e" v sovremennom russkom yazyke,' in *Russkaya i sopostavitel'naya filologiya: sostoyanie i perspektivy. Mezhdunarodnaya nauchnaya konferentsiya, posvyashchennaya 200-letiyu Kazanskogo universiteta* (Kazan' 2004), 268–9; V. V. Kolesov, "Sud'ba' i "schast'e" v russkoi mental'nosti' in *Razmyshleniya o filosofii na perekrestke vtorogo i tret'ego tysyachiletii, Sbornik k 75-letiyu professora M. Ya. Korneeva. Seriya 'Mysliteli.'* Issue 1 (St Petersburg 2002), 98–106;

D. Shmelev, *Russkaya yazykovaya model' mira* (Moscow 2002), 175–80 and many other such publications.

5 See M. Fasmer, *Etimologicheskii slovar' russkogo yazyka*, vol. 3 (Moscow 1971), 816.

6 V. Dal', *Tolkovyi slovar' velikorusskogo yazyka* (4 vols.; Moscow 1955), vol. 4, 583.

7 A. A. Potebnya, 'O dole i srodnykh s neyu sushchestvakh,' in *Slovo i mif*, ed. A. K. Baiburin (Moscow 1989), 472–551. (This quote, 486.)

8 A. F. Zhuravlev, 'Dolya,' *Slavyanskie drevnosti: Etnolingvisticheskii slovar' pod obshchei redaktsei N. I. Tolstogo*, vol. 2 (Moscow, 1999), 113–15. (This quote, 114.)

9 Of course, this was not the only thing that held back the proliferation of individual definitions. Language itself places limits on such proliferation. As with any other phenomenon, one can only discuss happiness in the terms already available to one, and the drive behind language is towards making abstraction concrete, as Boris Uspensky has pointed out ('O veshchnykh konnotatsiyakh abstraktnykh sushchestvitel' nykh,' in *Semiotika i informatika*. Issue 1 (Moscow, 1974)). For example, it is possible to say in Russian *schast'e razbilos* ('my, etc., happiness has broken,' as one would say of glass or of a mirror) [cf. 'my heart is broken,' Trans.], but one cannot say *schast'e promoklo* ('my, etc., happiness is sodden') or *schast'e prosokhlo* ('my, etc., happiness has dried up'). Imaginative literature, and particularly poetry, is engaged in a constant struggle with such linguistic restrictions, but even poetry is to some extent the victim of pre-existing set phrases.

10 Vorkachev, 'Kontsept schast'ya;' Zalyaleeva, 'Kontsept "schast'e"'.

11 Ivan Bunin, 'Vecher', in Ivan Bunin, *Sobranie sochinenii* T. 2, (St Petersburg: TOO Biont 1909), 360.

12 Evgeny Baratynsky, 'Khor, petyi v den' imenin dyaden'ki B[ogdana] Andreevicha ego malen'kimi plemyannitsami Panchulizevymi' (1817).

13 Alexander Pushkin, 'Pora, moi, drug, pora,' 1834, in Alexander Pushkin, *Sobranie sochinenii*, T. 1 (Moscow: Khudozhestvennaia literatura 1985), 528.

14 On this see further Vorkachev, 'Kontsept schast'ya.'

15 Aleksander Pushkin, 'K Chaadaevu,' (1818), 194.

16 For example, Aleksei Gonchukov, an official at the Kirov factory, paraphrased Pushkin in a poem from his unpublished 1952 diary about his workplace, which reads: 'My friend [also the Soviet word for 'comrade'], have faith: she will arise/The dawn of captivating happiness/Our factory will arise from sleep/And once again on its scrolls/They will write wonderful deeds' (Central Archive of Political History, St Petersburg, f. 4000, o18, d. 335, l. 6). [Trans].

17 In the original: [Anon], *Schast'e—v dovol'stve zhizn'yu i v umen'e pol'zovat'sya darami bozhiimi* (Nizhny Novgorod: Bratstvo sv. Kresta 1908); 'Neizvestnaya' [pseud.] *Schast'e i bogatstvo, zdorov'e i sila. Postnoe deshevoe pitanie* (St Petersburg: Tip. D. I. Shumakher 1908); O. S. Kenin *Schast'e v zhizni i lyubov' ot vsekh* (Vologda, 1909); [Anon], *Schast'e v zdorov'e* (St Petersburg: Tip. Yu. Maiofel'd 1909); [Anon], *Schast'e sem'i* [pamphlet on insurance] (St Petersburg: Tip. Busselya 1909); [Anon], *Schast'e v zhizni do vysshei starosti—zdorovye, ustoichivye i vynoslivye nervy* (Vyborg, n. 1916).

18 The term 'social command' appears to have been invented by Osip Brik in the mid-1920s, but was adopted by the ideologues of Socialist Realism in the early 1930s. [Trans.].

19 On the gratitude formula, see especially Jeffrey Brooks, *Thank You, Comrade Stalin! Soviet Public Culture from Revolution to Cold War* (Princeton, NJ: Princeton University Press 2000); on the childhood theme, see Catriona Kelly's article in this volume.

20 Cf. the arguments of Irina Paperno, 'Personal Accounts of the Soviet Experience,' *Kritika* vol. 3 no. 4 (Winter 2002), 596–7.

21 It seems appropriate to mention here that this 'production of happiness on an industrial scale' was also manifested in the construction of one of the main symbols of the approaching socialist heaven—the seaside resort of Sochi. In 1934, the Soviet government gave the project the status of a 'shock building programme,' the same as the industrial giants of Magnitogorsk, Kuzbass and the Dneprostroi Hydro-Electric Power Station. In time it turned out that this 'resort' was actually a socialist heaven in the strictest sense—one to which only the chosen ones in Soviet society could gain access (Stakhanov, the writer Nikolai Ostrovsky, Vasily Blyukher) (see Elizaveta Listova's 2006 film *The Soviet Empire Sochi*).

22 There were in fact moments when Party leaders suggested that the fateful boundary would be crossed pretty well tomorrow morning. At the Twenty-second Congress of the Communist Party in 1961, Khrushchev declared that by 1980 'the current generation of Soviet people will be living under Communism.'

23 This argument is developed at length in Sheila Fitzpatrick, *Everyday Stalinism: Ordinary Life in Extraordinary Times: Soviet Russia in the 1930s* (Oxford: Oxford University Press 1999). See especially Chapter 2, 'Palaces on Monday,' and Chapter 4, 'The Magic Tablecloth.'

24 It has even been argued that people have lost the facility to speak critically about the past at all. See, e.g., Daniel Bertaux, Paul Thompson, and Anna Rotkirch, *Living Through Soviet Russia* (London/New York: Routledge 2003), 9.

25 http://www.school-city.by/index.php?option=com_content&task=view&id=5385&Itemid=141 (accessed 19 March 2009).

26 David Samoilov, 'Dnevnik schastlivogo mal'chika,' *Znamya*, no. 8 (1999), 157. See also http://magazines.russ.ru/znamia/1999/8/samoilov.html (accessed 19 March 2009).

27 Elena Kiseleva, *Pravda*, 14 September 2002: http://news.pravda.ru/culture/2002/09/14/47050.html (accessed 19 March 2009).

28 Galina Medvedeva, introduction to Samoilov, 'Dnevnik schastlivogo mal'chika,' 149.

29 Emma Gershtein, *Memuary* (St Petersburg: Impress 1998), 251.

30 There is a substantial literature, both in Russian and in Western languages, on the Soviet festival, particularly of the prewar era. See, for example, James von Geldern, *Bolshevik Festivals, 1917–1921* (Berkeley, CA: University of California Press 1993); Malte Rolf, *Sovetskii massovyi prazdnik v Voronezhe i Tsentral'no-Chernozemnoi oblasti (1927–1932)*, Voronezh: Izdatel'stvo Voronezhskogo gosudarstvennogo universiteta, 2000; idem, 'Constructing a Soviet Time: Bolshevik Festivals and Their Rivals during the First Five-Year Plan. A Study of the Central Black Earth Region', *Kritika: Explorations in Russian and Eurasian History* , Volume 1, Number 3, Summer 2000, pp. 447–473; Karen Petrone, *Life Has Become More Joyous, Comrades: Celebrations in the Time of Stalin* (Bloomington, IN: Indiana University Press 2000); Svetlana Malysheva, *Sovetskaya prazdnichnaya kul'tura v provintsii: prostranstvo, simvoly, istoricheskie mify (1917–1927* (Kazan': Ruten 2005). However, this material is devoted primarily to the institutional organisation and ideology of the festivals, rather than to their emotional resonance, the topic of our investigation here.

31 Other such sites included the park of culture and rest and the seaside resort, but holidays were much more accessible—not everyone could visit the seaside and not every town and village had a park of culture and rest. The infrequency of holidays for 'ordinary' Soviet people (in the broadest sense—those from outside the political elite—is an important social fact in the Stalin era. Aleksei Gonchukov, the official at the Kirov factory mentioned above, took his first holiday in 1940 and did not visit a *kurort* until after the Second World War (see Central Archive of Political History, St Petersburg, f. 4000, o18, d. 333, 1. 133, 1. 163). [Trans.]

32 Two further interviews with informants born in 1918 and in 1940, while not cited directly, form part of the background to the discussion.

33 All names of the informants have been changed in order to protect their anonymity. The full list of those cited is: PF1, Inf.1, female, b. 1940; Inf. 2, female, b. 1939; PF3, male, b. 1940; PF 4, Inf. 1, female, b. 1927, Inf. 2, male, b. 1929; PF5, female, b. 1931; PF6, Inf. 1, female, b. 1932, Inf. 2, male, b. 1933, PF8, male, b. 1931; PF9, male, b. 1929.

34 See, e.g., the recent discussion, 'Forum 4,' in *Forum for Anthropology and Culture*, No. 3 (St Petersburg: MAE RAN 2006), 319–431, especially the comments by Vitaly Bezrogov, Larry Holmes, and David Ransel.

35 Emphasis inserted (AB, AP).

36 The informant has mixed up the White House (the seat of the Russian government in Moscow, where the attempted uprising took place in September 1993) and the Big House, the colloquial name for the headquarters of the secret police in Leningrad-St Petersburg. [Trans.]

37 EU Pb-01, PF-10, female informant, b. 1939.

38 A jubilee is a 'round number' birthday, such as thirty, fifty, sixty, etc. (five-year intervals are often marked as well). These tend to be celebrated in much more style than ordinary birthdays, particularly at places of work. The term can also be used for important wedding anniversaries, e.g., twenty-five years, forty years, fifty years. [Trans.]

39 Interestingly, an informant interviewed in connection with the history of childhood explicitly recalled that 8 March was not a 'festival' in the ordinary sense back in the prewar days: 'The eighth of March, that was simply a day of international solidarity, it wasn't a special day for women. The two things are totally different.' He also recalled the exceptional importance of a revolutionary holiday 'forgotten' in the Stalin era, the anniversary of the founding of the Paris Commune (CKQ-M-03 PF5A, 4. Interview conducted by Catriona Kelly. See www.mod-langs.ox.ac.uk/russian/childhood (accessed 19 March 2009)). [Trans].

40 Victory Day had briefly the status of a state holiday after 'the Great Patriotic War' came to an end, but was then removed from this status, and reassigned it only in 1965. It is therefore excluded from discussion, because much of the testimony from informants relates to the 1940s and 1950s, which they saw as a 'heyday' of the festival.

41 This particular informant comes from a working-class background, but the attitude to holidays is typical of the urban milieu generally.

42 A description of the parade held in Pskov to celebrate the royal manifesto of October 1905 setting up the State Duma—a bust of the Tsar swathed in palms carried aloft, the reading of a telegram from the Tsar, shouts of 'Hurrah'—anticipates several elements characteristic of Soviet parades. See *Pskovskii Gorodskoi Listok*, 23 October 1905, 3. [Trans].

43 'It is the fault of the school at Bulavkina for taking portraits of Soviet leaders out into the village streets that this has happened: the local population thought it was a religious procession and started making the sign of the cross.' Malysheva 2005, 208, note 40.

44 David Remnick, *Lenin's Tomb*. (New York: Random House 1993), 25.

45 In Leningrad, marchers would converge from the different districts of the city on to Nevsky Prospect (known from 1918 to 1944 as Twenty-Fifth of October Prospect, from the date of the October Revolution) and process from thence on to Palace Square (Uritsky Square from 1918–1944), or, in the case of marchers from Vasilievsky Island, for example, march directly to Palace Square.

46 Our informants' memories do not stretch (even at the level of family tradition) back to the 1920s, when, according to some sources, workers and officials had to sign an official form

certifying that they had taken part in the *demonstratsiya*. In their recent social history, N. Lebina and A. Chistikov cite a letter complaining of this practice dating from 1925 (see their *Obyvatel' i reformy: Kartiny povsednevnoi zhizni gorozhan*. (St Petersburg: Dmitry Bulanin, 2003), 137): 'If they don't find your signature, then you're declared a counter-revolutionary. During the parade they divide you up into groups of ten and the leader of each group is warned that he'll be considered personally responsible if anyone slopes off before the end of the ceremony.' Indeed, in the 1920s, as Emma Gershtein remembered, even those without a job might feel they ought to take part—unless they happened to be away from their home city (*Memuary*, 11). This practice is not recorded in later eras (by then, people knew they were supposed to attend the demonstration). However, it is clear from our interviews (see below) that considerable pressure was placed on individuals to attend the ceremony.

47 People's free time was generally very limited. It was impossible to take time off work to celebrate non-Soviet festivals, such as birthdays or religious holidays. In the late 1920s, the introduction of the *dekada* (ten-day week) meant that days off could fall on any day of the traditional seven-day week, putting an end to the principle of a regularly occurring 'sabbath.' Both before this was introduced and after it was replaced, the organisation of *subbotniki* (compulsory work sessions held on Saturdays), the nature of shift work in factories and shops, and so on, meant that the only time off many people were guaranteed fell on state holidays.

48 The passport showed your address in the official *propiska* (note of registration). [Trans.].

49 *Obyazalovka*, an untranslatably contemptuous term for a much-resented duty, something like 'a dreary chore.' [Trans].

50 For a discussion of the festival noise environment in the general context of city sounds see Vladimir Lapin, *Zvuki i zapakhi Peterburga* (St Petersburg: Evropeiskii dom 2007).

51 Such an opportunity was welcome in a city with formidable regulations related to noise abatement. City regulations of 1970 forbade 'loud music, song, and other noise that disturbs the peace of the citizenry in streets and courtyards between 11 p.m. and 7 a.m.'; by 1972, such noise was forbidden at all times of day. See *Byulleten' Ispolnitel'nogo komiteta Leningradskogo gorodskogo soveta* No. 20 (1970), 16; ibid., No. 21 (1972), 14. [Trans.]

52 The parades themselves were suspended during the war years, but were revived once the Blockade ended. [Trans].

53 The word *kumachovyi* is impossible to render exactly. It refers to a harsh red cloth such as was used for official flags and banners in the Soviet era. [Trans.]

54 Cf. a comparable memory from a woman born into a working-class family in Moscow in 1936: 'On the First of May you could go out dressed up, that really was a holiday, we went to the demonstrations, and I remember that like nothing else! Mama always used to make us something. Vitalik would get a new shirt and I'd get a new dress, now New Year is considered a big holiday, but before, you went out on the streets, used to be. Well, 'before,' I don't know, but that's how **we** used to live. Because we didn't have the means to make anything for New Year. We did it for the First of May!' (Oxf/Lev M-03 (Moscow 2003), PF-19A. Interviewer Yuliya Rybina). [Trans.]

55 The main footwear factory in Leningrad. [Trans.].

56 Albert Baiburin, *Ritual v traditsionnoi kul'ture* (St Petersburg: Nauka 1993), 201–23.

57 *Ryumochnaya*, a shop selling wine and spirits by the glass for consumption on the premises. [Trans.]

58 A main street in the Moskovsky District of Leningrad, in the south of the city, now known as Malodetskosel'skii Prospect. [Trans.]

59 Bars were closed so that people did not wander off there rather than taking part in the demonstration, and also to make it more difficult for people to turn up at the parade already drunk.

60 This refers to official stalls set out for the day, not to private enterprise on the part of those living on the ground floors. [Trans.]

61 This ethanol was supposed to be used for various industrial purposes, such as cleaning machinery. However, only a small amount would be used this way, so that supervisors would have a good deal of surplus at their disposal. [Trans.].

62 See Jochen Hellbeck's discussion of her diaries in *Revolution on My Mind* (Cambridge: Harvard University Press 2006), especially 155–7.

63 Mayakovsky continues: 'It is impossible to commune more fully and purely/With that great feeling under the name of class!' The word 'commune' is the one used for the religious act of communion. [Trans].

Chapter Nine: The 'New Moscow' and the New 'Happiness': Architecture as a Nodal Point in the Stalinist System of Value

1 I am grateful to Lesley Milne for drawing my attention to this. The recent books include: Jonathon Haidt, *The Happiness Hypothesis* (Basic Books 2006), Darrin McMahon, *Happiness: A History* (Atlantic Monthly Press 2006) and Alain de Botton, *The Architecture of Happiness* (Penguin Books 2006).

2 John Lancaster, 'Pursuing Happiness. Two scholars explore the fragility of contentment,' *The New Yorker*, February 27, 2006, 80.

3 E.g., 'K. E. Voroshilov na IX s'ezde VLKSM,' *Pravda*, 22 January 1931, 2.

4 See, e.g., 'Pervomaiskaia vystavka arkhitektury i planiroki v Moskve,' *Arkhitektura SSSR*, no. 4 (1934), 76.

5 E.g., 'Uroki maiskoi arkhitekturnoi vystavki,' *Arkhitektura SSSR*, no. 6 (1934), 4–17.

6 As Victoria Bonnell points out, this is a *lubok* technique, in other words a technique of the prerevolutionary religious chapbook. Victoria Bonnell, *The Iconography of Power* (Berkeley: University of California Press 1997), 112.

7 L. M. Kaganovich, 'Rech' na iubileinom plenume TsK VLKSM 29 oktiabria 1933 g.,' cited in L. Perchik, 'Gorod sotsializma i ego arkhitektura,' *Arkhitektura SSSR*, no. 1 (1934), 3.

8 E.g., D. Arkin's keynote address to the Union of Architects, 'Tvorcheskaia diskussiia Soiuza sovetskikh arkhitektorov i problema arkhitekturnogo nasledstva,' *Arkhitektura SSSR*, no. 3–4 (1933), 6.

9 Walter Benjamin, *Illuminations. Essays and Reflections*, ed. Hannah Arendt, trans. Harry Zohn (New York: Schocken Books 1968), 241–2.

10 Boris Groys, *Gesamtkunstwerk Stalin: die gespaltene Kultur in der Sowjetunion*, trans. from Russian by von Gabriele Leupold (Munich: C. Hanser c1988).

11 Katerina Clark and Karl Schlögel, 'Mutual Perceptions and Projections: Stalin's Russia in Nazi Germany – Nazi Germany in the Soviet Union,' in *Beyond Totalitarianism: Stalinism and Nazism Compared*, ed. Sheila Fitzpatrick and Michael Geyer (Cambridge: Cambridge University Press 2009).

12 I. V. Stalin, 'Novaia obstanovka—novye zadachi khoziastvennikov na stroitel'stvakh. Rech' na soveshchanii khoziastvennikov, 23 iunia, 1931,' *Sochineniia*, vol. 12 (Moscow: Gos. Izd. Polit. Lit. 1951), 55–9.

13 See Katerina Clark, 'Little Heroes and Big Deeds: Literature Responds to the First Five-Year Plan' in *Cultural Revolution in Russia*, ed. Sheila Fitzpatrick, (Bloomington, Indiana: Indiana University Press 1978), 194–201 and Katerina Clark, *Petersburg Crucible of Cultural Revolution* (Cambridge, Mass.: Harvard University Press 1995), Chapter 12.

14 Pereverzev, Voronsky, Friche, Libedinsky, Trotsky and other formulators of the major theoretical positions of the twenties tended to use such terms as *literaturnovedenie* (the title of Pereverzev's collection of writings published in 1928), *Khudozhestvennaia platforma RAPP'a* (Libedinsky's main theoretical treatise for the organisation, likewise published in 1928) or Voronsky's *Iskusstvo videt' mir*, likewise from 1928. E.g., Iu. Libedinskii, 'Khudozhestennaia platforma RAPP'a,' *Na literaturnom postu*, no. 1 (1928), 1–19.

15 S. Dinamov, 'Moskva-boevaia tema tvorcheskoi perestroiki,' *Literaturnaia gazeta*, no. 32, 11 July (1933).

16 Terry Eagleton, *The Ideology of the Aesthetic* (Oxford: Basil Blackwell 1990), 3.

17 Ibid., 5, 14.

18 Ibid., 2.

19 Ibid., 14.

20 Ibid., 17.

21 Ibid., 15.

22 Ibid., 17.

23 Ibid., 20.

24 Ibid., 17.

25 Ibid., 21.

26 Ibid., 29.

27 Stephen Kotkin, *Magnetic Mountain: Stalinism As a Civilization*, (Berkeley, California: University of California Press 1995), 360.

28 Eagleton, *Ideology of the Aesthetic*, 93.

29 'O perestroike literaturno-khudzhestvennykh organizatsii (postanovka TsK VKP(b) ot 23 aprelia 1932 g.,' *Stroitel'stvo Moskvy*, no. 4 (1932), 23.

30 I. A. Fomin's contribution to 'Tvorcheskaia diskussiia Soiuza sovetskikh arkhitektorov i problema arkhitekturnogo nasledstva,' *Arkhitektura SSSR*, no. 3–4 (1933), 16.

31 Katerina Clark, *The Soviet Novel: History As Ritual*, 3rd ed. (Bloomington, Indiana: Indiana University Press 2000).

Chapter Ten: Andrei Platonov's *Happy Moscow*: Tolstoi, Stalin and the Soviet Self

1 N. V. Kornienko, '…Na kraiu sobstvennogo bezmolviia' [commentary to Andrei Platonov's 'Schastlivaia Moskva'], *Novyi mir*, 9 (1991), 58–74.

2 Andrei Platonov, 'Lyubov' k dal'nemu,' in *30 dnei*, 69–71, reprinted in *Starik i starukha: Poteriannaia proza*, ed. by Fol'ker [Volker] Levin (Munich: Otto Sagner 1934), 153–6.

3 Andrei Platonov, 'Schastlivaia Moskva,' *Novyi mir*, 9 (1991), 9–58. For a critical edition of the novel, see Andrei Platonov, 'Schastlivaia Moskva,' in *'Strana filosofov' Andreia Platonova: Problemy tvorchestva. Vypusk 3*, ed. N. V. Kornienko (Moscow: Nasledie 1999), 9–105; for an English translation, from which all references to the novel in this article are taken, see Andrei Platonov, *Happy Moscow*, trans. Robert Chandler et al (London: Harvill 2001).

4 See in particular, Pia-Susan Berger-Bügel, *Andrej Platonov: Der Roman 'Sčastlivaja Moskva' im Kontext seines Schaffens und seiner Philosophie* (Munich: Otto Sagner 1999); Philip

Ross Bullock, *The Feminine in the Prose of Andrey Platonov* (London: Legenda 2005), 134–45; Philip Ross Bullock, 'Andrei Platonov's *Happy Moscow*: Stalinist Kitsch and Ethical Decadence,' *Modern Language Review*, 101 (2006), 201–11; Natasha Drubek-Maier, 'Rossiia—"pustota v kishkakh mira": "Schastlivaia Moskva" (1932–36gg.) A. Platonova kak allegoriia,' *Novoe literaturnoe obozrenie*, 32 (1998), 251–68; Kheli [Heli] Kostov, *Mifopoetika Andreya Platonova v romane* Schastlivaia Moskva (Helsinki: Helsinki University Press 2000) [available at http://ethesis.helsinki.fi/julkaisut/hum/slavi/vk/kostov (accesssed 24 March 2009)]; Keith Livers, 'Scatology and Eschatology: The Recovery of the Flesh in Andrei Platonov's *Happy Moscow*,' *Slavic Review*, 59 (2000), 154–82; Eric Naiman, 'Communism and the Collective Toilet: Lexical Heroes in *Happy Moscow*,' *Essays in Poetics*, 26 (2001), 96–109; Svetlana Semenova, 'Filosofskie motivy romana "Schastlivaia Moskva,"' in *'Strana filosofov' Andreia Platonova: problemy tvorchestva*, ed. N. V. Kornienko (Moscow: Nasledie 1993), 54–90; Clint Walker, 'Unmasking the Myths and Metaphors of the Stalinist Utopia: Platonov's *Happy Moscow* through the Lens of the *Bronze Horseman*,' *Essays in Poetics*, 26 (2001), 119–67.

5 Platonov, *Happy Moscow*, 4. In Russian, honest is *chestnyi*, hence Moscow's surname of Chestnova.

6 It has been suggested that Platonov may have been referring to Carlyle's influential novel *Sartor Resartus* (Walker, 'Unmasking the Myths,' 164–5).

7 Emma Widdis, *Alexander Medvedkin* (London: I. B. Tauris 2005), 53.

8 Matthew Cullerne Brown, *Socialist Realist Painting* (New Haven: Yale University Press 1998), 147.

9 Sheila Fitzpatrick, *Everyday Stalinism: Ordinary Life in Extraordinary Times: Soviet Russia in the 1930s* (New York: Oxford University Press 1999), 7.

10 Platonov, *Happy Moscow*, 43–4.

11 Naiman, 'Communism and the Collective Toilet,' 96–109.

12 Joseph Brodsky, 'Catastrophes in the Air,' in *Less Than One: Selected Essays* (Harmondsworth: Penguin 1986), 286.

13 Andrei Platonov, *The Foundation Pit*, trans. Robert Chandler and Geoffrey Smith (London: Harvill 1996), 3.

14 Ibid., 14.

15 Ibid., 24.

16 Ibid., 29.

17 Ibid., 42.

18 Platonov, 'The River Potudan,' in *The Return and Other Stories*, trans. Robert and Elizabeth Chandler and Angela Livingstone (London: Harvill 1999), 105.

19 Ibid., 118.

20 Ibid., 134.

21 Mikhail Geller, *Andrei Platonov v poiskakh schast'ia* (Paris: YMCA-Press 1982).

22 Leo Tolstoy, *Anna Karenina*, trans. by Rosemary Edmonds (Harmondsworth: Penguin 1978), 13.

23 Andrei Platonov, *Zapisnye knizhki: Materialy k biografii* (Moscow: Nasledie 2000), 118.

24 Audun J. Mørch, *The Novelistic Approach to the Utopian Question: Platonov's "Čevengur" in the Light of Dostoevskij's Anti-Utopian Legacy* (Oslo: Scandinavian University Press 1998).

25 Alexander Zholkovsky, 'The Codes and Contexts of Platonov's "Fro,"' in *Text Counter Text: Rereadings in Russian Literary History* (Stanford: Stanford University Press 1994), 279–82.

26 David Bethea and Clint Walker, 'Platonov's Revisiting of Pushkin's Sculptural Myth: Notes for a Violin with Silent Orchestra,' *Essays in Poetics*, 27 (2002), 63–96; Walker, 'Unmasking the Myths,' 119–67.

27 Intriguingly, the scene in *Happy Moscow* in which Sambikin performs an autopsy in search of the human soul is borrowed with astonishing fidelity from Leskov's *Cathedral Folk (Soboriane)* of 1872:

> The doctor, in the execution of his official duty, performed an autopsy on the body of a man who died suddenly, and school-master Varnavka Prepotensky brought several pupils from the district school to the autopsy, in order to show them the anatomy, and then, in class, he said to them: 'Did you see the corpse?' They answered, 'Yes.'—'And did you see the bones?'—'Yes,' they answered, 'we saw the bones.' 'And did you see everything?'—'Yes, we saw everything,' they replied.—'But you didn't see a soul?'—'No, we didn't see a soul.'—'Well, then, where is it?' And he settled the question for them by telling them that there is no soul. [Nikolai Leskov [Nicolai Lyeskov], *The Cathedral Folk*, trans. Isabel F. Hapgood (London: John Lane, 1924).]

Sambikin and Sartorius, however, both find the soul in the digestive system, Sambikin in 'the empty section between the food and the excrement' and Sartorius in 'the remnants of excrement and food' and in 'the cramped, impoverished layout of the whole body' [Platonov, *Happy Moscow*, 74]. These references also suggest another text by Tolstoi, 'The Death of Ivan Ilyich' ('Smert' Ivana Il'icha', 1886), where the hero's existential crisis, questioning of the conventional markers of happiness and success, and eventual embrace of his own mortality are precipitated by the diagnosis of a series of potential digestive ailments: 'floating kidney, chronic colitis, problem with the blind gut' (Leo Tolstoy, 'The Death of Ivan Ilyich,' trans. Anthony Briggs, in *The Death of Ivan Ilyich and Other Stories*, trans. Ronald Wilks, Anthony Briggs and David McDuff (London: Penguin, 2008), 183). The Russian for 'blind gut' (or *caecum*, as it also known) is *slepaia kishka*, and it is precisely in such *kishki* (here, the intestines more generally) that Sambikin and Sartorius search for the human soul.

28 Ayleen Teskey, *Platonov and Fyodorov: The Influence of Christian Philosophy on a Soviet Writer* (Amersham: Avebury, 1982).

29 Evgenii Iablokov, 'Kommentarii,' in Andrei Platonov, *Chevengur*, (Moscow: Vysshaia shkola, 1991); Evgenii Iablokov, *Na beregu neba: Roman Andreia Platonova 'Chevengur'* (St. Petersburg: Dmitrii Bulanin, 2001); Eric Naiman, 'The Thematic Mythology of Andrej Platonov,' *Russian Literature*, 21 (1987), 189–216; Eric Naiman, 'Andrej Platonov and the Inadmissibility of Desire,' *Russian Literature*, 23 (1988), 319–65.

30 A. A. Kharitonov, 'Arkhitektonika povesti A. Platonova "Kotlovan,"' in *Tvorchestvo Andreia Platonova* (St. Petersburg: Nauka 1995), 76–82.

31 For a cursory treatment of the relationship, written before any of Platonov's major works had been published in the Soviet Union, see A. L. Kisilev, 'L. Tolstoi i A. Platonov' in *Tolstovskii sbornik, vyp. 5. Doklady i soobshcheniia XII tolstovskikh chtenii* (Tula: Ministertsvo prosveshcheniia RSFSR; Tul'skii gosudarstvennyi pedagogicheskii institut im. L. N. Tolstogo, 1975), 228–38.

32 Platonov, *Zapisnye knizhki*, 74 and 77.

33 Tolstoy, 814.

34 Platonov, *Happy Moscow*, 99.

35 Robert Maguire, *Red Virgin Soil: Soviet Literature in the 1920s* (Princeton: Princeton University Press 1968), 294.

36 Komienko, '…Na kraiu sobstvennogo bezmolviia,' 60.
37 Geller, 236.
38 Tolstoy, 63.
39 Ibid., 736.
40 Platonov, *Zapisnye knizhki*, 128.
41 Harold Bloom, *The Anxiety of Influence: A Theory of Poetry*, 2nd ed. (Oxford: Oxford University Press 1997).
42 Eric Naiman, 'What If Nabokov Had Written "Dvoinik"? Reading Literature Preposterously,' *The Russian Review*, 64 (2005), 575–89.
43 Platonov, *Zapisnye knizhki*, 74.
44 Tolstoy, 49.
45 Platonov, *Zapisnye knizhki*, 119.
46 Platonov, *Happy Moscow*, 137.
47 Tolstoy, 179.
48 Ibid., 54.
49 Platonov, *Happy Moscow*, 74.
50 Ibid., 75.
51 Tolstoy, 822.
52 Ibid., 824.
53 Ibid.
54 Fitzpatrick, 133.
55 Tolstoy, 507.
56 Platonov, *Happy Moscow*, 140.
57 Andzhela Livingston [Angela Livingstone], 'O perevode prozy Platonova v angliiskie stikhi,' in *Strana filosofov' Andreya Platonova: problemy tvorchestva. Vypusk 4*, ed. by N. V. Kornienko (Moscow: Nasledie 2000), 111.
58 Catriona Kelly, *Refining Russia: Advice Literature, Polite Culture, and Gender from Catherine to Yeltsin* (Oxford: Oxford University Press 2001), 133.

Chapter Eleven: 'But Where is Your Happiness, Alevtina Ivanovna?': New Debates About Happiness in the Soviet Films of 1956

1 L. Pazhitnov and B. Shragin, 'Kogo liubit'?' *Iskusstvo kino* 3 (1967), 72. All translations from Russian are my own.
2 S. Zemlianukhin and M. Segida, *Domashniaia sinemateka. Otechestvennoe kino 1918–1996* (Moscow: Dubl'-D 1996), 8.
3 Petr Vail'. 'Kubanskie kazaki v poiskakh radosti. Byt,' *Iskusstvo kino* 4 (1996), 127.
4 I take the official production and release dates from *Sovetskie khudozhestvennye fil'my. Annotirovannyi katalog*, vol. 2, *Zvukovye fil'my (1930–1957)*, ed. A. Macheret et al. (Moscow: Iskusstvo 1961), and from *Sovetskie khudozhestvennye fil'my. Annotirovannyi katalog*, ed. N. A. Glagoleva, vol. 4 (Moscow: Iskusstvo 1968). Some other films made just before or after 1955–1956 are also referred to for comparison.
5 Petr Vail' and Aleksandr Genis, *60-e. Mir sovetskogo cheloveka*, third edition (Moscow: Novoe literaturnoe obozrenie 2001), 132.
6 A. Usmanova, 'Povtorenie i razlichie, ili 'Eshche raz pro liubov'' v sovetskom i postsovetskom kinematografe,' *Novoe literaturnoe obozrenie* 69 (2004), 198.

7 Juliane Fürst, 'The arrival of spring? Changes and continuities in Soviet youth culture and policy between Stalin and Khrushchev,' in *The Dilemmas of De-Stalinization. Negotiating cultural and social change in the Khrushchev era*, ed. Polly Jones (London: Routledge 2006), 135–53.

8 Marietta Chudakova, '1956 god (K vospominaniiam V. Kuznetsova)' in *Tynianovskii sbornik*. Vyp.10. *Shestye - Sed'mye - Vos'mye Tynianovskie chteniia* (Moscow: 1998), 805.

9 I. Shilova, ... *i moe kino. Piatidesiatye. Shestidesiatye. Semidesiatye* (Moscow: NIIK, Kinovedcheskie zapiski 1993).

10 The move into a new apartment, the *novosel'e*, is a commonplace both of the life and the art of the time. Such scenes recur in other films of the period, like *Spring on Zarechnaia Street*, to be discussed subsequently. For a late Stalinist version of the trope, see Aleksandr Laktionov's painting *To a New Apartment*, 1952. Laktionov's family members already have far more possessions of their own than the young characters in the films under discussion here. For a close reading of the significance of this painting, see Svetlana Boym, *Common Places: Mythologies of Everyday Life in Russia* (Cambridge, MA: Harvard University Press 1994), 5–11.

11 Dmitrii Bykov, 'Blud truda,' *Iskusstvo kino* 4 (1996), 123.

12 Ibid., 124.

13 Oleg Kharkhordin, *The Collective and the Individual in Russia: A Study of Practices* (Berkeley: University of California Press 1999), 282–5.

14 It is amusing to note, and may even be revealing in terms of ideological and cultural history, that 1954, the year in which Leonid Agranovich began work on the script that would become *A Person is Born*, was also the year of the Hollywood release of George Cukor's remake of the 1930s film *A Star is Born*. As the Soviet student Gleb met the unmarried mother Nadia, so the movie star on the skids, Norman Maine (played by James Mason), met the showgirl, Esther Blodgett (played by Judy Garland).

15 *"Shirokoekrannogo goria u nas net...'. K istorii fil'ma 'Chelovek rodilsia,"* introduced by A. S. Troshin, *Kinovedcheskie zapiski* 77 (2006), 52.

16 Ibid., 55.

17 Ibid., 60.

18 L. Agranovich, 'Bez strakhuiushchei setki,' in *Ivan Pyr'ev v zhizni i na ekrane. Stranitsy vospominanii*, ed. G. B. Mar'iamov (Moscow: Kinotsentr 1994), 197.

19 Josephine Woll, *Real Images: Soviet Cinema and the Thaw* (London: I. B. Tauris 2000), 43.

Chapter Twelve: Easy on the Heart; or, 'Strength Through Joy'

* 'Strength Through Joy' is *Kraft durch Freude*, a favorite Nazi slogan. It was the motto of a Third Reich sports and educational organisation that occupied the leisure time of German laborers; it was also the name of a faction of the German Labor Front in the Reichstag.

1 Jean-Louis Servan-Schreiber, *The Power to Inform* (New York: McGraw-Hill 1974), 25.

2 Anatoly Vishnevskii, *Serp i rubl': Konservativnaia modernizatsiia v SSSR* (Moscow 1998), 31–2.

3 Aleksandr Rodchenko, *Opyty dlia budushchego* (Moscow: Grant' 1996), 282.

4 These distributors provided food only for high-ranking Party officials. [*Ed.*]

5 Servan-Schreiber, 25.

6 TEZhE was the 'Trest Efirno-Zhirovykh Essentsii' ('Essential-Oil Extracts Trust Company'), a state-run enterprise. The acronym was popularly interpreted as 'TZh', 'Tainy Zhenshchiny' ('The Woman's Secret').–*Ed.*

7 Anatoly Lunacharsky, 'The USSR is Building a Life Worthy of Mankind,' in *Ogonek* no. 4 (1930), 4.

8 Vishnevskii, 53–8.

9 Katerina Clark, 'Polozhitel'nyi geroi kak verbal'naia ikona.' In *Sotsrealisticheskii kanon*. (St Petersburg: Akademicheskii proekt 2000), 569–84.

10 Bernice Rosenthal, 'Sotsrealizm i Nitssheanstvo.' In *Sotsrealisticheskii kanon* (St Petersburg: Akademicheskii proekt 2000), 62.

11 K. A. Zalesskii, *Imperiia Stalina* (Moscow: Veche 2000), 428.

12 Vadim Rogovin, 'Stalinskii neonep.' *Moskovskaia tipografiia*, no. 4 (1994).

13 An open letter signed by 'V. Khetagurova' appeared in the press in February 1937, calling for young women to participate in the 'taming' of the Soviet Far East; her letter evoked a response from about 250,000 young women.–*Ed.*

14 *Berlin-Moskau, 1900–1950* (München: Prestel 1995), 358.

INDEX

www.ingramcontent.com/pod-product-compliance
Lightning Source LLC
Chambersburg PA
CBHW022348280326
41935CB00007B/117